ERNST RÖHM

Ernst Röhm at the Hitler Putsch trial, 1924 (Mary Evans Picture Library).

ERNST RÖHM

Hitler's SA Chief of Staff

Eleanor Hancock

palgrave
macmillan

First published in hardcover in 2008 by PALGRAVE MACMILLAN® in the United States - a division of St. Martin's Press LLC, 175 Fifth Avenue, New York, NY 10010.

Where this book is distributed in the UK, Europe and the rest of the world, this is by Palgrave Macmillan, a division of Macmillan Publishers Limited, registered in England, company number 785998, of Houndmills, Basingstoke, Hampshire RG21 6XS.

Palgrave Macmillan is the global academic imprint of the above companies and has companies and representatives throughout the world.

Palgrave® and Macmillan® are registered trademarks in the United States, the United Kingdom, Europe and other countries.

ISBN: 978-0-230-12050-1

Library of Congress Cataloging-in-Publication Data

Hancock, Eleanor
   Ernst Röhm: Hitler's SA chief of staff / Eleanor Hancock
     p. cm.
   Includes bibliographical references and index.
   ISBN 0-230-60402-1
   1. Röhm, Ernst, 1887–1934. 2. Nationalsozialistische Deutsche Arbeiter-Partei. Sturmabteilung.—Biography. 3. Soldiers—Germany—Biography. 4. Gays—Germany—Biography. 5. Germany—Politics and government—1918–1933. I. Title.

DD247.R56H36 2008
943.086092—dc22   2007052851

A catalogue record of the book is available from the British Library.

Design by Scribe Inc.

First PALGRAVE MACMILLAN paperback edition: December 2011

10 9 8 7 6 5 4 3 2 1

Printed in the United States of America.

Transferred to Digital Printing in 2011

In loving memory of

Gunther Erich Rothenberg

(1923–2004)

Contents

List of Illustrations

Preface to the Paperback Edition

Errors in translation and transcription have been amended for this edition. The full footnotes and bibliography on my website have been updated to take account of relevant literature that has appeared since the manuscript initially went to the publisher in mid-2006.

While this book was already with Palgrave Macmillan before initial publication, *Hitler's Gay Traitor: The Story of Ernst Röhm, Chief of Staff of the S.A.* by Tony Atcherley and Mark Carey was published by Trafford Publishing (Victoria, British Columbia, 2007). It is based extensively on memoirs, including Röhm's autobiography, but gives only minimal references and makes very little use of archival research.

My thanks and acknowledgments go again to those mentioned in the Preface and to the Granger Collection for permission to reproduce the photographs in this edition.

Acknowledgments

By gracious permission of His Royal Highness Prince Franz of Bavaria, Duke of Bavaria, I was given access to the papers of Crown Prince Rupprecht, in the Geheimes Hausarchiv, Abteilung III of the Bayerisches Hauptstaatsarchiv. I am grateful for this. I also wish to thank Dr. Ernst Röhm very much for allowing me to consult the Röhm family's private papers, and for sharing family memories of his uncle, Ernst Röhm. I am indebted to Dr. Röhm and his family for their support of my research. Professor Reinhard Meyers of the Institut für Politikwissenschaft, Westfälische Wilhelms-Universität Münster, kindly let me read the Magister work of Andreas Walter Schmitz on "Die SA und ihr Selbstverständnis. Das Beispiel Viktor Lutze."

I am grateful to the editors and publishers of those works from which I have quoted extracts, and the owner of the copyright for the photograph reproduced in the frontispiece for permission to publish them. Quotations from Holger Herwig, *The First World War: Germany and Austria-Hungary 1914–1918* (Edward Arnold, London, 1997) and Ian Kershaw, *The Nazi Dictatorship: Problems and Perspectives of Interpretation* (Edward Arnold, London, 1997) are reproduced by permission of Edward Arnold (Publishers) Ltd. Every effort has been made to contact all copyright holders. The publishers will be glad to rectify any errors or omissions brought to their notice in future editions.

As a non-expert, I received generous help from specialists in the history of Bolivia and Turkey. For advice on Bolivian history and research in Bolivia, I wish to thank Professor James Dunkerley, Department of Politics, Queen Mary's College, University of London, Professor Herbert S. Klein, Institute for Social and Economic Research and Policy, Columbia University and Professor Charles W. Arnade, Emeritus Professor, Department of Government and International Affairs, University of South Florida at Tampa. At an early stage of my research, I was aided by the advice of Colonel Julio Sanjines Goitia in Bolivia. For guidance on Turkish history and sources, I thank Professor Erik J. Zürcher, Professor of Turkish Studies, University of

Leiden, and Dr. Adrian Jones, School of Historical and European Studies, Latrobe University.

This project has taken over ten years and required research on four continents, both by me and by my research assistants. I have been fortunate in the high quality of my research assistance: I thank Paola Méndez de Huber and Hans Huber Abendroth for their research for me in Bolivia; Julie Burbidge, Susan Cowan, Elizabeth Greenhalgh, and Michael Spurr for their research in Australia; Anthony Bidgood for the research he did in Britain and Germany; Alper Demir, Ebrew Demir, and Gungor Meric for their research assistance in Turkey; Alex Otto-Morris for his research in Germany; and Dr. Gregory Weeks, Webster University, Vienna for his research assistance in Austria. In addition, I am grateful to Generaldirektor Hofrat Dr. Kurt Peball for his assistance in finding documents in the Austrian State Archives. My research assistants in Bolivia were aided in particular by Ms. Martha Paredes in the archive of the Bolivian Ministry of Foreign Affairs, and in Germany, Alex Otto-Morris was assisted by Mr. Klaus Johann Pidde from the Hapag-Lloyd AG; I wish to record my appreciation of their help.

Over the years, I have drawn on the expertise and cooperation of staff in a variety of archives, mainly in Germany. It is a pleasure to work in Section IV of the Bayerisches Hauptstaatsarchiv, the Kriegsarchiv, with its friendly atmosphere and welcoming and helpful staff. I am very grateful to its successive directors, Dr. Rainer Braun and Dr. Achim Fuchs, and to its staff, particularly Mrs. Rudiger, Mrs. Jakobi, and Mrs. Köhler.

I wish to thank the directors of the following archives for their assistance: Dr. David Marwell at the then Berlin Document Center; Dr. Jürgen Wetzel, director of the Landesarchiv Berlin; Dr. Beatrix Schönewald, director of the Stadtarchiv Ingolstadt; and Dr. Tausenpfund, director of the Staatsarchiv München. In addition, I received expert counsel from the following archivists to whom I am grateful: Dr. Hartmut and Dr. Korn in Section II of the Bayerisches Hauptstaatsarchiv; Mrs. Lolo Anwander of the Bayerischer Landesverein für Familienkunde; Mr. Fischer, Mrs. Schleicher, and Mrs. Martens in the Bundesarchiv Koblenz; Mr. Zarwel in the then Bundesarchiv Abteilung Potsdam, and later at the Bundesarchiv in Berlin-Lichterfelde; Mr. Chris Murphy, African and Middle East Reference Room, Near East Section, and Mr. Fred Baumann, Manuscript Reading Room, Library of Congress; Mrs. Richter-Nachtigal in the Munich Evangelische Kirche Registeramt; Dr. Maria Keipert at the Politisches Archiv des Auswärtigen Amtes; Dr. Bachmann in the Staatsarchiv München; Mrs. Bauernschäfer in the Staatsarchiv Nürnberg archive; Mr. Edmund Hausfelder and Mrs. Doris Wittmann in the Stadtarchiv Ingolstadt; Dr. Hertl, Dr. Hecker, and Mrs. Angermaier in the Stadtarchiv München; and Mr. Manfred Baumgardt at the Schwules Museum Archiv.

For their helpfulness and efficiency, I wish to thank the following reading room staff: Mr. Kastner, Mr. Leipniz, and Mr. Schinhan in Sections II, and the Sammlung Personen of the Bayerisches Hauptstaatsarchiv; Mrs. Ilde, Mrs. Wolff, and Mr. Schulze at the then Berlin Document Center; Mrs. Grüner, Mrs. Hessel, Mr. Krüger, the late Mr. Lange, Mrs. Müller, and Mrs. Weller in the reading room of the Bundesarchiv in Berlin-Lichterfelde; Mrs. Hoffmann, Mrs. Jakobi, Mrs. Kaiser, Mrs. Nägele-Dreher, and Mr. Scharmann in the reading room of the Bundesarchiv Koblenz; Mr. Moritz, Mrs. Notzke, and Mrs. Waibel in the reading room of the Bundesarchiv-Militärarchiv in Freiburg; Mr. Berger and Mrs. Eggert in the Bundesfilmarchiv Berlin; and Mr. Werner in the reading room of the Staatsarchiv München. In Berlin, I also wish to thank the obliging staff of the Schwules Museum Archiv and the Prinz Eisenherz bookshop. In addition, I am grateful to the staff of the Amtsgericht München for allowing me access to Robert Bergmann's de-Nazification file.

I am indebted to Mr. Kronzucker, the director of Stadelheim Prison, for permitting me to consult prison records and view the layout of the prison. Mr. Josef Lederer, the owner of the Hotel Lederer am See in Bad Wiessee (the former Hotel Hanselbauer), allowed me to view those rooms of the hotel that played a part in the events of June 30, 1934; I thank him for this and for his generous hospitality.

Both Dr. Reinhard Weber in the Staatsarchiv München and Mr. Hermann Weiss in the Institut für Zeitgeschichte not only provided help as archivists, but also expert advice as historians of the period. I am grateful to them both for the many leads they gave me and for our stimulating conversations. In addition, I thank Mr. Weiss for putting me in contact with the Röhm family. The late Dr. Otto Gritschneder allowed me to use the entire archive he had assembled for his book, "*Der Führer hat Sie zum Tode verurteilt . . .*" *Hitlers "Röhm-Putsch"—Morde vor Gericht*, to draw on his memories of the period, and his historical expertise. I am indebted to him for all this, and for his and Mrs. Gritschneder's hospitality. Dr. Elke Fröhlich of the Institut für Zeitgeschichte kindly advised me on the contents of the unpublished Goebbels' diaries for 1934. Mrs. Bäumler-Holley of the Bavarian Finance Ministry briefed me on the copyright of Eher Verlag publications. Mr. Winfried Bauer of the Maximiliansgymnasium advised me on its records of Röhm's schooling. I thank them all for their assistance.

For sharing their expertise, I am grateful to Professor Bruce Campbell, Dr. Andreas Dornheim, Professor John Fout, Dr. Ted Harrison, Dr. Manfred Herzer, Professor Bernhard R. Kroener, Professor Lothar Machtan, Professor

Gerhard Schulz, and Dr. Hans-Rudolf Wahl. Professor Machtan and Mr. Robert Brockmann allowed me to read their unpublished manuscripts on Prince August Wilhelm and on Röhm's stay in Bolivia respectively: I thank them for their generous help.

To fit the word limit, archival references in the endnotes are minimal citations only. When a direct quotation has been referenced, other sources for the paragraph have been reduced. Fully itemized lists of references for each note and a full bibliography have been placed online at http://www.unsw.adfa .edu.au/hass/staff/hancock.html.

Hans Huber Abendroth, Elizabeth Greenhalgh, Paola Méndez de Huber, Robin Prior, Gillian Robinson, Michael Spurr, and Edward Wilson have read and commented on various drafts of the manuscript, which I appreciate very much. For valuable discussions and suggestions, I thank my friends and colleagues, Associate Professor Bain Attwood, Dr. David Blaazer, Professor David Chandler, Professor Ian Copland, Dr. David Cuthbert, Professor David Garrioch, Ms. Philippa Horner, Professor Bill Kent, Professor Robin Prior, Professor John Rickard, Mr. Michael Spurr, and Dr. Evan Zuesse. As well, I wish to acknowledge the stimulating comments of the various audiences who have listened to papers on the subject at the Schools of History at Monash University, the University of New South Wales@ADFA and High Point University, and at the following conferences—the Australasian Association of European Historians, the Australian Historical Association, the German Studies Association, the American Historical Association, and the Association of Iberian and Latin American Studies of Australasia.

In Berlin in 1997, the language institute Lingua Franca and its Spanish teacher, Mr. Jaime Fernando, helped me learn the Spanish needed for research on Röhm's two years in Bolivia. I am grateful to Ms. Renata Grossi and Professor Bill Kent for their help with my translations from Italian, and to Dr. Adrian Jones for his help with my translations from Turkish. For advice on the nuances of translations from German, I wish to thank Mr. Hans Huber Abendroth, Dr. Michael Hau, and my late husband, Gunther E. Rothenberg.

I am very grateful to Professor Robert King, the former Rector of the University College of the University of New South Wales@ADFA, for the value he placed on research, for his encouragement of my research in particular, and for his role at the University College in providing the atmosphere, terms, and conditions of work that allowed me to complete this biography. I wish to thank successive heads of department and school at Monash University—Professor Barbara Caine, Professor Graeme Davison, Professor Bill Kent, Professor Andrew Markus, and Professor Merle Ricklefs—for furthering my research. Above all, though, I owe a great debt to Professor Robin Prior, head of the School of History, and then head of the School of Humanities and Social Sciences at the University of New South Wales@ADFA, for his professional and personal support over the past few years.

Grants from the Arts Faculty at Monash University, the Australian Research Council, the Rector's Start Up Fund of the University College, the School of Humanities and Social Sciences at the University of New South Wales@ ADFA, and the University of New South Wales helped finance the research needed for the project. Dr. Elanor Huntington, School of Information Technology and Electrical Engineering, University of New South Wales@ADFA, was a significant mentor in 2004–5. I thank Professor Tom Griffiths and his colleagues at the History Program, Research School of Social Sciences, Australian National University, Canberra, for granting me a research fellowship for the last six months of my writing. I am grateful to Mr. Glenn Large, of the University of New South Wales@ADFA library, for his help, and to Ms. Jo Muggleton, School of Humanities and Social Sciences, for her invaluable administrative support at the end of the project. I wish to thank Ms. Lynne Weaver and Ms. Cathy Bennett for keying in the final manuscript. Professor Peter Dennis, Ms. Philippa Horner, and Mr. Michael Spurr gave expert advice and help in preparing the manuscript for publication: I am grateful to them.

Until his sudden death in early 2004, my late husband Gunther E. Rothenberg generously supported and assisted my work on Röhm. My friends Sue Jones and Edward Wilson, Christopher Diffey, Michael Fuery, Ian Hancock, Philippa Horner, Heather McIntyre, Robin Prior, Michael Spurr, and Liz Reed all helped me at difficult times after Gunther's death. Edward Wilson was present at the book's origins and has backed it throughout. I also thank Adamu Abbas for all his support and encouragement.

I am indebted to all those I listed above for their help. They bear no responsibility for the interpretations advanced in the book: these are mine alone.

Eleanor Hancock

CHAPTER 1

Introduction

E rnst Röhm was Chief of Staff of the National Socialist *Sturmabteilung* (SA), the attack section or stormtroopers, from the beginning of 1931 until the end of June 1934, and he was killed on Adolf Hitler's orders on July 1, 1934. The SA was a paramilitary organization designed for defense of Nazi Party meetings and attacks on its political opponents. It formed the workforce for the unceasing Nazi political activity in the lead up to the take-over of power in 1933. In 1933–34, the SA provided the violence and the threat of violence necessary for the party to take over and consolidate power.

Röhm played a crucial role in two periods of Nazism's history. From 1919 to 1923, as an officer in the Bavarian army, he was the party's patron, pro-moter, and protector. Bennecke claimed:

> In all important events of the National Socialist Party up to 1 May 1923 Röhm played an important, if not quite decisive role. The development of Hitler and also of his party is scarcely imaginable without Röhm's help and exertion of influence.[1]

Between 1931 and 1933, Röhm's authority and organizational skills allowed him to expand the SA successfully, hold it under party control, and organize it to contribute to the Nazi election campaigns of 1932 and 1933. Röhm kept the undisciplined SA under sufficient restraint for the party's purposes. Even after Röhm had been killed on his orders, Hitler reportedly commented that when the time came to write the history of National Socialism, Röhm would take second place in significance after himself.

Who was Ernst Röhm? He was of medium height for the period—1.7 meters or five foot five inches tall. As a young man, he had been thin. By the early 1920s, after years of deskwork and political activity in beer halls and cafés, he was stocky. In the late 1920s, he struggled to keep his weight down.

By 1933, he was solid and overweight, fat at times, but never as heavy as his fellow Nazi leader, Hermann Göring. One British press report in 1934 compared him to the film star Oliver Hardy in size and appearance.[2]

His hair was dark and short. For most of his life he wore it parted in the middle. Sometime in the early 1930s, he changed this to a more flattering high side part. His eyes were green. He had a short moustache. When not in uniform, he dressed like a respectable bourgeois. He smoked both cigarettes and cigars.[3]

After 1914, anyone who met him first noticed Röhm's disfigured face. A scar ran from his cheek across his shattered nose, which had been reconstructed by primitive plastic surgery. These scars were the signs of his war service and his courage. Less visible were the wounds to his body, over twelve incurred in 1916 at Verdun. Their effects on his health are unknown. By the 1930s, Röhm was suffering regular bouts of illness, including neuritis and heart problems, and was often under medical care.

Röhm had an unremarkable career as a junior officer in the Bavarian Army before World War I. After distinguished frontline service and severe wounds, Röhm spent the last two years of the war as a staff officer. In this role, he discovered his organizing capacity. After the war, in the Weimar Republic, Röhm's superiors in the army drew on his organizational skills to put him in charge of illegal weapons holdings in Bavaria, and thereby evade the Treaty of Versailles' restrictions on German military capability. Röhm himself was politicized by the German Revolution of 1918–19. He used his position to support right-wing paramilitary and extremist groups. In the course of this, from 1919 to 1923, he came to favor Hitler and the NSDAP over other right-wing organizations. Röhm became Hitler's personal friend and was the only member of the Nazi leadership who could address Hitler with the familiar "*Du*" ("thou"). In November 1923, he participated in the unsuccessful Nazi attempt to take over power in Munich—the so-called Beer Hall putsch.

Released from prison while Hitler and other putsch leaders were still serving their sentences, Röhm led the SA in 1924–25 while simultaneously trying to set up an "umbrella" paramilitary organization—the Frontbann. This attempt foundered not least on Hitler's opposition to it. Röhm accordingly resigned his offices and returned to private life before resuming political activity for the Nazis in 1928. He then spent a successful two years as a military officer in the Bolivian army. He returned to Germany for good at the end of 1930 to take up the position leading the SA that Hitler had been offering him since 1925. From 1931 to 1933, Röhm was under constant political attack from both Nazi opponents and within the party because of his almost-open homosexuality. He remained as Chief of Staff because of Hitler's unwavering support.

Yet, his personal friendship with Hitler, and Hitler's backing of him from 1931 to 1933, did not protect Röhm in 1934, when the question of the future role for the SA in the National Socialist state combined with a more widespread crisis of the National Socialist regime. On June 30, 1934, and during the days after, Hitler purged the leadership of the SA, including Röhm, who was killed on Hitler's orders on July 1, 1934. Hitler opted to resolve the crisis of the regime by decisively weakening the SA as well as striking at other threats to National Socialist control of government. Hitler sided with the leadership of the armed forces to secure their continued support for the regime at the expense of the SA. The purge of the SA has been seen as marking the final stage of the Nazi consolidation of power.

The manner of Röhm's death, and the power struggle in the regime that led to it, has influenced historians' assessments of Röhm. In the post-1945 historical study of the SA and National Socialism, there has been strong support for a view of Röhm as the leader of those who wanted a "second revolution," a more radical transformation of the existing German economic and political structures, as well as an army imbued with Nazi ideology through the SA. In the immediate postwar era, historians were excessively influenced by the testimony of senior military leaders, who were hostile to the SA. More recent studies of the SA, and of the lead up to June 30, 1934, have tended to move away from this interpretation, though it still has support.[4]

The emphasis now is more on Röhm as a political soldier or a soldier in politics, a man limited and constrained by his military and paramilitary experience. Because Röhm came to Nazism through his military position and paramilitary activities, he has also been seen as an "indispensable outsider" in Nazism.[5] His role as Hitler's early patron has led as well to an interpretation that he was "the man who invented Hitler."[6]

The scandals and publicity about Röhm's sexuality in the early 1930s have combined with changing historiographical trends to arouse interest in Röhm as "the Nazi as homosexual." Academic audiences seem more interested in this aspect of his life than in his role as a German or Nazi political figure. Is our belief that sexuality forms the key to a person's character as justified as we currently think it is? Does our interest in Röhm's sexual life tell us more about us than him? The attacks on Röhm and in Röhm's position as a homosexual in an officially homophobic movement have also interested historians for what they reveal about Nazi attitudes toward homosexuality and the history of homosexuality in Germany.[7] Even during his life, Röhm came to have a symbolic significance.

Röhm played a key role in National Socialism before it came to power and while it consolidated that power. While the SA itself has been the focus of increased historical study in recent years, this is the first academic biography of Röhm's life. Jean Mabire's earlier *Röhm l'homme qui inventa Hitler* is, at times, perceptive, particularly in its interpretation of Röhm's character, but Mabire gives no sources for any of his claims. The book's lengthy passages of undocumented dialogue mean that parts of it are effectively fictionalized.

The absence of biographical study of Röhm reflects, in part, the lack of interest of German academic historians in biography as a genre. Their focus has been on broader issues in the history of Nazism. Yet Hitler's authority, both within National Socialism and beyond it, was the authority of a charismatic leader. As a result, at the highest level of decision making in the Nazi movement and regime, power relations in the Third Reich were also personal relations between leaders. Biographical studies of Nazi leaders, by studying how they operated in this system, illustrate how it worked, how and why policies were arrived at, and how their power and decisions interacted with those of Hitler. Equally, the nature of Hitler's charismatic authority sometimes cast successive leaders into similar roles in the regime.[8]

The second reason for the absence of previous biographies of Röhm is the difficulty of the project. After June 30, 1934, all Röhm's private papers, as well as the records of his ministerial office, were seized. They have since vanished, and may have been destroyed in 1945, if not earlier. Only fragmentary personal papers survive.[9]

Röhm wrote and published his own autobiography, *Die Geschichte eines Hochverräters (The Story of a Traitor)*, in 1928. It was reissued in various editions until 1934. Röhm claimed that seldom had an autobiography been written more frankly. While the autobiography is ostensibly open and frank, it often conceals important issues, is self-serving, and not very reflective. The autobiography is how Röhm wanted to present himself to the world. It is not without its problems as a source.[10]

As a result of these gaps in the evidence, some of Röhm's ideas, actions and motives, and equally those of his opponents, have been impossible to reconstruct. This is particularly the case for the period from January to July 1934. This means that, up to a point, Röhm, like Hitler, "is for the historian unreachable, cocooned in the silence of the sources."[11]

There are aspects of Röhm's life that can only be grasped incompletely. Unfortunately, this particularly applies to his personal life. His inner life cannot be recaptured. The details of his day-to-day life are often unclear. These gaps in the record may, at times, make him seem a more complex or contradictory figure than he perhaps was. As a result, this is necessarily far more a study of Röhm's public rather than his private life, focusing, in turn, on his military and political careers—his career as an army officer from 1906 to 1923, and his political career from 1919 to 1934. Because of these gaps in the historical record, this biography is, more than most, an introductory portrait of its subject. I hope that its publication will encourage those who hold additional sources to come forward and allow me to expand on it.

CHAPTER 2

The Making of a Young Officer
1887–1914

From my childhood on I had only one thought and desire—to be a soldier.[1]
Ernst Röhm

Ernst Julius Günther Röhm was born at 1:00 a.m. on Monday November 28, 1887, in Munich, the capital of the kingdom of Bavaria in the German Empire. He was the third child of forty-year-old Guido Julius Josef Röhm and twenty-nine-year-old Sofia Emilie Röhm, née Baltheiser. His older brother, Robert Heinrich Bernhard, had been born on April 29, 1879, and his sister, Meta Eleonore (Lore), on May 14, 1880, in Schweinfurt, northern Bavaria.[2]

Röhm was baptized on December 11, 1887, by the Evangelical Church's town curate Rohmeder. His godfather was a successful relative on his mother's side of the family, Julius Baltheiser, a senior district judge in Herieden. As Protestants, the Röhms were members of a minority in a predominantly Catholic state. Protestants in Bavaria were better educated than the norm, more likely to hold official and civil service positions, and more likely to be army officers. Nonetheless, Röhm was sensitive to, and aware of, subtle prejudices against, and barriers to advancement for, Protestants in Bavaria.[3]

At the time of Röhm's birth, Julius Röhm was a railway inspector, the second oldest of eight children of an estate forester. As a middle level railway official, he had status to uphold, but little money on which to do so. His family had been officials in Thuringia, and then Franconia, for centuries. He travelled widely as a young man and made his own way in life. He eventually rose into the senior ranks of the railway service, retiring as a railway chief inspector. While Röhm was growing up, the family lived near the railway district.[4]

In later life, Röhm indicated that he never felt particularly close to his father or brother. He described his father as strict, but conceded that—once Julius Röhm realized that he achieved better without exhortation—he gave him much freedom and allowed full scope to his interests. In contrast, Röhm was very close to his mother and his sister. Both in public and in private, for Röhm, his mother was "the best wife and mother in the world. As her youngest, who loves her above all, I can say no more."[5] Ernst's position as the youngest child, and the large gap in age between his sister and him, may have influenced his family relations and character. As the baby of the family, he may have been indulged by his mother and sister. Family memories indicate that as a child he was strong-willed.

From his early youth on, Röhm wanted to be a soldier, and spent his free hours playing war games or visiting barracks and parade grounds. He grew up surrounded by large troop parades and patriotic festivals. There were so many parades of the Munich garrison in this period that they were no longer listed in the files of the War Ministry. The prominence of the army in Munich reflected the city's status as Bavaria's political and administrative capital and royal residence.[6]

As was common in such civil service families, the Röhm family's resources went into securing a good education for their sons. Robert Röhm eventually studied law and went into the railway service like his father. From autumn 1897, just before he turned ten, to spring 1906, Ernst Röhm attended the prestigious Königliches Maximiliansgymnasium on the Ludwigstrasse in Munich's administrative and official district. The school fees began at thirty marks a month in 1890–91. The class lists indicate that, as a railway official, Julius Röhm was of lower social status than the fathers of the majority of his son's fellow pupils. By the 1905–6 school year, when Röhm was in his final ninth year, most of the fathers of the other thirty-two students were factory owners or senior professionals.[7]

The Bavarian education system gave preeminence to the Gymnasium, the classical grammar school, with its minimum nine-year course. Röhm received a thorough education from well-qualified teachers at one of Munich's leading boys' schools. He studied German and classical literature, Latin, Greek, French, history, geography, nature studies, mathematics and physics, drawing and calligraphy, and gymnastics. Whether at school or privately, he also learned to play the piano very well.[8]

He himself described his achievements at school as "rather varied" and admitted that he was never a particularly good student. Röhm quoted an extract from a report he received in his seventh year: "'His conduct gave repeated cause for reprimand on account of [his] inclination to disorder and unrest.'" Röhm added, in 1928, that "this inclination has continued . . . to the present day."[9] In his last report before matriculation (Easter 1906), his conduct was described as "praiseworthy but he should be quieter and pay more attention. His tendency to chatter is recurrent."[10]

Röhm matriculated in July 1906. He claimed that his final results were good without his having made particular effort. The report his headmaster gave the army about Röhm's academic achievements on July 13, 1906 described him as having good results in the upper form examinations for religion, German, Latin, French, mathematics and physics, history and gymnastics, and adequate results in Greek. A separate report stated that the school knew of nothing detrimental to his honor.[11]

By 1906 when he matriculated, Röhm's family had prepared him for the future by paying for the best education available at the time. In becoming an officer, he was completing his family's rise into the upper middle, or even upper, class. Appearance at court was a privilege granted to all officers, together with the rectors of universities and technical universities, the president of the Chamber of Deputies, and the Knights of the Maximilian Order for art and science.[12]

In 1928, Röhm commented that "the dream of my youth was fulfilled"[13] on July 23, 1906, the day he became an ensign in the Tenth Royal Bavarian Infantry Regiment "*Prinz Ludwig*" (later "*König*") in the garrison town of Ingolstadt. He successfully completed his training in 1907, but his departure for cadet school was delayed by an outbreak of meningitis in his battalion. The reports of his training indicate that he had been diligent, hard working and full of a sense of duty. He had good intellectual gifts and his ability to execute orders demonstrated his interest in military service. No disciplinary problems were noted. He had been trained as a noncommissioned officer and deserved promotion.

Röhm attended the War School (*Kriegsschule*) from March 1, 1907 to January 25,1908. At this time, the Kriegsschule was located in a modern red brick building facing the Blutenburgstraße on the Marsfeld, the traditional place for infantry and cavalry exercises in Munich. Training was very strict and punishments were frequent. Röhm was punished three times for speaking at roll call, for careless posture (presumably on parade), and for insulting a comrade. His own account in his autobiography suggested he found the discipline hard. He claimed things were more difficult for him because he arrived late, and this seemed to disturb the smooth running of the institution. He described his own result as "not exactly the best,"[14] and indicated that he felt he deserved a better report.

While Röhm was at the Kriegsschule, he and his family were investigated for his political and social acceptability as an officer. The report noted that "his father is esteemed in official circles as a very impartial, loyal official who lives in good circumstances."[15] Röhm had had a good education and had good manners. He was modest, obliging, and thrifty. His monthly allowance was paid regularly.

One hundred and thirty-three ensigns and officer aspirants attended the Kriegsschule course in 1908. Of the 124 who completed the course, Röhm graduated ninety-eighth. His graduation certificate indicated he had received the overall grade of tolerably good and the following grades in specific subjects: 8 (very good) for leadership, 7 (good) for service with the troops, 6 (relatively good) for riding, signals, and for zeal, 5 (satisfactory) for fencing, drill, shooting, and gymnastics.[16]

In 1908, Ernst Röhm graduated from the Bavarian War School to be commissioned as an officer in the Bavarian Army. His superiors assessed the twenty-year-old as follows:

> A not yet completely firm character, who however works on himself with good will. His conception of the profession has become more serious. Intellectually of normal capacity, even if partially distracted. Zeal adequate. Physically strong and sufficiently dexterous. Attitude good: he still lacks assurance and certainty of bearing when facing formations. Off duty conduct and social manners are good. Needs supervision. Financial conditions are settled.[17]

On February 17, 1908, the officers of the regiment voted unanimously to find Röhm "completely worthy"[18] of being accepted in the estate of officer. On March 14, 1908 in Ingolstadt, he swore the oath of allegiance to the King as a lieutenant of the regiment.

His regiment had a long and illustrious history. It had been founded in 1682 and was one of the oldest Bavarian regiments. Its battle honors included the taking of Belgrade in 1688, commemorated in its regimental march, called variously either the Belgrade March or the Prince Eugene March. Röhm strongly identified with regimental traditions.[19]

Röhm had become an officer in the Bavarian army.[20] Since German unification in 1871, the Bavarian army was a separate formation of the German army under the military authority of the Bavarian king, who retained supreme command and had his own complete general staff. Bavaria was obliged to conform in pay, training, organization, and units to the norms of the federal army. Bavaria had had universal male military service since 1805. In wartime, the mobilized army came under the supreme command of the German Emperor as federal commander. Bavarian officers did not enjoy the socially privileged positions of their Prussian counterparts, but the reputation of the officer corps was rising. Bavarian officers envied the status of their Prussian counterparts and welcomed the introduction of Prussian norms. Officer status was a vehicle for upward social mobility for men from the Bavarian middle class. While noble officers were promoted more quickly and higher than middle class officers, Röhm could hope to make a career without requiring political or aristocratic connections. Unlike the Prussian army, the Bavarian army required its officers to have university matriculation. Officers were more likely to be Protestant than the Bavarian population as a whole.

The one remnant of distinctive Bavarian values was the officer corps' attachment to the royal family. The colonel-in-chief of Röhm's regiment was His Royal Highness Prince Ludwig of Bavaria, who became Prince Regent on December 12, 1912, ruling in place of his insane brother Otto, and controversially ascending to the throne in 1913 while Otto was still alive.[21]

Röhm spent his prewar military service in the small town of Ingolstadt, north of Munich. Ingolstadt had been a Bavarian fortress since 1860, with large scale fortifications and a permanent garrison. The Tenth Infantry Regiment was housed in the Kavalier Spreti, a nineteenth-century fortification in the north of the inner city. Ingolstadt's economic life centered on the garrison and the railways. Soldiers were almost 25 percent of the population in 1890. By 1910, the town's predominantly Catholic population numbered 23,716.[22]

For the next six years of his military career, Röhm would be on duty in Ingolstadt, apart from short-term secondments and medical and annual leave. From 1913 on, he was being trained as an adjutant, and in the winter of 1913–14, he completed a revision of the regiment's mobilization timetable.[23]

As a young lieutenant, he was poorly paid—1,500 marks a year in April 1908, rising to 1,700 marks on March 1, 1909. From this salary he was expected to pay for his own clothing and equipment. A junior officer could not expect to live off his pay until he reached the rank of captain after some eighteen years of service. In social prestige and consciousness, junior officers belonged to the upper classes, but their income was that of the lower classes. As a result, an officer's life was described as one of "splendid misery."[24]

Röhm himself noted that officers had to be thrifty and that they managed because meals in the officers' mess were cheap. He claimed that no officer in his regiment received more than twenty to forty marks subsidy from home a month, and some received no support. This seems unlikely. Regiments expected officers to have additional financial support from home.[25]

In his autobiography, Röhm painted an idyllic picture of social life in Ingolstadt, and of his working life as a young lieutenant. He was nostalgic about the social life of the garrison—the meals in the officers' mess, the afternoon concerts of the regiment's senior music master Max "Vater" Schott, who had composed the regimental march and was an excellent interpreter of Wagner, the games at the officers' tennis club, the festive dinners at the house of the fortress commandant, and the house balls and masquerades in the winter. His recollections may have been all the more idealized and nostalgic because, by the time he was writing, he was looking back on a vanished world. Yet his picture of a stable, deferential, and confident society in which entertainment and relaxation followed the seasons, is recognizable in the Ingolstadt newspapers of the period. These show a firm annual social calendar based on the ball season and ice-skating in winter, concerts given by the various regimental bands, plays, operas, operettas, and musical performances. The life of the town centered on the garrison, with its maneuvers, troop deployments, and exercises all reported. As late as 1934, Röhm still kept up friendships with Ingolstadt families from that time. One of his dancing partners, Miss Liesl Schneider, maintained contact with Röhm, and then his family, for the rest of her life.[26]

In his autobiography, Röhm praised some senior officers and contemporaries as well as mentioning by name an officer with whom he clashed over disciplinary issues. While he claimed that he later understood the reasons for the officer's decisions, he also conceded that he (Röhm) became calmer with the passage of time.[27]

Röhm claimed that he most enjoyed training new recruits. "No profession can be as pleasant as that of an officer, who leads man to man, to whom fate places responsibility in his hands for young men's hearts and lives."[28] Yet, Röhm's interactions, both with his troops and with Ingolstadt civilians, were sometimes troubled. On March 9, 1911, Röhm was found guilty, by a court of the Sixth Division, of mishandling a subordinate by repeatedly pushing him lightly in the side during musketry training and giving him a smack on the back of the head. Röhm's financial situation was such that he could not pay the legal costs awarded against him out of his own pocket. He was sentenced to three days' confinement to quarters, but the punishment was later suspended and he was pardoned.

Conviction on a charge of mistreatment of subordinates could end an officer's career. Both the number of cases of mistreatment and complaints about them were rising at this time, and the issue was politically sensitive. As an indication of how seriously such cases were viewed, a report on Röhm's case went to the War Ministry. In a report to the Brigade, the commanding officer von Kirschbaum rejected Röhm's excuse that he was overtired because he had been supervising on the shooting ground for over three hours, which was excessive. Röhm's defense was to point to a requirement that supervising personnel should be shifted. It is possible that the breaching of this requirement, as well as the favorable evidence of Röhm's company commander, meant the conviction did not damage Röhm's career.[29]

He was less fortunate a year later when he and other officers successfully brought a charge of defamation of officers against three Ingolstadt civilians—one woman and two men—who were convicted and tried on August 30, 1912. Röhm withdrew a further charge of defamation against one of the civilians, possibly under pressure from his superiors. The various regimental honor courts of the three officers concerned—Lieutenants Röhm and Mantel of the Tenth Infantry Regiment and Stark of the III Army Supply Battalion—and senior army commanders all claimed the officers were in the right.[30]

Nonetheless, his superiors considered that Röhm's own behavior had provoked the incident. Röhm and his fellow officers were in the Hotel Adler in Ingolstadt on April 22, 1912. Röhm had insisted that the civilians vacate a table usually reserved for officers, a *Stammtisch*, in such a manner that the civilians were provoked into making a series of insulting remarks. Röhm countered these remarks and then left the hotel. Röhm himself was sentenced to two days' confinement to quarters for his role in provoking the incident.[31]

Of the annual qualification reports that had to be prepared for every Bavarian officer by their direct superiors, only Röhm's 1909 and 1912 reports survive. The 1909 report was similar to his report from the Kriegsschule. In the 1912 report, Röhm's company commander assessed Röhm as:

> a vigorous, cheerful, capable officer with a well developed military spirit. Mentally of normal gifts and physically sufficiently dexterous that he is easily deployable in all aspects of service and forms a reliable support of his company chief. He fervently endeavors to fulfill his duties with diligence and conscientiousness. His military knowledge is appropriate for his time of service: his oral and written orders are good. Possesses in addition a good knowledge of French. He is very employable as a platoon leader, understands quickly and circumspectly, sensible and energetic. He treats his subordinates calmly and benevolently.[32]

He had had particularly good results in explaining what he had learned on a riding course to his men. His company commander claimed that Röhm's out-of-hours conduct was very good, apart from his "unlucky slip"[33] in the Stammtisch affair, which he attributed to Röhm's inexperience. He considered that Röhm's character would stabilize. His regimental commander also attributed Röhm's offense to inexperience: "He must show himself more amenable to instruction and greater self-discipline, before he can be proposed as an instructor at the Cadet Corps."[34]

The Stammtisch affair suggests that there were tensions between civilians and the army in Ingolstadt. Röhm and his fellow officers may have fallen victim to the unrealistic demands of the officer's honor code. An officer who failed to defend his honor could be dishonorably discharged. This created a certain touchiness and sensitivity. Only legal charges could be brought against civilians who came from classes that were not capable of giving satisfaction in a duel.[35]

These charges, the charge against him a year earlier of mistreating a subordinate, and his clashes with his superior officer raise questions about his personality. At this time, Röhm was in his mid-twenties. Did he have difficulty controlling his temper and dealing with frustrations? Was he a little immature? Were his senior officers correct in suggesting that his character needed to stabilize? These incidents suggest that his difficulties with authority, already seen in his school days, persisted. Röhm's attitude toward discipline and authority was ambivalent. In later years, he would frequently praise discipline, but he also needed to rebel against it.

Looking back, after 1945, at least one friend and fellow officer suggested that, at this time, Röhm was not taken seriously. When he joined the regiment, Karl Schreyer recalled, his company commander, Captain Vögel, advised him to make friends with all his comrades except Röhm:

> Röhm was then considered to be the most decided "fop" in the entire garrison, always indulging in eccentric ploys, especially where his clothing was concerned. He wore the highest collars, his cap at his own purposefully exaggerated angle, and the lightest blue uniform jacket in the whole Bavarian army. He counted as one of the regulars of the Ingolstadt brothels, and also led junior officers there. He had the clap seven times; and even the regimental commander himself, Kieffhaber, who was very much admired by Röhm, repeatedly asked him in jest: "Is it running again?" [Röhm was] the original dandified young peacetime lieutenant.[36]

Another friend and comrade, Franz von Hörauf, described Röhm as remaining a "daredevil"[37] where women were concerned.

Hörauf also claimed that, by 1914, Röhm was engaged to Miss Auguste Bauer, daughter of the Ingolstadt academy director, Karl Bauer, and sister of Röhm's friend Lieutenant Karl Bauer. Röhm visited the Bauer home and knew Auguste Bauer, but neither the Bauer nor Röhm families recall any engagement. There are no records of an engagement, and it is unlikely that

Röhm, as a self-conscious Protestant, would have chosen to marry a Catholic. Hörauf's claim must be regarded as not proven.[38]

In 1929, Röhm told Dr Karl-Günter Heimsoth, "I can also remember . . . a series of homosexual feelings and acts back to my childhood, but have had sexual relations with many women as well. To be sure, never with particular pleasure; also I earned three cases of gonorrhea from this, which I later considered to be nature's punishment for unnatural intercourse."[39] It has been suggested that homosexual men were attracted to an officer's career because the army was an all-male institution. At the time Röhm made his career choice, almost all professions in Imperial Germany were all male, so this was not necessarily a consideration. Being a military officer, however, represented the peak of masculinity. It may have been a reassurance to a bisexual young man in a society where male homosexuals were considered effeminate. Was some of Röhm's immaturity due to the difficulty of coming to terms with his sexuality?

As an officer, Röhm had a high status in a society where the military and military values were preeminent. Concepts such as patriotism, honor, loyalty, comradeship, and discipline were accepted and advanced in the officer corps. What political and social ideas did he absorb as an officer in the Bavarian army? His strong support for the Bavarian monarchy was shared by his family and reinforced in the army, where officers saw themselves as servants of the king. His autobiography noted every official and social occasion he spent with the king, with the Kaiser, and at the court. Unlike earlier generations, by Röhm's time, officers combined loyalty to the Bavarian royal family, the Wittelsbachs, and to Bavaria with loyalty to the Reich.[40]

Anti-Semitism, too, was part of the value system of most Bavarian officers. It increased perceptibly in the early twentieth century. There were only six active Jewish officers in the Bavarian army between 1871 and 1914, and Jews were less likely than others to become reserve officers.[41]

As a Bavarian officer, Röhm was expected to be above politics. Serving officers did not vote. Their very lack of interest in politics was of course, in itself, a political stand in favor of the status quo and a political and social system in which they were preeminent. The officer corps has been described as largely politically uneducated.[42]

Bavarian politics were relatively moderate, and before World War I, the adult male franchise was established in elections for the Landtag as well as the Reichstag. Yet, the confident and conservative world presented in the Ingolstadt press was only part of the reality of Imperial Germany. The pace of economic and social change had created political, economic, and social tensions. This was visible even in less industrialized Bavaria. In the 1912

Reichstag elections, the SPD made considerable gains in Bavaria, receiving 27 percent of the vote.[43]

Almost all the elements of modernity were present in Imperial Germany, but as an army officer stationed in Ingolstadt, Röhm could continue to be unaware of them. The Bavarian army tried to keep Social Democratic influences away from recruits. Ingolstadt, too, was a Catholic Center Party stronghold. Of the 3,290 votes cast in the town for the 1912 Reichstag elections, 2,000 were for the Center, 633 for the National Liberals, and 643 for the SPD.[44]

In summer 1914, when he went to Herrsching am Ammersee for his holidays,[45] Röhm was almost twenty-seven years old and a lieutenant in the Royal Bavarian Army. He was committed to and enjoyed his choice of, profession, which had marked a further advance in his family's social status. As a junior officer, his achievement had been undistinguished. He had made various blunders attributable to inexperience or immaturity. If he had any noticeable individual characteristics, they were a certain temper or impatience, sensitivity to criticism, foppishness, and an ambivalent attitude toward discipline. His position and experiences as an officer had protected him from a full awareness of the complexities and stresses of Wilhelmine Germany. Unlike Adolf Hitler, who was a failure in the pre-war world, Ernst Röhm was, and felt himself to be, at home in it. To those of his standing and profession, this was a comfortable, prosperous, and seemingly stable world. Within a month, it was to begin to change irrevocably for him and all his contemporaries.

CHAPTER 3

The Transforming Experience of World War I 1914–18

The National Socialist movement was born on the battlefields of World War I.[1]
Ernst Röhm

From a foolish dandy, Ernst Röhm "changed overnight into an extremely decent comrade, who was popular with all who associated with him. . . . It was this changed Röhm then whom we, his old comrades from peacetime and wartime, would follow."[2] In later life, Röhm would often describe World War I as transformative for his generation. The political lessons he drew from this were based on his own hard-won experience of the war, which profoundly affected him both physically and mentally. It was in the war, as well, that he first discovered his organizational skills.

On June 28, 1914, Archduke Franz Ferdinand, the heir to the Austro-Hungarian thrones, and his wife Sophie, Duchess of Hohenberg, were assassinated in Bosnia. The international crisis arising out of the Austro-Hungarian and German responses to the assassination accelerated in late July. On July 30, 1914, Röhm broke off his summer holiday to return to his regiment and go over its mobilization timetable. On August 1, Kaiser Wilhelm II, as supreme commander of the German armed forces, proclaimed a "threatening state of war"[3] and ordered the mobilization of the German armies. In Ingolstadt, as in other German cities, lively crowds flocked the streets.

At the outbreak of war, Bavaria put an army of 406,000 noncommissioned officers and men, 9,670 officers, 3,083 officials, medical professionals, and veterinarians into the field. The Tenth Bavarian Infantry Regiment was part of the Sixth Bavarian Division, which, with the Fifth Bavarian

Division, formed the Third Bavarian Army Corps under the command of General Ludwig Freiherr von Gebsattel.[4]

Röhm's regiment left Ingolstadt at 9:00 p.m. on the first mobilization day, August 2. It reached its initial destination, Remelach (Rémilly), in Lorraine on the Franco-German border, on the evening of August 3. In the event of war, Germany's military strategy, the Schlieffen Plan, called for the main German attack to be made on France through Belgium. German troops crossed into Belgium on August 4. On the southwestern border, the predominantly Bavarian forces of the Sixth Army, under the command of the Bavarian Crown Prince, Prince Rupprecht, initially had a defensive role—to protect the left flank of the advancing German forces. The Tenth Infantry Regiment was among Bavarian troops guarding positions behind the lines, while fighting was underway with French forces seeking to attack Germany via Lorraine, as outlined in France's Plan XVII.[5]

Ninety-two Allied, and seventy German, divisions clashed between August 14 and 25 in four simultaneous engagements known as the Battle of the Frontiers. Toward the end of this period, the Tenth Bavarian Infantry Regiment was ordered to cross the border. For the first and last time in the war, almost the entire Bavarian army attacked the enemy at the same time.[6]

Röhm was wounded near Spada in the fighting for Maixe and Crévic on August 25 when a shot lightly glanced his forehead. He claimed his immediate superior recommended him for the Iron Cross Second Class for bravery in the battle, when Röhm took over a unit to urge the attack forward. The Brigade Commander, Colonel Freiherr von Tautphoeus, however, rejected this recommendation, arguing, according to Röhm, that as an adjutant, Röhm's place was with his commander.[7]

Röhm's regiment suffered heavy losses in continuous fighting from August 25 to September 10, 1914, in the fighting around Gellenoncourt, which the regiment captured on September 8. Just after this, on September 9, 1914, as a result of the battle of the Marne, German troops began a partial withdrawal on the Marne. This marked the failure of the Schlieffen Plan. It was "an operational defeat of the first magnitude"[8] for Germany, as Germany had no alternative strategy. The defeat and its consequences were not made public.

On September 19 and 20, Röhm's regiment again saw action in the German advance on the Côtes-Lorraines, participating in the capture of both Haudronvilles and Hattonchâtel. On the morning of September 24, 1914, the regiment was ordered to withdraw from its position and attack the hills near Spada that night. On September 24, 1914, five officers and 67 men were killed; eight officers and 322 men were wounded; and over 100 men were missing. During the battle, while he slept in the front line, Röhm was hit by a shot that tore away the upper part of his nose.[9]

He was evacuated behind the lines, then to Metz and Kaiserslauten. Despite recurring wound erysipelas, a bacterial skin infection, his wound healed and a replacement nose was created for him. He was then transferred to the military hospital in Bad Reichenhall in Bavaria. He slowly learned to breathe through his nose again, and he claimed that he recovered quickly. Medical reports on his personal file described his surgery as successful, but in 1916, he was still experiencing breathing difficulties that necessitated further operations on his nose.[10]

The wound disfigured Röhm. Before the wound, his appearance had been normal, with a round face and regular features. Plastic surgery was in its infancy and he was left with a flattened or almost nonexistent upper nose, a small button of a lower nose, and a scar across his cheek. The scar gradually became less prominent, though it was always visible. Röhm claimed that the wound had no lasting side effects. Yet, as a result, he suffered from recurrent medical problems for the rest of his life. The wound was "constantly festering,"[11] according to his friend Robert Bergmann.

There is no clear evidence to indicate what the psychological effects of the wound were. It may have put an end to his prewar dandyism. Franz von Hörauf claimed that Miss Bauer broke off her engagement with Röhm after he was wounded because she did not want to live with a man who was so disfigured. Two of his friends and contemporaries, Hörauf and Hanns Betz, claimed that the facial wound accounted for his homosexuality, even though Röhm's own comments indicate that this was not the case.[12] These speculations probably cast more light on their conceptions of homosexuality than on Röhm's own reaction to his wounds. They may indicate, as well, that Röhm sought out the company of women more before 1914 than afterward, possibly because in the war, he proved his masculinity to himself and others by other means—through his courage in combat.

On October 19, 1914, Röhm was awarded the Iron Cross Second Class for "brave conduct in the face of the enemy,"[13] and on December 3, 1914, he was promoted to First Lieutenant. By April 1915, he had recovered enough to resume duties in the regiment's replacement battalion, and on April 17, 1915, he returned to his regiment at Spada as adjutant to its commander. From November 1914 to June 1916, the regiment had remained in the sector of the St. Mihiel Salient (Chauvoncourt-Spada-Lamorville). Trenches were built up in October 1914, and second and third lines of fortifications were built in May 1915. Within a few weeks, Röhm returned to frontline duty. In May 1915, he fought in Ailly Forest to repulse a French attempt to retake the salient.

On June 2, 1915, Röhm took command of the Tenth Company. As late as 1933, he claimed that his year as a company commander had been the best year of his life. Regimental practice was to spend nine days in the front line, followed by three rest days behind the lines at Chaillon. The one kilometer between the German and enemy lines was patrolled every night. German trench conditions were more comfortable than the British, and the regiment was stationed on a relatively quiet section of the front. Nevertheless, each day, both officers and men faced death or wounds on patrols, from enemy shells or from sniper fire. This was a pattern of casualties by attrition, rather than the heavy losses of a major battle. Combatants were often psychologically worn down by the constant danger, noise, and the discomfort caused by cold, mud, vermin, lack of sleep, and illness.[14]

In his autobiography, Röhm presented trench life as a matter of routine. His account emphasized his role as company commander and leader of his men. He may have felt that to admit to anything else would have cast doubt on his courage or his competence as an officer, and was not in keeping with the behavior expected of a commander. In his articles and speeches of 1933–34, he was more open about the demands of the front experience, and of the "pitiless zone"[15] of the foremost front of the war of material.

Röhm's own account suggested that he was a conscientious officer, perhaps even a martinet. He emphasized strict discipline, cleanliness, and the maintenance of peacetime standards of drill and training. He was concerned about his men's welfare in a paternalist way, but also maintained the privileges of rank. He claimed that he inherited a tired and fought-out company, and transformed it in a few months into the regiment's elite company. Röhm, at times, exaggerated his own achievements, claiming that he originated a system of aggressive night patrols in 1916. This was wider regimental practice, though his company was singled out for praise for its patrolling.[16]

He painted an idealized picture of his relations with his company and their soldierly camaraderie. The bonds between them all had lasted, he argued, proved by their tenth anniversary reunion in Feuchtwangen on September 4, 1927. The company held a further reunion in June 1933, and an informal reunion in May 1934. He was closest to the Altdorf senior teacher, Robert Bergmann. Bergmann, a year older than Röhm, had already served under him in peacetime as a reservist. The two men would become lifelong friends as a result of their wartime service. In 1933, Bergmann dedicated an article on these experiences to "my most loyal and best comrade, my only friend for life, Captain Röhm in silent loyalty and deep affection."[17]

The impact of trench warfare on Röhm at the time was more profound than he admitted in his autobiography. Bergmann noted that "a deep, almost aching melancholy lay in his [Röhm's] manner; his cheerfulness seldom broke through also in joyous, carefree times."[18] Bergmann described Röhm as a connoisseur of the German poetic classics as well as a student of military literature. Together with the leader of the ninth company, Lieutenant Karl Bauer, they recited Wallenstein's last words from Schiller's *In Wallensteins Lager* one evening in the earth house the officers of the two companies shared. On October 25, 1915, just after the three men parted to return to their companies, Bauer was killed. Bergmann noted that he and Röhm were deeply affected by Bauer's death, Röhm writing that it was "the only time in the field that I shed bitter tears."[19]

* * *

The Chief of the German General Staff, General von Falkenhayn, aimed at destroying the French army by wearing it down in a battle of attrition. The German attack on the French fortresses around Verdun began on February 21, 1916. On June 1, 1916, a German offensive opened, aimed at capturing the jumping-off positions for a final attack on Verdun: the stronghold of Thiaumont, the ridge at Fleury, Fort Souville, and Fort Vaux. After the attack was halted on June 12, it resumed on the evening of June 22, 1916.[20]

The First Bavarian Infantry Division, to which the Tenth Infantry Regiment was attached, was assigned to a frontal attack on the armoured fortification of Thiaumont, and a French trench defense identified by the Germans as the Z-work on the high ridge Froideterre *(Kalte Erde)*. The Tenth Infantry Regiment was on the right of the line, with the tenth and eleventh companies in the front line.[21]

Fighting at Verdun was a battle of small units from shell hole to shell hole, a chaotic experience for those who fought there. So it was for Röhm on June 23, 1916. His company was torn apart and intermingled with men from other companies. Röhm, Bergmann, and the ten to fifteen men who remained with him attacked, cleaned out, and captured various French trench defenses *(I-Werke)*, taking two French officers and some sixty-five men prisoner. Röhm and his men captured I-Werke 147, which his superior officers believed was the successful precondition for the advance on Froideterre. Röhm, Bergmann, and others were badly wounded. Röhm made his way back behind the lines, with Bergmann and Röhm's batman Gößl. In the casualty clearing station, doctors discovered that Röhm had been hit by a projectile that passed near his lungs and left the body near the shoulder. Röhm's group set off further behind the lines with Bergmann, Gößl, two other wounded members of his company, and the French prisoners. The group came under French artillery shelling, and Röhm was hit again. Röhm called farewell to Bergmann and Gößl, who were also wounded once more, but Bergmann refused to give Röhm up for lost and eventually succeeded in helping him take shelter behind a small hill. Eventually, "with superhuman effort,"[22] Bergmann and Gößl dragged Röhm to a connecting trench. Röhm lost consciousness there and came to later the next day on a stretcher in a meadow. He had over ten shell splinters in his body. Bergmann had sent his comrades and medical orderlies to carry him back overnight. "I was saved."[23] Röhm always regarded Bergmann as the man responsible for saving his life.

His regiment, together with the Bavarian Infantry Life Guards Regiment, had captured the armoured fortification Thiaumont and occupied the greater part of the village of Fleury. Röhm commented, "I bled from many wounds and was greatly weakened; but I felt full of pride, that I had been there. The 23rd of June, the regiment's greatest day of victory, is also the proudest day of my life."[24] The regiment was highly praised by the king and in the Supreme Army Command communiqué. Victory, however, came at a great cost. Ten officers, 140 non-commissioned officers and men were dead; seventeen officers and almost one thousand men were wounded.

Immediately before the battle, Röhm had been awarded the Iron Cross First Class for his outstanding actions and bravery since the beginning of the war. On the basis of his actions on June 23, and, he claimed, at a suggestion from his former battalion commander, Röhm put his name forward for Bavaria's highest military decoration, the Militär-Max-Joseph-Orden (MMJO), for conspicuous achievement over and above the dictates of duty. The order carried with it a knighthood, with the title Ritter von. Röhm's case was strongly supported by his commanders, though they had to admit that they were dependent on Röhm's own account of the fighting, since so many of the witnesses to his acts were dead.[25]

Röhm was not awarded the MMJO. Although the order's chapter voted four to three in favor of the award, War Minister von Hellingrath followed the advice of the Chancellery Office of the order and recommended the king reject the award on the grounds that actions like Röhm's occurred frequently, and were therefore not over and above the dictates of duty. The king accepted this advice. It may have become harder to win the decoration as the war progressed.[26]

Röhm claimed he was rejected because the War Ministry was trying to restrict the giving of medals for financial reasons. He may have found this out through his contacts in the War Ministry, but it is also possible that this was advanced to him as a face-saving explanation. Disappointment at not getting the title and entry into an elite order played a role in the anger Röhm admitted to feeling. Some of his friends, like Hörauf, had already won it. Röhm's uneven disciplinary record before 1914 did not affect the decision.[27]

Röhm's career as a frontline officer ended on June 23, 1916. He had proved himself to be a brave and decisive junior officer. He had met the standards of the profession he chose and the supreme test of masculinity as defined by his society. Supporting Röhm's nomination for the MMJO, the Commander of the Eleventh Infantry Brigade, Major General von Tautphoeus, described him as "one of the 10th Infantry Regiment's best officers, whose sang-froid, bravery and constant dash had an exemplary effect on his subordinates."[28]

Whatever the physical and psychological costs of his wounds, Röhm's character steadied in this period. This may, of course, have been the result of maturity. By 1916, he was almost thirty. Equally, personal characteristics that caused problems for him in peacetime—his touchiness and readiness to take offence, willfulness and insubordination, a tendency to find fault with superior and subordinate alike—now showed their obverse—bravery, willingness to take decisions on his own initiative, readiness to demand and get a lot from his subordinates, ability to lead men and inspire them.

Röhm spent the rest of 1916 recovering from his wounds before resuming work in the War Ministry in October. He spent two days in the field hospital at Romagne and six days in a war hospital at Montmédy before being transferred to a reserve hospital in Frankfurt and, finally, the reserve hospital at the Kriegsschule in Munich. In Montmédy, six shell splinters were removed from his back, upper thigh, chest, arm, and face. A further two splinters were removed from his upper back and thigh in Frankfurt. During the entire period he was under medical treatment, additional large and small shell splinters were removed from his body. During his convalescence, Röhm complained repeatedly of unsteadiness, sleeplessness, poor memory, loss of appetite, general exhaustion, and great nervous instability. In addition, he reported heart palpitations. His doctors characterized these as neurasthenia, nervous complaints as a result of combat experience. It is not clear what treatment, if any, they gave this condition, which tended to be diagnosed among officers as the equivalent of shell shock. In his autobiography, Röhm did not mention his neurasthenia. In general, he made light of his injuries and of his period of recovery, which his medical notes show to have been more difficult than he acknowledged.[29]

He spent time convalescing in a hospital at Hohenaschau in Upper Bavaria and at home, and started working from home, handling requests for reserve status. By October, he approached a relative at the War Ministry, Colonel Koller, for alternative employment. Soon he was made adjutant to the head of the army section, Lieutenant Colonel Freiherr Gustav Kreß von Kressenstein. Röhm, who was promoted to captain in April 1917, worked in this section from October 1916 to May 1917. It was von Kreß who taught him how to work, Röhm claimed.[30]

The army section handled all general army and service matters, as well as keeping an eye on domestic political developments. Röhm's responsibilities included viewing, checking, and submitting the work of all experts in charge of the various sections of the Ministry, as well as handling any issues raised by deputies in the Bavarian Landtag. For the first time, however indirectly, Röhm was involved in domestic German politics. At the end of his period in the War Ministry, von Kreß assessed Röhm as "a lively, sympathetic officer who was tirelessly active, with good understanding, intellectually lively, and with particularly pronounced initiative. Energetic, tactful and with a very good military manner, he filled his position excellently." [31]

In May 1917, Röhm returned to frontline service as an active staff officer for the Twelfth Bavarian Infantry Division, commanded by Major General Freiherr Nagel von Aichberg and stationed in Romania. The Twelfth Bavarian Infantry Division had been created in 1916 out of three infantry regiments all formed that year—the K.B. Twenty-sixth, Twenty-seventh, and Twenty-eighth Infantry Regiments—and the Twenty-second Field Artillery Regiment. [32]

Röhm was appointed second orderly officer in the divisional staff under Captain Kieffer, head of the Section 1B, at Focşani in Romania. Röhm's posting may have been organized by his regimental friend von Hörauf, who was the division's first general staff officer. Röhm soon became Hörauf's first orderly officer. From May 1917 to April 1918, the division remained in Romania, with its headquarters in Focşani. Between August 6 and September 3, 1917, the division attacked Romanian forces over the River Siret (Sereth) to the north and east of Focşani in the battle of Mărăşeşti, but the attack was brought to a standstill. [33]

In Romania, Röhm began to develop his skills as an organizer. His responsibilities included replacement and supply, accommodation, provisions and catering, and health and veterinary matters. He was helped by Bergmann, whom he arranged to have accompany him. In February 1918, von Nagel assessed Röhm as "a very zealous, lively officer with an open, straightforward character and cheerful disposition. He comprehends promptly and works quickly and thoroughly." [34]

After an armistice was agreed with Romania and Russia in early December 1917, the division advanced over Brăila and Galaţi (Galatz) in eastern Romania. It was then prepared and trained in the area around Mizil for a transfer to the western front. On April 17, 1918, it left Romania and went by train on a nine-day journey to Rethel in northern France. On the way, Röhm made a quick stop in Vienna to visit his sister and brother-in-law, Lore and Adolf Lippert. [35]

On arrival in Rethel, Röhm was appointed second general staff officer in the division. By the time the division arrived on the western front, the last major German offensive in the west, Operation Michael—the so-called Ludendorff offensive—had failed, exhausting and demoralizing German forces. Ludendorff continued to shift the focus of German attacks, aiming for a breakthrough. The Twelfth Bavarian Infantry Division took part in the last two of these battles—the battle of Soissons-Reims, from May 27 to June 13, 1918, and the offensive against the eastern edge of the Marne salient on July 16.[36]

Immediately after Soissons-Reims, Röhm met Quartermaster General Erich Ludendorff for the first time at Lagéry. Röhm claimed in his autobiography that, much to the horror of the senior officers present, he pointed out the division's inadequate equipment and weapons to Ludendorff. Röhm's contemporaries testified to his tendency to speak frankly to his superiors.[37]

In his autobiography, Röhm's account of his experiences as a staff officer on the western front in 1918 omitted any of the difficulties the division was encountering. Its fighting ability was faltering. Its staff knew troop discipline was loosening. Enemy intelligence saw the division as third class, with low morale.[38]

Supply difficulties worsened morale. Röhm's responsibilities included allocating quarters, bringing up the baggage train, setting up traffic police, establishing ammunition dumps, organizing the catering, medical and veterinary services, protection against air and gas attacks, and economic exploitation of the countryside. "Here I was in my element and I prided myself that no one could challenge me. With this there was always unrest and disorder, and this suited me."[39] Röhm commented that the troops were right to demand what they needed and to take no account of the staff officer's difficulties. He did not indicate that it was Allied artillery and air superiority that restricted the transport of German food supplies to the front.

The Allied counteroffensive on the Marne, the so-called second Battle of the Marne, began on July 18, 1918. The German Seventh Army, of which the Twelfth Bavarian Infantry Division was a part, retreated to a new defensive line. By the end of August, the division was pulled back still further. After two or three weeks rest at Le Cateau, on August 26 it became reserve for the Army Corps Crown Prince Rupprecht, and was transferred to Roubaix on the Flanders front.[40]

Before this, Röhm had accompanied General Nagel von Aichberg on a visit to the head of the General Staff of the Sixth Army, Oberstleutnant Herrgott, in Tournai from August 24 to 30, 1918. Röhm himself sought and received Herrgott's permission to move equipment held behind the lines— clothing kept for the troops and sutlery—back to Germany.[41]

The division returned to the Flanders front at the beginning of September. From this time on, it was retreating continuously with heavy losses. On October 6, the division, which had lost over 3,300 men, 40 guns, and 250 machine guns, was relieved and evacuated to the Sixth Army in the area around Lille. The troops learned that Germany had sought an armistice.[42]

By October 2, 1918, because so many general staff officers had fallen ill from influenza, Röhm has been seconded to the staff of the Prussian Guard Corps. He was given a new area of responsibility—evaluating all reports and messages from the front, making proposals for the use of aircraft and balloons, and employment of the communication troops. He enjoyed working in the Prussian staff where everything was under control, he later wrote.[43] This comment suggested that he was not immune to the Bavarian officer's inferiority complex vis-à-vis his Prussian counterpart.

By mid-October 1918, Röhm returned to the staff of the Twelfth Bavarian Infantry Division when it was transferred from Flanders to France. The mood at the front was depressed, he admitted, though he attributed this to the poisoning of the soldiers' minds by the home front. Soon after this, Röhm, too, fell ill with influenza. A further wave of Spanish influenza had hit German forces in late October. On October 21, Bergmann, now Röhm's orderly officer, wrote to Emilie Röhm that her son had a very high fever and was physically and psychologically exhausted. The same day, Röhm was sent first to Field Hospital 38, and then to a hospital at Hall near Brussels. It was at this time that Nagel von Aichberg reportedly said of Röhm "'Röhm was the best general staff officer I ever had.'"[44]

Röhm returned from hospital on November 3, only to collapse with influenza again. He applied for, and was granted, ten days leave in Munich. The day he was due to leave, November 8, 1918, he learned the news both of revolution in Munich and of the Kaiser's abdication.[45]

Röhm was a few weeks short of his thirty-first birthday when the entire world of Royal Bavaria and Imperial Germany on which he had based his life to that point began to collapse around him. The state and society into which he was born was disintegrating. Röhm was about to be abruptly thrown out of his chosen path in life and have his assumptions and values challenged. His future was open, more open that it had been since he left school. Like millions of others, he stepped into an unknown world. Equally like millions, he went into this new world unwillingly. The new world could not offer him the certainty and prestige of the old.

CHAPTER 4

The Trauma of the German Revolution 1918–19

I am of the opinion that if we had had political officers in November 1918 the revolution would not have triumphed. [1]

Ernst Röhm

During World War I, Ernst Röhm matured, demonstrated his bravery, and discovered his organizational skills. For these reasons, it was a key experience for him. His transformation was completed by the German Revolution of 1918 and 1919, which politicized the thirty-one-year-old. The revolution was a traumatic, as well as a radicalizing, experience. Röhm spoke and wrote less of this aspect of his development, and his claims in the autobiography about his actions at the time were, at times, misleading. The story he told reflected both the prevailing interpretation of the revolution on the *völkisch* right by 1928 and, in some ways, his own image of how he wanted to have acted rather than how he did act. His interpretation of the reasons for the revolution had some distinctive elements.

From January 1918, despite increased surveillance, Bavarian workers participated in strikes, demonstrations, and protest movements. On May 22, 1918 in Ingolstadt, uniformed soldiers participated in riots in which the town hall was stormed and set on fire. Soldiers' riots followed in other towns. In July and August, there were large demonstrations by women in Munich protesting about the lack of food. On November 2, King Ludwig III conceded full democratization and responsible government.[2]

The revolution began in Bavaria on November 7, 1918. At the end of a mass SPD and USPD public peace demonstration on the Theresienwiese in

Munich, a breakaway group led by USPD intellectual Kurt Eisner won over various groups of soldiers in the city and seized power. By 7:00 p.m., the government no longer controlled any troops in Munich, and at 1:00 a.m. on November 8, Eisner proclaimed the Bavarian Republic. No officers or officer cadets offered to protect the Bavarian royal family, and the king and his family left for the Chiemsee. The first German monarchy fell in Bavaria.[3]

The causes of the revolution in the army and the home front originated in the way the war was waged. Social tension, inequality, and political divisions characterized the organization of both the German armed forces and the home front, and helped bring about strikes and unrest at the home front in 1917 and 1918, and mutinies and revolution in 1918. The rigidity of some aspects of the Empire weakened the German war effort in the field and at home.[4]

Bavaria made an unprecedented military effort, but—as elsewhere in Germany—its home front preparations were improvised. Munich and Bavaria industrialized rapidly. Food supply was a problem as early as 1916. Inequality in the distribution of rations led to popular unrest. War weariness, political radicalization, and social conflict were combined with hostility to control of the war economy from Berlin, and anti-Prussianism.[5]

Röhm spent almost a year on the home front in 1916–17, the last seven months working in a government department in Munich. Reports prepared for the War Ministry made it clear that morale on the home front was deteriorating and that it was worsened by the comments made by soldiers in their letters and on leave. Röhm made no direct mention at all of political, economic, or social conditions inside Germany in his autobiography. This omission was significant and politically motivated, whether consciously or unconsciously. To write of the conditions of the life on the home front would remind his readers of the hardships of 1916–18 and would cast a more negative light on the generally positive picture he had painted of royal Bavaria and imperial Germany. It would make the outbreak of the revolution more explicable.[6]

It has been suggested that Röhm's defensiveness at not taking action against the revolution led him to stress the seriousness of his influenza. This defensiveness was related to Röhm's own explanation for the success of the revolution—that it triumphed because of the ineffectiveness of officers' resistance to it. On November 8, on his way home to recuperate, he received the news of the Kaiser's abdication. By the time he arrived back in Munich, the war was over and the city was ruled by its revolutionary soldiers' and workers' council.[7]

While Röhm claimed only to have discovered revolutionary feeling among shirkers in the étappe in October-November 1918, the fighting ability of his own division was weakening by mid-1918. He claimed that the over-throw of the imperial regime was not a revolution but a mutiny on the home front, and that it had succeeded because senior officers had not taken decisive enough action against it. It was "the most shameful overthrow of the system, which had chosen for itself feeble and old men as supports, by the demands and noise of the streets."[8] He claimed the revolution had succeeded in Bavaria because of the failure of the Bavarian War Minister, and the War Ministry in general, to take energetic measures of resistance. He criticized senior com-manders on the home front for cowardice, lack of decisiveness, neglect of duty, and lack of character, above all, in their failure to take a stand against the revolution, even if this meant death.

By attributing the failures of the army leadership and officers to their individual character flaws and weaknesses, Röhm avoided facing any military or political factors that contradicted his presentation of the course of the war. His focus on an army mutiny ignored any contribution to the revo-lution at home made by the political, social, and economic problems and tensions of Imperial Germany. He avoided acknowledging that attempts to use troops, even Prussian troops, to suppress the uprising foundered on the troops' unwillingness to fire on fellow soldiers.[9]

His explanation drew on the "stab in the back" myth—that the unde-feated army in the field was stabbed in the back by the revolution at home—but had its own distinctive flavor. Röhm's emphasis on the revolution as a mutiny in the army is, in some ways, reinforced by the recent historiography of the German Revolution, which emphasizes the concept of a strike by the army against the war.[10]

Röhm's emphasis on mutiny also reflected the trauma that the soldiers' turning against their officers was for him. The German Revolution was marked by soldiers tearing badges and insignia of rank from their officers' uniforms and by other acts of hatred directed against the caste that led them in war. In addition, Kurt Eisner, the first Minister President of Bavaria, was an intellectual and pacifist of Jewish origin. Eisner was the antithesis of military discipline and efficiency. Eisner's success in winning the support of Bavarian troops was a reminder to Röhm that, despite his professed concern for the ordinary soldier, many of these soldiers rejected the values of the officer corps and the army.[11]

Yet, Röhm's insistence that the army mutiny and unrest on the streets could easily have been brought under control if senior commanders had acted decisively meant that anti-Semitism was less salient in his explanation of the revolution and its causes. It also meant that Röhm could see the solution in a remilitarization and politicization of the army in the right direction.[12]

In his autobiography, Röhm claimed to have triumphed over representatives of the revolution in arguments, or to have defied them. There is no independent evidence for any of these statements. Where he touched on aspects of the revolution that others had personal experience of, the behavior he admitted to was less assertive. He took off his cockade in the imperial colors at Munich railway station to be allowed off the train by the station guards.[13]

Röhm recovered at home under his mother's care, and by late November or early December, reported to the Ministry of Military Affairs. He volunteered to serve as a briefing officer to explain the current situation to returning frontline troops. On December 4, 1918, he traveled to the headquarters of the First Bavarian Reserve Corps, and from there to the Twelfth Bavarian Infantry Division in Elberfeld-Barmen. They were soon ordered home to Landshut, and the division staff was dissolved. Röhm was then appointed adjutant of the Eleventh Bavarian Infantry Brigade in Ingolstadt on January 1, 1919. On January 2, he returned to Ingolstadt to take up this position for just over three months until early April 1919. Röhm later described this as a period of resistance, mainly passive, on his part, to the demands of the revolutionary soldiers' councils.[14]

As Minister President, Kurt Eisner led a provisional SPD-USPD government until Bavarian state elections were held on January 12, 1919. Eisner's government was relatively moderate, emphasizing order and giving the royal family permission to return to Bavaria. The treatment of returning officers by the government was initially generous. Like the other officers he later criticized, Röhm took no immediate action against the revolution, but was rather able to continue employment under its auspices.[15]

In the Bavarian state elections of January 12, 1919, the USPD received a severe defeat. The two Socialist parties together won an overall majority in Munich, but in Bavaria as a whole, they only won 35.5 percent of the vote. Together with the Farmers' League (*Bauernbund*), this was a vote of 45 percent for the provisional government. The new government would not be a socialist government. Similar results were recorded in the elections for the National Constituent Assembly on January 19, 1919.[16]

Röhm's own public or traceable actions against the revolution, as reported in his autobiography, all date from February 1919, that is, *after* the elections made it clear that the wider Bavarian electorate did not support the revolution. In *Die Geschichte eines Hochverräters*, Röhm gave extracts from three leaflets that he prepared and distributed among the troops in February 1919. In the first—"Sleepers, awake!"—he called on Germans to awaken and rebel to express their national pride. In the second—"*Quousque tandem Catalina?*" ("How long still, oh Cataline?")—Röhm attacked Eisner for opening Bavarian files on the origins of the war to demonstrate Germany's guilt in starting the war. In the third leaflet—"Soldiers!"—Röhm attributed the revolution to the actions of "commercial Jews and knaves"[17] paid by Germany's enemies to bring about the revolution just before France and Britain collapsed themselves. These traitors continued to receive foreign pay to ensure anarchy ruled in Germany. He called on soldiers to save their honor and atone for their crime of breaking their oath to the Kaiser.

This final leaflet already showed Röhm advancing aspects of the myth that the German army, about to be victorious in the field, was stabbed in the back, in Röhm's version, by traitors and Jews in the pay of Britain and France. While his anti-Semitic comments were mild in comparison with the usual form these took on the extreme right, they marked his first recorded support of anti-Semitism. Equally, they marked the first explicitly political anti-Semitic remarks in his autobiography.[18]

Röhm's pamphlets also showed an inability to move outside of his own social and political standpoint. The arguments could only appeal to men who already shared his view of the world. They adopted a top-to-bottom approach and drew on religious metaphors. God deserted Germany when its soldiers broke their oath, he argued in "Soldiers!" for example.[19]

In his own account of this period, Röhm emphasized every piece of evidence of popular opposition to the revolution. Ingolstadt press reports indicate that he exaggerated this. Wartime industrial development temporarily changed the political landscape in the town. In the Landtag elections, the SPD won 49.3 percent of the votes, and the USPD 2.8 percent in Ingolstadt—the two socialist parties had a bare majority of 52.1 percent.[20]

Röhm claimed to have been so angry when Eisner visited Ingolstadt on January 5 and gave a provocative speech against officers that he demanded the soldiers' council personally take the officers under its protection. He asserted that he engineered an officers' strike in protest at the garrison soldiers' council's attempt to stop him recruiting soldiers for a popular home guard. On February 12, despite opposition within the government, the Minister of Military Affairs, Rosshaupter, had called for all Bavarian men capable of bearing arms, to enter a popular home guard to prevent any threat of civil war.[21]

On February 21, on his way to the opening of the Bavarian Constituent Assembly, where he planned to offer the resignation of his provisional government, Kurt Eisner was assassinated by a young officer, Graf Anton von Arco auf Valley. Unrest broke out in Munich, and a Central Council of the Bavarian Republic took power. At the time of the assassination, Röhm claimed to have been on his way to Munich to a meeting at the Military Affairs' Ministry on the issue of the officers' strike.[22]

Eisner's huge public funeral took place in Munich on February 26. In Ingolstadt itself, there was a meeting at which the commandant condemned the murder in the officers' mess. While Röhm assured his readers that he did not want to give up the fight, he refrained from taking a public stand. From his own account, Röhm was not one of the officers who left the room in protest. On March 1, 1919, he resumed his activities as an adjutant, despite the opposition of the revolutionary soldiers of the garrison council and the fortress commandant, whom Röhm criticized for being too cooperative with the council.[23]

Röhm began to look elsewhere for employment. In early April, he surreptitiously left for Ohrdruf in Thuringia, where the "Bavarian Free Corps for the protection of the Eastern borders" (*Bayerisches Freikorps für den Grenzschutz Ost*), later known as the Freikorps Epp, was being formed under the command of Colonel Franz Ritter von Epp, who had led the elite Bavarian Infantry Leib-Regiment in World War I. By May 1, Röhm had been joined there by Bergmann.[24]

From November 1918 on, the army leadership had encouraged the formation of volunteer units intended to be more politically reliable than the army; this was later supported by Defense Minister Gustav Noske. Freikorps, or free corps, were usually led by officers from the imperial army—sometimes junior officers—and recruited students, young men too young to fight in the war, and some former soldiers. The government condoned the violence and brutality with which the Freikorps proceeded against the revolutionary forces. This gave rise to a more violent and radicalized form of soldiering. The Freikorps mentality combined a desire to continue or experience the war with hostility toward the new Republic and a readiness to use violence against internal political opponents. Many of its activists later moved into right-wing paramilitary organizations and the Nazi Party.[25]

The Freikorps Epp was a small part of a much larger phenomenon. Its commander was a highly decorated Bavarian officer who had served in China, German South-West Africa and World War I, where he won both the Pour le Mérite and the Militar-Max-Joseph-Orden. While Röhm admired Epp, some of his Bavarian military contemporaries were more critical of him. As the one Bavarian military leader of any note involved in the suppression of the Council Republic, Epp would later gain an undeserved prestige as the liberator of Munich.[26]

With the formation in Munich of the more radical Second Council Republic on April 7, 1919, the SPD-dominated Hoffmann government fled to Bamberg and soon appealed for federal help. South of the Danube, Bavaria had no troops loyal to the government. Defense Minister Noske permitted open recruiting for the Freikorps Epp. The number of volunteers was small and mainly composed of officers. By April 16, the federal government had decided that troops from northern Germany would move against the Second Council Republic. The newly renamed "Bavarian Rifle Corps" (*Bayerisches Schützenkorps*) left Ohrdruf on April 22 to travel to Ulm. Accompanied by Röhm, Hörauf, and Rittmeister Weingart, Epp traveled to Ingolstadt by special train on April 26, 1919, to have discussions with General von Möhl. That evening, they returned to Ulm and the corps was placed under Gruppenkommando West, led by General Haas.[27]

The Freikorps Epp, numbering between 700 and 900 men, was a small contingent of the 46,000-man force that attacked Munich from the west, north, and south. Operations began on April 30, and the first troops under General Deetjen reached Munich on May 1. By the evening of May 2, Munich was in the hands of the government troops, after bitter fighting.[28]

Röhm's own role in the liberation of Munich was not a prominent one. On the morning of May 2, he was appointed to be the chief of staff of Lieutenant Colonel Herrgott, who was to be the new city commander of Munich. The two men drove into Munich, avoiding the fighting, to the Hotel Vierjahreszeiten, where the overall commander of the troops attacking Munich, Lieutenant General von Oven, had made his headquarters. The fighting in Munich ended quickly. A bloody and indiscriminate counterrevolutionary purge of the city began in which historians estimate as many as one thousand people were killed under martial law.[29]

Röhm started work on May 3 in the army museum. His responsibilities were the administrative reorganization of the city's emergency services, purging of the police, creation of a guard regiment for Munich, and setting up a Munich self-defense force. Röhm worked closely with the new Police President of Munich, Ernst Pöhner, in the political "cleansing" of the police, and in arresting suspected leftists.[30]

Röhm claimed to have met strong opposition from the Bavarian government because of his plans for an armed *Einwohnerwehr* (residents' defense force), even though he allegedly won the support of the local SPD. On May 13, 1919, he wrote a personal report to von Oven justifying the arming of the Einwohnerwehr. Among other things, the Einwohnerwehr was a last reserve in the event of revolution. "If today the federal troops withdrew, this would be the signal for the beginning of destructive activity among the less independent and easily influenced Bavarian troops,"[31] he warned. Röhm was not alone in his lack of confidence in the political reliability and discipline of the ordinary soldier at this time.

Röhm claimed that the Hoffmann government decided to remove Herrgott from the position of City Commandant and replace him with Major von Seisser. In an act of solidarity, Röhm stood down from his own position.

In May 1919, he returned to the staff of the Rifle Corps Epp, which was now known as the large Bavarian Rifle Brigade 21 *(große bayerische Schützenbrigade 21)*. It now incorporated various other Freikorps units and cavalry and artillery units.[32]

In 1928, Röhm claimed that he had come to recognize, in his short period in the city commandant's office, that officers had to think and act politically. The belief that the armed forces had been apolitical in Imperial Germany was incorrect. The soldier's oath of allegiance required a clear political will to protect the throne and fatherland in all circumstances. The stability of the old system allowed some to think they did not need to bother with political issues, but this was a false assumption. The events of November 9, 1918 were the reckoning for the army officers' and NCOs' political lack of judgment. No other profession or estate gave as much blood in the war, yet no other profession and estate had been so deprived of its rights after the war. Before the war, the army had at its head a soldier who also had the right to take political decisions, the king or other princely head of state. "The officer was at least then spared taking orders from a non-soldier."[33] In the Weimar Republic, with a civilian parliamentarian in charge, political influence on the army could not be fended off as it had been in the imperial system. Röhm conceded that most officers chose to remain apolitical, but "I at least was not prepared to give up my right to think and act politically in the framework of the service activity that was given to me."[34]

The passage indicated that Röhm saw his appointment to the city commandant's office as a key step in his politicization. It was also, clearly, a self-justification. His own prewar military career had been as apolitical as those of the officers he criticized. He had to explain and justify his change.

Röhm's outrage at the fact that the achievement of responsible government in Germany meant that officers would have to follow the orders of civilians also suggested that his political attitudes came from his heightened consciousness of his rights as an officer. His opposition to the revolution came in part from "*social* horror, the bewilderment of the ruling class when the lower orders suddenly, inexplicably, get out of hand."[35] Röhm may have found the revolution all the more threatening because his position in this ruling class was not yet fully established.

The actions of ordinary soldiers and sailors in 1918 and 1919 were an explicit rejection of the old army and the old regime. Röhm wrote about such men as if they were the dregs of society or misled by Jews in the pay of Germany's enemies. His own proposal on the need for an Einwohnerwehr in Munich, specifically the section that suggested that Bavarian troops could still be easily subverted by leftist agitation, suggested his confidence in his men was far more shaken that he could admit for political, and perhaps also psychological, reasons in 1928. The privileged position of Bavarian officers before the war meant that Röhm could not comprehend why many Bavarians had turned against the imperial system.

Röhm presented himself as having been politicized by the 1918 revolution. More accurately, Imperial Germany had allowed his political attitudes and assumptions to remain implicit and unchallenged. In 1918, they were challenged, and he reacted strongly against this. Röhm's reaction was so strong that it altered his entire career. Over the next five years, he would pursue both military and political activity.

CHAPTER 5

"Machine-gun King" of Bavaria 1919–22

Twelve years ago today I met Captain Röhm. It was in a cellar where we racked our brains over how to oppose the revolutionary movement.[1]

Adolf Hitler

In May 1919, Ernst Röhm rejoined the Freikorps Epp, then renamed the Rifle Brigade Epp. From then until December 1922, Röhm served as a staff officer for Epp. In this capacity, he had both official, public duties and secret duties, where public and private, defense and politics blurred together. These secret duties, and his own response to the revolution, led Röhm to increasingly independent political activity.

By early 1922, an article in the Social Democrat (SPD) newspaper, the *Münchener Post*, titled "Attack columns against the *Münchener Post*," detailed Röhm's activities and those of his friends. This article described Röhm and Captain Heiß, the overall leader of the Reichsflagge, as "machine-gun kings"[2] of Bavaria. The article claimed Röhm had a network of thirty other current and former officers in Vienna who regulated weapons smuggling from Bavaria to Austria and Hungary. The Bavarian weapons smugglers met almost daily in the Witteschen Weinstube, Barerstrasse 55, with Röhm as their chairman. The article noted that Röhm was a member of various right-wing political organizations, despite this being strictly forbidden for officers. Röhm reported the story's claims extensively in his autobiography, and only denied its allegation that he had enriched himself from his weapons holdings.

Röhm's secret duties originated as a result of the restrictions of the Treaty of Versailles on the size of the German Army and its armaments. The military exploited various means of evading these provisions. Röhm's secret military activities began on the orders of his commanders. Equally, his unofficial political activities were tolerated, and often encouraged, by his immediate superiors—Epp and, over him, General von Möhl.

The atmosphere in Munich following the overthrow of the Council Republic was febrile, and further left-wing unrest was feared. Under military rule in Munich, which continued until November 1919, extreme rightist groups were tolerated, and even promoted, by the army, whose increased political role contributed to Bavaria's overall move to the right.[3]

On May 12, 1919, the national law to form a provisional army *(Reichswehr)* came into effect, and the preexisting Bavarian army was dissolved. In the course of May and June, Reichswehr Section Command 4 (Möhl) was formed from Bavarian Schützenbrigade 21 (Epp) in Munich, and Bavarian Reichswehr Brigades 22 in Augsburg, 23 in Würzburg, and 24 in Nuremberg. The army was gradually reduced in size in conformity with the treaty provisions: on October 1, 1919, to a transitional army of 200,000 men; on September 1, 1920 to 150,000 men; and by January 1, 1921 to 100,000 men. In Bavaria, the military authorities used this to purge the army of any soldiers supporting the left, including the SPD. [4]

Röhm's formal administrative responsibilities as a staff officer, and, after September 1, 1920, as Epp's orderly officer, included lodgings, transport, financial decrees, procuring equipment and weapons, lorries, and the use of transport. This was largely the same area of responsibility that he had in World War I as a staff officer. His responsibilities extended to drafting routine and important correspondence, reports, and orders.[5]

Even as his secret military duties and his own political activities increased, Röhm continued to complete his normal administrative workload as well. The Schützenbrigade's headquarters were in the Prince Leopold barracks, where he worked long hours, and lived nearby in the Pension Isabella, Teng Street 33. On occasion, he drafted orders for, and acted for, Epp in areas outside his own formal area of responsibility. When Röhm countersigned a memorandum for accuracy, this usually indicated he had drafted the memorandum concerned.[6]

Röhm's personal friendship with Epp would continue for the rest of his life, interrupted only by a temporary estrangement in 1923. Karl Schreyer noted that, in his relations with his superiors, Röhm was "a man with particularly pronounced views of his own and his own will."[7] One of Epp's military contemporaries criticized Epp for indecisiveness. Did Röhm play for Epp, the role Göring later played for Hitler—did Röhm make Epp feel and act more decisively? Epp certainly gave Röhm particular trust and left him plenty of initiative. As a result, "it was hard to say who was the master in the staff of Infantry Commander VII."[8] According to Röhm, Epp left all work on the

Einwohnerwehr to him. On a more personal level, did Epp, who was some nineteen years older than Röhm, become a surrogate father figure?

The need to maintain law and order internally against any further threats from the left, together with the policy of evading the disarmament provisions of the Treaty of Versailles, combined in the Bavarian Government's support for the Einwohnerwehr. The first Bavarian Einwohnerwehr had been local civil guards or self-defense forces organized in country districts for self-protection during the revolution. From June 1919 on, Forestry Councillor Georg Escherich's proposals for unifying these forces won the support of Gustav von Kahr, the president of the district government of Upper Bavaria, then of the Hoffmann state government and national Defense Minister Gustav Noske. While the Hoffmann Government wanted the Einwohnerwehr constituted on the basis of the broadest possible support, in practice, SPD supporters were reluctant to join. Working class opposition meant that even the middle class was reluctant to join in the cities and the Einwohnerwehr was strongest in the countryside. Escherich and his chief of staff, Lieutenant Colonel Kriebel, intended the organization to play an independent political role.[9]

As head of section Ib of Epp's staff, Röhm was responsible for providing the volunteer units—of which the Einwohnerwehr was the most important—with weapons, ammunition, and other equipment. Röhm placed one of the officers from his supply camp into the Einwohnerwehr's administrative section. Epp agreed that the Schützenbrigade would pass on a number of arms to the Einwohnerwehr each month. The Schützenbrigade would write these arms off as no longer functioning and obtain replacements. From time to time, Röhm accompanied Epp on his journeys of inspection of Einwohnerwehr units in the countryside, including one in the Chiemgau by national Defense Minister Noske, Bavarian Interior Minister Endres, and Kahr. While the Einwohnerwehr came to regard the weapons as theirs, Röhm was concerned to maintain the army's control over the weapons holdings. From the beginning, it was recognized that this work had to be kept secret and violated the peace treaty.[10]

By the beginning of 1920, the Einwohnerwehr was the one civil guard in Germany that was independent of state control. In February 1920, it was 224,000 men strong, with over 150,000 rifles and 1,000 machine guns. The first Allied demands for dissolution of the Freikorps, the Einwohnerwehr, and the temporary volunteers were made in December 1919. The national government responded by disbanding the Freikorps, temporary volunteers, and the central Einwohnerwehr office, but allowing local units to continue.[11]

The Bavarian army itself, as well as the various volunteer units, moved more and more to the right. Röhm and Epp used the government's post-Council Republic concern about the political reliability of the troops to push their own political views. For example, in January 1920, Röhm drafted, for Epp's signature, a memorandum calling on the government to take the psychology of the troops into greater account. The troops, he claimed, had been placed under strain by the verdict in the trial of Graf Arco, Eisner's assassin, and in reaction to a mass USPD demonstration in Berlin.[12]

Röhm was also searching for a political home. He joined various right-wing organizations, despite the ban on serving Reichswehr officers voting or otherwise engaging in political activity. After a brief period of membership of the monarchist German Nationalists (DNVP), he rejected them because they did not sufficiently appeal to all classes.[13]

Röhm joined the German Workers' Party (*Deutsche Arbeiter Partei* or DAP) after attending a meeting in 1919 in the hotel "Deutsches Reich." He claimed to have been among the first seventy members, in other words, to have joined the party at about the same time as Adolf Hitler. Party records suggest he was member 122. He recounted in his autobiography that he attended almost every meeting and persuaded many of his friends to join.[14]

The DAP had its origins in a "Free Working Committee for a Good Peace" founded by the locksmith Anton Drexler in March 1918 to persuade German workers to support the war effort. Its first public meeting was held in October 1918. On January 5, 1919, the DAP was founded in the Fürstenfelder Hof, and Anton Drexler elected its first chairman. On September 12, 1919, Adolf Hitler visited a party meeting in his capacity as an army political education speaker. Hitler's first speech for the party was given on November 12, 1919. By December that year, Drexler had drawn up the party program, which was revised in consultation with Hitler. At the beginning of March 1920, the party had added "National Socialist" to its name (NSDAP). The party's speakers of this period were strongly anti-Semitic. Röhm commented, with approval, that the early founders of the party spread "enlightenment" about "the destructive work of Jewry."[15]

Röhm reported that he took a particular interest in the SA. The SA had begun in January 1920 as an organization to protect Nazi party meetings. By 1921, it was a paramilitary organization that used force against opposition in Nazi meetings and broke up opponents' meetings. Röhm may have been the intermediary who secured Captain Ehrhardt's involvement in training the SA. Epp provided the money for the NSDAP to buy the newspaper *Völkischer Beobachter* in 1920. Röhm was probably "the decisive influence"[16] in the early growth of the NSDAP.

Röhm's first personal encounter with Hitler, he reported, came in early 1920, when he met Hitler at a meeting of the "Iron Fist," a nationalist organization that met periodically in the home of Captain Beppo Römer. Hitler's commanding officer, Captain Karl Mayr, information officer at the

Wehrkreiskommando, brought Hitler into this circle. Mayr was Hitler's discoverer. He had selected him for training as a speaker, and was the initial patron and supporter of his career.[17]

Röhm and Hitler became friends. Röhm's sister, Lore Lippert, claimed that Röhm proposed that Hitler use the familiar "Thou" to him to make Hitler socially acceptable in officers' circles. From 1920 on, Hitler frequently visited the Röhm family and was often invited to meals at their home.[18]

Röhm's political activities led circles around Wolfgang Kapp to approach him in March 1920, requesting support in Bavaria for an overthrow of the Reich government. In October 1919, Kapp—a founder of the wartime ultra-nationalist Fatherland Party—and Ludendorff set up the National Union and began seeking support for a *putsch*, an armed takeover. They won the backing of General von Lüttwitz, who commanded all troops east of the Elbe.[19]

At the beginning of March 1920, the national government had ordered the dissolution of the Ehrhardt Brigade, a Freikorps stationed near Berlin. Lüttwitz was dismissed on March 10 after he tried to force the resignation of President Ebert and the government. On March 13, under Lüttwitz's command, the Ehrhardt Brigade occupied Berlin's administrative district, and proclaimed Kapp Chancellor. The putsch collapsed as a result of a go-slow by the civil service, the incompetence of the putsch organizers, and a general strike called for by Ebert and the SPD ministers in the government. On March 18, Kapp and Lüttwitz fled to Sweden. The role of the Freikorps and the attitude of the army leadership led to political upheaval. There were communist uprisings in Thuringia and Saxony, and the proclamation of a breakaway socialist republic in the Ruhr.[20]

In Bavaria, the putsch moved Bavarian politics decisively to the right. There are some indications that Bavarian organizations may have been more involved in the putsch than Röhm was willing to admit. Epp and Röhm participated in meetings that eventually led Escherich and Kahr to approach Möhl to call for a transfer of government powers to Möhl as a military commander. At 3:00 a.m. on March 14, Möhl went to see Hoffmann, accompanied by Kahr, Pöhner, Escherich, Kriebel, and representatives of the volunteer units. The Hoffmann government was forced to resign; Möhl was given complete power in Munich; Kahr was named civilian commissioner. He gained this position because he had the support of the Einwohnerwehr.[21]

Despite the ambiguous attitude of the army leadership, the national government was forced to call the army in to suppress the Ruhr Republic. Bavarian troops under Epp's command were among those deployed. On March 19, 1920, Epp and his staff, including Hörauf and Röhm, set off by train for the Ruhr, arriving in Rehda in Westphalia on March 20. On March 23, the final transport of Bavarian troops arrived and they were given the name Bayerische Schützen-Brigade Epp.[22]

The army action against the Ruhr Republic involved many Freikorps units. The Bayerische Schützen-Brigade Epp encountered resistance in Pelkum, in particular, before they occupied Dortmund. Röhm, Hörauf, and Captain Stemmermann were part of the Brigade's mobile staff, and were responsible for supply including the transport of munitions.[23]

The Ruhr campaign provided evidence of the different political atmosphere existing in Bavaria. Anti-Semitic incidents by Bavarian troops led to complaints in Dortmund and Hamm. When asked by higher authorities to take action against this, the Brigade staff temporized. They did not take action but asked for more information to see if the allegations were justified.[24]

Looking back in 1928, Röhm claimed that the army could have taken charge in Germany at this time. He was outraged by press criticism of the role of the Reichswehr in the Ruhr.[25] Here again, he showed his sensitivity to any diminution in the position of the army and its officers. In the same section of his memoirs, Röhm became increasingly critical of senior German officers for their failure to act as he thought necessary.

Hans von Seeckt, the new head of the army command, protected the army from attempts to introduce republican values into it. He was also concerned about reducing the overt politicization of the army. As early as December 1919, his office had recognized that young officers had been given too much independence, and that army discipline had suffered as a result. Even Möhl seemed to make a temporary concession to this, when he sent Röhm to cool off for a period as liaison officer to the general state commissioner's office in the Police Direction.[26] More generally, though, the Bavarian section of the Reichswehr continued with its political role, protected by the Bavarian government.

At this time, Röhm had difficulty managing financially, possibly because of the postwar inflation. In April 1920, he received 500 marks in support from the 1919 war fund. He received further financial support of 4,000 marks from the Military Funds Commission. He had to begin repaying this at a rate of 83.50 marks a month beginning on August 1, 1920,[27] which suggests that he was not enriching himself from his secret weapons dealings.

His personal life came to merge more and more with his professional life and political activities. After long hours in the office, he attended political meetings or went to beer halls and cafés with his personal and political friends. He formed a group called "Black-White-Red" *(Schwarz-Weiss-Rot)*, which would meet in Munich cafés wearing badges in the imperial colors, and "nationalize" the cafés by asking for the "Deutsches Flaggenlied"—a song of the Imperial Navy—to be played, and forcing guests to stand up and sing along. Here, he had the support of Captain Josef (Beppo) Seydel, with whom he attended the Kriegsschule. They met again during maneuvers and in the early part of the war, and were brought together by their shared political views. Seydel was a press officer in the Einwohnerwehr leadership. Lore Lippert described Seydel as "one of Röhm's closest friends."[28]

Röhm's autonomous role in controlling illegal weapons and his increasingly independent political role both strengthened in the period from 1920 to 1922. As the federal government moved against the Einwohnerwehr under allied pressure, the Bavarian government continued to protect it. In May 1920, Escherisch gathered rightist groups in Germany together in the Organisation Escherisch (Orgesch). In southern Bavaria and Austria, his deputy Rudolf Kanzler encompassed similar groups in the Organisation Kanzler (Orka). Epp and Kahr strongly supported Escherisch, while Röhm provided Orgesch and Orka with weapons, equipment, and munitions. Orka transported weapons on a large scale to Austria. In July 1920, Kahr announced the formation of an Einwohnerwehr border protection force on Bavaria's southern, eastern, and northern borders to prevent outside unrest spilling into Bavaria.[29]

In May 1920, Orgesch was banned nationally. It continued only in Bavaria. The Bavarian government refused a federal government request to dissolve the Einwohnerwehr in May 1920. Allied pressure on the German government to disband the Einwohnerwehr and seize their weapons increased, culminating in a formal note from an inter-allied conference to the German government. These pressures forced Orgesch leaders to meet on May 30, 1921, to announce their disarmament. Already, in May 1921, the central government banned the unauthorized formation of military-style units; in June 1921, Reich Chancellor Wirth announced the dissolution of the Bavarian Einwohnerwehr under Section 1 of the Law to Implement Articles 177/178 of the Peace Treaty of May 22, 1921. The dissolution of Orka followed in July.[30]

This increased Röhm's role in concealing weapons. Dissolution of the Einwohnerwehr meant that Bavarian armaments offices in Bamberg, Ingolstadt, and Munich were closed, and their workers dismissed. Röhm won Epp's approval to set up a new, completely equipped field procurement service (Feldzeugmeisterei or FZM) and its subsidiary, the Faber Motor Vehicle Rental Service. Ostensibly owned by Major Faber, this provided a cover organization for the activities of the FZM, whose nominal head was Colonel Freiherr von Botzheim. Röhm was in actual control and operated virtually autonomously. The FZM's purpose was to register and administer all weapons under the control of the paramilitary units, but originating from the Reichswehr.[31]

Some Germans who betrayed hidden weapons holdings were killed in so-called Feme murders. Political violence was also directed at leading representatives of the Weimar Republic. Röhm helped hide the killers of Germany's former Finance Minister Matthias Erzberger for Organisation Consul, an underground organization formed from the remnants of the Ehrhardt Naval Brigade. In Bavaria, by 1922, the organization was led by Otto Pittinger, aided by Professor Stempfle; Röhm acted as a go-between.[32]

Röhm frequently met with Captain Ehrhardt, who had moved to Munich after the failure of the Kapp Putsch. His political ties extended to Captain Beppo Römer's Bund Oberland and Captain Adolf Heiß's Reichsflagge. Once the Einwohnerwehr was disbanded, Röhm and Heiß transferred some of its weapons to Reichsflagge, whose Munich branch Röhm was persuaded to lead.[33]

Kahr had rejected the implementation of the first Law to Protect the Republic, introduced after Erzberger's murder. As a result of a compromise reached between the federal government and the Bavarian People's Party on the issue, he was forced to resign, and on September 21, 1921, stood down as Minister President. Escherich and Kriebel also withdrew from public life. On June 1, 1921, Escherich had ordered the Einwohnerwehr to disarm, and on June 27, to dissolve. After numerous conferences in which Epp and Röhm were advisors, Dr. Otto Pittinger, formerly Einwohnerwehr Kreisleiter in Regensburg, formed the "Organisation Pittinger," which would be known as the League Bavaria and Reich *(Bund Bayern und Reich)* after the summer of 1922. Most Einwohnerwehr leaders transferred to Bund Bayern und Reich. Pittinger himself was trusted by Crown Prince Rupprecht. Möhl kept the patriotic movement united by refusing to arm or train groups other than Bund Bayern und Reich.[34]

On October 18, 1921, King Ludwig III died on his estate in Sárvár, Hungary, aged seventy-six. His body was returned to Munich where it lay in state in the Ludwigskirche before a state funeral on November 5, 1921. Röhm was bitterly disappointed that Crown Prince Rupprecht did not announce he was ascending the throne. Epp, Möhl, and Pittinger allegedly attempted to persuade Rupprecht to do this before the funeral. On Kahr's advice, Rupprecht restricted himself to stating that he had succeeded to his father's rights. He refused to exploit his father's death to proclaim himself king and was only willing to assume the throne with popular support.[35]

Röhm's political activity was starting to gain hostile press attention. On January 27, 1922, Röhm and the members of "Schwarz-Weiss-Rot" met at the Witteschen Weinstube in the Barerstrasse and celebrated the Kaiser's birthday. The SPD paper, the *Münchener Post*, claimed this was a separatist Bavarian meeting. From this circle, together with members of Organisation Consul living in Munich, Röhm founded the local Munich chapter of the National Organization of German Officers *(Nationalverband Deutscher Offiziere— NDO)*. He also continued to lead the Munich branch of Reichsflagge.[36]

He was involved in various anti-government activities, including, he claimed, activity on the fringes of a plan by Pittinger to seize power on August 25, 1922. According to Röhm, Pittinger lost his nerve and did not go through with his plan to seize power. Steger has refuted this and argued that it was Röhm, as intermediary, who ensured that the planned putsch failed, because he considered that Pittinger did not have the full support of the paramilitary groups. From this time on, Röhm lacked confidence in Pittinger.[37]

The right believed the Lerchenfeld government, which had followed Kahr, did not oppose the law to protect the republic strongly enough. They forced its resignation. The successor government under von Knilling sought the support of the patriotic organizations.[38]

The socialist press had begun to attack Epp for his role in supporting the NSDAP and the *Völkischer Beobachter*. Epp and Röhm believed that socialist leader Erhard Auer wanted to secure SPD control over the weapons holdings. The killing of Foreign Minister Walther Rathenau on June 24, 1922, by men from Organisation Consul, led to a crackdown on the extreme right, and the passage of a law for the protection of the republic. Bavaria refused to recognize this law. Epp and Röhm's opposition to it led Röhm, on July 20, to circulate a right-wing publication, *Heimatlandbriefe*, to the various troop commanders under Epp's name with the comment, "These letters give an accurate picture of the current situation."[39] This came to the attention of the SPD paper *Freiheit*, and the Reichswehr Ministry started an enquiry. Möhl defended Epp against the charge that he was seeking to influence the troops, and Epp and Röhm countered that the leaking of the memo indicated Spartacist infiltration of the army through NCOs, whom they claimed had leaked the letters to USPD deputies. Seeckt intervened, and on August 12, 1922, Möhl issued a decree stating that von Epp had been punished with a simple reprimand.

The *Heimatlandbriefe* affair seems to have been the last straw for Seeckt and the national government. On November 25, 1922, Reich Defense Minister Dr. Gessler and Seeckt ordered Epp to exchange Röhm with Captain von Hanneken. Röhm would move to the General Staff of VII Division, and Hanneken would take his place. Again, Röhm and Epp saw this as an SPD-inspired push aimed at control of the Bavarian weapons holdings.[40]

Epp and Röhm resisted initially. Epp refused to use Hanneken, and Röhm did not report to his new position. Epp asked Möhl to reverse the transfer, but Möhl, who himself was being moved to Kassel, could not effect a change.

Möhl did concede that Röhm could continue to retain his responsibilities for the weapons holdings as well.[41]

Röhm began concealing and maintaining German weapons holdings at the request of his immediate superiors in Bavaria—Epp and Möhl. He may have started these tasks as an ambitious young officer, and may have seen them as a valuable, if unorthodox, contribution to his military advancement. Despite the support of his superiors, he had to act on his own so that they could maintain their "deniability." This submerged aspect of his official duties gave him increasing independence and autonomy, and a growing political profile. He played an influential, but not prominent, role in Bavarian affairs during this period. On a number of occasions, he had been one of the driving forces behind the political changes that favored the right. The SPD press recognized his growing significance.

Röhm was initially a minor figure, but used his key position to play a more freelance role. Rather than simply maintaining the arms caches for Einwohnerwehr or army use, Röhm began to use them as a bargaining counter within the extreme right and to strengthen Reichsflagge. As a result of his secret duties, he gained a position of political influence in Bavaria. In this period, he became the political soldier in the way that he claimed the revolution had taught him was necessary. He reflected, and drove forward himself, the politicization of the Bavarian Reichswehr. He supported and participated in various abortive attempts to overthrow both the Bavarian and the national government and replace them with more radical right-wing and monarchist alternatives.

During these years, Röhm also became involved in extreme right-wing political organizations, joining, forming, and supporting a variety of them. It is clear that, at this time, of his life he was not solely a National Socialist and not even a National Socialist first. For him, his membership in the NSDAP ran alongside membership of other similar organizations. He was a supporter and patron of the NSDAP, to which he was moving closer by the end of 1922. In 1923, he would intervene to protect the party again.

CHAPTER 6

Political Soldier
January–September 1923

I am as well a political soldier and am one consciously, with conviction.[1]

Ernst Röhm

Ernst Röhm's transfer to the Seventh Division as a staff officer at the end of 1922 was one of a series of postings designed to reduce the independent political activity of Bavarian army officers. It placed Röhm directly under the control of the army group headquarters, responsible to Lieutenant Colonel Freiherr von Berchem, the chief of staff of Army Group VII. The move, designed to reduce Röhm's political role, had the paradoxical effect of spurring him onto greater political involvement.[2]

By ensuring that no one else had an overview of the location of the secret weapons' camps, Röhm retained control of them and had to be allowed to continue to oversee them, even in his new position. Removed from the restraint that Möhl and Epp had previously exercised over his actions, he sought to use his control of the weapons holdings to intervene directly in extreme right-wing politics. By 1923, he struck a fellow officer as "more politician than officer, an adventurer."[3]

In 1923, Germany was in crisis. In January 1923, both France and Belgium occupied the Ruhr in retaliation for Germany's default on reparations payments. The German government's response was to call for passive resistance in the Ruhr, and to continue paying its civil servants there while they were on strike. This unleashed hyper-inflation that was not brought under control until the end of the year.[4]

Röhm's political opinions were moving closer to those of Hitler and the NSDAP. The NSDAP and its strongly anti-Semitic propaganda was gaining support in Munich, including from people who had once supported the Council Republic. While most German political parties gave priority to national unity in face of the threat posed by the occupation of the Ruhr, the extreme right put a seizure of power first. Röhm shared this view of the crisis with Hitler. On January 17, Röhm prepared a memorandum on the internal political situation in which he argued that the punishment of Ebert, and of the November criminals, as well as an end to the policy of fulfilling the demands of the Treaty of Versailles, all had priority before an armed struggle against France or Poland.[5]

Röhm sought to urge the new Commander of Wehrkreis VII, General Otto von Lossow, to give closer support to Hitler and the NSDAP. He intervened to win Lossow's backing for the annual Nazi Party conference in Munich on January 27 and 28. The Bavarian Government had placed restrictions on the meeting out of fear of a Nazi putsch. When the Nazis threatened to go ahead as planned, it proclaimed a state of emergency in Bavaria right of the Rhine. At meetings of troop commanders and officers of the Munich garrison, Röhm recalled "I gave open expression to my feverish indignation about the attitude of the Bavarian Government."[6] He helped induce Epp to speak to Lossow, who ordered Röhm to bring Hitler to him. In a conversation with Lossow and the head of the Landespolizei, Colonel Hans Ritter von Seisser, Hitler promised he would ensure a peaceful party day. Lossow then gave Röhm the task of intervening with the Bavarian Government in Lossow's name to lessen the restrictions. Enlisting the help of Kahr, Röhm and Hitler then went to Munich Police President Nortz, who agreed to allow some of the meetings. Röhm was proud of his success. The party day passed peacefully, though Hitler did not keep to the details of his agreement with Nortz.

In the midst of these events, Röhm was beset by professional and personal problems. His transfer had brought about an estrangement with Epp, who believed Röhm had sought to remove himself from his influence. Röhm claimed that other officers jealous of his role aggravated the tension between the two men for their own ends. In his memoirs, Röhm described 1923 as "a really unlucky year,"[7] beginning with his separation from Epp, which was followed by a series of attacks from his enemies and those who envied him. Military courts of honor were abolished, in theory, in the Weimar Republic. In practice, the Reichswehr retained them, concealed as commissions of inquiry. Officers brought cases of alleged breach of honor to their superiors, who would institute commissions of inquiry. In the course of 1923, Röhm had a number of honor cases brought against him. Some of these cases suggest that, over the years, fellow officers had come to resent his position of autonomy. Once Epp's protection was removed, he was vulnerable. Other cases may indicate that Epp had exercised a restraining influence on Röhm and that Röhm's own independent judgement was more erratic.

In January, Röhm brought the first of his honor charges against Captain Ritter von Radlmaier and his wife. In various conversations over the New Year, both Radlmaiers had stated that Röhm financially profited from his position. Röhm rejected an apology offered by the Radlmaiers and made his financial records available to the commission of inquiry to refute the charge of embezzlement. The commission of inquiry found the Radlmaiers' claims "completely unsubstantiated."[8] The Radlmaiers retracted their allegations.

The Radlmaiers voiced suspicion and jealousy of Röhm's financial dealings that was more widely shared. Mrs. von Radlmaier commented that Röhm "was not clean. He needs much money for women and he also has to get that from somewhere."[9] Röhm had told Mrs. von Radlmaier that he had to leave his apartment because he could not receive women there. He offered the Radlmaiers' niece a monthly allowance if she moved out of her parents' home and made their relationship physical rather than platonic.

The Nazi Party conference also led, indirectly, to further honor charges. When Pittinger did not support Hitler on the issue, Röhm decided to withdraw his own support from Pittinger, against whom he had been intriguing for some time. In a two-hour meeting in Röhm's office on the evening of January 27, Röhm asked Pittinger to free him from his promise of collaboration. When Pittinger refused, Röhm produced a written declaration on January 30 stating that he saw his connection with Pittinger as ended. Heiß joined Röhm in this step. Röhm then sent a memorandum to his political supporters, justifying his declaration, explaining why he thought Pittinger was an unsuitable leader, and accusing him of "cowardice."[10]

In turn, Pittinger accused Röhm of "disloyalty,"[11] partly because Röhm's departure led to Reichsflagge as a whole leaving Bund Bayern und Reich. Röhm temporarily denied the Bund access to the weapons stores. Pittinger formally complained that, in issuing his memorandum, Röhm had violated the officers' honor code, but in bringing the complaint, he may have been trying to force a reconciliation. The cost of Röhm's departure was high. It led to wider divisions among the patriotic organizations, several of which followed Reichsflagge out of the Bund.

The resulting commission of inquiry established by Lossow examined four questions—whether Röhm was guilty of disloyalty to Pittinger; whether, in issuing the memorandum against Pittinger, Röhm violated the honor code; whether Röhm made defamatory comments in the memorandum; and whether Röhm claimed that the weapons in his charge belonged to him and not to the Reichswehr or the patriotic organizations. The court of inquiry cleared Röhm on all charges, though it considered that he should have given

Pittinger a copy of his memorandum. The one exception was the accusation of cowardice that Röhm had not made face-to-face. Röhm believed the accusation to be true; therefore, it could not be a question of defamation. His evidence for the accusation was insufficient and it was made behind Pittinger's back. The commission believed that Röhm saw Pittinger's conduct as justifying the accusation, and he was always ready to give personal satisfaction. Accordingly, Röhm was not guilty of a breach of the honor code. Conversely, the commission found that Pittinger had insulted Röhm by accusing him of disloyalty. Lossow considered it inappropriate to give the dispute further publicity by the two men fighting a duel, and insisted on mutual written apologies.[12]

The Röhm-Pittinger dispute worsened relations between Epp and Röhm and led to further honor cases. Röhm had refused to show Epp his memorandum about Pittinger because Röhm was upset that Epp had not defended him in a conference where Pittinger had accused Röhm of breaking his word. Epp accused Röhm of deliberately making the army's position in its negotiations with the patriotic organizations more difficult.[13]

A further honor case arose out of this when former Justice Minister Christian Roth challenged Epp to a duel with sabers on May 11, 1923. Röhm had acted as a tale-bearer between Roth and Epp. The reasons for his behavior were unclear, but appear to have been related to his estrangement from Epp. In early March 1923, Epp commented to Röhm that Roth was always lying. Epp based this judgement on a report by Röhm that Roth had deliberately lied about an allegation that Pittinger had received fifty million marks from industry to maintain his weapons holdings. Roth withdrew this claim when he realized he had been mistaken, but Röhm did not tell Epp about this retraction. Röhm then promptly reported to Roth Epp's description of him as a liar. The commission of inquiry proposed a compromise of mutual retractions between Epp and Roth. It went on to find that Röhm's behavior had not met the requirements expected of an officer of his age and position. He was at fault first because he told Roth about a confidential conversation with a senior officer, thus causing the entire dispute, and secondly, because he had not reported to Epp that Roth had corrected his statement, as a result of his "cooling relationship" with Epp. The commission found that Röhm's negligence in "careless reporting of information" had caused the trouble, and found him to have displayed "a lack of openness and conscientiousness."[14]

In addition, Röhm asked Lossow to sort out a dispute between him and Lieutenant Colonel Adam and Epp. Epp had used a report by Adam that described Röhm's behavior, in his negotiations with Bund Oberland, as equivocal. Lossow rejected Röhm's claim that Adam had violated his honor. Rumors, which were spread in Bund Bayern und Reich, that Röhm sold weapons to the Tyrol to earn more money for FZM employees were also found to be baseless.[15]

The cases culminated in Lossow issuing a letter of reprimand to Röhm on June 29, 1923, making serious remonstrations because of Röhm's lack of discretion and loyalty to Epp. "I enjoin you strongly to exercise rigorous self-criticism of yourself so that slips like this no longer happen."[16] Lossow pointed out that Röhm's position and the Feldzeugmeisterei were funded by the state, and that the weapons belonged to the state and not to him or any outside organization. Lossow concluded that Röhm's "nerve-wearying activities" had led to "a certain dimming or confusion of ideas."[17]

Röhm's behavior in these disputes may have been prompted by the desire to gain more freedom of action, as well as to make trouble for Epp in the light of what he saw as Epp's lack of support. By 1928, when he was writing his autobiography, Röhm presented them very circumspectly. This suggests that he may have come to realize that his own behavior did not always show him in the best light.

Röhm also sought to influence Lossow and win his support for the right-wing organizations. In February and March, he drew up several memoranda for Lossow that set out his assessment of the political situation. In the first of these, handed to Lossow on February 1, he described his approach as "radically nationalist."[18] Before and during the revolution, he had been in a hospital, life-threateningly ill with influenza. Nonetheless, he felt that he was an accessory to the revolution and wanted to make good his personal shame. It was his duty as a soldier to say what he thought to his superior. He had always had this courage and it often made him unpopular.

Röhm continued that the Germans would only be able to succeed in their fight to restore the nation when they made the workers nationalist again. Consequently, strengthening the Nazi movement was an essential precondition for a patriotic fighting front. In a subsequent discussion with Lossow, he urged him to maintain close links with the nationalist youth, and oppose the ban on Reichswehr members belonging to these organizations. He convinced Lossow on this point, and the relevant decree of the Reichswehr Minister was not put into effect in Bavaria.[19]

As part of national preparations for a possible war with France, the Reichswehr tried to increase its strength by training and integrating the right-wing paramilitary organizations into the Reichswehr. From February to mid-April, the Bavarian Reichswehr and these organizations negotiated a statement of obligation by the leaders of the units that they would place them under Lossow as state commandant. These negotiations led to members of the organizations being given military training. They delivered their weapons for this purpose and were given the word of honor that the weapons remained their property. This military training continued in Reichswehr barracks from March 1923 until the end of the Ruhr conflict.[20]

In March 1923, in a further memorandum, Röhm suggested to Lossow that incorporating the existing volunteer units would be the first step in mobilizing for any future war. The army would have to meet the volunteer units halfway on the question of offices and insignia. He criticized those army commanders and their advisers who were critical of the Freikorps' spirit of the units, and believed they should take over leadership by virtue of their professional authority. The psychology of struggle was foreign to these men. Yet, he then foreshadowed submerging the units by restoring the old regiments with their traditions. He also called on Lossow to intervene against alleged unpatriotic stories in the *Münchener Post*.[21]

Röhm put his assessment—that a military clash with France would not be hopeless and might be Germany's sole salvation—to Reich Chancellor Cuno's staff when Cuno visited Munich. He brought Hitler along to give a political analysis. Röhm also claimed to have ensured that Hitler met with Seeckt on March 11, 1923, though Seeckt was not willing to commit himself to act against the government.[22]

Röhm was playing an increasingly independent political role. On January 31, 1923, Heiß named Röhm as a member of the working staff of the state leadership of Reichsflagge and Heiß's deputized representative in Munich. Both Röhm and former Bavarian Justice Minister Roth claimed the responsibility for organizing a more radical right-wing umbrella organization, the Working Community of Patriotic Fighting Organizations *(Arbeitsgemeinschaft der vaterländischen Kampfverbände)* that was founded in late January 1923. Röhm's claim to have had an originating role is strengthened by the fact that the Arbeitsgemeinschaft's meetings took place in his office.[23]

The Arbeitsgemeinschaft included the NSDAP, Reichsflagge, Vaterländische Bezirksvereinen Münchens (VVM), Bund Oberland, Bund Unterland, and the Zeitfreiwilligenkorps München. Roth was its political leader, and Kriebel, its military leader. Röhm conducted the negotiations that ultimately resulted in Bund Oberland joining the Arbeitsgemeinschaft. Röhm's military superiors knew of his negotiations, but not of developments inside the Arbeitsgemeinschaft.[24]

Röhm no longer restricted his role to giving advice on the sidelines, but participated actively. He opened and chaired the first meeting of the Arbeitsgemeinschaft on the evening of February 4, 1923. He indicated that their goals must be the struggle against Marxism, the military creation of a strike force, and making *Heimatland* their intellectual weapon. Hitler's suggestion that the Arbeitsgemeinschaft would stand behind a united national government was accepted.[25]

The Arbeitsgemeinschaft held exercises in Forstenrieder Park on March 25, and a further exercise on the Fröttmaninger Heide on April 15. Lossow and Berchem saw these exercises as being of little military value. In an illustration of the extent to which Röhm was moved by nonmilitary considerations, he noted that from "our"[26] point of view, the exercises served to weld their people together and assure them of their strength. They had a political and psychological purpose, rather than a military one.

Röhm used successive Arbeitsgemeinschaft meetings (March 13, April 7, April 11, and April 12) to give Hitler a more prominent position, asking him in a memorandum to set out the purpose, tasks, and political goals of the Arbeitsgemeinschaft. His justification of his unilateral action was that "after all, I was the host and had made my rooms available."[27] In his memorandum, Hitler placed the cleansing of the nation at the center of Germany's national interest. The patriotic units had to make Bavaria a national state in the borders of the corrupt German nation to force the government to take a stand. Their goal had to be to free Germany from its internal and external enemies and to unite all Germans. It took Röhm some time to get agreement on Hitler's memorandum being adopted as the Arbeitsgemeinschaft's political program.

Röhm's role in the exercises of the Kampfverbände on the Fröttmaninger Heide on April 15 led to national government intervention. As leader of Reichsflagge München, Röhm issued an order mentioning some other Reichswehr officers by name as leaders of the exercises. The *Münchener Post* published the letter, and called on the government to investigate the Bavarian Reichswehr's flouting of Gessler and Seeckt's bans on their political activities. The *Rote Fahne* called on Gessler to intervene on April 19.[28]

On April 25, 1923, Reichswehr Minister Gessler ordered a ban on any further participation by the members of the Reichswehr in such exercises. According to Röhm, Gessler's order continued: "In particular I request that Captain Röhm be removed from work on such matters."[29] Gessler called for the connections with the right-wing organizations to be dissolved and for Lossow to hold himself aloof from politics. After this, Lossow banned members of the Reichswehr from joining the Vaterländische Verbände. Röhm handed over the leadership of Reichsflagge München to Seydel.

In his memoirs, Röhm claimed he removed himself from active participation in the Arbeitsgemeinschaft at this time, but this was not so. He continued to attend its meetings, including a discussion on April 26 about stopping any planned SPD or KPD procession for May Day. On April 27, the Arbeitsgemeinschaft and the Vereinigten Vaterländischen Verbänden Bayerns presented the state government with a declaration, warning of damage to the population from the proposed left-wing demonstrations, stating that they would stop them or would support the government if it decided to suppress them. The Bavarian government decided to disallow a large procession, but allow seven smaller ones. The Arbeitsgemeinschaft tried, but failed, to have these processions banned, and then decided to proceed independently and occupy the bridges across the Isar to stop the demonstrations reaching central Munich.[30]

At a third meeting, on the morning of April 30 at Röhm's office, the leadership of the Arbeitsgemeinschaft decided to ask Lossow to release weapons for the National Socialists. Hitler, Kriebel, Zeller, and von Lenz called on Lossow and told him they planned to use all the means at their disposal to stop the processions. Lossow countered that the Reichswehr and Landespolizei would maintain the authority of the state, if necessary by force. Despite having previously promised he would make their weapons available to the organizations at any time at their request, Lossow refused to release the weapons. At a separate meeting with Seisser, Seisser told Hitler that any arbitrary forceful action would lead to a clash with the Landespolizei.[31]

The Arbeitsgemeinschaft leadership, including Röhm, met again on April 30, and demanded aggressive action against the processions. The military leaders of the units—Kriebel (VVM), Göring (NSDAP), Hoffmann (Unterland), and Lenz (Lenz)—then had another meeting with Röhm. Those present subsequently refused to testify to a Bavarian Landtag inquiry to avoid self-incrimination. They discussed Lossow's refusal to give out the weapons, Röhm reportedly telling Seydel and Faber that he had been expressly ordered by Lossow not to give them any further orders.[32]

Even though Lossow had given orders that weapons were not to be released to the units, subordinate offices did not obey them. Röhm had already ordered an armored car to be brought from the Reichswehr's concealed holdings and transported to the rooms of the Faber car rental company on the night of April 30. From 5:00 p.m. on, cars with weapons were driven to the firm's office.[33]

Early on May 1, about three thousand men assembled, the National Socialists and Reichsflagge on the Oberwiesenfeld, while Oberland gathered at the Maximilianeum. All units at the Oberwiesenfeld were armed, with the distribution of weapons from trucks taking all morning. Kriebel commanded the overall operation from the Ring Hotel, while Hitler was in charge on the Oberwiesenfeld.[34]

Röhm claimed that he held himself aloof from any of these developments, and that on going to his office at his normal time, he discovered that his telephone calls were being intercepted. Lossow stationed an officer at the WKK switchboard to prevent unauthorized use of the phone. While Lossow denied this measure was directed against Röhm, Gordon considered that

Röhm was one of its targets. Röhm claimed to have also refused requests from Police President Nortz to negotiate with the Kampfverbände. After handing over their weapons, the Kampfverbände moved off in a procession from the Oberwiesenfeld via Leopoldstrasse and Ludwigstrasse to the Siegestor. Röhm asserted that the units had succeeded in removing the pressure of the left. Later historians suggested the opposite. The police were so preoccupied with the Kampfverbände that the left was able to violate the terms of its marching permits.[35]

The demonstrations on May 1 were a trial of strength between the paramilitary organizations and the Bavarian government. It revealed the extent to which both the Reichswehr and Landespolizei contained many supporters of the patriotic organizations, so that not all orders given were carried out. As a result, Lossow became more suspicious of the Arbeitsgemeinschaft. Police President Nortz was transferred from Munich and replaced by Karl Mantel. The Bavarian government began legal proceedings against the leaders of the Verbände, which were not suspended until 1927.[36]

"May Day brought Röhm to the end of the road as a free-wheeling politician operating from a safe and influential base."[37] On May 3, 1923, in the presence of Epp, General von Danner, Freiherr von Kreß, and Lieutenant Colonels Freiherr von Berchem and Meier, Lossow told Röhm that he was being transferred to be company commander in Bayreuth. Lt. Col. Meier would take over his work in the Wehrkreiskommando. According to Lossow, the reasons for the transfer were Röhm's responsibility as a commander for the events in the offices of the firm Faber in the night of April 30–May 1, his misuse of the offices of the FZM for political meetings in the lead-up to May 1, and his involvement in the political activities of the Kampfverbände, despite the ban on Reichswehr members joining the Kampfverbände.

Lossow rejected Röhm's complaint that he had cast doubt on Röhm's honor. The same day, Röhm requested his release from the army and went on leave until a decision was made on this request. Seydel and Faber also resigned their positions in the FZM as an act of solidarity with Röhm. These resignations made it easier for Lossow to bring the FZM back under Reichswehr control.[38]

On May 29, after a discussion with Lossow, Röhm withdrew his resignation request. He asked for, and was granted, four weeks leave at a cure in the military rest home at Bad Reichenhall to restore his health. He spent mid-June to mid-July there, though he returned to Munich on July 4 to attend a large Reichsflagge evening in the Bürgerbräukeller organized by Seydel.[39]

Röhm asked Lossow for secondments to the artillery and cavalry to broaden his professional experience. Lossow agreed, and on August 15, 1923, Röhm arrived at Grafenwöhr to serve with the Seventh Artillery Regiment.

From September 12, he was attached to the Sixth Reiter Regiment 17, also at Grafenwöhr.[40]

Yet, Röhm had not renounced his political activities. On September 2, despite a Reichswehr Ministry ban on Reichswehr participation, he personally led Reichsflagge Südbayern in a parade before Ludendorff, Prince Louis Ferdinand, Kriebel, and Hitler at the "German Day" *("Deutsche Tag")* in Nuremberg, with almost all Reichsflagge and the greater part of the SA and Oberland participating.[41]

At this meeting, the German Fighting League *(Deutsche Kampfbund,* also known as the *Kampfgemeinschaft Bayern)* was formed to replace the Arbeitsgemeinschaft. Weber (Bund Oberland), Heiß (Reichsflagge), and Hitler signed a declaration drafted by Wilhelm Weiss and Gottfried Feder, announcing their intention to fight for national freedom and against Marxism and the International, and "Jewry" as a cause of putrefaction in national life and pacifism. Röhm saw this as a great step forward because it signaled the willingness of the patriotic organizations to think and act politically. Röhm claimed that he tried, unsuccessfully, to get Weber and Heiß to give Hitler political leadership.[42]

Röhm claimed that he returned to Munich in mid-September 1923, eager to see where he would serve next. But within a week, on September 26, he renewed his request to resign from the army, this time permanently. Röhm's own explanation emphasized political factors. Röhm had attended a meeting of the leaders of the Deutsche Kampfbund on September 25. Hitler presented the political situation and the imminence of German liberation so powerfully in a speech at this meeting, Röhm claimed, that he decided to resign from the army to devote all his strength to the salvation of the fatherland. Hitler was appointed political leader of the Kampfbund at this meeting.[43]

The next day, the Bavarian government appointed Kahr as general state commissioner. The Kampfbund saw this as a declaration of war against them. Hitler wanted immediate Kampfbund action against Kahr, but both Röhm and Scheubner-Richter, the general manager of the Kampfbund, knew that their forces were not strong enough for an immediate clash. In the Reich, full power was transferred to the Reichswehrminister, and in Bavaria, to Lossow, who voluntarily subordinated himself to Kahr.[44]

Crown Prince Rupprecht required officers of the former royal army to support Kahr. On September 27, Heiß named Röhm as his deputy in Reichsflagge and sent him to Nuremberg to instruct the leaders and units there, where the Reichsflagge leaders had declared their support for Kahr. Röhm and Heiß then traveled to Bayreuth to attend the Deutsche Tag on September 30. Heiß came under pressure from the spokesman of the DNVP to support Kahr and issued an order to the Reichsflagge district groups, promising support for Kahr and his policies as long as they did not touch the basic principles of the Kampfbund. Röhm agreed to this unwillingly.[45]

In deciding to leave the army, Röhm may have been aware that his prospects for further preferment in the army were poor. Promotion rates in the Reichswehr overall were glacial in the Weimar Republic. Röhm had attracted the unfavorable attention of both the Reichswehr Minister and the army leadership for his disobedience of their orders. He was not alone: most politically active officers in the Bavarian Reichswehr were, in fact, forced out of the army in 1923–24.[46]

At almost thirty-six, Röhm was abandoning the career that had engaged his energies since his youth. In a sense, this decision had been foreshadowed by his increasing double life over the previous three years as officer and political activist. His actions in the summer and autumn of 1923 showed he was unwilling to relinquish a political role. Although this was a vital decision for Röhm's professional and personal future, he possibly did not recognize it as the decisive break in his life that it would become. From September 1923, he expected a Nazi takeover of power in Germany, and with it, his triumphant return to the army.

CHAPTER 7

Putschist
September 1923–April 1, 1924

Likewise I was not only such a close friend of Hitler, but I placed such confidence in him in political matters, that I merely said to him. . . . "You need to say to me only, for example on the xth the Reichskriegsflagge stands at the start at the Siegestor, then it stands there. You can count on this."[1]

Ernst Röhm

The German political and economic crisis peaked toward the end of 1923. The Bavarian Government sought to maintain its control by appointing Kahr as General State Commissioner with emergency powers on September 26. Ernst Röhm had already responded to the political atmosphere. He was on leave from the army, pending his resignation—a resignation brought about by his desire to contribute to the nationalist revolution, which he believed to be imminent.

The hyper-inflation continued and would reach its high point in early November. On October 21, Röhm's lunch cost him one thousand million marks. Germans were experiencing economic hardship and many feared for the future. Attempted Communist uprisings in Saxony and Thuringia led the national government to proclaim a state of emergency, and to send troops into Saxony to ensure that the Saxon Minister President dropped the Communists from his cabinet. The grand coalition government under Gustav Stresemann as Chancellor ended passive resistance in the Ruhr and resumed the payment of reparations on September 26, which began the process by which inflation was brought under control. To nationalists, however, it amounted to a surrender to the French.[2]

In appointing Kahr, Bavarian Minister President Knilling hoped to weaken the right wing by taking over some of their policies. During October

1923, conflict between Bavaria and the Reich government intensified. Kahr again invalidated the law to protect the republic. He began a policy of deporting non-Bavarians that was applied in particular to foreign Jews, and he also prevented the execution of Federal Constitutional Court (*Staatsgerichtshof*) arrest warrants for Ehrhardt, Heiss, and the former Freikorps' leader, Gerhard Rossbach.[3]

Under the Bavarian state of emergency, General Otto von Lossow was appointed executive officer of the Bavarian government. On September 27, Reich Defense Minister Gessler ordered him to implement a ban on the *Völkischer Beobachter*; Kahr issued a counter-order. Lossow obeyed Kahr. The Bavarian government appointed Lossow as State Commandant and had the troops of the Seventh Division swear an oath of loyalty to Bavaria. Kahr now controlled all civilian and military power in Bavaria, including the Bavarian Landespolizei under Colonel Hans Ritter von Seisser.[4]

Kahr's appointment led to changes in the Kampfbund. On October 6 and 7, Reichsflagge held a meeting in Nuremberg, which was also attended by Hitler, Kriebel, Göring, Brückner, and Weiss. At the beginning of the meeting, Heiß declared his support for Kahr. According to Röhm, Heiß's decision was probably influenced by Crown Prince Rupprecht's views. The Crown Prince believed that restoration of the monarchy was not yet possible and supported Kahr.[5]

It was characteristic of Röhm's "non-conformist" monarchism that, unlike Heiß, he did not alter his political stance to fit in with the Crown Prince's wishes. At the meeting in Nuremberg, Röhm read a declaration on Hitler's behalf that Hitler withdrew his confidence in Heiß, and was supported by the leaders of Reichsflagge in Augsburg, Memmingen, and Schleissheim. Heiß declared these groups dissolved.[6]

Röhm then reconstituted the dissident groups as Reich War Flag *(Reichskriegsflagge* or RKF) under his leadership. The whole of Reichsflagge München supported him, and held its founding parade on October 12. On October 17, Röhm tried unsuccessfully to win the Crown Prince's support for the Kampfbund.[7]

Röhm's hopes for national political change were encouraged by a crisis in the Reich government. On November 2, the SPD left the coalition because Reich action against Bavaria had been insufficiently forceful. As a result, Stresemann no longer had a Reichstag majority. Seeckt, Gessler, and leading industrialists, notably Friedrich Minoux, sought to overcome the crisis by creating an independent Reich directory to solve the crisis using the president's powers under Article 48. Seeckt planned to act legally with the consent of President Ebert. Other more radical right-wing organizations in north Germany wanted to take more forceful and less constitutional action.

Negotiations between these north German organizations and the Bavarian triumvirate of Kahr-Lossow-Seisser continued until November 8. The triumvirs sought to use the more radical north German organizations to bring pressure on Seeckt to act.[8]

At the same time, Lossow and Seisser conducted parallel negotiations with the leaders of the Kampfbund. On October 24, Lossow called a conference of the Verbände at which a possible expansion of the Reichswehr was discussed to increase the forces available to the triumvirs and to prevent internal unrest. During this meeting Lossow spoke of a right-wing dictatorship as desirable. Afterward, he issued a secret order codenamed "Autumn Exercise" to incorporate the Verbände into the Seventh Division in case of internal unrest. On October 27, Röhm advised the Augsburg RKF that the Kampfbund would be participating in the WKK's preparations to strengthen the Bavarian Division, and that they should obey the relevant orders of the garrison commanders.[9]

The leaders of the Kampfbund conceived of the planned action as a "March on Berlin," using force to overthrow the republic. They were influenced by pressure from their own economically desperate followers, and by the successful recent examples of Mussolini's "March on Rome," and Mustafa Kemal's consolidation of his rule in Turkey by setting up a rival government in Ankara and taking over government in Constantinople from there, spoken of in Germany as the "Ankara solution." Mommsen argues that Röhm, in particular, favored the Ankara solution of using Bavaria as a stepping stone to seize the Reich government and overthrow the peace settlement. [10]

The leaders of the Kampfbund tried to pressure the triumvirate to launch a common "March on Berlin." At the same time, they tried to ensure that this was directed according to their own wishes. In their negotiations with both the north Germans and the Kampfbund, the triumvirs delayed. They put such conditions on their cooperation with the north German organizations that any successful action was unlikely.[11]

The negotiations increased expectations of a putsch or other dramatic action. Röhm saw himself as preparing for a great cause—the liberation of his country—and gathered around him a group of mainly youthful followers, some of whom had already worked for him in the FZM. Men like Carl Léon (Leu) Graf du Moulin-Eckart and Rolf Reiner would remain his friends and political colleagues for life.

Röhm was active in training and organizing the RKF, holding two parades of RKF Munich on October 26 and 27, and having RKF Augsburg and Munich swear allegiance on October 30 and November 2, respectively. Röhm's access to weapons, and the nature of its membership, meant RKF was probably better armed and drilled than other Verbände. Röhm claimed over

300 RKF members in Munich, but other evidence suggested there were some 170 members in Munich. The overall strength of the RKF was between 250 and 500. While Röhm claimed its members came from all classes and professions, its members were predominantly young men from the middle classes, with many students and former employees of Röhm in the FZM. Röhm's nephew, Robert Lippert, who was studying in Munich, was a member. Both Röhm and Rossbach moved in student circles, spoke to student groups, and worked through student organizations, in Röhm's case, the Corps Palatia.[12]

Since Röhm was still a Reichswehr officer, he operated the RKF through Seydel and Karl Osswald. Röhm's deputy and Ortsgruppenführer for Munich was the twenty-eight-year-old technical university student, Karl Osswald. The opening passages of a letter Osswald wrote to Röhm while the latter was in prison in December 1923, using the familiar "Thou," suggests that the two men may have been even closer:

> Dear Captain! Dear Röhm! Excuse the stupid salutation. But since my letter must mix official reports with private ones, the first greeting refers to my revered commander, the second to my Röhm—here I really cannot say any more—for this word really expresses everything that you are and will remain for me.[13]

Reichskriegsflagge had an assault detachment of men of military age, a recruits' section for young men with no previous military training, and a cadre section of older men led by the retired Captain Hildolf Freiherr von Thüngen. Inside the assault detachment, Gruppe Stark, headed by Captain Wilhelm Stark of the Landespolizei, was comprised of active soldiers and policemen. In addition, Walther Lembert, a retired lieutenant, led the Batterie Lembert, a semi-autonomous organization that had left Bund Oberland for the RKF. Like other patriotic Verbände, RKF München trained in the evenings every week in Reichswehr barracks—in the drill hall of the Nineteenth Reichswehr Regiment, in the engineers' barracks and in the barracks of the transport section.[14]

The Kampfbund leadership had been contemplating a putsch for some time. There may have been plans to kidnap Bavarian leaders on November 4 during a ceremony to lay the foundation stone for a memorial to the war dead in Munich. On November 6, Kahr, Lossow, and Seisser spoke to most of the leaders of the Bavarian Verbände, Kahr telling them it was crucial that a nationalist government independent of the Reichstag be set up in Berlin. He would give the order to act if such a government needed armed support, and he would not tolerate independent action by any organization. Both Lossow and Seisser stressed their support for Kahr and their willingness to suppress any putsch by force.[15]

Hitler then decided to act independently in a decision taken with a few other leaders, probably Max von Scheubner-Richter, the business manager of the Kampfbund, and the retired judge Theodor von der Pfordten. Hitler was possibly concerned that action was imminent and would occur outside Kampfbund control. In Endres' opinion, Röhm was as much an instigator of the putsch as Scheubner-Richter or Göring, because he convinced Hitler that the Reichswehr, or large sections of it, sympathized with Hitler and would not take up arms against him. This was a mistake.[16]

On the morning of November 7, senior Kampfbund leaders met at Kriebel's house to confirm the decision. Hitler, Weber, Göring, Scheubner-Richter, Kriebel, and probably Ludendorff attended. Those who attended denied that Röhm was present, but this may have been to protect Röhm's legal position, as he was still a serving Reichswehr officer. In an account given in 1937, Scheubner-Richter's manservant claimed Röhm was there. In denying that Röhm attended, Weber commented:

> I knew that on the one hand a close personal friendship existed between Röhm and Hitler, [and] on the other hand complete agreement on the goal and also the means. So one could assume—I personally also assumed this—that Captain Röhm would agree absolutely with the fact that it would take place on the evening of 8 November without previous advice.[17]

The prosecutor's office concurred.

On November 7, Lossow called his senior commanders together and advised them that the Reichswehr would stop any right-wing putsch. He named Hitler as the likely putsch leader, warned them against falsified orders, and asked the officers present to tell their subordinates of his position. A number of officers present proclaimed their support for Ludendorff and Hitler.[18]

The putschists may have believed that the triumvirs would cooperate when faced by an accomplished fact, particularly because Kahr, Lossow, and Seisser had been compromised by their previous dealings with them. The decision was taken to strike on the evening of November 8, while Kahr was addressing a meeting at the Bürgerbräukeller on the fifth anniversary of the revolution. Partly because of the short time span and a desire for secrecy, planning was sketchy. The leaders of the paramilitary groups met at the NSDAP headquarters at the Schellingstrasse in the evening of November 7 to finalize their plans. Röhm probably attended this meeting; he refused to answer questions about it in later interrogations. The various Kampfbund groups were to meet for training or propaganda meetings on the evening of November 8. Their leaders received sealed written orders to be opened that night.[19]

The Kampfbund planned to force the cooperation of the triumvirs to proclaim a nationalist government and then use the Bavarian Reichswehr to march on Berlin, gathering support of other nationalist forces outside Bavaria. The goals of the new nationalist government included the creation of a central dictatorship, a purge of their political opponents, and, after the overthrow of the peace settlement, the creation of a greater Germany. Jews were to be excluded from German political life. A draft constitution was drawn up by Theodor von der Pfordten, which included the creation of assembly camps to house "all persons dangerous to security and useless eaters."[20]

The Kampfbund could mobilize some 4,000 armed men: 1,500 from the SA Regiment München, some 125 from the Stosstrupp Hitler, and about 300 SA men from southern Bavaria; 2,000 odd from Bund Oberland; 200 from the RKF; and about 150 from Kampfbund München. Opposing them would be some 1,800 men in the Landespolizei combat units and some 800 men in Reichswehr combat units.[21]

On November 6, Karl Osswald ordered RKF members in Munich to attend a Kampfbund meeting at the Löwenbräukeller on Thursday November 8, 1923. Osswald also ensured that RKF weapons were brought out of storage to the Corps Palatia in an order the same day. This order suggests that Röhm knew of the putsch plans before the meeting at Kriebel's house on November 7.[22]

The evening of November 8 was dark and starless. The first snow of the winter fell. Kahr spoke about his policies to a full hall at the Bürgerbräukeller starting at 8:00 p.m. Ten minutes later, the first SA men drew up outside in trucks, and shortly after 8:30 p.m. the Stosstrupp Hitler arrived. Together, they surrounded the Bürgerbräukeller and blocked the exits. Hitler and a small group of armed men then forced their way to the podium. Hitler, or one of his entourage, fired into the ceiling before asking the triumvirs to join him in a side room. For fifteen minutes, there Hitler tried to persuade them to support him. With the three men still resisting, Hitler returned to speak to the audience and persuaded the majority present to support the putsch. He then used the audience reaction to put pressure on the triumvirs, aided by Ludendorff and Pöhner. Lossow, Seisser, and finally, Kahr, agreed to support the putsch. They then returned to the hall and Kahr, Ludendorff, Lossow, Seisser, and Pöhner all spoke briefly.[23]

The same night, Reichskriegsflagge held an evening of comradeship at the Löwenbräukeller in Munich's west. Of an audience of between 1,500 and 1,800, some 600 were in uniform—not only RKF, but SA, Oberland, and Kampfbund München. Röhm opened the meeting with a short speech.

He stated that after the five-year disgrace following the revolution, it was time to break with Marxism, settle with the November criminals, and stand up for the German people. Röhm then handed over to Hermann Esser, who was taking Hitler's place as speaker, despite being ill with jaundice. Esser had only been speaking for ten minutes when Röhm appeared on the podium, tapped Esser on the shoulder and whispered something in his ear. Rolf Reiner had telephoned the news of the putsch from the Bürgerbräukeller to all participating locations soon after 8:40 p.m. using the code phrase "successfully delivered." Esser announced loudly that the Bavarian government was arrested, a new national government formed and the Reich government deposed. Members of the Kampfbund present were called on to march in formation to the Bürgerbräukeller to swear allegiance to the new government. This occurred between 8:45 and 9:00 p.m., that is, before Hitler had forced the agreement of the triumvirs.[24]

As the assembled Kampfbund units set off to march east to the Bürgerbräukeller, Röhm claimed he received orders to occupy the Wehrkreiskommando at the intersection of Ludwigstrasse and Schönfeldstrasse. These orders possibly came from a motorbike rider who encountered the marching column, but may also have been Röhm's initial objective from the beginning. The main body of RKF moved off to the Corpshaus Palatia to collect their weapons, while other Kampfbund forces moved off to different tasks. Röhm, together with the remaining men of RKF, Batterie Lembert, and Kampfbund München, arrived at the Wehrkreiskommando at about 10:00 p.m. Röhm asked the sentry to take him to the duty officer, Captain Daser, who then ordered the men let in. Unknown to Röhm, Daser had already alerted General von Ruith and the troops in Munich more generally about the putsch.[25]

The RKF forces occupied the entire building. The Stammabteilung took over the telephone, security, and guard duty while the Batterie Lembert stood guard, the RKF under Osswald, and Abteilung Binz, stood ready for special duty in the building, and Kampfbund Zeller was in readiness in the courtyard. Röhm set up his command post in the anteroom of the commandant.[26]

The men under Röhm's command settled down to wait for Lossow's arrival as the Reichswehr Minister in the putschist government. But Lossow did not come. Instead, Hitler arrived between 10:40 and 11:00 p.m. Hitler went up to Röhm and said "So Röhm, it's done. We have a new Reich government."[27] According to Röhm, Hitler embraced him and told him it was the most wonderful day of his life. Hitler gave a short speech to the men. Ludendorff and Kriebel also arrived later.

Hitler and Weber had earlier left the Bürgerbräukeller to sort out a dispute at the engineers' barracks, leaving Ludendorff in charge. Ludendorff released the triumvirs on their word of honor. Across the city, groups of putschists took independent action when no orders came—seizure of Jews and prominent members of the left as hostages, arrest of allied officers from the International Military Control Commission in the Hotel Vier Jahreszeiten, control of most bridges in Munich and seizure of money. Even before this the generals that Daser had alerted gathered at the Stadtkommandantur, the town commandant's headquarters, at the back of the Hofgarten, only some five hundred meters from the Wehrkreiskommando. They warned officers that they should only obey orders from the Munich commandant, General von Danner. Lossow arrived at 10:45 p.m. and stated that he did not feel bound by a word of honor given under duress. A number of steps were taken to thwart the putsch and the military headquarters were transferred to the infantry barracks in the north west of the city, away from the areas under putschist control.[28]

Röhm went with Seydel to the town commandant's office, having learned that Lossow was there, but found the door barred to him. Pöhner arrived at the Wehrkreiskommando and Röhm tried, in vain, to reach Lossow by phone. As the evening continued and rumors of difficulties grew, Röhm rested periodically.[29]

Although Röhm claimed the men under his command were disciplined and well behaved, the balance of the evidence of other witnesses suggests that this was not the case. The atmosphere inside the Wehrkreiskommando became tenser as the night wore on. Leaders and men were tired and keyed up; the leaders were beginning to sense that events were going against them. Toward midnight, Röhm seemed to one witness to be depressed. After 1:00 a.m. Röhm ordered the remaining Reichswehr officers in the building be placed under armed guard.[30]

On Röhm's orders, patrols were sent into town from 7:00 a.m. on the morning of November 9. He called the officers of the units to him and ordered them to prepare the building for defense. He barricaded Schönfeldstrasse with pointed steel obstacles, and the Ludwigstrasse entrance with barbed wire and a heavy machine gun. At 10:00 a.m. the phones were cut off. There was a "gloomy mood"[31] as the leaders of the units explained to the men that they faced a fight. Röhm ordered the men to take their positions but not to fire on the Reichswehr without express orders. Röhm himself took up position behind the barricades in the Schönfeldstrasse.

Landespolizei and Reichswehr forces were moving toward the Wehrkreiskommando from the south, the north, and the east. At about 10:00 a.m. two serving officers who were friends of Röhm and sympathetic to the putschists—Lieutenant Colonel Friedrich Haselmayr, commander of the second battalion of the Twentieth Infantry Regiment, and Captain Friedrich Ritter von Krausser of the divisional staff—visited Röhm. They left to go to Lossow to get him to negotiate. There, they met Lieutenant Colonel

Hans-Georg Hofmann, the commandant of Ingolstadt who had come to Munich to help the putschists without directly taking sides. Just before midday, Hofmann won Lossow's permission to offer Röhm an honorable withdrawal if the occupiers surrendered and gave up their weapons. Haselmayr and Hofmann returned to Röhm with the news. Meanwhile, Epp, who had recently retired, and Hörauf also arrived to urge Röhm to surrender. Röhm initially refused, saying Ludendorff had left him with orders to hold the building. He then agreed to a two-hour armistice, ordered by Hofmann on his own initiative, while Röhm went with Epp, Seydel, and Du Moulin-Eckart to negotiate with Danner in the infantry barracks in the Türkenstrasse.[32]

Danner told Röhm there could be no negotiations: Röhm had to surrender. When Röhm countered that he had orders from Ludendorff, Danner pointed out that since Röhm was still a Reichswehr officer, Ludendorff had no right to give him orders. Röhm asked for a messenger to be sent to Ludendorff to ask him to revoke the order.[33]

The discussion was interrupted by a police officer who brought news of an armed clash between the police and putschists at the Feldherrnhalle, and a false report of Ludendorff's death. The remaining putsch leaders had agreed on a march through the city for the purpose of relieving Röhm and winning the army over to their side. As they approached a police cordon at the Residenzstrasse before the Feldherrnhalle, a shot rang out and the police returned fire. When the firing ended, four policemen and fourteen putschists were dead. Back at the Türkenstrasse, the false report of Ludendorff's death was amended to one that Ludendorff was a prisoner. Röhm broke off negotiations to return to his men.[34]

Soon after Röhm left the Wehrkreiskommando, two shots were fired from the building, wounding two soldiers. A machine gunner from the Reichswehr returned fire, killing RKF member Martin Faust instantly and mortally wounding Theodor Casella. (The dying Casella mistakenly told a number of RKF members that he had been shot by Oberleutnant Maximilian Braun.) The troops facing the Wehrkreiskommando had not yet received Hofmann's cease-fire order.[35]

On his return, Röhm had to hold back some of his forces from surrendering at gunpoint. Captain Wilhelm Wimmer then arrived with the formal surrender terms—Röhm's arrest and a release of the men once the building and their arms had been given up. Wimmer also brought a message from Ludendorff rescinding his previous orders to Röhm. At about 1:30 p.m. on Friday November 9, the occupiers of the Wehrkreiskommando assembled to surrender. The remainder of the RKF then carried Faust's body through the Munich streets to his home before dispersing. Under arrest, accompanied by

Seydel and Du Moulin-Eckart, Röhm was driven in a staff car to Danner in the Prinz-Arnulf-Kaserne and then to the Police Direction.[36]

Röhm spent one day in solitary confinement and then November 10 and 11 in imprisonment with others involved in the putsch, Friedrich Weber, Major Hans Streck, and Oberleutnant Gerhard von Prosch. His first interrogation was on November 12 at Neudeck, and two days later he was transferred to the prison in the Munich suburb of Stadelheim.[37]

Reichskriegsflagge, the Nazi Party, and the other political and paramilitary units that participated in the putsch were banned on November 9. Osswald continued to lead the underground RKF. On November 14, Röhm issued a statement to RKF members thanking them for their loyalty, discipline, and bravery. On December 3, he issued a further message, saying they had lost the battle, but not the cause.[38]

At Stadelheim, Röhm was well treated and had numerous visits from his family and friends. He did not cooperate with his interrogators, and was touchy about his rights and prerogatives as a prisoner. Prison authorities described him as behaving "very arrogantly," being "easily excited,"[39] and highly status conscious. He paid other prisoners to clean his cell.

The trial of the putschists for treason began on February 22, 1924, in the former infantry school at 3 Blutenburgstrasse in Munich's west. The prisoners were held in the rooms there during the trial. It was the first time they had all met since the putsch. Röhm wrote that he was overjoyed to shake Hitler's hand again. The trial itself lasted from February 26 to April 1, 1924, with twenty-five days of hearings.[40]

The Bavarian government refused to have the putschists tried in Leipzig by the Staatsgerichtshof, in part because Bavaria did not recognize the Leipzig court's authority. The government was also concerned to ensure that material embarrassing to it or the triumvirs was not disclosed during the trial. Instead, controversially, the Bavarian government, particularly Justice Minister Franz Gürtner, used the People's Court of two professional and three lay judges. The chief judge in the trial, Georg Neithardt, was sympathetic to Hitler. The putschists, in particular Hitler, used the trial for propaganda. Hitler was allowed to dominate the trial with his speeches. The prosecutors, selected by Gürtner, were not forceful and did not use all the evidence and witnesses available.[41]

Unlike Hitler, Röhm did not take a major part in the trial. He was represented by senior counsel Dr. Christoph Schramm, the father of an RKF member. His fellow defendants and friends provided mitigating evidence for him, denying that he had been present at various meetings before November 8. Ludendorff stated that Röhm had acted correctly in understanding his comment when he left the Wehrkreiskommando on the morning of November 9—"Remain here for the time being"[42]—as an order.

Röhm only testified at length on the fifth day of the trial, March 5, presenting himself as a staunch nationalist and enemy of the revolution. His counsel, Schramm, also praised Röhm's selflessness and patriotism. Röhm spoke, in veiled terms, of his work with the patriotic organizations and criticized Reichswehr officers who participated in the work of the patriotic organizations without giving them full support. He specifically criticized Braun for an alleged comment that "'I don't care if Reichskriegsflagge has two dead men. I am a soldier and that's what I'm paid for.'"[43]

Röhm stressed he created the RKF as a purely military organization. In court, he presented himself as uninvolved in the preparations for the putsch but a willing supporter of the new government. He chose not to make a closing statement, commenting that he had nothing to add to "the statements of my friend and Führer, Adolf Hitler."[44]

In his testimony, Röhm criticized Braun's behavior during the cease-fire and surrender. Schramm maintained these criticisms despite the testimony of various senior officers and Braun himself that Braun had not shot Casella. In his evidence, Lossow's chief of staff, Lieutenant Colonel von Berchem, described Röhm's criticisms of Braun as "slander" and accused Röhm of "irresponsible agitation."[45] These comments led Röhm to challenge Berchem to a duel with pistols after the trial, a dispute that was later settled by an army court of inquiry. Braun's own conduct was cleared by a commission of inquiry of officers of his own regiment. Schramm continued to bring charges and accusations against Braun, even though these were in no way related to the charges against Röhm.

Röhm pressed his attacks on Braun in *Geschichte eines Hochverräters*, in which he devoted seven pages to a discussion of the shooting of Faust and Castella. He still claimed that Braun was responsible for the Reichswehr returning fire. This was followed by a strongly anti-Semitic passage in a secondhand account of the RKF procession that brought Faust's body through the Munich streets to his parents' home.[46]

Why did Röhm react like this? To a certain extent, criticism of Braun was part of a wider putschist tactic. By focussing on certain individuals in the Reichswehr and attributing responsibility to them, the putschists therefore exempted the majority of the Reichswehr from the criticisms.[47] The shock of the deaths also meant that RKF members wanted someone to blame.

Criticism of Braun may have served to repress awareness of Röhm's own failings. If Braun was responsible for the conduct of his troops, then so, too, was Röhm. The more strenuous his criticisms of Braun, the more they reflected an underlying unease at his own role. Röhm claimed that Braun "strutted about in a provocative, not to say theatrical pose with a slung rifle, felt it necessary to show a victor's manner continuously and did not treat his enemies as soldiers, but as criminals."[48] Braun's alleged behavior confronted Röhm with the distance between his own view of himself and the view of others. If Braun treated Röhm as a criminal, it was because Röhm had broken the law and his oath as an officer.

Similarly, the anti-Semitism of the passage may have reflected the views of RKF members, like Heinrich Himmler, who reported their experiences to Röhm. It may have been a further expression of his resentment of his defeat and a deflection of his anger from its real target, the Reichswehr, which he dared not attack openly.

The trial verdicts were delivered shortly after 10:00 a.m. on April 1, 1924, to a jubilant crowd. Hitler, Pöhner, Kriebel, and Weber were found guilty of treason and sentenced to a minimum sentence of five years' fortress imprisonment. Röhm, Brückner, Pernet, Wagner, and Frick were all found guilty of the crime of accessory to treason and sentenced to one year three months' fortress imprisonment. In Röhm's case, the four months and three weeks he had served under investigative arrest were deducted from his sentence. In addition to costs, the accessories were fined one hundred gold marks, or a further ten days' fortress arrest. Ludendorff was acquitted. Arrest decrees against Röhm, Frick, and Brückner were lifted. There were similar light sentences in the parallel trials of lesser participants in the Putsch.[49]

Violating the presidential guidelines for the wearing of uniforms, but with the permission of the trial judge, Röhm, Brückner, Ludendorff, and some of the other defendants appeared in uniform for the verdict. Questioned by the police later about this, Röhm became excited and showed distress. He commented that he considered it a matter of course to wear his uniform on such a day, "even if for me this was personally also the last time."[50]

After the main trial, Röhm, Brückner, Pernet, Wagner, and Frick were immediately released on probation until April 1, 1928. At the end of the trial, Röhm decided he would continue the political struggle for Germany's renewal rather than return to private life. Vowing to serve a people of fighters ready to die and live for freedom, he returned to political activity.[51]

CHAPTER 8

Frontbann Leader
April 1924–May 1925

The task I now saw facing me was a large one: I had to re-create from the shattered organizations banned by von Kahr an instrument for the movement that was fit for action.[1]

Ernst Röhm

On April 1, 1924, Ernst Röhm walked free on eighteen months' probation. Apart from Ludendorff, many other leaders of the völkisch movement in Bavaria were either in prison or in exile, thereby giving Röhm a potentially greater role in its affairs. Discharged from the Reichswehr, he could now play a more public political role than before.

In the dock on April 1, 1924, both Hitler and Kriebel gave Röhm unrestricted authority to rebuild the paramilitary movement.[2] In this period, Röhm became de facto head of the SA, and of a new successor organization to RKF—Old Reich Flag (*Altreichsflagge* or ARF). His main energies, however, were devoted to setting up the *Frontbann*, an organization he envisaged as uniting all völkisch paramilitary units. Particularly in the remaining nine months of 1924, Röhm was active in all these organizations as well as serving as a Reichstag deputy.

Against Hitler's wishes, the völkisch groups decided to contest the Reichstag elections on May 4, 1924. Röhm was nominated as a candidate, and in his speeches he indicated that he saw himself as a representative of the front fighter. He spoke in Ansbach at the instigation of a former school friend, Dr. Einsle. The völkisch movement won votes as a result of public support in Munich and Bavaria, and the publicity surrounding the putsch and the trial. Röhm and thirty-one others were elected to the Reichstag as candidates of the National Socialist Freedom Party (*Nationalsozialistische Freiheitspartei*). Reichstag deputies received passes for free rail travel throughout the Reich. Röhm was able to use this to support his activities in the paramilitary organizations.[3]

Röhm attended the second Reichstag's sessions every day it sat from May to August 1924. He only spoke once in the Reichstag, on May 28, to demand the release of Hermann Kriebel from Landsberg. He claimed to have persuaded his party to submit proposals to the Reichstag to create an investigative committee on prisoners of war, to call for intercession for Ruhr fighters held in French prisons, and to promote the rights of the front fighter by giving them special privileges, including a double vote. The Reichstag debated none of these motions.[4]

While Hitler was in prison, the völkisch movement itself divided and fragmented. Hitler appointed Alfred Rosenberg, then editor of the *Völkischer Beobachter*, to lead the Nazi Party when he was arrested. On January 1, 1924, Rosenberg formed the Greater German People's Community *(Großdeutsche Volksgemeinschaft)*, intended to be a successor to the still illegal NSDAP. Two other rival organizations were also founded—the Völkisch Bloc on January 6, 1924, in Bamberg, and the German Völkisch Freedom Party *(Deutschvölkische Freiheitspartei* or DVFP).[5]

Röhm saw his task as creating a fighting instrument out of the banned and demoralized paramilitary units. He spent the first few weeks after his release holding discussions on the issue, aided by Gerhard von Prosch and Kurt Lüdecke. Looking back, Lüdecke remembered Röhm at this time as:

> a brilliant leader of men, an excellent officer, fearless and straightforward. His massive, round head, battle-scarred and patched, looked like something hammered from rock. He was the living image of war itself, in contrast to his polished manner and exceptional and instinctive courtesy. That, with his naturalness, diplomatic tact and *savoir faire* distinguished him from leading Nazis then and afterwards, who for the most part were boorish and arrogant, or were bullies. For all his one-sided military mind, he was a passionate politician, having, for a soldier, a rare intelligence and understanding for politics. I liked his keen, open gaze and his firm hand clasp.[6]

Röhm remained in close contact with the imprisoned leaders in Landsberg. On April 10, with Dr. Frick and Wilhelm Brückner, he visited Weber and, with Brückner, Hitler and Kriebel.

Hitler had also entrusted Röhm with the general rebuilding of the SA. In April, Röhm visited Hermann Göring, nominally head of the SA at that time, in exile in Innsbruck, and Gerhard Rossbach in Salzburg to discuss the SA. Göring personally appointed Röhm as his deputy and gave him unrestricted authority. Rossbach became SA Chief of Staff, but could not return to Germany to take up the position, and resigned on July 26, 1924.[7]

Göring hosted a large SA leaders' conference in Salzburg on May 17 and 18, 1924, attended by representatives of all Gaus in Germany and Austria. At the meeting, Röhm was recognized as head of the SA. The distinctive mustard brown SA shirts, which had been earlier used by Rossbach's Freikorps, were adopted as the SA uniform at this meeting. At the same meeting, Röhm issued guidelines to govern the rebuilding of the SA. They described the SA as the "fighting troop of the NSDAP,"[8] and stressed its military organization and membership of the Kampfbund. Röhm attended meetings of NSDAP leaders in his capacity as SA commander. On August 15, 1924, he led the SA in a march past at the National Socialist party day at Weimar.

By the beginning of June, Röhm was also leader of the ARF. It had been formed in Nuremberg in December 1923 by Wilhelm Liebel and Karl Braun in a split from Heiss's Reichsflagge over Reichsflagge's attitude toward the Hitler putsch. By April 1924, Ritter von Krausser led a Munich branch. Almost all former RKF members joined the Munich branch and dominated the organization. By June, leadership, first of the Munich branch, and then of the entire organization, was transferred to Röhm.[9]

As a Reichstag deputy and prominent member of the attempted putsch, Röhm played a more public role in the völkisch movement. On May 6, he spoke in the Bürgerbräukeller at a festival to honor Hitler, stating that Hitler had to be the leader in the future struggle. On May 10 and 11, he participated in a rally, the Deutsche Tag, in Halle. On the evening of May 10, Röhm spoke to völkisch units assembled for the meeting in four halls in neighbouring Merseburg. There he met the former Freikorps Rossbach member, Wolf Heinrich Graf von Helldorf. Röhm spoke to Helldorf and others about his plans to combine fit young men into a new völkisch paramilitary movement that would develop into the Frontbann, which he envisaged as combining all völkisch units with a strong central organization.[10]

Röhm's concept of the Frontbann did not recognize that the political landscape had changed since November 8–9, 1923. It was as if he was recreating the 1923 Kampfbund, but seeking to make it more effective by strengthening its central organization. The similarity to the Kampfbund extended to the role Röhm envisaged for himself and Hitler. Röhm would be the military leader as Kriebel had been, and Hitler, the political leader. Röhm can be seen as a "slow learner," seeking to reproduce the patterns that worked before November 1923.[11]

On May 31, Röhm traveled to Landsberg to meet Kriebel and Weber together, and Hitler. Röhm brought with him a draft proposal for the Frontbann that foreshadowed a centralized leadership. All three "Landsbergers'" rejected Röhm's draft emphatically and without any prior coordination of their responses. Their rejection was on political and philosophical grounds as much as out of fear that any involvement might jeopardize their hopes of an early release. They opposed Röhm's proposed centralized control. Hitler told Röhm a new founding was psychologically impossible because existing organizations would never be prepared to dissolve into a new organization. Hitler preferred a looser organization protecting the independence of the Verbände. Röhm countered that Hitler was unable to judge the issues adequately in prison. That afternoon, when Ludendorff visited the three "Landsbergers," they presented him with a counter-draft prepared by Kriebel, setting out their objections, and asked him to give it to Röhm. They told Ludendorff they rejected Röhm's proposals. Ludendorff supported Röhm, saying Röhm already had the matter correctly underway.[12]

If the opposition of Hitler, Kriebel, and Weber from prison was not yet a decisive blow to Röhm's plans, the "Landsbergers" were correct in predicting why Röhm's concept would not work. Most völkisch paramilitary units refused to surrender their independence to the new organization. In 1923, as paymaster and arms provider to the Bavarian paramilitary units, Röhm could enforce a certain degree of unity; in 1924, he was just one among many völkisch leaders, and he could not.

Röhm admitted to Schramm and Helldorf that his plans had been rejected by the leaders in Landsberg. He told Helldorf, probably in August 1924, that Hitler's attitude had been one of complete rejection. He had, nonetheless, created the Frontbann, as he believed Hitler was not in a position to judge the situation in the Reich. He would take the reproach of disobedience on himself. To others, such as Liebel and his supporters in Nuremberg on June 1, Röhm was evasive about the attitude of the "Landsbergers."[13]

When Röhm visited Hitler again in June—probably on his visit of June 12 to Hitler with Ludendorff—Hitler's disagreement had strengthened. He told Röhm his plan was completely wrong. Hitler could not support it and could not advocate it to his followers. Röhm's response was that it had already been done and could not be changed. This was a surprising claim, as all that Röhm had done to that date was hold discussions with various völkisch leaders. He had taken no action that could not be revoked. Röhm appears to have assumed that Hitler would support a successful fait accompli, as he had supported the völkisch movement's electoral involvement once it won votes. Hitler also opposed Ludendorff's plan to unite the NSDAP and the DVFP, and told Ludendorff he was resigning the political leadership.[14]

Röhm visited Hitler, Weber, and Kriebel again on June 17. All three prisoners were angered by the draft Frontbann proclamation, particularly Hitler, whose name was used in it. In a later visit, Ludendorff made it clear to Hitler that he agreed with Röhm, whose position was strengthened because the three Landsberg leaders were not prepared to clash publicly with Ludendorff.[15]

When Röhm later wrote to Hitler asking him if he could visit again, Hitler did not reply directly but let it be known via other visitors that he considered such a visit pointless. Hitler commented to the police in December "the fact that I had to resort now to a purely formal relationship with Röhm was painful in itself, because a sincere relationship of friendship had existed until then between Röhm and me, which also continues still now."[16]

Ludendorff supported Röhm and let him set up the Frontbann along his own lines. At this time, relations between Ludendorff and Röhm:

> were governed by a particular relationship of trust . . . Ludendorff appreciated Röhm quite extraordinarily on account of his great organizational talent and his farsightedness, [Ludendorff] did not yet suspect anything of his abnormal inclination that he already certainly had then. . . . Looking back I remember many meetings with Röhm in pubs, where he always invited and drew together one or two young people of his staff. Then this seemed to the unsuspecting participant as exemplary care of these young men without means, but afterwards to be sure, with knowledge of Röhm's inclinations, it appeared in a different light.[17]

In June and July, Röhm continued his discussions with a variety of leaders of the Verbände, retiring officers, and others seeking their help in setting up the Frontbann. On July 10, Ludendorff chaired a meeting on the Frontbann at the Haus am Frauenplatz in Munich of some twenty men representing the various Wehrverbände. The proposals were rejected by Eugen Meyding, the Chairman of the Deutschen Schützen- und Wanderbund, a replacement for Bund Oberland, who was aware that the "Landsbergers" had rejected Röhm's proposed organizational structure for the Frontbann. The only Verbände that agreed to go into the Frontbann were the two under Röhm's control—ARF and the SA—and the Frontkriegerbund.[18]

Röhm sought to ensure that the Frontbann was permitted by the Bavarian government. He submitted a lengthy draft proclamation to Interior Minister Stützel and met with the Minister in late July 1924. The proclamation, drafted by Karl Schramm, was strongly influenced by völkisch racial thought, describing Jews as "the lingering poison in the body of the people."[19] The political goal of the Frontbann, according to the draft, was to free Germany from its internal and external enemies.

The Bavarian cabinet discussed Röhm's proposals on August 2 and rejected them. Stützel indicated that he thought Röhm was seeking an economically secure position through the Frontbann. The ministers were reluctant to trust the promises of loyalty from such organizations in the light of their bad experiences over the past few years.[20]

A planned meeting of Röhm and Stützel on August 5 fell through. In an earlier meeting with Ministerial Councillor Zetlmeier, Zetlmeier indicated to Röhm that the government was opposed to Röhm publishing his proposed proclamation. Röhm then claimed to Stützel that the sole purpose of the Frontbann would be to prepare young men for military service through physical exercise and accustoming them to obedience. This would be the cover story adopted by all Frontbann leaders after the first arrests in September.[21]

On August 16, the "Völkischer Frontkampfbund Frontbann" was founded and registered as a society in Berlin. On August 25, its name was notarially changed to "Frontbann." On the German Day in Weimar on August 15, Röhm and Helldorf spoke to a meeting of about fifty men who were leaders of the various Verbände, seeking to get them to join the Frontbann Gruppenkommando Mitte under Helldorf's leadership. The Stahlhelm refused to become involved because they did not want to give up their independence. According to Helldorf's deputy, Freiherr von Eberstein, this doomed the Frontbann Gruppenkommando Mitte, as the Stahlhelm was the strongest formation in the region.[22]

In all his activities designed to set up the Frontbann, Röhm put the best gloss on developments in an effort to drive the organization forward and convince the undecided to join. He led some men to believe that Hitler supported his endeavors, while he let others believe that the Bavarian government approved the founding of the Frontbann. For Röhm, the end justified the means. This sometimes caused him temporary embarrassment. In August, for example, he could not explain to Seydel in Nuremberg why he could not make Hitler's name more prominent in the draft proclamation.[23]

Using Ludendorff's prestige, Röhm was able to extend the organization beyond Bavaria, and win the support of many men who later took leading positions in the SA and SS. The Frontbann had thirty thousand members. Working under Röhm's direction, Osswald and Schramm created an extensive organizational structure for a paramilitary organization to encompass Germany and Austria by September 1924. Röhm prepared the lengthy Frontbann service regulations along strictly military guidelines.[24]

Now that Röhm was no longer in the army, however, he was not as effective a leader. He could not draw on the administrative backup he had in the FZM, and he could not deliver the funding he had been able to in 1923. Writing to Schramm on August 19, Osswald described the Frontbann as vegetating. They lacked the money to build up the organization, and Röhm kept him in the dark about developments in northern Germany. Röhm dawdled his time away, did not have the necessary decisiveness simply to sail through, and had no money. Earlier, Osswald had described Röhm as overly optimistic, and this letter reflected a more jaundiced view of Röhm's character than the hero-worshipping tone of Osswald's letter to Röhm in prison.[25]

By the end of August, Röhm was ready to make the creation of the Frontbann public. On August 27, he wrote to Stützel indicating that the proclamation was imminent. On August 28, while in East Prussia with Ludendorff to commemorate the tenth anniversary of the battle of Tannenberg, Röhm issued a short proclamation to the press announcing the creation of the Frontbann. It omitted the ideological emphasis of Schramm's earlier draft, and merely stated that those units and comrades basing themselves on National Socialist ideology and unconditionally following Hitler, Ludendorff, and Graefe, had joined together in the Frontbann. A copy of the proclamation was sent to Stützel, who responded that the Bavarian Interior Ministry had not changed its attitude.[26]

Following the public announcement of the formation of the Frontbann, organizational and recruiting activities on its behalf intensified. On September 5, Röhm reached an agreement with the Völkisch Bloc and the Großdeutschen Volksgemeinschaft that the Frontbann could recruit at their meetings. On September 12, Röhm issued an organizational staff order for the Frontbann, naming Seydel as his personal representative on the staff, and also giving staff appointments to Osswald, Schramm, Weiss, and von Prosch.[27]

On September 13, Röhm accompanied Ludendorff to Elberfeld and Münster to set out the military and political organization there. Ludendorff went on to Helldorf's estate at Wohlmirstedt, where Helldorf raised with Ludendorff the possibility that some of the orders Osswald was issuing might be illegal. In turn, Ludendorff mentioned the matter to Röhm, and on September 15, Röhm issued a special decree indicating that these orders no longer applied.[28]

Helldorf's concern was prescient. The next day, on September 16, the Munich police searched the Frontbann offices and the homes of nine men (Osswald, Brückner, Leo Stempfle, Prosch, Schramm, Krausser, Aechter, Karl Ludwig Reff, and Meyding). For the time being, Röhm's immunity from prosecution as a Reichstag deputy protected him. Osswald, Krausser, Prosch, Brückner, Schramm, Weiss, and then Seydel and Faber were arrested. The police concluded the ARF and the Deutsche Schützen- und Wanderbund were replacements for the illegal RKF and Bund Oberland. They judged Frontbann to be an organization designed to seize power by force and assumed that Röhm's dealings with the Interior Ministry were designed to disguise the Frontbann's real goals.[29]

Röhm returned from Berlin on September 18 to visit Stützel with Landtag deputy Gregor Strasser in an attempt to secure the release of those arrested. When he met Stützel on September 19, two men had been released, but three more had been arrested. On the weekend of September 21–22, the *Völkischer Kurier* published a statement by Röhm describing the founding of the Frontbann as completely above board and denying either Hitler or Ludendorff had anything to do with it. Schramm later claimed that he suggested this press statement to Röhm as a way of notifying those arrested of the correct "cover story" for their interrogations. Röhm also tried, unsuccessfully, to gain support from the Reichswehr by seeking a meeting with Lieutenant Colonel Kurt von Schleicher, chief of the military political section of the Reichswehr.[30]

The Bavarian authorities were convinced that the Frontbann represented a continuation of the banned organizations. Röhm believed the arrests were a pretext for the Bavarian government to delay the release of the remaining prisoners in Landsberg. In an attempt to forestall this, the leaders in Landsberg issued a statement indicating they had not supported the Frontbann. On September 29, the Bavarian State Supreme Court decided to hold the Landsberg prisoners, pending the outcome of the Frontbann investigation. Röhm was unsuccessful in winning any support for the Frontbann from the Bavarian Parliament's völkisch members on October 1.[31]

Röhm had first been interrogated as a witness on September 17. On October 17, he presented his interrogators with a lengthy memorandum justifying the founding of the Frontbann as designed to help the army fight Germany's external enemies. Frontbann members had to be loyal to the National Socialist ideology because that ideology alone promised the liberation of the fatherland. In this memorandum, he mentioned what would be a constant theme of his later speeches and writings: National Socialism was born on the battlefields of the World War.[32]

Röhm and Ludendorff also issued public statements on October 15, 1924 indicating—correctly—that Hitler, Weber, and Kriebel had no part in the Frontbann. By the end of October, the criminal proceedings against Osswald and the others were extended to Röhm and Ludendorff by the Staatsgerichtshof zum Schutz der Republik. The proceedings were eventually abandoned on September 26, 1925.[33]

On August 30, the Reichstag was dissolved after it adopted the Dawes Plan, an American initiative to stabilize the German economy. New elections were called for December 7, 1924. In this campaign, paramilitary units began to be used in electoral propaganda and activity. Röhm wanted leaders of the paramilitary groups to get prominent positions on the völkisch ticket but he was unsuccessful. He himself was placed so low on the list that he was not re-elected. Having lost his immunity from prosecution as a result of the dissolution of the Reichstag, he temporarily took shelter in Helldorf's castle.[34]

Röhm's perfect Reichstag attendance may have been partly monetarily motivated. Röhm was in a poor economic position while supporting others. Röhm's sister, Lore Lippert, claimed in 1952 that Hermann Göring, who was living in exile in Austria with his first wife, Karin, had turned to Röhm for financial help. Röhm had already moved back to live with his parents at Herzogstrasse 4/III in late 1922. On August 29, 1924, he applied to the Reichswehr Ministry for support. He was awarded 220.05 RM toward the cost of repaying an accidental pension overpayment. The money appeared instead to have been used by the Frontbann.[35]

Röhm's economic position had not improved by November 1924. He had been under the care of Dr. Emil Ketterer since the beginning of August for hemorrhoids and accompanying stomach ailments. This led to overall health problems, for which Ketterer recommended a sanatorium cure. Röhm commented that, in addition, his nerves were overstrained. He could not afford to go to a sanatorium and instead spent several days in a cabin in the mountains near Salzburg and saved money by staying with relatives in Salzburg and Vienna.[36]

Toward the end of the year, Röhm set out what he considered to be the guiding principle of leadership for the Frontbann—Ludendorff was to be its patron, and Hitler, the leader of the political movement. Ludendorff disagreed with this, and Hitler did not respond when Röhm reported to him shortly after his release from prison on December 20, 1924. On January 14, 1925, Röhm asked Hitler to release him from his leadership of the Frontbann; a few days later, Röhm made representations to Ludendorff along the same lines. A decision was postponed and Röhm temporarily remained leader.[37]

On February 12, Ludendorff gave up the national leadership of the völkisch movement. Graefe and Gregor Strasser also resigned from the national leadership. At a meeting of Frontbann leaders from February 28 to March 2, 1925, in Helldorf's castle in Wohlmirstedt, the leaders decided they would follow Hitler as Führer of the National Socialist movement, and Ludendorff as patron. In the meantime, Hitler had refounded the NSDAP and asked Röhm to take over the SA leadership, but Röhm refused. Hitler's new guidelines for the party saw the SA as an auxiliary organization, subordinate to the party. On March 27, 1925, Hitler published a directive in the *Völkischer Beobachter*, directing all questions concerning the SA to Röhm. The prospect of Röhm commanding the SA on Hitler's terms appears always to have been open to him.[38]

Röhm strongly supported Ludendorff's candidacy for the presidency after the death of Ebert in March 1925, even though he knew Ludendorff was

unlikely to win. Röhm and Hitler wrote some of Ludendorff's election proclamations, Röhm appealing to soldiers of the wartime army to vote for the man
who had raised the sharpest protest at the ingratitude for their sacrifices. On
March 28, Röhm and Hitler appeared with Ludendorff and other völkisch
leaders at the federal meeting of the Frontkriegerbund in the Bürgerbräu.[39]

Earlier, on March 22, Röhm accompanied Hitler to Weimar where Hitler
made Arthur Dinter Gauleiter, despite Frontbann resistance. Röhm felt that
while Hitler demanded the Frontbann acknowledge his orders unconditionally, he did not recognize the Frontbann as the National Socialist paramilitary
movement and place it under his leadership. This led Röhm to seek to clarify
matters with Hitler:

> I wanted to tell my friend Hitler in full openness everything I did not like.
> I know that many men cannot bear admonishers and warners. I have always
> taken the opposite view. As long as I have stood in a responsible position, I
> have always placed a loyal friend at my side, to whom above all I gave the task
> of raising all objections that could be raised against the measures taken by me.
> I consider the "spirit, which denies," an indispensable comrade along all paths
> of human striving and creation. Sincere friendship linked me to Hitler. Just
> because I saw that flatterers, who adored him unconditionally and dared no
> word of contradiction, pressed around him, I considered myself obligated as a
> loyal friend to speak openly to him.[40]

On April 16, 1925, Röhm met Hitler in Hitler's Munich home and gave
Hitler a comprehensive memorandum on the Frontbann. By his own account,
Röhm was willing to merge the Frontbann with the SA, but wanted to have
sole responsibility for the new merged organization and for issuing orders to
it. The Frontbann would be an independent paramilitary organization inside
the National Socialist movement.[41]

Hitler rejected Röhm's proposals and demanded the exclusive subordina-
tion and incorporation of the Frontbann in the framework of the NSDAP.
Hitler did not see Röhm's suggestion as an act of friendship, but as a conscious reduction of Hitler's effectiveness, which was not Röhm's intention.
Röhm wrote that the consequences for him were "obvious."[42] On April 17,
he wrote to Hitler, resigning from the leadership of the SA and asking Hitler
to agree to his resignation as Frontbann commander. Hitler did not reply.
On April 30, he wrote to Hitler again, stating that since he had received no
answer to his letter, he believed he would have Hitler's agreement to give an
attached statement resigning his position to the press. He asked Hitler not to
withdraw his personal friendship. Röhm also wrote to Ludendorff advising
him of his decision. Ludendorff wrote back to thank him for his message;
Hitler did not.

On May 1, 1925, Röhm gave the National Socialist press a statement indicating that he was resigning from the Frontbann and SA leadership. Brückner resigned with him. All queries concerning the SA were to be directed to the NSDAP headquarters in Munich, and all questions concerning the Frontbann to Helldorf. In a statement that went to his close colleagues, he said that he could not win support for his concept of the Frontbann from either Ludendorff or Hitler. "I do not think of leading a formation that is focussed on National Socialism without the support of these men or ever against their will."[43] Economic considerations also played a part in his decision.

Some historians interpreted the Hitler-Röhm dispute over the Frontbann in the light of later developments in the relations between the two men in 1933–34. It is more useful to understand Röhm's attitude by looking at his immediate past experiences of 1919 to 1923. Röhm had not yet adjusted to the realities of politics after the failure of the Hitler Putsch.[44] He was still seeking to repeat the formulas and approaches that he had used before September 1923, but without the support of the army, this attempt was less successful.

In his relations with Hitler, Röhm had not yet comprehended his own changed and diminished status. He was no longer patron or protector, but subordinate. Hitler, though, was not yet "Hitler." His position was not yet as strong as it would later be. It was the founderings of the various völkisch factions and their disagreements while Hitler was in prison that helped secure his role as Führer. Hitler's dealings with Röhm on his release from prison indicated his determination to prevail on issues of strategy and structure.[45]

The past two years had been full of upheaval in Röhm's personal and professional life. He had left the army, participated in the attempted putsch, been imprisoned, and stood trial before resuming independent paramilitary activity. In the Frontbann, Röhm had copied the organizational structure and approaches of the army. On May 1, 1925, Röhm became a civilian private citizen for the first time in his adult life.

CHAPTER 9

"Human, All Too Human": Private Life 1925–28

My paths have often led me where the honest Philistine blushes and shudders. And yet I would not want to have missed the impressions and experiences I have gained. I laugh at the fools who go through life without knowing it. And I accept life and will not allow myself to be robbed of my glad belief in this world of God in spite of everything.[1]

Ernst Röhm

In resigning the Frontbann leadership, Ernst Röhm announced that he was withdrawing from all political formations and societies to secure his complete freedom of action in the future. In his private statement to his ideological comrades, in addition to setting out his political reasons for leaving, he added that economic considerations forced him to secure a living.

For the first time in his adult life, Röhm had to earn a living as an ordinary civilian. Not all the details of his employment in this period are known, but his financial circumstances were not good. He began by working as a door-to-door salesman selling books for a right-wing publishing house, the Deutsche Nationalverlag. He struggled in this job, and often found it painful and humiliating.[2]

Late in 1926, Röhm was employed for two months in the Robel track-building factory, a position found for him by Princess Luise of Sachsen-Altenburg. Röhm claimed he did well and was considered for a leading position by the firm's founder. Yet, he did not remain there. He was employed for a time as a manual laborer, but where he worked in 1927 is not known. He spent some of the year writing his autobiography, hoping to make money from the book. By 1928, he had returned to political activity for the NSDAP and was writing occasional articles for the *Völkischer Beobachter*.[3]

Röhm's monetary problems continued. His earnings were supplemented by his military pension of RM 335.25 a month, but, even so, he could not manage financially, and repeatedly turned to the Reichswehr Ministry for support: between 1926 and 1928 he received a total of 1,100 marks in five one-off payments. This was further evidence that he was either in difficult economic circumstances or that he had a certain inability to manage money. Röhm's repeated requests for financial support indicate that he had not enriched himself from 1919 on, despite hostile claims to the contrary. In 1926, Röhm made his first abortive attempt to go to Bolivia as a military instructor. No doubt he was motivated as much by financial need as by a desire to return to military life. Röhm also did not appear to have gained any substantial inheritance from his father's estate when Julius Röhm died, aged seventy-nine, on March 3, 1926, at his home in the Herzogstrasse. Röhm's reduced circumstances meant that, after his father's death, he continued to share the apartment at the Herzogstrasse with his mother.[4]

Röhm could not escape the consequences of his past political involvement, and gradually began to be drawn back into völkisch affairs. In early 1926, the left-wing parties in the Reichstag succeeded in forming a Reichstag investigative committee—the Reichstag Committee for Feme Organizations and Feme Murders. The "Feme" was a term revived by Organization Consul for punishment detachments. In "Feme" murders, members and non-members were killed by radical right-wing organizations out of suspicion of treason or other offences.[5]

The Reichstag Committee held hearings in Munich from October 5 to October 13–14, 1926, amid much hostility in Bavaria. Its Munich hearings did not provide much new material because most witnesses claimed convenient lapses of memory when questioned. On the committee's return to Berlin, its chairman, Paul Levi, made it clear that three murders in 1920 and 1921 could be traced back to a group organized in the Einwohnerwehr's business office. In all cases, the perpetrators had the sympathy of, and, at times, help of, high-ranking civilian and military officials.[6]

Röhm and Epp both admitted to helping von Schweikart, the alleged murderer of the waitress Maria Sandmeyer in 1920. In the course of Röhm's interrogation, he refused to answer Levi's further questions and was fined three hundred marks by the committee for contempt. It is not clear what the questions were that Röhm refused to answer, and whether he refused because Levi's questioning was getting close to something legally incriminating. Röhm's own account in his autobiography was marked by anti-Semitic attacks on Levi,[7] which suggests that his anti-Semitism and consequent resentment of Levi's authority led him to refuse to answer the questions. Röhm did not pay the fine and refused to allow others to pay it for him. Instead he and the Nazi press publicized his serving of the sentence. On February 9, 1927, Röhm began his ten-day sentence in Stadelheim prison. Röhm claimed that he chose to serve the sentence in the hope of making an impression on frontline veterans who did not support the völkisch movement, to force them to recognize the reality of Germany's shame and loss of honor.[8]

Röhm also resumed contact with the SA. In 1927, the Rossbach Bicycle Section, under Edmund Heines' leadership, joined the SA. They held exercises over Easter, March 19–20, 1927, near Fürstenfeldbruck, and met Röhm in Pöcking, near Starnberg where Röhm was on holiday. On May 15, Röhm attended an SA meeting to show solidarity with Heines, who was being expelled because his activism clashed with the party leadership.[9]

Röhm continued to have close links to both Heines and Rossbach. In 1928, he defended Heines in an article in the *Deutsche Zeitung* during Heines' trial for a Feme murder. Heines was sentenced to fifteen years' imprisonment for second degree murder for the so-called Stettiner murder, but was released the following year in an amnesty. Röhm attacked the Feme murder investigations as the work of the Jews, the triumph of the trader over the soldier. Specifically, he saw Jews as the enemy of the German essence and as the leaders of the self-emasculation of Germany by dishonoring its soldiers.[10]

By 1928, Röhm reemerged in Nazi Party politics. By mid-year, the police intelligence service described him as "dedicating himself"[11] once more to the NSDAP. He may have been led back to politics by the failure of his efforts to make a success of civilian life. It is possible, though, that he underwent a period of reflection and reconsideration of his purpose in life, an early midlife crisis, possibly prompted by his father's death. In the period 1927 to 1928, he used his autobiography to reflect on his past life, his character, and his ideological views. He researched his ancestry on his father's side of the family, and he published a family tree. From 1924 on, he came to terms with his sexuality and consciously adopted a homosexual identity.

At the age of forty in 1927, what kind of man was he? According to Max Werner, Röhm "was a 'chap', an over-emphasized masculine character, hypermasculine."[12] He struck a sympathetic Italian observer, the Italian fascist Giuseppe Renzetti, as "'jovial, intelligent. . . . Correct and loyal. . . . All things considered, he was and remained an official who wanted to be in politics but did not quite have the capacity.'" [13]

He was his mother's favorite and she kept a household for him for the rest of his life. Renzetti recalled visiting Röhm "in his home, a tiny and modest apartment, where his mother, who treated Röhm with the tenderness and affection one would a child, offered us coffee."[14] Although Röhm consciously rejected bourgeois values and never married, he enjoyed a loving and conventional home life whenever he wanted it. His mother kept open house for Röhm's friends. He gave her flowers and went to church with her. She supported and shared his political views, although, true to his principle that women should not mix in politics, he did not discuss such issues in detail with the women in his family.

His interests extended beyond politics. He collected engravings, read the German literary classics, and befriended artists like Carl Anton Reichel and opera singers like Hans Beer. He was an excellent piano player and frequently entertained his friends with spontaneous piano recitals.[15]

Like Adolf Hitler, he was a passionate Wagnerian. In the period from 1926 to 1928, he was repeatedly the guest of Siegfried and Winifred Wagner in Haus Wahnfried at Bayreuth, combining his musical and ideological interests. He was a go-between for Siegfried and Winifred Wagner in their relations with Crown Prince Rupprecht. The strength of his reactions to Wagner can be seen in his comments on the experience of watching performances at Bayreuth in the autobiography. These remarks also suggest a concealed romanticism. His favorite singer was the Romanian tenor Joseph Schmidt, even though Schmidt was Jewish. He also collected records of the Italian tenor Beniamino Gigli, Wagner, and Beethoven, and the operetta composer Carl Zeller.[16]

Throughout his professional and political life, Röhm demonstrated a high level of organizational and bureaucratic skill, and was extremely hard working. His friend Bergmann described him as "the most gifted general staff officer, an extraordinarily talented organizer and a man of clear judgement and single-minded will."[17] The Nazi agricultural theorist Walther Darré testified to his ability to listen carefully, and then clearly identify and analyze problems. One SA leader described him as:

> open, upright but self-willed. Consequently from the beginning of his military career he was a difficult subordinate for his superiors. He was not inclined to think much of another's opinions and thoughts, if he considered they were lacking in ability and insight. He had an aversion to everything civilian, non-military, and was critical of the non-soldier . . . Röhm was comradely to his colleagues and subordinates. Therefore he always had a great influence on those he led.[18]

Another recalled "Röhm was one hundred per cent a comrade. He had the right tone that one expected from a decent commander."[19] The Frontbann experience showed, however, that he was unskilled in political maneuvering. In politics, he was a follower, even if, at times, an insubordinate one, rather than a leader.

Friendship and loyalty to his male friends was extremely important to him. He maintained many of his friendships—with Bergmann, Seydel, von Epp, Heines, and Du Moulin-Eckart—for his entire adult life. His friends remained loyal to him even when they were accused of homosexuality as a result.[20]

It was also important for Röhm to see himself as generous and broadminded, willing to see the good in the other side. On a number of occasions in his autobiography, he made a point of stressing his excellent relations with people whom he might not be expected to get on with, such as the SPD deputy Franz Schmitt, or his ability to see the point of view and concede the strengths of his ideological enemies, such as Communist Reichstag deputies. His political opponents could confirm that he could listen to and accept criticism. His former lawyer reportedly observed in 1935 that Röhm "had a soldierly toughness, like the mercenaries of old who wished to live and let live; he also possessed that remarkable form of tolerance that, while allowing respect for an adversary, does so simply to fight him all the more stubbornly."[21] Röhm's critics accused him of an inability to keep his mouth shut when discretion was advisable. "Röhm was as indiscreet in his talk as he was uninhibited in his pervert libertinism."[22]

In his autobiography, as its title indicated, Röhm presented himself as a traitor to the Weimar Republic. He prided himself on his conscious onesidedness and wrote of his inclination to disorder and unrest. He displayed a strong aversion to the words "prudent" and "mature." He described his temperament as "effervescent."[23] He presented himself as always speaking frankly to friends and superiors. He made it clear that, rather than compromise on an issue that he felt strongly about, he would walk away, as he had done in 1919, 1923, and 1925.

Röhm has often been seen as a revolutionary, but he might more accurately be described as having the temperament of a rebel. All his life, there was a conscious tension between his praise for, and his felt need for, discipline and his actual indiscipline. He appears to have needed order and discipline to rebel against them and test their limits. He would, at times, engage in childish provocations and rebellions, but back away from firm opposition. His relations with his superiors were most successful when they recognized this, gave him scope for his initiative, and forgave his transgressions. This appears to have been the key to his long friendship with Epp. He would rebel rather than overthrow the authority that he temporarily disobeyed or disregarded. He still needed that authority to be there.[24]

Röhm's approach to all his loyalties was always protestant or non-conformist. That is, his actions were determined by his individual conscience. It was allegiance in his way. His monarchism was genuine, yet *he* decided when he would obey the Crown Prince and when he would not. Crown Prince Rupprecht's official biographer, writing while the Crown Prince was still alive and with his approval, commented, "Röhm showed in his attachment to the monarchy—even still after 1933—more character than many others."[25] Far more than Epp after 1933, Röhm was "courageous enough"[26] to intervene to protect Crown Prince Rupprecht.

Röhm claimed in his autobiography that he saw no inconsistency between his loyalties to the Bavarian monarchy, and to Hitler and Ludendorff. He may have thought this was the case, but his actions belied it. By the time he wrote this passage, his loyalty to Hitler and National Socialism had triumphed over his loyalty to Ludendorff (whom he no longer followed after 1925) and to the Crown Prince.[27]

Röhm saw himself, and was seen by others, as a man of the world, aware of and tolerant of human weakness. He was a bon vivant, liking his food and drink. After June 30, 1934, he was criticized for the lavishness of his entertaining. This led his family to claim that his lifestyle was modest and not luxurious.[28]

He provoked strong feelings. Some hated him because of his politics, found him ugly, or were viscerally repelled by his homosexuality. Others found that he was "an interesting, sympathetic conversational partner. One quickly got used . . . to the disfiguring scar on his face."[29]

For many people, what most differentiated Röhm from other Nazi leaders was his sexuality. His homosexuality divided opinions about him within the Nazi movement itself. The attitude of some leaders, notably Hitler, mirrored Röhm's own man-of-the-world attitude, though sometimes this "tolerance" was patronizing and self-conscious. Some accepted his sexuality without really understanding it, while others were strongly and lastingly hostile to him for this reason.[30]

Röhm wrote that he first really recognized his homosexuality in 1924 after a series of same-sex feelings and experiences since his youth.[31] It is not clear whether this happened in prison, or after he left the Reichswehr. Did leaving the Reichswehr remove a certain pressure to live conventionally from him? Did his time in Berlin as a Reichstag deputy and political leader give him the opportunity to explore Berlin's more open homosexual subculture? We do not know.

In January 1925, while he was still Frontbann leader, Röhm's suitcase was stolen by a seventeen-year-old youth he met in the Marien-Kasino, a homosexual bar in Berlin. The young man whom Röhm had invited back to his hotel room in Berlin stole a luggage check and then his suitcase, presuming that because of the circumstances of the theft Röhm would not take action. Röhm did not yield to this implicit blackmail and reported the theft to the police. When the thief was apprehended, he revealed that Röhm had requested a form of sexual relations of him that he would not agree to. The thief was prosecuted successfully. Knowledge of this case did not stop Hitler from continuing to offer Röhm the leadership of the SA.[32]

Under Section 175 of the German criminal code in the Weimar Republic, sexual relations between men that were similar to intercourse—oral and anal sex—were punishable under law. Mutual masturbation was not. Consequently, provided both partners denied having committed punishable acts, successful prosecution was difficult. In public discussion, homosexual orientation, identity, and acts—whether illegal or not—were usually conflated. German society was hostile to homosexuality, yet by the 1920s, the country had the largest homosexual rights movement in the world and the most open homosexual life in Berlin. Röhm's financial difficulties did not stop him from exploring this life in a city he described as unique in this respect. "The bath house there is however still in my view the peak of all human happiness. At any rate the type and manner of intercourse there pleased me exceptionally." [33]

Röhm's family did not appear to have accepted or understood his sexuality. As a result, his life was partly compartmentalized between his family, his personal and political friends and colleagues, and his homosexual or bisexual friends. These compartments were not watertight. Some men moved between them or shared them all, such as Gerhard von Prosch, and Karl Zehnter—or knew of and accepted them all—such as Seydel and Du Moulin-Eckart. Röhm did not conceal his sexual inclinations from his friends or from more casual contacts. The British journalist Sefton Delmer recalled how, in 1931, Röhm took him out for an evening in Berlin's night spots, including the homosexual night club, the Eldorado. At the Eldorado, a transvestite hostess sat down at their table and began to talk to Röhm about a party they had been to together. When Delmer commented on the indiscreetness of such an approach to an ex-client in front of a stranger, "Röhm, who normally was open and unashamed about his pickups and enjoyed joking about his 'weakness' was suddenly huffy. 'I am not his client. I am his commanding officer,' he said with complete seriousness. 'He is one of my stormtroopers!'" [34]

There is no evidence whether Röhm ever sought or found long-term emotional, as well as physical, relationships with men. After 1931, he compartmentalized his life further, finding and paying his sexual partners through an intermediary and therefore keeping them at a distance.[35]

As a homosexual, Röhm knew the hypocrisies of German society from personal experience. This knowledge is behind his recurrent use of the metaphor of tearing down and removing masks and veils.[36] He no doubt felt that his family and German society forced him to mask his real inclinations.

Röhm drew political conclusions about his sexuality. By 1929, he was a member of the League for Human Rights, the largest of the three German homosexual rights organizations that campaigned for repeal of Section 175. In his autobiography, Röhm criticized the hypocrisy and prudishness of German society and the willingness of völkisch circles to share these false values. He condemned state efforts to regulate innate human drives by law. "The struggle against the cant, deceit and hypocrisy of today's society must take its starting point from the innate nature of the drives that are placed in men from the cradle. . . . If the struggle in this area is successful, then the masks can be torn from the dissimilation in all areas of the human social and legal order."[37] This was a barely coded plea for the repeal of Section 175.

It was recognized, as such, by the völkisch nationalist, psychologist, and homosexual rights campaigner, Dr. Karl Günter Heimsoth, who was the first doctor to argue that homosexuality was a non-pathological condition in his doctoral dissertation, *Hetero- und Homophilie*, in 1925. He was active on the radical right and a frequent contributor to *Der Eigene*, the journal of another homosexual rights' organization, the Society of the Individual. After the publication of Röhm's autobiography, Heimsoth wrote to Röhm concerning its sections on hypocrisy. Röhm responded that Heimsoth had understood the purpose of these passages correctly, as being directed against Section 175. He had a more detailed statement in the first draft, but altered it on the advice of his friends, probably Seydel. Röhm indicated to Heimsoth that he made no secret of his position.[38]

Röhm's laissez faire attitude to issues of sexuality and reproduction ran counter to the main emphasis of völkisch and Nazi thought on this issue. The homosexual rights movement's literature may have also influenced his hostility to what he saw as women's excessive role in modern German society. Here, he reflected views expressed by many contributors to *Der Eigene*, who wanted women's social roles to be restricted to the family, reproduction, and meeting daily material needs.[39]

In his speeches and occasional writings, Röhm displayed conventional völkisch anti-Semitism. When he developed his political views at length in *Die Geschichte eines Hochverräters*, he gave anti-Semitism less emphasis than Hitler had in *Mein Kampf*. Röhm's anti-Semitism was conventional rather than obsessive. "Röhm placed little importance on racial questions."[40] Jews were innately handlers and dealers, Röhm argued, therefore, they had come to the top in a postwar society that embraced these values and rejected manly strength and military values. That dominance would be removed when German values—which he associated with martial ideals—were restored. Röhm's emphasis on the "rough war hero" as the leader at a time of national greatness also drew on ideas developed by male homosexual rights activists in the 1920s.

In spring 1934, when Hans-Joachim Schoeps asked him whether he had anything against the Jews, Schoeps recalled that Röhm answered, "'The question is idiotic. I have neither something against the Jews nor something for the Jews; they are a matter of complete indifference to me.'"[41] He continued that he could imagine the national revolution without anti-Semitism, but warned Schoeps that Hitler was not approachable on the issue.

Röhm combined nostalgia for the pre-1914 world with his National Socialism. Rather than being a social revolutionary, he was a supporter of hierarchy and social status. His monarchism was genuine, and recognized as such by Crown Prince Rupprecht. He cultivated his social contacts with members of the nobility. He wrote of his experiences in the factory in 1926 that the Nazi movement had to improve the hard conditions of the German industrial worker. Yet, it had also to be made clear to the worker that his poor living conditions were due to the peace settlement and the Dawes Plan, and not his employer's choice. Strikes and class hatred would not improve the workers' living conditions; only getting rid of the yoke of the enemy powers would achieve that. He claimed in his autobiography that officers in the prewar army were heralds of social justice.[42]

Röhm was not an original political thinker. He adopted ready-made ideas rather than developing them further. He never really explored the implications of the concepts he relied on, like the political soldier, which he seemed to model on Ludendorff's role in World War I.[43] He did not have the clear sense of his opponents' political or psychological weaknesses that Hitler often demonstrated.

Röhm's autobiography was published in 1928. Writing it may have been part of restarting his political career, as it raised his profile again on the radical right. He may also have hoped to make money from its publication; his letters from Bolivia revealed a continuing interest in its sales.[44]

That year, he also played the main part in persuading Epp to stand as a National Socialist candidate for the Reichstag in the elections of May 20, 1928. Epp's candidacy was a significant propaganda victory for the party and contributed to a rise in the party vote in Bavaria. Epp topped the poll in the Upper Bavarian-Swabian electoral district. While the overall national vote for the National Socialist and Völkisch Bloc candidates fell from 3 percent to 2.6 percent, in Bavaria the vote rose from 5.1 percent to 6.4 percent.[45]

Röhm was involved as a go-between in Nazi negotiations with the Crown Prince. It may have been at this time when Röhm undertook a passionate attempt to win the Crown Prince's support for National Socialism, in which he fell to his knees before the Crown Prince in entreaty. "Such theatricality was of course the most certain method to be dismissed quickly and abruptly."[46] The witness to this, Graf von Soden, left different accounts of when this happened. In 1949, Soden claimed that it occurred in 1925–26, but stated that this was after Röhm's return from Bolivia; in his memoirs, he recalled the meeting as taking place in 1923; Sendtner suggested that the meeting took place in the mid-1920s. Soden speculated that this was an effort by Röhm to free himself of the "mental burden" caused by clashes between Hitler and the Crown Prince, because Röhm was "enslaved" to Hitler but had a "sincere veneration" for the Crown Prince.[47]

Röhm refounded Reichskriegsflagge in August 1928 with the aim of leading its members into the NSDAP. On July 25, 1928, the original section of Altreichsflagge München met in the Arzbergerkeller. Freiherr von Thüngen began the meeting by saying that Röhm, who could not attend, wanted everyone to gather around him. The former RKF should arise again under Röhm's leadership. On October 18, 1928, the reconstituted RKF held a reunion celebration in the Restaurant Bürgerbräu. Röhm announced that he was not proposing to reconstitute RKF as a paramilitary organization. Rather, he set up a new organization called the Flag Club, of which he was the first chairman. Its members would begin by meeting once a month for comradeship and discussions. After the meeting, Röhm and some twenty younger members marched to a NSDAP meeting in the Mathäserfestsaal. At the end of this meeting, Röhm gave a long speech in which he pointed out that the members of the former Reichskriegsflagge still belonged to the National Socialists in comradeship and brotherhood of arms. He wanted the National Socialist movement to be strong and consolidated. The police report concluded, "The actual purpose of Röhm's calling this evening of comradeship was undoubtedly solely that of bringing about this corporative transfer into the NSDAP."[48]

In early November, Röhm undertook a long journey throughout Austria visiting Nazi Party leaders there on Hitler's behalf. On November 9, he spoke at a public meeting in Vienna, and took part in Nazi ceremonies in Nuremberg and Altdorf that month.[49]

Röhm also attempted to use his contacts to act as a link between the NSDAP and the Reichswehr on military issues. In a leaflet dated November 28, 1928, Röhm announced that the Defense Policy Organization (*Wehrpolitische Vereinigung* or WPV) had been formed on July 25, 1928. (This was the date of the meeting of Altreichsflagge München.) It was based on the former RKF, it would meet monthly, and members would pay a monthly contribution. "Jews and Freemasons of any description cannot belong to the organization."[50] It would feature talks by military professionals and discussion evenings, "with particular emphasis on the political aspects of preparation for, and leadership in, war."[51]

The first formal meeting of the WPV was held in the Wittelsbachergarten on December 12,1928. Konstantin Hierl addressed the meeting on the war of the future, including the important role to be played by motorized forces. Some fifty-five men attended, including Hitler, Hess, Himmler, former Reichskriegsflagge members, and current and former officers. Röhm, who was the WPV's leader until further notice, was not present. The police report noted that he had departed a few weeks previously. The police believed erroneously that he had left for Argentina for a long stay of some four months.[52]

Röhm's attempts to make a life in Germany for himself outside politics had been fruitless. By early 1928, he had resumed his political activities for the Nazi Party. In 1926, he had unsuccessfully attempted to go to Bolivia as a means of returning to military life. This application was revived unexpectedly by the Bolivian Government in 1928. This took him away from the NSDAP and back to the military career he had abandoned in 1923. In December 1928, Ernst Röhm left Europe for the first time in his life to travel to Latin America to take up a position as a military officer in the Bolivian Army.

CHAPTER 10

Lieutenant Colonel in Bolivia
1928–30

I want to be a soldier. . . . I believe that I can widen my military skills best in a foreign army.[1]

Ernst Röhm

In December 1928, Ernst Röhm left for Bolivia to serve in the Bolivian army as a military instructor for two years. He was away from Germany at the time that the Nazi Party began to record its breakthrough electoral successes, despite repeated efforts by Adolf Hitler and the party to secure his return. By working in Bolivia, he had resumed his military career, but in a different culture, to which he adapted effectively.

By mid-1928, Röhm had been engaged to work in Bolivia by Major Wilhelm (Guillermo) Kaiser, a former German officer who was temporarily Bolivian Military Attaché in the Netherlands and who had been entrusted with "various missions"[2] in Europe by the Ministry of War. The offer of an actual position came so quickly that Röhm claimed he had only forty-eight hours notice to embark in Hamburg. Bolivian authorities agreed to count Röhm's service as beginning on December 5, 1928. Around this date in Berlin, Röhm finalized the administrative engagements for his departure. He left Du Moulin-Eckart in charge of representing his interests with the Bolivian embassy in Berlin, caring for his mother, and maintaining contacts for him.

Röhm had decided to take a companion with him to Bolivia so as not to be too lonely. A nineteen-year-old student at the Academy of Fine Arts in Munich, Martin Schätzl, accompanied him at Röhm's expense. The men met in Straubing in 1928. Their friendship may have arisen through shared political views. Describing Schätzl as his companion, Röhm indicated frankly to Heimsoth that Schätzl was not a potential sexual partner for him. This was not only because Schätzl was heterosexual, but also because Röhm felt no desire for him, though he considered Schätzl good-looking. Schätzl referred to Röhm as "Uncle Röhm."[3]

On December 14, 1928, Röhm and Schätzl transferred to the Hotel Atlantik in Hamburg until their ship, the Hamburg-Südamerikanische Dampffahrtsgesellschaft's *Cap Polonio*, sailed at 4:00 p.m. Röhm traveled first class for 1,800 marks, while Schätzl traveled second class for 520 marks. The Chief of the Bolivian General Staff, General Hans Kundt, whom Röhm had met in Berlin before his departure, traveled with them from Germany. After stops in Boulogne, Lisbon, Rio de Janeiro, and Montevideo, the *Cap Polonio* reached Buenos Aires on December 31. Röhm, Kundt, and Schätzl left Buenos Aires on January 1, 1929 on a five day train trip to La Paz. They crossed the Bolivian border on January 3, and arrived in La Paz on the afternoon of January 5.[4]

In 1929, Bolivia had an area three times as great as that of the Weimar Republic, with a population of slightly over 3.2 million. Ninety percent of its predominantly Indian population lived in the west of the country on the Altiplano, a high interior basin surrounded by the Andes. In the 1920s, some five percent of the population was European, a ruling elite descended from the Spanish conquerors. They and the mixed-race Cholos dominated politics in the 1920s. Germans were the largest group of more recent European immigrants to Bolivia.[5]

Most of Bolivia's population worked in subsistence agriculture. The country's main export was tin, of which, in 1920, Bolivia produced 23 percent of the world's output. This dependence on international raw materials markets meant Bolivia was hit hard by a steep decline in the world price for tin beginning in 1929.[6]

As a result, the state budget had structural weaknesses. Recurrent financial crises meant the government resorted to heavy borrowing from foreign lenders. Thirty-seven percent of the budget in 1929 went to servicing foreign debt, 20 percent to the military, and the remaining 43 percent had to cover all other government responsibilities.[7]

Under the constitution in force from 1877 to 1938, Bolivia was a unitary republic with two houses of parliament elected by direct male suffrage. Literacy tests meant that only a small minority—seventy thousand voters in the 1926 elections—of the population voted. The army's political profile was low. It intervened in politics in 1899, 1920, and 1930, only to uphold the constitution and manage the transfer of power from one civilian government to another. Officers generally accepted the ethos of military professionalism.[8]

In 1929, the Bolivian Army had some five hundred officers and twenty thousand men on active duty, divided into six divisions, with thirteen infantry regiments, three cavalry regiments, three field artillery regiments, three sapper battalions, and one aviation squadron. While, in theory, all Bolivian men aged between nineteen and forty-nine were liable for military service, in practice, only a small number of men were called to the ranks annually. De facto the army was racially divided with predominantly European officers and mainly Indian recruits.[9]

Bolivia's relations with Paraguay worsened in 1928. Both Bolivia and Paraguay were expanding their military forts in the Gran Chaco, where the border between the two countries was not clearly defined. On December 8, 1928, Paraguayan forces attacked the Bolivian Fortín Vanguardia in the Chaco. A temporary government of national unity was formed in Bolivia and Bolivian President Hernando Siles ordered the retaking of Fortín Vanguardia in the Chaco and the capture of the Paraguayan Fortín Boquerón. After this had occurred, Siles accepted U.S. mediation. In September 1929, both countries accepted an act of conciliation and Bolivia returned Fortín Boquerón to Paraguay.[10]

The tensions with Paraguay appear to have renewed Bolivian interest in hiring German military advisers for the Bolivian army. Before World War I, an official German military mission was sent to Bolivia in 1911. The mission concentrated on purely military tasks, especially training, and its members returned to Germany on the outbreak of war.[11]

Article 179 of the Treaty of Versailles prohibited the dispatch of German military missions overseas and required Germany to ensure that its citizens did not leave Germany to serve in foreign armed services or train them. As the German armed forces were reduced in size, this provision was evaded by many former officers. Bolivia had ratified the Treaty of Versailles by the end of 1920, and was a founding member of the League of Nations. By mid-1920, however, Bolivia had resumed the employment of Hans Kundt, the head of the prewar mission. Kundt renounced his German citizenship, assumed Bolivian citizenship, and returned to Bolivia by June 1920. Initially, he was employed in a civilian position and gave military advice surreptitiously. Bolivia rejected French protests at his employment. France objected alone, as both the British and U.S. governments saw Kundt's return as an assurance of discipline and efficiency, while, by the end of the 1920s, British diplomats regarded Kundt as more Bolivian than German in his reactions and loyalties.[12]

Both the Bolivian government and Kundt himself tried to increase the numbers of German officers working in Bolivia in the 1920s. In addition

to the return of some other members of the prewar mission, and some isolated hiring of individuals, in 1926, a "Danzig Mission" of nineteen officers
and NCOs was recruited. The German officers hired transferred into the
Danzig police to avoid international protests. Three members of the mission
became involved in an espionage scandal when they offered to spy for Paraguay because they were unpaid. The Danzig mission was unsuccessful and, by
September 1929, only seven men from it remained in Bolivia.[13]

On February 9, 1921, President Saavedra appointed Kundt as Chief of
the Bolivian General Staff. This placed him on the same level as the Minister
of War. Kundt answered only to the President. Kundt's role in Bolivia in the
1920s was politicized in a way that his prewar employment had never been.
Successive presidents used him to protect themselves against opposition, and
he operated a system of espionage within the army. Kundt's position aroused
hostility. Members of the officer corps resented his generous pay and his
political influence, and still saw him as a foreigner. Kundt was also unpopular
with his fellow German officers. In 1926, President Siles sent Kundt overseas to avoid further tension, but recalled him from Europe in 1928 because
of the border clashes with Paraguay. The partial mobilization of the Bolivian army had been disorganized and Kundt's replacement, José C. Quirós,
was blamed.[14]

Röhm's hiring probably was also prompted by the tensions with Paraguay.
His final contract was signed in La Paz in 1929. He entered the Bolivian
Army with the rank of Lieutenant Colonel, and a monthly salary of 1,000
Bolivianos in his first year of service, rising to 1,100 Bolivianos in the second year. The value of the Boliviano was set at one-and-a-half gold marks.
This was double the salary of a Bolivian lieutenant colonel, but one-third
of Kundt's monthly salary. Röhm's contract ran from January 1, 1929, to
December 31, 1930. Röhm was paid three thousand Bolivianos to cover the
cost of his trip to La Paz, and seven hundred Bolivianos for his uniform and
equipment. At the end of the contract, he would be paid a bonus of two
thousand Bolivianos. If he renewed the contract, his starting pay would be
three thousand Bolivianos a month.[15]

Röhm gave a variety of reasons for his decision to accept the contract. In
keeping with his self-image as a warrior, Röhm suggested in the fifth edition
of his autobiography that he had hoped to see action in the Gran Chaco
fighting. He added ironically: "Since I am an immature and wicked man, war
and unrest agree with me better than the good bourgeois order."[16] To Crown
Prince Rupprecht, Röhm stated that it was not possible for him to be a soldier
in the German army at that time. Financial motives also contributed—he was
grateful to have employment.

Röhm's political reputation preceded him. While the German ambassador in Bolivia, Hans Gerald Marckwald, had supported the Danzig mission, his experience with it and the Bolivian hostility to Kundt led him to change his mind. In July 1928, he told the German Foreign Ministry (Auswärtiges Amt or AA) that it was not advisable that further German officers should be hired. Noting that he had heard that Kaiser had engaged Röhm, Marckwald remarked: "Is this gentleman really the right German military representative for here?"[17]

Röhm's notoriety may indirectly have made him more valuable to Bolivia. He was aware that the Chilean and Argentinean military attachés saw him as a danger to their countries. He and Marckwald also knew of the French Ambassador's opposition to Röhm's employment. The French Ambassador, Mr André le Mallier, bombarded the Bolivian government with formal and informal protests about Röhm's employment. Eventually, on May 2, 1929, the Bolivian government responded with a bland factual note, stating that Röhm was employed as a professor at the military college and ignoring the wider issues le Mallier had raised on the Treaty of Versailles and Röhm's political role in Germany. Le Mallier could only express the French government's regret at Röhm's employment, but, as the British ambassador noted in a different context, the Bolivian government had little respect for the Treaty of Versailles, and such protests were useless.[18]

Röhm's period as a professor in the military college appeared designed to give him time to learn Spanish. He mastered Spanish quickly, aided by his earlier command of French and Latin. Since the Bolivian army had been modeled along German lines, he found it easy to adjust, and, by June, he was capable of exercising an independent command.[19]

Initially, Röhm and Schätzl lived in the home of a socially prominent Bolivian, José Manuel del Carpio. La Paz, the de facto administrative center of Bolivia, was then a city of almost 150,000, at an altitude of 3600 meters. Röhm was quite homesick and he and Schätzl were dependent on each other's company. To start with, he found no homosexual life or potential sexual partners in La Paz. By August 1929, however, "after great efforts I have actually brought about some change, and with modest demands one can live."[20]

Röhm maintained his political friendships and ties with Germany. Writing to Crown Prince Rupprecht, he continued his efforts to win the Crown Prince for the National Socialist cause. On February 1, 1929, he wrote to "my dear Adolf Hitler,"[21] thanking him for the offer Hitler had conveyed to him before he left, presumably a further offer to lead the SA. Röhm assured Hitler that the two men remained linked but that financial necessity meant he had

had to reject the offer at the moment. Du Moulin-Eckart had advised him that Hitler wanted him to return quickly and then work with him.

By late April 1929, Röhm was accompanying Kundt on an inspection of recruits, his first official trip outside La Paz. From June to September 1929, he was an inspector of troops himself. He asked for his first command in Sucre, the official capital, to help Schätzl, whom he believed would have more opportunity to sell his pictures there. Röhm spent from June 18 to July 25 in Sucre before returning to La Paz, and traveling from there to Uyuni in the southwest for a month to inspect another regiment. At the beginning of September, he returned to La Paz.[22]

Röhm was then appointed Chief of Staff at the divisional command of the First Division in Oruro under General Carlos de Gumucio. He left for Oruro on September 15, and soon found himself an apartment. His Spanish was now proficient, as can be seen from the surviving reports he wrote. With General de Gumucio, he inspected the garrisons at Challapata, Uyuni, and Potosí from September 30 to October 7, 1929, to check their preparedness for the large October war games, in which he participated on October 22 as chief of command of the Blue Division, which won.[23]

In December 1929, Röhm went on holiday to Chile, spending four days in Santiago and returning via Valparaiso and Antofagasta. In Chile, too, his past meant that he attracted more attention than his rank would suggest. The local newspaper in Antofagasta, *El Mercurio*, interviewed him. Diplomatically, Röhm praised both the Chilean and Bolivian armies.[24]

Röhm made friends easily, both in the German community and with his fellow Bolivian officers. For the first and only time since 1919, contemporaries judged him uninfluenced by his political role. General Oscar Moscoso recalled: "He was a cultivated and agreeable man, who was fond of music. He played old ballads and German lieder on the piano. As an officer he impressed me with his efficiency . . . We never suspected whom we had amongst us."[25] Colonel Luis E. Saavedra commented: "He was an exceedingly intelligent officer, to the point that he aroused the jealousy of his superior, General Kundt, who sent him to Oruro to remove him from the General Staff. He was undoubtedly more capable than Kundt and that was the origin of their rivalry."[26]

Surprisingly, Röhm did not appear to realize that Kundt was jealous of him. To begin with, he believed he was getting on well with Kundt, but by April 1930, he recognized that his relations with him were not as good as he would like. He confided to the Crown Prince that Kundt saw him as a Bavarian, and therefore as second-class, and added that Kundt resented Röhm's many supporters.[27]

Röhm remained at the divisional command in Oruro until August 1930. In January 1930, he trained recruits; in May, he led the division while the commanding general was away; and, in June, he participated in the garrison's war games. Röhm and Schätzl shared an apartment in Oruro, employing a female servant. In January 1930, Röhm was elected second president of the German club there, and he attended its meetings until early July. He claimed that, as a result of support from younger members of the German community, a purely Nationalist board was elected, which did not please those club members of Jewish origin.[28]

Röhm maintained his continuing interest in German politics. He wrote to Crown Prince Rupprecht, telling him he hoped for a German resurrection because he believed that Germany had reached its lowest point. He wrote to the Crown Prince that his ideal was a free fatherland under the strong and responsible leadership of the hereditary princes. "A decent Germany must once again have a monarch at its head."[29]

This letter leaves no doubt of the authenticity of Röhm's monarchism and of his emotional tie to the Crown Prince. How did he reconcile this with his Nazism? He appeared to do so by denying the existence of any such conflict. The very genuineness of his royalism may have been useful to the NSDAP. Because his monarchism came from the heart, he could be a persuasive intermediary.

Röhm indicated to the Crown Prince that his concern for developments in Germany was such that he did not intend to remain in Bolivia after his contract expired. He was coming under pressure in Bolivia to stay on since he had made his intention of returning home known. He was not prepared, however, to break his contract. In July, he wired his refusal of an offer from the NSDAP for him to return to stand in the September 1930 Reichstag elections.[30]

Röhm advised the Crown Prince that the Bolivian president wanted to stay in office and that there might be political unrest in the coming weeks. "Naturally I personally also refrain from any political comment here."[31] Ultimately, he did not care who ruled Bolivia. "Yet General Kundt is considerably affected by it, for he stands and falls with the current President."[32] Röhm's private and public comments and views on Bolivian affairs give no support to the interpretation that he planned the June 1930 coup against Siles' government for General Carlos Blanco Galindo.

Siles' term was due to end in August 1930. Kundt began by opposing any unconstitutional extension of Siles' term. Within months, Kundt's position had changed. On May 28, 1930, Siles turned over power to a Council of Ministers, controlled by Kundt and Colonel David Toro. The Council of

Ministers called for elections for a Constituent Assembly to amend the constitution and to allow Siles to serve another term. There was much opposition to Siles' moves in the officer corps. Student demonstrations against Siles began on June 12; on June 22, a student was killed in La Paz when soldiers fired on demonstrators. Protests spread. On June 24, the garrison at Oruro proclaimed itself in revolt, followed by coordinated uprisings in other cities. The next day in La Paz, cadets from the Colegio Militar rose against the government. After three days of bitter fighting in the city, the Council of Ministers resigned. A military junta led by General Carlos Blanco Galindo was formed on June 28. On June 27, Siles took refuge in the Brazilian Embassy, Toro and some other members of the Council of Ministers in the Chilean Embassy, and Kundt and his family in the German Embassy.[33]

Public anger focused on Kundt, who was blamed for the order that soldiers should fire on the cadets. Threatening crowds gathered around the three legations sheltering members of the former government, and strong anti-German feeling was expressed. German businessmen felt compelled to publish a statement of loyalty to Bolivia in the press to appease the population. Kundt was not able to leave the country until July 28.[34]

The June 1930 coup was a further intervention by the Bolivian Army to prevent the constitution being subverted. The junta's decree of June 29 established mechanisms for a return to civilian rule in six months. After eight months, civilian government resumed, and Daniel Salamanca became the next elected president in February 1931.[35]

The new military government publicized the details of Bolivia's poor budgetary position, and allowed the press to draw attention to the generous salaries of the German officers. The budgetary crisis was genuine. By July 23, 1930, Marckwald considered that the official influence of Germans in the government had collapsed. He expected that all Germans employed in the civil service would be dismissed immediately, though it was not yet clear whether this would apply to the officers. He noted that "Röhm is said to strive to succeed Kundt."[36]

Röhm's claim that he was so trusted by the officers of the Oruro garrison that they offered to put him at the head of the uprising seems unlikely in view of the fact that he was a foreigner. He was, however, friends with one of the leading figures in the new government, Colonel Filiberto Osorio. Shortly after the coup on July 3, he was recalled to La Paz to take up a position on the General Staff since Kundt no longer blocked his employment. In August, he was appointed technical advisor in the General Staff because of his "diligence and work ethic. . . . [He had] distinguished himself by his discipline and technical knowledge."[37]

On his return to La Paz, Röhm shared a house in the centre of La Paz, on the intersection of Camacho and Loayza Streets, with Schätzl and the German civilian engineer Bagger. Röhm and Bagger gave musical evenings. The two men debated the merits of their favorite composers on these evenings and "on these occasions Röhm's joy in strong argument confirmed the instinctive authority and faculties of his character."[38]

By August 1930, Röhm seemed to be wavering in his decision to leave Bolivia at the end of his contract. He told the Crown Prince that he now had more scope for his efforts, as he was first advisor in the General Staff. He claimed that if he stayed on he would be able to maintain the German influence, while accepting that the Chief of the General Staff had to be a Bolivian. Röhm wrote to Heinrich Himmler that he was planning to be in Germany on leave at the beginning of 1931. "Perhaps by then it will have occurred to Hitler, what he can use me for."[39] If not, he would return to Bolivia. His telegram in September 1930 to Adolf Hühnlein—"Returning November notify mother and Hitler Roehm"[40]—did not indicate whether he planned to return permanently or not.

By October, Röhm had pitched his demands too high. In mid-October, Marckwald reported that, apart from Röhm, Lt. Col. Scherlau and Major Birnbacher, all other German officers had been urged to end their contracts on financial grounds. The Bolivian authorities

> dearly wanted to keep Lieutenant Colonel Röhm himself here in order to have at least one man in the General Staff who understands the work and also gets it done. Röhm however was only willing to stay if he was given the position of deputy *(stellvertretende)* Chief of the General Staff. Since in the current conditions that was not possible he then preferred to follow the call of his National Socialist friends at home.[41]

Did Röhm deliberately raise his demands too high, to be forced to return to Germany?

Röhm wrote that three things had attracted him to Bolivia—a desire to get to know the world, to view Germany from the outside, and to be a soldier again. He claimed never to have regretted his decision. Perhaps as a result, the U.S. foreign correspondent Louis P. Lochner considered that Röhm's views on Germany's external relations were more realistic than those of others in the party leadership. Röhm's political opinions were also strengthened by his experiences in Latin America, as the Germans he met overseas were either still loyal to Imperial Germany or supported the völkisch movement.[42]

Röhm maintained his links to Bolivia through the Bolivian Embassy in Berlin. He noted in the revised edition of his autobiography published in

1933, that he remained an active officer of the Bolivian Army on extended leave in Germany. Even his insignia as Chief of Staff of the SA was adapted from his insignia in the Bolivian army. Röhm kept his Bolivian options open. In 1931 and 1932, he punctiliously advised the Bolivian Embassy that he could not return to Bolivia. In February 1932, there appears to have been an abortive attempt to recall him by the then Chief of the Bolivian General Staff. This may have implicitly given him a continuing alternative to his life in Germany—a "Bolivian option." When Röhm came under political attack in Germany from 1931 to 1933, he and Nazi publicists were prone to exaggerate the role he played in Bolivia. Even though he had warned the Chief of the General Staff against war with Paraguay in a memorandum before he left Bolivia, Röhm made known his personal support for Bolivia's cause in the Chaco War that began in July 1932, despite Germany's official neutrality on the conflict.[43]

Röhm's intellectual superiority to Kundt and Kundt's career in Bolivia may also have strengthened Röhm's hopes that he could play a leading role in the German Army after a Nazi seizure of power and combine his military and political ambitions. While the Bolivian junta was concerned to ensure a quick transfer to civilian rule, Röhm expressed the hope that they would stay in power longer. Marckwald reported to the Auswärtiges Amt:

> When I said to him jokingly on parting—he is personally a very pleasant and sociable man—that he should however keep his hands away from politics at home, then he answered me quite seriously, "Officers are the best politicians!" I could only reply to this, "Yes, 1,000 years ago!" [44]

Röhm and Schätzl left Bolivia in mid-October 1930. Before they left, Schätzl held a large exhibition of landscapes, portraits, and architectural studies in the rooms of the Club Bancario in La Paz from September 27 until at least October 3. By October 14, they were aboard the Hamburg-Amerika line's *Sachsen*. They returned via Peru, passing through the Panama Canal on October 15, and arrived in Munich on November 6, 1930. Hitler, other party colleagues, and friends greeted Röhm at the station. According to the *Völkischer Beobachter*, Röhm was "still the old, indestructible front soldier."[45] Röhm's almost two years in Bolivia had been successful on balance, but they had come to an end. He returned to take up a leading role in the SA as Adolf Hitler intended.

CHAPTER 11

Chief of Staff of the SA
1931–33

If you have followed my path through life, then you know what difficult times, persecutions and slanders I have been through. [1]

Ernst Röhm

A dolf Hitler recalled Ernst Röhm from Bolivia at the end of 1930 to entrust him with a leading position in the SA. The next two years would be a period of great instability in German politics and intense struggle on Germany's streets. Under Röhm's command, the SA would make a significant contribution to the growing Nazi electoral strength, but Röhm's success came at considerable personal cost, as he was under constant political attack both within and outside Nazism.

On Röhm's return in early November 1930, his immediate role in Nazism was unclear. He was "tumultuously greeted"[2] on November 10, when he attended a meeting of the Wehrpolitische Vereinigung, and, on November 22, he spoke at the Nuremberg Kolosseum with Hermann Esser. On November 30, Hitler called a SA leaders' conference in the Allianzkonzern office in Barerstrasse in Munich. Fifty senior leaders, as well as Röhm, attended. When it became clear that North German SA leaders objected to his appointment, Röhm left the meeting in order not to influence its deliberations. Hitler strongly advocated Röhm's reemployment, and prevailed. He reserved for his own decision how Röhm would be utilized. On January 5, 1931, Hitler announced Röhm's appointment as Chief of Staff of the SA, reporting to Hitler as Supreme SA Leader.

Conditions in Germany were markedly different from when Röhm had left in December 1928. The country was in the middle of the Great Depression, the effects of which were being worsened by the deflationary policies of Chancellor Heinrich Brüning. Brüning's cabinet was the first presidential cabinet, relying on the president's emergency powers under Article 48 rather than a Reichstag majority to pass its laws. President von Hindenburg and his advisors had already begun to undermine representative government.[3]

The NSDAP started to win electoral support as a result of the agricultural crisis that was the first sign of the Depression. From 1928 on, it began to pick up votes in Protestant rural areas. The party responded by altering its political approach from the "urban plan" of seeking to win German workers away from the SPD and KPD to one of rural nationalism. The crucial breakthrough came in the September 1930 elections when the NSDAP received 18.3 percent of the vote and became the second largest party in the Reichstag.[4]

The NSDAP embarked on a series of propaganda campaigns aimed at saturating districts judged ripe for the Nazi message. This increased tensions between the party and the SA, whose members provided the bulk of the labor force for such campaigns. Until November 1923, and under Röhm's leadership in 1924–25, the SA was designed to assist in a forceful takeover of power. In February 1925, when Hitler issued fundamental guidelines for the party, he gave the SA an ideological rather than a paramilitary role. It should be the NSDAP's instrument in the ideological and political struggle. Nonetheless, the Oberster SA-Führer from November 1926 on, Franz von Pfeffer, continued to follow a military model in the order and structure of the SA. The SA leaders understood the SA to be soldiers, as distinct from the party's politicians, and wanted the SA to be largely independent of the party leadership. In private, Hitler may have assured the SA leadership a role leading the German army, at the same time as he made no public promises to this effect. Speaking to a course of SA officers in September 1931, however, Hitler saw the role of the SA in the Third Reich as a propaganda troop paid for and armed by the state.[5]

In the period 1926–28, when the party was following the "urban plan," the SA used force to carry the party's message into enemy strongholds. This tactic originated with the Berlin SA. In the cities, SA men were rough fighters. In the country, where violence was used less, they won support and impressed the population with their ordered discipline.[6]

By autumn 1930, the SA had some sixty thousand members. SA men were predominantly young, most under thirty years old, and many were unemployed. They were more likely to be working class than the party membership as a whole. Under Röhm as Chief of Staff, the SA grew in an unprecedented way. By the end of 1932, it had expanded to some 427,000 men, but there was a high membership turnover.[7]

The SA's constant activity and clashes with its opponents led to the development of a SA subculture and a "SA-spirit." The SA was characterized by marches and public appearances that were as military and disciplined as possible, and by violence and aggression directed at political enemies on the left and Jews. The SA's social world centered on SA *"Sturmlokale"*—rooms in hotels and bars allocated to local SA groups as regular customers—and from 1930 on, "SA homes" for unemployed or homeless SA men. These homes provided a standing troop of young men with free time for party activities. As the Depression progressed, most SA men were unemployed—the structures and activities of the SA exerted a powerful attraction for them. The SA man thought of himself as a member of a community welded together by a common fighting experience. SA training and activities were characterized by action rather than ideological education. Rough masculinity was the ideal. Edmund Heines, and arguably Ernst Röhm, symbolized this in their own careers and personalities.[8]

The SA's finances were a constant source of friction with the party organization. They helped provoke the first "Stennes crisis" of summer 1930. On August 1, Pfeffer put the Berlin SA leadership's demand for places on the party's electoral list for the Reichstag to Hitler. The salaries and benefits that Reichstag deputies received would be a great help. Hitler refused this request. Pfeffer, who was under considerable pressure for financial assistance from Walther Stennes, OSAF-Stellvertreter Ost, resigned on August 12. The Berlin SA then effectively went on strike. Hitler traveled to Berlin to resolve the crisis. He announced on September 1 that he would take over the position of OSAF and that the SA's financial condition would improve. Temporarily, Hitler had Otto Wagener act as SA Chief of Staff.[9] The Stennes crisis prompted Hitler to renew his offer to Röhm to lead the SA.

Hitler made this decision even though he was aware that Röhm could be outspoken, would not hesitate to express his disagreements with Hitler to his face, and could be indiscreet. Röhm had been away from Germany for two years and was therefore out of touch with developments inside the Nazi movement. From the Frontbann period of 1924–25, Hitler also knew that Röhm had a different concept of the role of a paramilitary organization than his own. Yet, between 1925 and 1930, Hitler repeatedly offered the position of leading the SA to Röhm, and he appointed him after a crisis in which it was clear that many in the SA would support Röhm's views.

Röhm's homosexuality, which Hitler already knew about, would give Röhm's opponents a ready point of attack. Röhm's appointment met with criticism both inside and outside the NSDAP. Within a month, Hitler had to issue a statement defending Röhm from internal attack because of his sexuality. He commented that the SA was "not a school to educate the daughters of the upper classes but a formation of rough fighters."[10] When this statement was leaked to the SPD newspaper *Vorwärts*, further attacks from the German left and right followed.

Yet, there was no doubt that Röhm had the organizational and administrative skills to handle the SA's expansion. He commanded respect because he was a Nazi of the first hour, because of his crucial services to Nazism between 1919 and 1925, and because of his wider links in the völkisch movement. His name and reputation would draw men from the other paramilitary organizations to the SA. The fact that he had not held a position of leadership in the party since 1925, and his two years away from Germany, meant that he had not been involved in any recent internal disputes. His man-of-the-world manner, his hostility to "respectability," and his sociability would help him relate to the average SA man. Röhm still had contacts in the Reichswehr that might be useful to the NSDAP. His long personal friendship with Hitler meant that, for Hitler, Röhm was a known quantity. Röhm's predecessor, Pfeffer, argued with the benefit of hindsight: "Röhm, whose gifts were restricted to the military and organizational, was moreover not equal to the game that was played out in the sophisticated areas of politics and probably had no inkling at all of the two-edged and dangerous task he took on."[11]

Röhm's homosexuality also offered Hitler benefits by making him more reliant on Hitler. Lüdecke and Pfeffer both considered that Hitler appointed Röhm SA Chief of Staff *because* of his homosexuality. Lüdecke claimed Hitler told him "'quite apart from Röhm's great achievements, I know I can absolutely depend on him.'"[12]

Hitler also ensured that Röhm's position was not as strong as Pfeffer's had been, by making Röhm Chief of Staff only while reserving the OSAF position for himself. The Chief of Staff's powers were also reduced. Röhm lost access to independent sources of finance for the SA because Party Treasurer Xavier Schwarz was given control of the SA's Quartermaster Service, which sold equipment to SA men, and of its Aid Fund, which provided insurance cover for SA men in the event of death or injury. SA discipline was transferred to the party's investigative and arbitration committee, the Uschla; Gauleiters were given the power to supervise Gau SA leaders' expense accounts; and the SS was increased in size at the expense of the SA. Tensions already existed between the mass organization of the SA and the smaller SS, which was developed as an elite force.[13]

As Chief of Staff, Röhm extended and elaborated on the military structuring of the SA under Pfeffer, and that he had foreshadowed in his organizational planning of the Frontbann. Röhm professionalized the SA's administration, especially at its higher levels, and intensified its bureaucratization and militarization. He centralized much power in the SA's Munich headquarters, the Oberste SA-Führung, and set up a Reichsführerschule for the SA. A flood of orders came from the SA's Munich headquarters, and service regulations regulating all aspects of SA life in detail were drawn up in 1931. He exerted greater control over the SA by setting up an Inspectorate-General to visit and report on regional and local SA units, and by himself making flying visits to SA units across Germany.[14]

Röhm brought men he knew from the Bavarian Army, Reichskriegsflagge, and the Frontbann into the senior ranks of the SA and SS. Röhm's staff was almost all men he had worked with in Munich before 1923. These appointments included his friends and former army comrades—Karl Schreyer, Josef Seydel, Franz Ritter von Hörauf, Hans-Georg Hofmann, Friedrich Ritter von Krausser, and Robert Bergmann. From Reichskriegsflagge and the Frontbann, he appointed Hans Peter von Heydebreck, Edmund Heines, Carl Léon Graf Du Moulin-Eckart, and Karl Ernst. Dornheim has argued that Röhm's personnel appointments "show his organizational talent and a crafty political cunning, combined with unhesitating ruthlessness, an inclination to pomp and excessive 'holding court' and an incapacity to seek allies outside his own following."[15]

These men were not—as is sometimes suggested—appointed by Röhm because they themselves were homosexual. They were, however, his personal friends, men he trusted, men who had shown themselves unperturbed by Röhm's sexuality, and would therefore be more loyal to him than his internal SA critics. Their appointment over the heads of long-serving SA leaders was resented, but Röhm rejected complaints. He emphasized that he considered the former military officers he appointed in particular to be more qualified for higher command. His appointments created a senior SA leadership that was socially distinct from the rank and file—older, better educated, from a higher social class, often former Reichswehr officers finding a substitute for a disrupted military career. This made senior SA leaders less likely to side with their men against the leadership.[16]

The message from the top of the SA to its rank and file was one of obedience to Hitler. At the time of the second Stennes' revolt in April 1931, Röhm strongly supported the party leadership. Röhm held unsuccessful negotiations with Stennes in Berlin in late March. Stennes rejected Hitler's order that the party obey a government decree to seek twenty-four hours permission for political rallies, and attempted to place the party and SA in Berlin under his control. On April 4, 1931, all SA leaders were ordered to submit declarations of loyalty to Hitler, Stennes was expelled from the party, and the autonomy of the SA leadership was further reduced. Hitler appointed Wilhelm Loeper, Gauleiter of Halle-Merseburg, to the position of party personnel manager. Loeper was given the power to screen all appointments to the positions of Gauleiter, deputy Gauleiter, and regional SA leader. SA funding was temporarily cut and the SA was prevented from accepting new members until July 1. Stennes unsuccessfully attempted to have Röhm killed in July–August 1931.[17]

The SA's weakened position prompted Röhm to take independent steps to secure financial support for the organization and to secure his own sources of intelligence. In November 1930, Röhm met Georg Bell, whom he had known in the early 1920s, once again through Bell's fiancée, Hildegard Huber, a friend of the Röhm family. Bell claimed to have far-ranging connections with intelligence services, particularly British intelligence. Sometime after January 1931, Röhm and Bell reached a verbal agreement that Bell would make connections with leading German and foreign political figures, and keep Röhm informed of any significant developments. In exchange, Röhm would reimburse Bell's expenses and support him financially. On March 21, 1931, Röhm and Bell formalized this agreement with Du Moulin-Eckart as a witness. For a monthly salary of 350 marks and all costs reimbursed, Bell would create and organize an SA intelligence service, set up an SA press office and paper, create a propaganda office for the SA inside and outside Germany, and seek out financial help for the SA.[18]

Röhm may have chosen Bell because he knew him from outside Nazism and felt that Bell would therefore be more loyal to him. Röhm's reliance on Bell was also an indication of Röhm's isolation within Nazism. Bell was an unqualified and unsuitable choice for the wide range of responsibilities that Röhm gave him. Until coming into contact with Röhm, Bell had worked as an engineer in Munich. He had been fined three hundred marks for his involvement in the so-called *Tscherwonzen* affair, an attempt to flood the USSR with forged ten-ruble notes and create political instability there. Bell was a combination of confidence man and fantasist, who succeeded in convincing many others apart from Röhm that he was more widely traveled and better connected with foreign intelligence services than was the case.[19]

From April to June 1931, and again in February and March 1932, Bell traveled overseas to France, Switzerland, and Britain, seeking financial support for the SA, gathering information for Röhm, and seeking to overcome foreign suspicions of Nazism. At the end of April 1931, Bell also arranged that the British journalist Sefton Delmer meet Röhm. At their first meeting, Röhm indicated to Delmer that he wanted to reassure foreign opinion that the West had nothing to fear from an expansion of the SA under his command. The SA would prevent the German unemployed from coming under Communist influence. Röhm introduced Delmer to Hitler a week later. Bell and Röhm believed Delmer to be an agent of British intelligence, and cultivated contacts with him to reassure the British about the rise of Nazism. Bell claimed that British and French financial groups were willing to offer Röhm credit, providing he led the NSDAP, brought the NSDAP under English influence, and that he set up a foreign and defence policy along particular lines. Bell claimed Röhm agreed to these conditions. This claim is doubtful since Röhm never took action along the lines requested by the financial groups.[20]

Röhm did agree to a memorandum on future Nazi foreign policy, which Bell drew on in his discussions in London. The memorandum stressed that the SA was in no way a military force and would, at some time in the future, become superfluous. The Nazi Party, it continued, emphasized agreement with Britain, followed by rapprochement with France. The memorandum stated that Germany saw itself as a European power and opposed any German cooperation with Russia or the United States. Although Röhm himself signed the memorandum, the memorandum may have been drawn up by Bell rather than Röhm. Aside from the emphasis on good relations with France, there was no difference of emphasis in the memorandum with Hitler's stated foreign policy views of the period. Röhm himself favored good relations between Germany and France. Röhm also approached Delmer in 1931 with a plan he claimed originated from von Schleicher to expand the army by including 250,000 SA men and 50,000 Stahlhelm men. Röhm sought Allied approval for the plan and wanted to travel to London to negotiate it. Germany would then conclude an anti-Bolshevik alliance with France, Italy, and the United Kingdom.[21]

It has been argued that Röhm's goal was to use the money he hoped Bell would raise for the SA and the growing strength of the SA as a bargaining counter to achieve his goal of becoming Reichswehr Minister. It is probable, however, that Röhm's main interest was to secure financial support for the SA and thereby strengthen his position within Nazism.[22]

Bell also prepared a thirty-page plan for a SA intelligence service to help Röhm's position within and outside Nazism. This plan does not survive. Both Bell, and the intelligence service that was set up under Du Moulin-Eckart, were used to defend Röhm as attacks on him intensified from June 1931 on. [23]

On June 2, 1931, the SPD newspaper, the *Münchener Post*, began a series of critical stories on Röhm. The first story sought to discredit Röhm as a profiteer from the republic by publicizing the financial support he had gained from the state from 1925 on. On June 22, 1931, in an article entitled "Homosexuality in the Brown House. Sexual Life in the Third Reich," the paper shifted its focus to Röhm's sexuality. The stories drew ostensibly on an alleged report sent to Röhm by a Nazi intelligence officer, Dr. Meyer. On June 24, as part of the *Völkischer Beobachter*'s counter-attack, it published a statement by Röhm stating that he had rejected Meyer's offer of his services as an intelligence officer and had never received the report published by the *Münchener Post*. Further stories followed in the Berlin SPD press as well as the *Münchener Post*.[24]

Shortly afterward, on July 13, 1931, police in Berlin seized copies of Röhm's letters to Heimsoth in a raid on Heimsoth's home. Since Röhm had written frankly about his sexuality in the letters, he was potentially even more vulnerable to attack. In August 1931, a police intelligence report noted that since the press articles were largely based on fact, neither the NSDAP nor the individuals involved could publish factual rebuttals. Hitler had forced Röhm to pursue a defamation action against the *Münchener Post*, "even though, as he himself says, he is already completely convinced it will fail."[25] The police claimed that Röhm immediately went on leave and left Munich for a few weeks. Later the same month, Röhm sent Bell to Berlin in an unsuccessful attempt to win support for Röhm from Gregor Strasser, the NSDAP organizational leader, and Strasser's deputy, Paul Schulz.

Röhm's personal links with Hitler remained strong. He was closer to Hitler socially at this time than he would be after January 30, 1933. He regularly attended Hitler's daily gatherings in his favorite cafés in Munich—the Café Weichand near the Volkstheater, the Teesalon-Carlton in the Briennerstrasse, and the Café Heck in the Galeriestrasse. On September 18, 1931, Hitler's niece Geli (Angela) Raubal committed suicide in Hitler's Munich apartment on the Prinzregentenstrasse. On September 26, 1931, Hitler obtained a special dispensation from the Austrian authorities to allow him to visit her grave in the Central Cemetery in Vienna. In addition to the Raubal family and members of Hitler's entourage, Röhm accompanied Hitler on this trip.[26]

In this period, the German economic crisis worsened, with the failure of the Darmstädter und Nationalbank on July 13 and a two-day bank holiday. The formation of the second Brüning cabinet on October 9, 1931, was followed on October 11 by a rally of the "National Opposition" in the "Harzburg Front." The Stahlhelm, the German Nationalists (DNVP), and the NSDAP held a rally at Bad Harzburg to support the overthrow of the Brüning Government and a vote of no confidence against Brüning in the Reichstag.[27]

Röhm cultivated the SA's connections with the Reichswehr. On March 31, 1931, he reached agreement with General von Schleicher, then head of the Ministerial Office in the Reichswehr Ministry, that the SA in the east should be trained to defend Germany's border with Poland. The Reichswehr feared Polish military strength and encouraged local border defense organizations, which were trained and equipped by the Reichswehr to support the army in the event of a Polish attack. The SA in East Prussia and the border provinces of Posen and West Prussia participated willingly; cooperation in Pomerania and Silesia was less successful.[28]

Röhm's connections with the Reichswehr were used to organize Hitler's first meeting with von Schleicher, and through Schleicher, Hitler's first meetings with Brüning and President von Hindenburg in autumn 1931. Schleicher used Werner von Alvensleben as his intermediary with Röhm, and Röhm used Graf von Helldorf, then leader of the Berlin SA.[29]

Several witnesses reported Röhm's goal was to be Reichswehr Minister.[30] This ambition, and his belief that he had the capacity to fill it, had been strengthened by his stay in Bolivia. General Kundt had de facto held a similar position there for ten years off and on. Röhm's self-confidence had been reinforced by his ability to establish himself and create a following in Bolivia, away from his German reputation, allies, and connections. Röhm may well have been a capable Reichswehr Minister for the foreign and military policy that he appeared to envisage for Germany: a Germany that was militarily strong and nationally assertive, but with good relations with Britain and France, and an army weighted toward defense rather than offense.

Röhm himself would not have considered his sexuality any obstacle to his appointment. The attitudes of the time meant, however, that once it was publicized, he was unacceptable in the position to von Hindenburg and the army leadership. He was too political an appointment for the Reichswehr to accept. In addition, he had a fellow National Socialist rival for the position, Hermann Göring, who probably would have been more acceptable to the Reichswehr than Röhm.[31]

Although Schleicher was willing to use Röhm for his political contacts with the NSDAP, according to Brüning, the senior Reichswehr leadership, including Schleicher, regarded Röhm with "unbounded disdain."[32] When Schleicher approached Röhm in December 1931 to seek NSDAP support for a parliamentary extension of Hindenburg's position as president, and Röhm demanded the position of Reichswehr Minister for himself in return, Schleicher rejected his demand.

The *Münchener Post* continued to attack Röhm. In November 1931, the paper turned its focus to the SA intelligence service under Du Moulin-Eckart, using material gained from a former NSDAP member, and claiming Du Moulin-Eckart had prepared lists of people to be purged by the Nazis. Eventually, Hitler successfully sued the editor of the *Münchener Post* for defamation because the story cast doubt on Hitler's commitment to the legal path to power. On January 25, 1932, Röhm responded by shifting responsibility for intelligence to the Reichsführer-SS from February 1, 1932, and Du Moulin-Eckart was temporarily transferred to Berlin in April 1932.[33]

The campaign against Röhm intensified in the 1932 election year. The NSDAP's political opponents, initially in the SPD, and later, more generally on the left and right, still saw this as a means of discrediting Nazism. In February 1932, Hitler delayed making a decision on whether to run as president against Hindenburg. He did not announce his candidacy until February 22. The party and SA threw themselves into frantic weeks of campaigning before the first presidential election on March 13, 1932, in which Hindenburg won 49.6 percent of the vote; Hitler, 30.1 percent; Thälmann (KPD), 13.2 percent; and Düsterberg (Stahlhelm), 6.8 percent. In the run-off election on April 10, Hindenburg won a second seven-year term with 53 percent of the vote, while Hitler won 36.8 percent, and Thälmann, 10 percent.[34]

Two major attacks were directed against Röhm linked to the presidential elections. In March 1932, Dr. Helmuth Klotz, a former Nazi who had become a SPD publicist, published the full text of Röhm's letters to Heimsoth in a booklet eventually entitled *Der Fall Röhm (The Röhm Case)*, three hundred thousand copies of which were distributed throughout Germany in March and April 1932. Publication of the letters was accompanied by a hostile press campaign that combined calls for Röhm's dismissal with salacious speculation about his sexuality.[35]

From the beginning of these attacks in 1931, Röhm trod a fine line in response to the scandals around his sexuality. On the one hand, he chose not to lie about his sexual inclinations. In police interrogations, he always admitted to bisexuality. He was forced to bring court cases against Klotz for distributing the letters, which were unsuccessful because he never denied the authenticity of the letters. In court, he admitted the letters to Heimsoth were his; he did not seek to claim that they were forgeries. Yet, he could not be completely honest or open, particularly where such openness would bring him into conflict with the law.[36]

The unwelcome publicity led Röhm to regulate his sexual life. It was too risky for him to frequent the bath houses of Berlin, which he had indicated to Heimsoth were his preference before 1928. Before he left for Bolivia in 1928, he had met the twenty-year-old clerk Peter Granninger, with whom he began a sexual relationship after his return from Bolivia. Within a few months, Röhm had reached an arrangement with Granninger. Over Easter 1931, Röhm employed Granninger in the intelligence service of the Oberste SA-Führung, and subsidized the cost of his frequent changes of apartment. In exchange, Granninger selected and groomed youths between the ages of fourteen and twenty as potential sexual partners for Röhm, paying them money and teaching them Röhm's own preferred sex practices in his own sexual relations with them. Usually in Granninger's own quarters and in Du Moulin-Eckart's flat in Munich, Röhm met these youths for sex sessions, either as a couple or in sessions with multiple partners. Granninger, Karl Zehnter, the owner of the *Nürnberger Bratwurstglöckl*, a Munich restaurant, and after mid-1933, Gerhard von Prosch also participated in some of these sessions. After Granninger and Röhm fell out and Röhm sent Granninger to a position in the SA in Silesia in March 1934, Röhm's servant Johann Holtsch took over the role of procurer for Röhm. While Röhm denied breaching Section 175 of the German criminal code to the police, these encounters did involve oral sex, as well as other acts, which, while not illegal under Section 175, would have shocked conventional public opinion at the time (urination into the mouths of his partners, licking their anuses). Röhm gambled correctly that Granninger's precautions—his selection and preparation of Röhm's potential partners, their payment, and Granninger's frequent changes of apartment—would all protect him from blackmail and publicity.[37]

Hitler ignored the campaign against Röhm, indicating privately that to bow to it would be a sign of weakness. Hitler's response depended on the attitudes and motives of those who approached him. To Heinrich Hoffmann, he stated that Röhm's private life was of no interest to him. On April 6, 1932, Hitler issued a statement declaring that Röhm would remain SA Chief of Staff, both before and after the presidential election. Yet, on May 13, 1932, Hitler removed the Hitler Youth from Röhm's area of responsibility, by making the Hitler Youth leader Baldur von Schirach directly responsible to him. In part, this was to prevent the Hitler Youth being caught up in any bans of the SA and SS, but it was also to deflect criticism that Hitler left the homosexual Röhm in charge of a youth organization.[38]

Other Nazis did not see the publicity Röhm was attracting in the same way. On March 13, 1932, NSDAP member and former SA-Standartenführer Emil Danzeisen ordered a fellow Nazi, the architect Karl Emil Horn, to travel to Munich and kill Du Moulin-Eckart, Bell, Ingolstadt SA leader Julius Uhl, who later led Röhm's staff guard, and, finally, Röhm. The head of the Party Court, Walter Buch, and others were behind the plot.[39]

Rather than carry the plan out, Horn contacted Du Moulin-Eckart, and Du Moulin-Eckart, in turn, ensured that the police were notified. According to Du Moulin-Eckart's postwar testimony, Hitler was annoyed that Du Moulin-Eckart had made the Horn-Danzeisen plot known to the police, and thus public. Hitler pressured Röhm to remove Du Moulin-Eckart from the Oberste SA-Führung. The police investigation into the plot did not probe into the wider background or the instigators of the plot. Emil Danzeisen was found guilty of two charges of ordering a crime in July 1932 and sentenced to six months' imprisonment.[40]

The plot was dramatic evidence of hostility to Röhm inside Nazism. It seems to have unsettled Röhm. Bell claimed that Röhm commissioned him to kill Paul Schulz in March–April 1932, but that he never attempted to carry it out. Bell's account is improbable in that Röhm would have been able to command the assistance of men more suited to carrying out such a murder than Bell.[41]

Röhm was so shaken by the planned attempt on his life that he turned to his fellow Bavarian army officer, Karl Mayr, now a leader of the SPD dominated paramilitary organization, the Reichsbanner. Bell was the intermediary in setting up the meeting. When the meeting became public in October 1932, the two men published completely contradictory accounts of the meeting. Delmer suggested that Bell double-crossed Röhm, leading Röhm to believe that Mayr had sought the meeting to see if he and a section of the Reichsbanner could come over to the Nazis.[42]

According to Mayr, Röhm had come to seek support from him against enemies in his own camp, including Schulz. The Röhm Mayr depicted was recognizable and believable. Röhm blamed the politicians, "the civilians," for the fact that the SA and Reichsbanner faced each other in struggle. Mayr observed that when he made strong points about the conditions the Nazis would have to accept for any political truce, Röhm "peacefully accepted these and other much stronger judgements and statements."[43] Even Röhm admitted in his account of the meeting that Mayr had pointed out the dangers Röhm faced in his own ranks, "that I was—as he expressly said—already 'a dead man.'"[44] It is not clear what advantage Röhm gained from this meeting. Röhm may have also sought Mayr's support in calling off the SPD attacks on him. Perhaps the meeting, of which Röhm claimed he had notified Hitler, also served to pressure Hitler to support Röhm.

The Horn-Danzeisen case also led to Röhm to part with Bell. Bell broke with Du Moulin-Eckart on March 15, 1932, on the grounds that their conceptions of the intelligence service were so different. On April 5, the federal and some state governments banned the SA and SS. On April 19, Röhm used the ban on the SA and the resulting financial pressures on the SA to end his employment of Bell. By May, Röhm had forbidden his adjutants from having any contact with Bell, who had become an embarrassing liability to Röhm, whose situation in the party at the time was described as desperate.[45]

On May 12, 1932, four Nazi deputies, led by Edmund Heines, had attacked Klotz in the restaurant in the Reichstag building. Klotz continued his criticisms of Röhm, publishing a written interview with Ludendorff on May 17. Ludendorff attacked Röhm's homosexuality and Hitler's toleration of it, not only in this interview but also in a booklet entitled *Heraus aus dem braunen Sumpf (Out of the Brown Morass)*.[46]

On May 30, von Hindenburg dismissed Brüning as Chancellor and replaced him with Franz von Papen. The Reichstag was dissolved on June

4, and new elections were set for July 31. Röhm was the main Nazi negotiator in the lead-up to the dissolution of the Reichstag. On June 8, when Röhm visited the Chancellery for discussions on lifting the ban on the SA and SS, Papen was reported as having said earlier, "If one has dealings with Mr. Röhm, one should sit on a chair as much as possible."[47]

On June 16, Papen's government lifted the ban on the SA and the SS. The next day, Hitler confirmed Röhm as his chief of staff. The SA threw itself into frantic electioneering, based on the expectation that the NSDAP would win government in this election. The NSDAP won 37.3 percent of the vote and gained 230 seats, becoming the largest party in the Reichstag for the first time. The attacks on Röhm had not had the desired wider effect, for they made no inroads on the Nazi Party's electoral support or SA membership.[48]

Following the election, Hitler made it clear to Schleicher that the NSDAP would no longer "tolerate" the Papen government, and demanded the position of Chancellor. Röhm played a key role in the negotiations that led up to Hitler's interview with Hindenburg on August 13, 1932. On the afternoon of August 12, Röhm and Helldorf called on Papen, and the next day, Röhm accompanied Hitler in his calls on Schleicher, Papen, and Hindenburg. That month, according to Delmer, Röhm claimed that he was prepared to stage a putsch if Hindenburg did not make Hitler Chancellor, but that Hitler had decided to hold to the path of legality. SA frustration at the Nazi failure to win government led to outbreaks of terror and violence in East Prussia and Silesia. While Röhm saw such acts as an outlet for the mood of the SA, they also showed how easily the officers could lose control of their men. While the violence against Jews and the left in East Prussia appeared to be the work of lower levels of the SA, the Silesian campaign originated with Heines and was sanctioned by Röhm. Most of the incidents in Silesia were planned in advance, executed on the orders of the regional SA leadership and, according to the statements of such leaders, intended to exert pressure on the negotiations to form a new Reich government.[49]

In the course of the violence in Silesia, at Potempa on August 9–10, a group of SA men murdered a laborer with Communist sympathies. The Reich government responded by introducing two emergency decrees against political terrorism. Five of those who participated in the attack were sentenced to death at the end of their trial in Beuthen on August 22, 1932, where the verdict led to serious riots. Continued activity without anything to show for it was putting pressure on the SA and the SS, and there were signs of disintegration in the formations.[50]

Röhm's own position and character had been under attack since June 1931. His life had been threatened, details of his private life published widely, and only Hitler's support kept him in his position. In public, Röhm claimed to be unmoved by the attacks of his political opponents: they showed that he was dangerous. The attacks on Röhm were not without their effect, though few contemporary observers noticed this explicitly. Meeting Röhm again in September 1932 after seven years, Kurt Lüdecke noted:

> outwardly he had changed but slightly, yet his demeanor was not quite the same. He was a little less definite, less positive, less sure of himself than I remembered him. His judgement was still sound, his mind still showed the realist, with a wide grasp of things; in certain aspects, he had grown. He still had his poise and his winning personality. But there was something vaguely disturbing. Perhaps the vicious attacks on him had sickened his healthy ego, perhaps the tarnish on his reputation had eaten too deeply. It was as if a sense of guilt hovered over his countenance, which now and then looked forced.[51]

Lüdecke claimed Röhm told him he had lost his independence forever and could only follow Hitler loyally. A Munich police report of a SA meeting in October 1932 described Röhm as having "a somewhat morose face" and receiving a "subdued" reception.[52]

The failure of Hitler's negotiations with Papen and Hindenburg led to the Nazis combining with the KPD to vote no confidence in the government. A further round of national Reichstag elections followed on November 6. Röhm's position came under renewed pressure. Bell left the NSDAP on October 8 and began attacking Röhm. He then sued Röhm for money he claimed was owed to him, claiming implausibly that Röhm broke with him, among other reasons, when he had to make it clear to Röhm that he was not homosexual. Further salacious press reporting followed.[53]

The election results showed a slump in the Nazi vote of some 4 percent. Political negotiating and lobbying continued. On December 2, Kurt von Schleicher became the next presidential Chancellor. Schleicher's attempts to split the Nazis by offering Gregor Strasser the deputy chancellorship failed. On December 8, frustrated at Hitler's all or nothing stance on the chancellorship, Strasser resigned all his party offices.[54]

Röhm did not play a prominent public role in this period. He was ill with a heart complaint in November and went on three weeks convalescence leave. While Röhm and other Nazi witnesses in court trials would use illness and other excuses to delay the trials, in this instance Röhm genuinely appeared to have been ill. Speculation continued that Hitler was about to replace him.[55]

In January 1933, negotiations between the National Socialists and von Papen continued with the aim of forming a national government. By mid-January, these negotiations had the support of von Hindenburg. On January 28, Hindenburg refused Schleicher's request to dissolve the Reichstag and von Schleicher resigned as Chancellor. Together with other Nazi leaders, on January 30, Röhm waited at the Kaiserhof Hotel in Berlin for news of Hitler's appointment as Chancellor. The NSDAP stood just before its goal.[56]

Over two difficult years, Röhm had succeeded in holding the SA together. He enabled it to undertake a constant round of electoral and political activity. He had done so while under continuous attack from both within and outside the NSDAP. The political campaign against Röhm had weakened him in the Nazi movement, and only Hitler's steadfast support kept him in his position. The unrelenting pressure on Röhm meant he had focussed on his immediate tasks, following Hitler unquestioningly, and had not given much attention to what his and the SA's future would be after a successful Nazi takeover of power.[57]

Figure 1. Ernst Röhm as a captain in the Reichswehr (Archiv Gerstenberg-ullstein bild/
The Granger Collection, New York) [0171938]

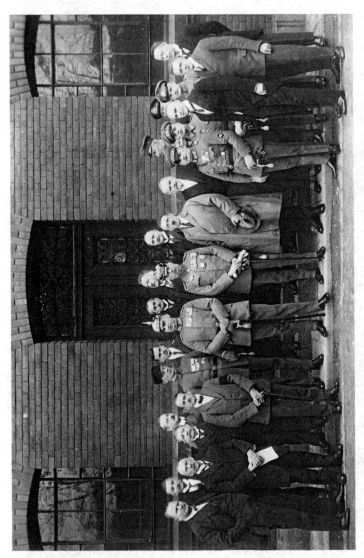

Figure 2. Adolf Hitler and others at the trial following the Beer Hall Putsch at Munich, Germany. From left (in uniform): Friedrich Weber, Hermann Kriebel, Erich Ludendorff, Hitler, Wilhelm Brückner, Ernst Röhm, Heinz Pernet, Wilhelm Frick (in civilian clothes), and Robert Wagner. Photographed February 26, 1924. (ullstein bild/The Granger Collection, New York) [0084684]

Figure 3. Ernst Röhm as SA Chief of Staff—undated drawing by Karl Bauer, with Röhm's signature (Archiv Gerstenberg-ullstein bild/The Granger Collection, New York) [0171939]

Figure 4. The wedding of SA-Gruppenführer Karl Ernst on April 15, 1934. From left: Hermann Göring, Ernst Röhm (witnesses), Minnes Ernst (née Wolff), and Karl Ernst (ullstein bild/The Granger Collection, New York) [0171937]

CHAPTER 12

The Seizure of Power
January–June 1933

It was due to you in the first instance that this political instrument could develop such strength within a few years that it made it possible for me to win the struggle for power by overpowering the Marxist enemy.[1]

Adolf Hitler

January 1933 began, for Ernst Röhm, with speculation about his possible dismissal as Chief of Staff of the SA. It ended with the realization of the goal for which he had returned from Bolivia. On January 30, the night of Hitler's appointment as Chancellor, the SA and Stahlhelm paraded past Hitler in front of the Reich Chancellery building from 7:00 p.m. to 1:00 a.m. That day, persuaded by Franz von Papen that this would secure a nationalist government with a Reichstag majority, President Paul von Hindenburg appointed Adolf Hitler Chancellor of a minority cabinet dominated by Nationalists and other conservatives. Papen was Deputy Chancellor. Apart from Hitler, there were only two other Nazis in the Cabinet, Wilhelm Frick as Minister of the Interior and Hermann Göring as Minister without Portfolio and Prussian Minister of the Interior. Papen hoped to use the Nazis' popular support to bring about an authoritarian regime. Initially, the appointment of another presidential government seemed, to many Germans, to be no different than the appointment of other such governments in the past. The Nazi leadership, however, had no intention of leaving office. At the second Cabinet meeting on January 31, in persuading the Cabinet to agree to new elections, Hitler promised these would be the last elections. "A return to the parliamentary system will be completely avoided."[2]

Hitler made this decision known to senior army and navy commanders on February 3, when he met them for the first time as Chancellor. The internal guiding principles of the new government would be "the strictest authoritarian leadership of the State, removal of the cancer of democracy,"[3] he told them. Hitler had promised Hindenburg to refrain from any interference with the army. He promised the army leadership that the party organizations would be responsible for the internal political struggle, and the army would remain apolitical. Unlike in fascist Italy, there would be no mixing of the army and SA. Reichstag elections were set for March 5, 1933.

In the period from 1931 to 1933, Nazi officials were banned by Hitler from planning for a takeover of power after the November 1931 "Boxheimer Hof" affair. In September 1931, officials from the Hesse Gauleitung met at a farm, the Boxheimer Hof, to draw up practical plans for a Nazi takeover of power, including dictatorial powers. The documents were leaked to the SPD by a defector, and a furor resulted. Hitler was concerned, lest such plans be used by the government as evidence that the party was departing from its promised course of legality. In an order to the SA on December 9, 1931, banning all further such planning, Hitler noted that "it is a matter of course, and does not need to be mentioned, that after the takeover of power National Socialism will act with inexorable rigor against all parasites on the people and fatherland."[4] In 1932, in a meeting with von Bredow on July 26, Röhm and Göring told him that "they believed however that they had the right to retaliate for the harm Marxism had done. The SA had been trained for this revenge for years. Marxism had to be completely destroyed."[5] The SA rampages in East Prussia and Silesia in 1932 had already illustrated how the average storm trooper interpreted this aim.

The new government's initial measures reflected not just its desire to remain in power but also its belief that Marxism was a feared and dangerous enemy to be countered ruthlessly. Communist calls for a general strike against the new government led Hindenburg to approve an Emergency Decree to Protect the German People, allowing for police restrictions on public meetings and temporary detention, without trial, for treason or weapons offenses. In Prussia, under Göring as Interior Minister, it was made clear that this was to be directed against the SPD as well as the KPD.[6]

In Prussia and in states where National Socialists already had government positions, SA leaders were gradually appointed to head police organizations, and on February 22, a secret decree from Göring stated that the only organizations from which auxiliary police in Prussia could be recruited were the SA, SS, Stahlhelm, and Deutschnationalen Kampfring. By mid-February, the states of Thuringia, Mecklenburg-Schwerin, Oldenburg, Braunschweig, Anhalt, Lippe, and Mecklenburg-Strelitz were under Nazi control.[7]

Even when they were not enrolled as auxiliary police, the SA and SS in Prussia sought out and held their political enemies on the left in SA headquarters and other buildings that became the first "wild" concentration camps. Throughout most of this process, the local SA and SS acted without specific orders from their leadership and without unified directions or control. They took action spontaneously, dominating the streets in public and pursuing their enemies both publicly and privately. In the opinion of the ordinary SA and SS man, this was the day of revenge against Germany's enemies.[8]

On the evening of February 27 in Berlin, the unemployed former Dutch anarcho-syndicalist, Marinus van der Lubbe, set the Reichstag on fire as an anti-Nazi act. Van der Lubbe was captured at the burning building, but Hitler, Göring, and Goebbels, who arrived at the Reichstag, were convinced that this was part of a wider Communist uprising. Göring ordered the immediate arrests of Communists and all their associates. On February 28, Hindenburg enacted the Decree to Protect the People and State. This was a response to the perceived Communist threat that amounted to the introduction of a state of emergency and suspension of almost all democratic rights. The Nazi leaders themselves genuinely appear to have believed that the fire was a Communist plot. Their worldview—that Germany was being subverted by dangerous enemies—predisposed them to believe that their enemies were capable of such steps.[9]

Immediately after the fire, because its timing was so electorally convenient for the Nazis, left-wing circles abroad alleged, in turn, that the Nazis had started the fire to give themselves a pretext to move against the KPD. Göring or senior SA leaders were alleged to have been the organizers. After considerable historiographical debate and investigation, it is now generally accepted that van der Lubbe acted alone.[10]

Göring claimed that van der Lubbe had links with the SPD and used this to ban all SPD publications in Prussia for fourteen days. In those states not under Nazi control, such as Bavaria, the police moved against the KPD after February 28. The Bavarian government, however, rejected a demand from the federal government on March 1 for a general ban on the SPD press in Bavaria.[11]

The conditions under which the March 5 Reichstag elections were contested therefore varied. The KPD could not campaign freely in any state in the country. The SPD could only campaign freely in those states not under Nazi control. While other parties were generally undisturbed in their electioneering, the NSDAP and their ally, the DNVP, were favored by their control of the federal government. On March 1, the NSDAP election proclamation even appeared in the internal Prussian government gazette. The claims that a Communist coup had been imminent were widely believed. The country was already "under conditions of semi-dictatorship."[12] Violence against SPD members and offices, as well as against the KPD, intensified from the evening of the election, with the SA taking the lead.

In the elections, the Nazis achieved 43.9 percent of the vote nationwide. Together with their Nationalist allies, they had 51.9 percent. Hitler was confident that the Reichstag would pass an Enabling Act that would give him the power to issue decrees bypassing the Reichstag for four years, even though this required a two-thirds majority and a two-thirds quorum.[13]

On March 23, the Reichstag met at the Kroll Opera House, its temporary location, to pass the Enabling Act. As presiding officer, Göring illegally reduced the quorum from 432 to 378 by not counting the legally elected Communist deputies. Not only did the remaining deputies have to run a gauntlet of SA and SS men as they arrived, but they also took their places in the Chamber, surrounded by armed SA and SS men. Only the ninety-four SPD deputies who could turn up voted against the Act.[14]

In the period following the March 5 election, mass SA demonstrations, combined with intervention by Interior Minister Frick, were used to "coordinate," that is, take over, state governments. New Nazi governments were formed in Hamburg, Baden, Saxony, Bremen, Lübeck, Hesse, and Württemberg. State commissioners were appointed by Frick, who replaced the elected governments with a Nazi appointee and police commissioners with local Nazis on the pretext of a direct Communist danger. The army leadership, Blomberg as Reichswehr Minister and von Reichenau as head of the Ministerial office in the Reichswehr Ministry, supported this process.[15] Röhm and others in the SA leadership again did not play a prominent or initiating role in these activities.

On March 10, Hitler publicly denounced violence against foreigners, which he attributed to Communist infiltration of the SA, and he exhorted the SA to stop harassing individuals and disturbing businesses. Yet, he added that the SA should not be sidetracked from its task, the annihilation of Marxism. The national uprising would continue to be carried out from above and the SA should act to crush resistance to the orders from superior authority.[16]

Röhm himself only played a prominent role in the Nazi takeover of power in Bavaria. The Bavarian government, recognizing the significance of von Papen's takeover of the Prussian State government, had tried to secure its position by an unsuccessful plan to appoint Crown Prince Rupprecht as general state commissioner like Kahr. This plan alarmed the federal government. On February 25 and 27, an emissary of Reichsführer-SS Heinrich Himmler, Oberführer Freiherr von Malsen-Ponitzau, met with the leader of the Bavarian Homeland and King League, Freiherr Enoch von Guttenberg, to ascertain the Crown Prince's attitude. Guttenberg suggested that Röhm or Himmler meet with the Crown Prince, but no such meeting took place.[17]

Once again, when faced with a potential conflict between his monarchism and his National Socialism, Röhm chose National Socialism.

After this plan failed, the Bavarian government, under Minister President Heinrich Held, tried to enlist the support of President Hindenburg and to remove any pretext for intervention by maintaining order. The Bavarian ambassador in Berlin, Sperr, had already accurately noted that affairs in Berlin had already slipped so far into tyranny that action in Munich could no longer stop them.[18]

On the afternoon of March 8, the Held government became aware of SA and SS plans to force it to stand down. Early on the morning of March 9, Sperr advised that he could no longer reach Röhm or Adolf Wagner, Gauleiter for Munich and Upper Bavaria, in Berlin. At 10:00 a.m., Frick assured Sperr that there were no plans to appoint a Reich commissioner in Bavaria. Meanwhile, in Munich, large numbers of SA and SS massed in the city. Between 12:15 and 12:30 p.m., Röhm, Wagner, and Himmler appeared with a large entourage at Held's office in the Außenministerium and brought him an ultimatum to appoint a Bavarian Generalstaatskommissar immediately and equip him with wide powers. They suggested Epp for the position. When Held refused and accused them of putting him under pressure, Röhm claimed that he would immediately suppress any attempt to use force. A communication came from Frick stating that if the Bavarian government did not appoint a Generalstaatskommissar by 3:00 p.m. that day, the federal government would appoint Epp. Held told the Nazi leaders that he could not take such a decision on his own and would call a Ministerial Council meeting at 2:30 p.m. and leave the decision to them.[19]

The Ministerial Council began its meeting, knowing that Röhm's promises had not been kept. SA men were gathering at the railway station, and the SA and SS had occupied the Marienplatz. Efforts were made to get the Reichswehr to send out street patrols and move to a state of readiness, but later in the afternoon, the Reichswehr advised that it judged the issue to be a matter of internal Bavarian state politics into which it could not intervene. In any case, as was desired by Berlin, they would take no action against the SA and SS. This news came shortly after Epp, Röhm, Wagner, and Himmler appeared in the room at 3:40 p.m. to learn of the decision. Held had decided in the meantime to reject the proposals of "Röhm and accomplices."[20] According to Röhm, who telephoned Hitler, Hitler, Brückner, and Frick all denied having assured Held that there were no plans to change political conditions in Bavaria. At 5:00 p.m., the Nazis broke off negotiations, pointing out that the SA would march according to plan and Held would be responsible for any ensuing bloodshed.

Frick called Röhm, who had returned to the Braunes Haus, and said he would immediately appoint a Reich commissioner for Bavaria himself. Held was notified. Frick sent a telegram authorizing Epp to take over the powers of the state authorities in Bavaria. The Bavarian Government received a telegram notifying it of this decision at 8:45 p.m. At about 9:00 p.m., Epp appeared with Röhm, Wagner, and Himmler, placed a copy of Frick's telegram before Held, and sought a transfer of powers. Epp pledged that ministers, and their homes, would be secure.[21]

That evening, Epp appointed Röhm and Esser as State Commissioners for particular purposes, Adolf Wagner as State Commissioner for the Interior Ministry, Ludwig Siebert as State Commissioner for the Justice Ministry, and Heinrich Himmler as Commissioner Police President in Munich. Later, on April 12, Epp formalized the various Ministerial positions. On April 13, Röhm was appointed Epp's State Secretary. Considering the key roles they had played in the take over of power in Bavaria, both Röhm and Himmler did not gain prominent positions in the new regime. Symbolically, Epp, accompanied by Röhm and other Nazi leaders, gave a speech at the Feldherrnhalle at 11:00 p.m. on March 9.[22]

At 10:30 a.m. on March 10, the entire Bavarian cabinet met and Held formally transferred power to Epp. The official takeover of police power and inspection of the police took place at 3:00 p.m. in the courtyard of the Türkenkaserne. That afternoon, Epp sent a radio message to the police instructing them to take various Communist and Reichsbanner leaders into "protective custody," to search for weapons. and to hoist the swastika flag on public buildings. A meeting of the State Commissioners followed at the Staatsministerium des Äußern.[23]

The Bavarian government had been unable to resist a takeover that combined deception and a pincer movement of "legal" pressure, as well as the threat of the use of force. Despite Epp's pledges, on the evening of March 9, Interior Minister Stützel and Staatsrat Schäffer were taken from their homes by force and taken to the Braunes Haus. There, Stützel was hit on the head with a steel bar. The Munich rabbi Dr. Bärwald and Stadtrat Ostermaier were also subjected to mistreatment that evening.[24]

On the evening of March 12, Röhm had told police and Interior Ministry officials that he would make special commissioners available to take the necessary measures in his name. The same day, he named regional SA leaders as special commissioners and special deputies. Party officials were also appointed to these positions, which continued until July 1934. Their task was to supervise all political organizations and military groups, and to seize all weapons and ammunition. At the same time, they were to report any lack of discipline or failure to follow the decrees of the new government to the Interior Minister.[25]

In Munich, because it was the Nazi leadership's home, pursuit of personal opponents was keen and swift. On March 9, Max Amann arrived at the editorial rooms of the anti-Nazi *Gerade Weg*, which had already been stormed by the SA, and personally attacked its publisher, Fritz Gerlich, before Gerlich was taken into protective custody. Georg Bell, who was with Gerlich, hid from the SA. The next evening, he and the *Gerade Weg* editor, Major Hell, escaped across the border to Austria. From Austria, Bell sought reconciliation with Röhm, writing to him and one of Röhm's lawyers, Franz Mayr. Mayr recommended Bell stay in Austria. On April 3, one of Bell's friends, Paul Konrad, appeared at the Gasthaus Blattl in Durchholzen, where Bell and Hell were staying, and urged Bell to surrender to the political police. He was followed by five men who claimed to be representatives of the Munich political police. Bell agreed to return to Munich with them, and as he was putting on his shoes, he was shot with six or seven shots by one of the men, aged about forty, a brutal-looking, somewhat pale man, with a beard that was possibly glued on. The shots missed Hell. Richardi and Schumann, and Dornheim, suggest the murderer was SA-Standartenführer Julius Uhl. Uhl's age, and the fact that the assassin was not identified in a postwar trial, argues against this. Bell's murder was probably at Röhm or Reinhard Heydrich's instigation. An attempt to poison Du Moulin-Eckart in Vienna at about the same time most likely arose from a desire to remove him as a political embarrassment, but did not originate with Röhm. From Berlin, Helmuth Klotz fled to Prague on March 15, 1933. [26]

Other opponents of Röhm ended up in protective custody. The prominent Munich lawyer and SPD member, Max Hirschberg, whose firm had appeared for the *Münchener Post* in its cases against Röhm, was held in police custody from March 10 to 11, before being transferred to prison, and held there until August 23, 1933. Hirschberg later claimed that his was "'the only case of real protective custody in all Bavaria.'"[27] The police held him for such a long time to protect him from Röhm, who wanted him transferred to Dachau and killed there. The wife of another protective custody prisoner, Niura Lorant, found her husband's car had been taken by the SA High Command for its own use, including by Robert Bergmann.

Heimsoth, who joined the Nazi Party in 1933, was not arrested by the Gestapo until March 1934, for alleged political activities. He disappeared on his release from Gestapo custody in Berlin on March 16, 1934; the date of his death is unknown. He could, therefore, have been killed either at Röhm's instigation or at that of Röhm's opponents in the regime. Both groups had a motive for removing an embarrassing witness.[28]

By the end of March, Wagner had made the auxiliary police an ongoing institution. Over 4,000 SA men were employed in this capacity by the end of March. On May 1, 1933, a formal Bavaria-wide organization had been set up, with a center for the security police led by Röhm, with Gruppenführer von Krausser as his deputy and Gruppenführer Fuchs as liaison officer with the Interior Ministry. Disputes over the payment of the auxiliary police were not resolved until mid-June when the Reich Interior Ministry agreed to pay some of their costs.[29]

Senior SA leaders increasingly occupied the positions of police president, special commissioner, or senior president and administrative president in state ministries. The smaller SS tended to take over the political police. By spring 1933 on, some of the SA's long-standing financial problems as an organization had also been solved by the provision of financial support by I. G. Farben and other industrialists.[30]

After the passage of the Enabling Act, the party leadership, SA, and SS began to move against other non-National Socialist political organizations across the country. From mid-March, any open activity of left-wing parties was stopped. Then, the Nazis turned against other parties. By May, the meetings of the Bavarian People's Party (BVP) were banned. In a wave of arrests at the end of June, BVP leaders, elected representatives and Catholic priests well known as BVP supporters were arrested.[31]

Unrestricted and undisciplined SA and SS terror often had a greater effect on the lives of the population than the decrees of the central government. First "wild," and then more official, concentration camps were established. Bessel suggests that SA violence in eastern Germany arose at the initiative of Nazi militants, and was a legacy of the years of struggle rather than a plan by the Nazi leadership. The SA had lost its previous main occupation—electoral campaigning—and was therefore free to attack its "enemies" quickly. The SA's frustration and disappointment was unleashed on an enemy whose resistance was less effective than had been expected. [32]

Most SA and SS action occurred without direct orders from their leaders, who nonetheless furthered it by refusing to intervene. When violence directed against foreign citizens, often Jews, led to repeated protests by their governments to the Foreign Ministry, Nazi leaders blamed the attacks on Communist provocateurs in SA or SS uniform. This was both an excuse, and also an expression, of the Nazi worldview that someone whose actions objectively damaged Nazism must be acting in the interests of its enemies. SA leaders called for greater SA discipline and an end to abuses of power, but no serious steps were taken to implement this.[33]

The SA and SS also used force and the threat of force to attack Jews and to force Jewish lawyers and judges out of courts. On April 1, they provided the manpower to enforce the daylong boycott of Jewish shops, businesses, and professionals. Röhm encouraged efforts to counter foreign "atrocity propaganda" on the treatment of German Jews. On May 2, the SA and SS provided the force to take over the left-wing trade unions; on May 10, the regime seized SPD assets, and on June 21, it banned the SPD. In June, the regime moved against the Center Party. That month, Alfred Hugenberg, the leader of the DNVP, resigned as a minister. The remaining leaders of the DNVP dissolved the party.[34]

Franz Seldte, Reich Labour Minister since January 30, 1933, who led another right-wing paramilitary organization, the Stahlhelm, had joined the NSDAP on April 26 and placed the organization under Hitler's political leadership. This proved to be too indeterminate an arrangement. On June 21, Hitler and Seldte agreed that the Stahlhelm's youth organization should become part of the Hitler Youth, and the Jungstahlhelm (men between eighteen and thirty-five) should become the Wehrstahlhelm under the SA leadership. A stage-by-stage incorporation of the Stahlhelm was agreed, a move strongly, but unsuccessfully, opposed by many members of the Wehrstahlhelm. In taking over the Stahlhelm, the SA leadership had eliminated a major potential rival.[35]

By mid-1933, Röhm and the SA leadership could look back with satisfaction to the contribution the SA had made to Nazi control of Germany. On July 14, 1933, a law made the NSDAP the only legal political party in Germany. This symbolically marked the end of this process.[36]

The organization Röhm headed had made three crucial contributions to the consolidation of power. First, the SA had provided the force that backed up Hitler and the party and that destroyed its opponents, "guided but hardly controlled from the top."[37] The SA indiscipline and insubordination, which had caused trouble for Hitler and the party before 1933, delivered political control through the use of violence without explicit orders needing to be given. Secondly, the SA was one of the main means of coordinating non-Nazi organizations, particularly the police and the remaining paramilitary organizations. Thirdly, as the numbers of men joining the SA grew, it therefore contributed to the Nazification of German society.

Aside from the takeover of power in Bavaria, Röhm's own role in this process had been indirect. The contribution of the SA as an organization was crucial. By June 1933, however, Röhm faced the question: What would the future role of the SA be in the Third Reich?

CHAPTER 13

The Search for a Role: Ernst Röhm and the SA June–December 1933

Where would the Government be if the S.A. were abolished? The Jews and Marxists would come back over the frontiers in droves, and everything would be undone in a few weeks. For that matter Bavaria, at the slightest provocation, if Bavarian interests were involved, would go her own way.[1]

Ernst Röhm

The Nazi consolidation of power had largely been completed by June 1933. Ernst Röhm and the SA had to find new roles. What would Röhm himself do? What would the SA do? The problem was recognized by some other leaders and outsiders. In the second half of 1933, a temporary solution was achieved. Hitler designated the SA as the upholders of National Socialist values inside Germany. At the same time, the SA was to be used surreptitiously as a reservoir of support for the army. This second function aroused pressure from and concern among foreign governments.

Röhm was "the second man after Hitler" in the regime, and his position at the time was "commanding,"[2] according to Darré. Röhm continued the expansion of the SA in this period. As early as the end of March 1933, Röhm had indicated that the SA and SS had to complete what they had won by gaining a foothold in every area and among those who had until then had been in the camp of the enemies of National Socialism. "Every true German man should be welcome as a fellow fighter to us."[3]

The absorption of the Stahlhelm continued, despite much opposition in Stahlhelm ranks, motivated by its members' sense of distinctive corporate identity and distaste for the SA's greater militancy. In late June, Röhm had to appoint Edmund Heines, then SA-Obergruppenführer in both Pomerania and Silesia, as "Special Plenipotentiary for the Reorganization of the Stahlhelm in Pomerania" to overcome the Stahlhelm resistance to the merger. The SA, SS, and Stahlhelm leadership met at Bad Reichenhall from July 1–3, 1933. After this meeting, the entire Stahlhelm was subordinated to the SA, though it remained independent in theory. Had the Stahlhelm joined the SA at once, its membership would have outnumbered the SA. Instead, it was taken over step by step. On September 23 and 24, a large Stahlhelm meeting was held in Hanover, attended by Hitler, Seldte, and Röhm, and intended to seal the reorganization of the Stahlhelm. Nonetheless, tensions between the former Stahlhelm and the SA continued into 1934. Röhm also moved to take over the other right-wing paramilitary groups. On August 10, he ordered the incorporation of the Brigade Ehrhardt into the SS, for example.[4]

These moves removed any possible reserves of manpower for conservative opponents of the Nazis. Campbell concludes that "the coordination of the Stahlhelm and others probably did as much to stabilize the new Nazi regime as any other action of the SA in 1933 or 1934."[5] Yet, such moves meant that the SA had become a less politically reliable instrument for its leadership. Many men in the Stahlhelm were opposed to the "SA spirit." Tensions between the SA and the Stahlhelm continued into mid-1934. If the SA's expansion stabilized Nazism by depriving its conservative allies of a force to support them, then, as Bessel points out, the price of this was the weakening of the SA itself.

The new expansion created organizational and financial problems. In response, Röhm reorganized the OSAF staff in May and the entire SA structure between July and September, 1933. Brigades linked to the geographical organization of the Reichswehr were created in place of the earlier Gaustürme that had been linked to NSDAP Gau boundaries.[6]

The SA did not have enough lower- and middle-level officers to staff its new structure. This intensified the organization's pre-existing disciplinary problems. While pre-January 1933 members were promoted or given priority in work creation, new members often had unrealistic expectations that the SA leadership would find them employment. As the period of the active seizure of power drew to an end, thousands of newly joined SA men were left with no purposeful activity. Some—too many—continued acts of violence and harassment that now seemed to serve little political purpose.[7]

The financial problems of the expanded SA led Röhm to demand three million Reichsmarks a month to arm the SA, according to Reich Finance Minister Schwerin-Krosigk. Hitler used Schwerin-Krosigk as a pretext to claim that the money was not available and, instead, the SA received some large sums to pay off its debts.[8]

By the end of May, Röhm told the SA that "feasts have been celebrated enough."[9] The SA and SS needed to stop celebrating the takeover of power and to focus on the tasks in front of them. According to Röhm, these tasks were to be the embodiment of the National Socialist revolution and the continuation of the fight against Marxism and reaction. The German Revolution was still in its early stages.

Soon after, Hitler's message changed. At the Bad Reichenhall meeting, Hitler told the assembled SA, SS, and Stahlhelm leaders that he would brutally suppress any efforts by reactionary or other circles to overthrow the Nazi system. He would proceed equally ruthlessly against the "second revolution," which would have catastrophic consequences. The change in Hitler's views has been attributed to increasing awareness of the detrimental effects of continued Nazi and SA intervention in the economy.[10]

On July 5, *The Times* reported that Hitler had also told the Statthalter that Germany faced a period of consolidation. On July 10, Interior Minister Frick more strongly proclaimed the revolution over and issued a circular stating that talk of it continuing in fact sabotaged the national revolution. This led to restrictions on the activities of the auxiliary police.[11]

The last non-National Socialist political organizations were dissolving themselves. On July 6, the monarchist Bavarian Home and King League disbanded. On July 14, the Law against the Establishment of Political Parties was passed, making the NSDAP the only legal party.[12]

At Bad Reichenhall, Hitler had praised Nazism as an example of a spiritual and ideological revolution. The SA leadership's most important task would be to educate Germans in the National Socialist outlook. It had to be a solid supporter of the Nazi worldview. Röhm took up, and repeated, this claim throughout the year in his speeches and articles. The SA's purpose, Hitler continued at Bad Reichenhall, was to shape the new German state spiritually on the basis of the National Socialist idea and spirit and to educate the German man to be a living member of this state.[13]

Neither the SA, as an organization, nor Röhm as a leader, was well suited to the new ideological role Hitler had allocated them. Röhm maintained the self-protective distinction he drew between public and private life, and his accompanying "man-of-the-world" attitude. In September, he issued a decree calling on the SA not to interfere in issues of private life. It was of no concern to the SA whether women smoked or wore makeup.[14]

The SA's role was poised between the old and the new. In July, the organization played its Weimar role of getting out the vote in the Protestant Church elections. Pro-Nazi groups within the German Evangelical churches, such as the German Christians, sought to Nazify the church from within. Hitler supported moves to unify the various Protestant churches into a single Reich church and appointed Ludwig Müller as his delegate. After months of maneuvering, the Cabinet approved the new constitution of the Reich Church on July 14, 1933, the same day that it approved Germany's Concordat with the Catholic Church. Hitler then announced that elections for positions in the new Evangelical Reich Church would be held on July 23. The Nazi Party and the SA were mobilized to aid the German Christians in the vote. The German Christians were largely successful, and Müller was confirmed as Reich Bishop on September 27, 1933.[15]

The SA leadership tried to keep the SA occupied as much as possible. It held a large autumn parade of the SA in Berlin. In September, in Nuremberg, the SA under Röhm participated in the Victory Party Congress. Röhm was present at various parades and rallies throughout the rest of the year. On October 6, for example, he gave a speech to a rally of the Silesian SA at the monument to the battle of Leuthen, Frederick the Great's victory over Austria in 1757.[16]

The SA leadership was concerned to find jobs for SA men and to find ways of improving their discipline. In Prussia, they set up their own equivalent of a military police, the *Feldjägerkorps*, to handle disciplinary offences. This was considered a success and, for the rest of the year, negotiations continued to set a similar organization up for Bavaria. The financing of the new organization was the main stumbling block.[17]

In spite of having told the SA that there had been enough celebrations of the Nazi coming to power, Röhm himself showed no reluctance to celebrate. In early June, while on convalescent leave, he traveled to Turkey, where he met Kemal Atatürk. On June 24 and 25, in Munich's town hall, he attended a reunion of his tenth company of the Tenth Infantry Regiment. Over two hundred men from the company, as well as Bavarian, Nazi, and Reichswehr, and police dignitaries, attended. In his speech, Röhm claimed that Hitler had brought about a change that allowed "the old genuine soldierly spirit"[18] to be the common possession of all Germans once again. On June 29, he opened the Ernst-Röhm-Haus, the offices of the SA-Gruppe Franken, in Nuremberg. On October 22, both Hitler and Röhm were given honorary citizenship in a ceremony at Rathaus Kelheim.

Like other Nazi leaders, Röhm also continued to gain positions. On July 2, 1933, Epp reconfirmed him as his State Secretary. This role appears to have been largely symbolic without any substantive duties. Röhm rarely took an active part in the Bavarian Ministerial Council (*Ministerialrat*) meetings he attended, although he often traveled with Epp on official journeys. On July 19 and 20, Röhm and his staff accompanied Epp from Hof to Chaim and, a month later, Röhm, Himmler, and their staffs traveled with Epp to Grafenwöhr to dine with officers of the regiments stationed there.[19]

Hitler also ruled on the SA's role in Reich defense. It was to be used in border protection, mainly in the eastern border provinces. Initially, Walther von Reichenau, the head of the ministerial office in the Reichswehr Ministry, had favored developing a rearmed Reichswehr as an elite force and attaching the SA to it as a Swiss-style militia. On July 5, Röhm announced the appointment of Obergruppenführer Friedrich Wilhelm Krüger as Head of Training (Chef AW) and main liaison between the SA leadership and the Reichswehr. By the end of the month, Defense Minister Blomberg issued a decree indicating that the SA would be in charge of premilitary training. The Reichswehr leadership involved the SA in a broad structure of premilitary training. By October these plans had developed to involve some 250,000 SA men a year in over two hundred SA sport schools.[20]

While the government and army were already drawing up rearmament plans, Germany was still officially a member of the League of Nations, bound by the armaments restrictions of the Treaty of Versailles and participating in an international disarmament conference at Geneva. The government and army leadership were aware that Germany was still militarily weak, and they needed to avoid any preventive attack by other powers. Accordingly, there was concern to avoid publicity being given to the SA and SS that might attract adverse foreign attention.[21]

From August 18 to 21, SA, SS, and Stahlhelm leaders met again at Bad Godesberg for further consideration of the incorporation of the Stahlhelm. Both Hitler and Röhm spoke at the meeting. Both men stressed that the army alone would be the arms bearer of the nation, and that it would never be replaced by the political soldiers.[22]

Seeking to allay the disquiet of the French government, on September 15, Hitler told the French Ambassador, André François-Poncet, that the SA were a party troop and militarily valueless. Yet, at about the same time, the British military attaché considered the SA to be superior to, and more numerous than, Britain's Territorial Army.[23]

Hitler emphasized these concerns in a meeting with the Reichsstatthalter on September 28. The government's goal, he told them, was national rearmament, which must be hidden, and the development of German strength, as much as possible. The most dangerous time was the period that had to pass before Germany was strong enough to prevent any other state from attacking. The press had to refrain from publicizing rearmament and showing pictures of the SA.[24]

In September, Blomberg's assessment of the collaboration with the SA was positive. On September 15, he told officers of the Sixth Division that the army need not fear rivalry from the SA. The SA's task was to maintain what had been achieved in the internal political struggle, while the armed forces were to educate German youth as soldiers in peacetime and to defend Germany's borders in wartime. The Chancellor agreed with this. Soon after, Blomberg directed that collaboration with the SA at the local level should intensify.[25]

On October 14, 1933, Germany left the disarmament conference and the League of Nations. The government announced a Reichstag election and a referendum on the decision to be held on Sunday, November 12. The election campaign itself began on October 17. The party, the SA, and the SS were mobilized for a series of election rallies. Röhm stood on the Nazi Party list, for the first time, to be elected as a deputy.[26]

The decision to leave the League of Nations increased the government's sensitivity about international perceptions of the SA. Before it was announced, Röhm gave interviews to foreign newspapers, emphasizing that the SA's role was ideological and internal rather than military. These assurances did not reduce the suspicions of other powers. The British Ambassador, Sir Eric Phipps, described Röhm's comments in one such interview as "so unconvincing as to be alarming."[27] On October 24, the British Foreign Office noted that the British military attaché suggested that the paramilitary forces as a whole (SA, SS, and Stahlhelm), which he estimated to number some 1.5 million men, should be regarded as part of the German defense force.

Röhm and the SA leadership were also involved in German policy toward Austria, which was directed by Hitler through the Austrian Nazi Party leader, Theo Habicht. Hitler may have hoped that a Nazi government could come to power in Austria and that, like the Free City of Danzig, Austria could be Nazified while remaining nominally independent. As a first step, Germany introduced a 1,000-mark fee on travel to Austria, which effectively stopped German tourism. After a bombing campaign by Austrian Nazis began on June 12, Austria banned all government officials from being members of the Nazi Party, arrested known Nazi Party leaders, and deported Habicht to Germany. Austrian Nazis began to flee the country to avoid arrest and arrived in Germany as refugees. Attempts by Papen and Neurath to change Hitler's policy had failed by July 30. Habicht told the Auswärtiges Amt on July 31 that the collapse of the Dollfuss government in Austria was imminent.[28]

The Bavarian government housed the male Austrian refugees in barracks near the German-Austrian border and encouraged their formation into the "Austrian Legion" of the SA. By the end of August 1933, some 3,500 to 4,000 men were enrolled. To reduce the likelihood of border clashes, the Austrian Legion was moved from Lechfeld to camps further away from the border in October.[29]

The available evidence does not substantiate speculation that Röhm was involved in pursuing an independent policy toward Austria. In the last weeks of October, Werner von Alvensleben, president of the socially exclusive Berliner Herrenklub, visited Vienna on private business. While in Vienna, he made contact with Vice Chancellor Emil Fey and others in the Austrian government. It has been suggested that this visit was at Röhm's initiative because he wanted his own sources of information about Austria. Habicht's access to Hitler meant that alternative views of Austria did not reach Hitler and therefore did not influence German policy. Habicht certainly reacted as if this had been an attempt to outmaneuver him. The Dollfuss government had not fallen, nor had German-Austrian relations improved by November.[30]

Although Hitler's deputy, Rudolf Hess, also called for an end to celebrations, this did not stop the Nazi elite from marking the tenth anniversary of the 1923 Hitler putsch with great ceremony. Röhm and Göring played a prominent role in the commemoration. On November 8 in the Königsplatz in Munich, a ceremony attended by Hitler, Epp, and other leaders marked the handover of flags from the former Freikorps to Röhm and the SA. Afterward, the leaders visited Hitler's flat in the Prinzregentenstrasse. On November 9, a reenactment of the march to the Feldherrnhalle took place. Hitler reviewed a parade of twenty thousand SA men, including one thousand armed SA men and five hundred armed SS men from the SA and SS-Reichsführerschulen. Hitler, Göring, Röhm, Wagner, and Siebert all gave speeches. The appearance of these armed formations excited the attention of the foreign press and diplomats. Plans to include the Landespolizei in the parade were cancelled "'out of regard for foreign susceptibilities.'"[31] As part of the celebrations, Hitler approved various promotions, including that of Du Moulin-Eckart to Brigadeführer. Earlier, on November 2, Röhm had appointed SS-Brigadeführer Robert Bergmann as his personal adjutant and Sturmbannführer Hans Erwin Graf von Spreti-Weilbach as his first adjutant.

Further celebrations followed for Röhm on November 27 and 28, to mark his forty-sixth birthday. The evening before his birthday, the Munich SA held a parade and tattoo in front of his residence at the Prinzregentenstrasse 7. The next day, the leaders of the SA and SS gathered to honor him at a reception there.[32]

By November, the British ambassador concluded that "the S.A. has not become superfluous, but for the moment it is not the power it was."[33] Hitler had offered foreign powers a German army of three hundred thousand men serving short-term, with defensive weapons only, if disarmament negotiations failed. This suggested that the SA might be sacrificed for foreign policy purposes.

In this context, Röhm's appointment as Minister without Portfolio on December 1, 1933, with an annual salary of RM 30,428.40, could be seen as an attempt to anchor him and the SA within the administrative apparatus.

Speaking to the Reichsstatthalter on September 28, Hitler had foreshadowed this, indicating that he planned to lead the party into the Reich power structure and was contemplating creating a SA ministry. Röhm's appointment was part of this wider process. Rudolf Hess was also made Minister without Portfolio, and the Nazi Party and SA were officially incorporated into the state. Röhm gave up his position as Bavarian State Secretary, though he remained State Commissioner for Particular Purposes, and therefore a member of the Ministerialrat. French Ambassador André François-Poncet was disturbed by Röhm's inclusion in the cabinet, and the possibility that this would confer official status on the SA. The British Foreign Office wanted the SA and SS incorporated into the army, and not continuing as separate organizations.[34]

In response to these concerns, Röhm gave a speech to the diplomatic corps in Berlin on Thursday, December 7, entitled "Why SA?" The speech was widely publicized both inside and outside Germany. In it, Röhm emphasized that the SA was a volunteer political organization and that it had nothing to do with the army. He claimed that no SA men were trained by the Reichswehr.[35]

"Throughout the delivery of the latter part of the lecture it was evident that Röhm's heart was not in his task . . . Röhm failed to relish his task of explaining that the S.A. were henceforth merely a political force."[36] Röhm complained to a British diplomat after the speech about the French attitude to his appointment as a Minister. It was only natural that the head of the SA should be a Cabinet Minister. The SA, he added, kept young men off the streets. Röhm scorned the foreign fear that the SA was militarily significant. "They were still a horde without any conception of what Prussian military discipline meant."[37] Röhm's comments, which were designed to allay British suspicions, also indicated the role he saw the SA playing in maintaining the regime.

On December 8, Hitler met the British Ambassador, Sir Eric Phipps, in the presence of Foreign Minister von Neurath. Describing Hitler as "less strained and more normal than usual,"[38] Phipps reported that Hitler's only outburst came when Phipps suggested the SA and SS be absorbed into a twenty thousand-man army. Hitler compared the SA and SS to the Salvation Army, to Phipps' laughter. Hitler claimed the SA and SS had no military function and he would allow periodic and automatic supervision of them to confirm this. Phipps considered Hitler's loss of composure to be unsurprising, as the SA and SS were indispensable to Hitler for internal reasons, and the regime would collapse if they were dissolved.

Röhm's public appearances decreased soon after he gave his speech to the Diplomatic Corps. On December 10, the Oberste SA-Führung announced he had influenza and had to be nursed at home. Subsequently, on December 13, it announced that he would be taking a three-week holiday to recover his health. On Thursday December 14, Röhm flew to Rome and then went by car to Naples and Capri for a short, private holiday. [39]

While Röhm was away, his mother celebrated her seventy-sixth birthday on December 15. Röhm's mother was publicized as the female influence in his life. An article written by "J. S.," presumably Josef Seydel, for the *Völkischer Beobachter*, wrote of her warm heart, her strong support for the Nazi struggle, and her interest in the SA, her son's life work. She had maintained her cozy living room throughout all her moves. An article in the *Münchner Illustrierte Presse* described Röhm's love of German Shepherd dogs, the closeness of his relations with his mother, the simplicity and good taste of his home, and his deep understanding of classical music. He held musical evenings at home. The same month, Renzetti characterized Röhm as follows: "Röhm is a soldier, an excellent organizer, loyal to Hitler; intelligent, possessing also considerable ambitions. He is sensitive and very susceptible: taken as you find him, he can be a good friend."[40] Röhm and Hitler were still close enough to attend a concert of the soprano Maria Müller together in Munich in late November.

By December 1933, Ernst Röhm was Minister without Portfolio in a government and society increasingly under Nazi control. Hitler recognized that Röhm and the SA had played a major part in ensuring this. At the end of the year, Hitler sent public letters of thanks to Nazi leaders for their role in the seizure of power. In his letter to Röhm, Hitler commented that when he appointed Röhm Chief of Staff, the SA had been in a serious crisis. Röhm had overcome this and made the SA strong enough to make the Nazi revolution possible—by the SA's consistent crushing of the Marxist terror. It was the SA's task to secure the state internally while the army secured it externally. Röhm echoed this in his New Year order for 1934, in which he called on the SA to be "the guarantor of the victory of the revolution and the emissary of their belief in Germany."[41]

While Röhm had achieved much, his future and that of the SA was unclear. The crushing of the parties of the left meant the SA's prime purpose had been realized. It had increased in size, bringing more men under the influence of Nazi ideology. While this increase, and the absorption of the Stahlhelm, had stabilized the regime, it had weakened the SA, and the continued absorption of disparate elements diminished the SA's standing in the community.

It was the SA's potential military role that most concerned other powers and the Reichswehr leadership. Initially, the Reichswehr leadership had been willing to give the SA training and use it as a supplementary force in border protection. Many SA officers, however, were found to be unsuitable for command. Rivalry with the SA encouraged the army to develop the idea of a conscript army under Reichswehr officers. By the end of December 1933, Hitler and Blomberg had agreed that universal military service would be introduced in 1935. Hitler had agreed with Blomberg that the Reichswehr had responsibility for all areas apart from premilitary training.[42]

It was not clear to the Reichswehr leadership whether Hitler could be relied on to hold to this if he came under sustained pressure from Röhm. Could the SA succeed in its claims to play a military role? This question would occupy Röhm and the rest of the leadership at the beginning of 1934.

CHAPTER 14

Crisis Approaches
January–June 1934

I was then, and I am now, firmly convinced that Röhm, for all his independence
of thought, was loyally devoted to Hitler and that he had planned no putsch.[1]

Hermann Esser

A t the beginning of 1934, the future of the SA and its relations with
the army remained unclear. The issue would become more acute
as the year progressed. The size of the SA remained a potential problem for German foreign policy. Röhm had adopted Hitler's guideline—that
the SA should carry through a revolution in the hearts and minds of the
Germans—but this proved inadequate to motivate and occupy the SA.

The SA leadership faced the problem of pressure for meaningful activity
and employment from the large numbers of men who had joined the SA and
were still joining. These problems found more sympathy in the Bavarian state
government than in the central government. The SA had not only absorbed
the Stahlhelm and men from other smaller paramilitary groups. It had also
gained members from men who joined to avoid political suspicion or persecution, who wanted to curry favor with the new regime, or who thought that
joining the SA would help them find a job. Even before the seizure of power,
Munich police had noted the unrealistic expectations held by many SA and
SS leaders and men of their future roles in a Nazi regime. Disappointment
at missing out on the gains of the National Socialist revolution and lack of
purposeful activity intensified SA indiscipline and rowdiness. The SA ideology, as expressed in Der SA-Mann, emphasized nationalism and the lessons of
the front experience more than völkisch racism.[2] As such, it provided an easy
mental transition from values more widely shared in German society to more
specifically National Socialist views.

Many of the SA men who had been members before January 30, 1933, had found political or other employment. The larger group of new recruits was less disciplined and less reliable. Their expectations were incapable of being fulfilled until a more general economic upturn began. Accordingly, Röhm and the SA leadership were concerned to ensure SA men were provided for in general employment policies.[3]

The size of the SA and its potential military use alarmed foreign powers. Since German rearmament was still in its initial secret stages, both Hitler and the military leadership took pains to allay fears on that score to halt any preventive attacks on Germany. Hitler had already made various offers to representatives of foreign powers that suggested a willingness to reduce the size of the SA or place it under international supervision.[4]

Röhm adopted a more public role in relations with foreign diplomats, seeking to overcome suspicions of the SA by direct contacts. He entertained, on a large scale, in his new residence in the Standartenstrasse in Berlin. Jüttner claimed later that Röhm also had repeated meetings with foreign military attachés in the winter of 1933–34 to reassure them about the SA. Röhm continued with his campaign to overcome foreign fears of any military role for the SA. In February, he met the French ambassador and, separately, the French military attaché. On Friday, February 23, he hosted a large dinner for the diplomatic corps, attended by Neurath, Blomberg, Phipps, U.S. ambassador Dodd, ten other ambassadors. and five military attachés.[5]

Röhm gave interviews to foreign correspondents in which he stressed that the SA's purpose was not military, but was to embody the ideology and will of the Nazi revolution and protect Germany against the internal Marxist enemy. Speaking to SA leaders at Friedrichsroda on January 20, 1934, Röhm told them that the SA remained revolutionary. It was the guarantor of the German revolution. He called on them to use all possible strength to build the nation and to create Hitler's people's community.[6]

Problems were emerging in the cooperation between the Reichswehr and SA on military training. Senior SA officers were not always up to the tasks set them by the military. Some in the SA blamed Krüger for the increasing difficulties in relations. Tensions between the Reichswehr and the SA over a delineation of their respective roles were discussed at Reichswehr senior officers' conferences in Stuttgart on January 15 and in Kassel on January 18. On January 18, Defense Minister Blomberg wrote to Röhm calling for all tensions between the two organizations to be removed.[7]

Röhm had contacts and sympathizers among younger army officers, particularly those from Bavaria. On January 24, on the anniversary of Frederick the Great's birthday, it was customary for a speech to be given at the

War Academy. In 1934, this honor fell to the young Bavarian officer Ritter und Edler von Xylander, one of Röhm's friends. Röhm arrived late, after the speech, perhaps intentionally. At the end of the speech, Xylander departed from his prepared text to praise the revolutionary attitude of the Prussian military leadership after 1806, and to call on the officers of 1934 to think in exactly the same revolutionary manner. The assembled senior officers were embarrassed. The next day, the army leadership called for a report on Xylander's speech, and at the end of the course, the War Academy commandant was replaced.[8]

Another officer recalled Röhm's arrival at the Reichswehr Ministry in January 1934 to speak:

> He appeared in civilian clothes. . . . He smelled considerably of scent. Despite certain off-putting characteristics, one could not deny however that Röhm had a certain "leader's charm." Clearly much wounded vanity played a role for him. Perhaps one could say that he would have been a different person if he had been awarded the Max-Josephs-Order in the First World War. The gap between the National Socialist and the representative of monarchist views was rather narrow in him.[9]

In May 1933, a British Embassy report on the Nazi leadership had characterized Röhm as "a notorious pervert and an unattractive character."[10] By January 1934, however, the British Consul General in Munich, Donald St. Clair Gainer, commented:

> In some ways Röhm is the most sympathetic figure, in spite of his personal moral reputation. He attends quietly and strictly to his duty, interferes little in politics and is an able soldier and administrator. He is not himself out for political aggrandizement.[11]

Röhm continued to attend official ceremonies and to play a prominent role as a leader of the regime. In February, he attended a dinner hosted by von Neurath for the visiting British politician, Anthony Eden, then Lord Privy Seal. Eden recalled that:

> Röhm, then very much a leading personality, was a more flamboyant figure, scarred and scented, with a jewelled dagger at his waist . . . he told me of his fighting experiences the world over, the last installments of which had been, if I recall correctly, in Bolivia. But he was not just a perverted swashbuckler, he had intelligence of a kind and, a rarity in the modern world, he was a man who boasted of his bravery, yet was brave. But he was hardly of the modern world; a *condottiere* of the Middle Ages might have looked and behaved like that.[12]

Outwardly, relations between the leadership of the SA and the army were cordial. On February 2, Blomberg held an all-male social evening, a *Herrenabend*, at his Berlin home, attended by senior army and police officers, and senior SA and SS leaders. Yet, the dispute between the two organizations came to a head in February. On February 1, 1934, Werner von Fritsch was appointed head of the army leadership. Fritsch supported a stronger stand by the army in defense of its own interests against the SA. In comments to a meeting of senior army commanders in Bonn on February 2 and 3, Blomberg indicated that attempts to reach an agreement with the SA had failed. The military leadership sought to reassure Hitler that they would be politically reliable servants of the new regime and that he therefore did not need to supplant them with the SA. In early February, the army leadership introduced a National Socialist insignia on army uniforms.[13]

On February 1, Röhm sent Blomberg a memorandum on the future relations between the Reichswehr and SA. The exact contents of Röhm's memorandum are unknown, as no copy of it appears to have survived. Knowledge of its contents comes from Blomberg, and it is possible that he exaggerated or distorted these for his own purposes. The military leadership claimed that Röhm made a bid for the SA to take over the army, with the professional skills of the existing officer corps being used in the capacity of General Staff officers, while SA commanders were rewarded with high rank. Writing after the war, Weichs claimed Röhm's comments were along the following lines:

> I consider the Reichswehr to be only still a training school for the German people. Waging war and therefore also mobilization will in future be the SA's responsibility.[14]

Those SA leaders who survived into the postwar period, and others close to Röhm in 1934, suggested instead that Röhm wanted the SA to form a separate militia army on Swiss lines for national defense. This would have been consistent with policy suggestions he had earlier made to Hitler in a March 1933 memorandum envisaging the SA forming the basis of a militia alongside the professional army. Some believed that he wanted this to be a parallel organization alongside the Reichswehr; others, that he wanted this to replace the Reichswehr. It is not clear either whether in his memorandum to Blomberg, Röhm was staking an ambit claim designed to pressure the army to concede more of a role in defense to the SA, whether the militia idea was a fallback position, or whether Röhm saw the militia as the first step toward an SA-dominated army.[15]

Two points should be noted in this context. Even if all that Röhm ever envisaged was that the SA should form the basis of a popular militia separate from a continuing Reichswehr, the Reichswehr leadership would have seen this as unacceptable. A militia based on the SA would still be a competitor for arms and other resources as Germany rearmed, and a political and military rival. In the 1850s, the Prussian army had seen off a potential contender along these lines in the Landwehr. Secondly, like the foreign policy conceptions he had Bell outline in 1931, Röhm's concept of a militia army was innately conservative. It would be an army of defense rather than offense.

Blomberg countered Röhm's memorandum with his own proposals. Again, no copy of these appears to have survived, but their gist can be reconstructed from Krüger's comments on them. Blomberg proposed that the SA should only have charge of premilitary training, military training of those capable of military service who were not in the army, and maintenance of the military capacity of former soldiers and those who had not served.[16]

Hitler was forced to intervene on February 28, calling a meeting of the heads of the Reichswehr, SA, and SS, and Göring in the Reichswehr Ministry headquarters in the Bendlerstrasse. In his speech to this meeting, Hitler clearly rejected Röhm's plans to form an SA militia. He had decided, instead, for a mass army to be created from the Reichswehr and based on the model of the pre-1914 army. A militia would not be adequate for national defense. The SA, therefore, had to restrict itself to political tasks. In the period of transition to the creation of a mass army, Hitler agreed with Blomberg that the SA would be called on for border protection and premilitary training. Hitler then spoke of Germany's need for living space and to strike decisive blows to its east and west. The army had to be ready for defense in five years and offensive action in eight years. In this speech, Hitler decisively put an end to Röhm's plans for a strong military role for the SA. It is not clear what he had in mind for the SA.[17]

The military leaders were satisfied. They saw Hitler's comments as signaling a crucial success over the claims of the SA. The same day, they made public their intention of introducing the "Aryan paragraph"—the legal provision requiring Aryan descent of officials—into the Reichswehr.[18]

After the meeting, Röhm invited all present to breakfast at his residence in the Standartenstrasse. Hitler did not attend. "The meal was good, the atmosphere was frosty."[19] After the military leaders left, Röhm criticized Hitler's decision to the SA and SS leaders. Viktor Lutze claimed later that Röhm had told the assembled leaders that Hitler's speech had no validity for him, and that if he could not reach his goals with Hitler, he would carry them through against Hitler. Lutze saw these comments as disloyal and reported them first to Rudolf Hess, and then when Hess refused to get involved, to Hitler, personally. Hitler reportedly told Lutze to let things ripen.

Röhm's comments in his anger at being checked so publicly were later interpreted by both Hitler and Lutze as evidence of his disloyal intentions. They may rather have been Röhm venting his anger and frustration, letting off steam at the rejection of his plans. As a Nazi of the first hour, he may have felt he could express his frustration about Hitler more freely than Lutze thought fitting. Within a week, Sir Eric Phipps was commenting of Röhm, when they met at dinner, that Röhm's "joviality seemed dimmed, and he conveyed to me an 'after the ball' impression,"[20] an allusion to the chorus of the popular song of the 1890s, "After the Ball": "Many the hopes that have vanish'd, after the ball."[21]

Röhm gave other indications that his comments had been rhetorical. On March 12, he issued service instructions for SA inspectors. These instructions indicated that defense preparations and national defense were the responsibility of the Defense Minister, whose directives were binding not only for the regional military authorities but also for the SA. Röhm directed the SA inspectors to secure "*frictionless cooperation*"[22] between the SA and the Reichswehr. Röhm succeeded in persuading Hitler to seek positions for SA leaders as Reichswehr officers, but this was rejected by Hindenburg. Hitler continued to use Finance Minister Schwerin-Krosigk to refuse to pay Röhm the large sums of money he asked for to equip the SA, sums that Röhm was able to persuade Hitler to agree to when the two men met alone.

As part of the continuing efforts to increase SA discipline, Röhm gained Hitler's approval in March to set up a separate SA tribunal to punish SA men who had committed serious offenses against discipline and order. The SA leadership saw this as a positive step, but it may have had the opposite effect. By removing SA discipline from any external control, it meant that critics of SA excesses were led to a clash with the entire organization.[23]

The Bavarian government supported Röhm's moves to set up special SA and SS courts, which they saw as designed to deal with disciplinary matters only, and not with offenses under the penal code. More than the Reich Government, the Bavarian government appeared to have understood the pressures on Röhm and the SA leadership from below. It also continued to back SA plans to set up a Bavarian *Feldjägerkorps*, a military police-style unit for the SA, partly as a means of policing the "militarily splendidly equipped"[24] Austrian Legion of the SA, which now numbered about eight thousand to ten thousand men, and whose border violations continued to be a problem for German-Austrian relations.

In March, Röhm had participated in a piece of political theatre that had probably been organized with the head of the Berlin SA, Karl Ernst, and Propaganda Minister Goebbels. The British film *Catherine the Great*, starring the Austrian actress of Jewish origin, Elisabeth Bergner, had its German premiere on March 8. It took place three days after Goebbels had announced that non-Aryans, whom he had banned from German theaters, had been reappearing. Goebbels had "requested" German authorities to prevent such lawbreaking and warned that if the request was ignored, the German public might take action itself. Rioters outside the premiere theatres, including Berlin SA men, shouted anti-Semitic slogans, threw eggs at posters in the lobby, and harassed cinema-goers, who had to be escorted into the theater. While Karl Ernst assured the demonstrators outside the cinema that the film would be banned, inside, Röhm took the stage at the premiere, said he was speaking for Hitler, and called on the audiences to remember that Germany was a land of law and order. The next day the film was withdrawn from distribution in Germany.[25] Such a demonstration would not have taken place without official collusion. Röhm's intervention was most likely, therefore, prearranged with Goebbels and Ernst.

Röhm spent early April abroad. He was not the only Nazi leader to travel in the spring of 1934. In May, Göring paid a private visit to Yugoslavia and Greece. Accompanied by an entourage of nine, including Bergmann, Reiner, and Krausser, Röhm spent Easter 1934 in Brioni in Italy. He then flew to Dubrovnik in Yugoslavia for a private holiday. He received an enthusiastic reception from Yugoslav officials and the local population. The visit was extensively covered in the press there and was seen by both Yugoslav and foreign observers as a sign of a Yugoslav desire for closer relations with Germany. [26]

Interviewed by the Yugoslav paper *Politika*, Röhm commented that the German revolution was not yet over because it required a complete spiritual change in the entire German people. They had to set materialism aside and create new economic and social conditions. The Reich's international position would improve as the world realized that National Socialism was not imperialist. Röhm returned to Munich by air via Venice on the evening of April 11.[27]

Röhm and Hitler appear to have met at the beginning of April. Further signs that Röhm was pulling back the SA's public profile came in early April, when the Party Treasurer, Xavier Schwarz, announced that the SA spring parade, planned for Berlin in May, would not now take place. The day after Röhm returned to Munich, he issued an order to the SA indicating that all SA officers and men would be sent on leave in July to allow them relaxation and time with their families. Participants in courses due to be run in July would get August off instead. The move appears to have arisen from the Röhm-Hitler meeting at the beginning of the month as a means of easing tension.[28]

Röhm continued with his round of public engagements. He and his staff were guests of honor at an official dinner given by the Italian ambassador, Vittorio Cerruti. The ambassador's wife, Elisabetta Cerruti, recalled that Röhm "was an extremely ugly man but the only Nazi of high rank with good manners; the others were all, without exception, boors."[29] Röhm told her at the meal that he was planning to leave Berlin for a holiday to cure the neuritis he had in his right hand. He had needed two injections to attend the dinner. "Throughout the whole meal he spoke of his devotion for the Führer and was so overcome with emotion that at the *poulet à La Richelieu* tears came to his eyes."[30] At this time, Röhm was seriously ill with heart problems, neuralgia, and complications from his nose wound.

On April 14, Röhm, Neurath, and Reich Justice Commissioner Hans Frank attended the annual meeting of the Society of the Friends of the Ibero-American Institute at the Hotel Atlantik in Hamburg. Röhm spoke in Spanish, praising the ardent patriotism of Latin Americans and their sympathy for Germany. The next day, he and Hermann Göring were witnesses at the wedding of Berlin SA Gruppenführer Karl Ernst and Minnes Wolff. On April 17, he attended a large SS concert in the Sportspalast in Berlin with Hitler, Papen, Blomberg, and Goebbels.[31]

The next day, Röhm gave his second major speech to the diplomatic corps in Berlin on the role of the SA. He presented the SA as designed to win the hearts and minds of German men for National Socialism rather than a military organization. It served to protect Germany at home and ensure that Marxism could not revive.[32]

To keep the SA occupied, Röhm held a large variety of exercises and inspections. On March 17 and 18, he attended a SA parade in Essen, and on March 24 and 25, the Gruppe Sachsen parade in Dresden. In the second half of April, from Weinheim, he made a trip in the Odenwald area, described as an exercise journey with SA leaders to assess the participating officers. In spring, he conducted a series of inspections: on May 7 and 8 in Regensburg, inspecting the SA-Gruppe Bayerische Ostmark; from May 12 to 14, inspecting Gruppe Franken in Franconia; on May 25 in Stettin; and from May 26 to 28, he carried out inspections in the area of Gruppe Pommern, and then on May 29 in Schneidemühl.[33] These inspection tours, which were motivated by the need to keep the SA busy, were later interpreted as sinister attempts to prepare the SA for a putsch. A personality cult of Röhm also developed in the SA as a means of binding the organization together.

Before he left for this series of inspections, Röhm had spent the weekend of May 5 and 6 in Ingolstadt. In June 1933, the Ingolstadt Town Council had bestowed honorary citizenship on Hindenburg, Hitler, Epp, and Röhm. Röhm was the only recipient who chose to accept it in person, on the

"Ingolstadt Day" on Sunday May 6. After June 30, 1934, in Ingolstadt, it was rumored that Hitler visited the town secretly on this day and took fright at Röhm's ambitions as shown at the celebrations. There is no evidence for this, nor would Röhm's comments at the ceremonies have given rise to any concern about his disloyalty. On May 6, Röhm was enthusiastically greeted with much ceremony, including SA parades and tattoos, and a reunion of his war time comrades from the tenth company of the Tenth Infantry Regiment, whose costs were paid by the council. Röhm also visited a number of Ingolstadt families that he knew. In his various speeches in Ingolstadt, Röhm stressed a strong and united Germany and the need "to work further according to Adolf Hitler's wishes, for we stand today first at the beginning of the German revolution."[34] Röhm spoke of the revolution continuing, of overcoming barriers of class and estate, of the National Socialist people's community, but never of a second or social revolution. His political ideas were far from socialist.

Between his inspections in Franconia and Pomerania, Röhm returned to Berlin. On Thursday May 17, he gave a reception in Berlin for various ambassadors and military attachés, which was also attended by Blomberg and Fritsch. One army officer who attended described the SA leaders present as very arrogant and showing little respect for Fritsch. Röhm spent Pentecost at an estate in Gross-Wuttige near Ratenau with his mother, his sister-in-law, Rolf Reiner, and SS-Sturmbannführer Scholz. Röhm did not feel well and complained of neuralgic pains in his right arm. "He could barely even raise his arm."[35] On May 24, Röhm met the French Ambassador, André François-Poncet, for dinner. According to François-Poncet, Röhm "looked absent-minded and ill, and mentioned that he had had to have medical treatment for neuritis."[36] Röhm's illness was genuine rather than feigned, though there may have been a psychological element in his illnesses, for his health tended to break down at times of personal and political stress.

Cooperation between the Reichswehr and the SA, particularly the training section under Krüger, continued. The aim was to have 240,000 men ready for the army and 7,300 for the navy by October 1935. Considerable care was taken to conceal this. Yet, distrust grew. On April 21, and again on May 7, Fritsch called on commanders to report any SA breaches of their agreement on cooperation. Röhm's alleged continued efforts to arm the SA also alarmed the Reichswehr. This may again have been a result of mutual suspicion. Jüttner claimed that Blomberg and Reichenau saw SA arming done at the request of other sections of the Reichswehr, such as in the Rhineland, as suspicious.[37] Röhm may have feared the Reichswehr was working against the SA and believed the SA needed the weapons to defend the revolution.

The sense that the SA was being outmaneuvered and pushed to the sidelines, and the growing political tensions in 1934 led some SA leaders and men to indulge in aggressive rhetoric about the need for a second revolution, a revolution that would sweep aside the last remnants of political reaction. This bluster was a product of their sense that they were losing out in a subterranean power struggle. The lack of a specific SA intelligence system meant that the leadership was blind to the nature of the moves against it. Röhm issued an order that each SA office should start to collect information on hostility against the SA. The time could come when this material was needed. "Röhm had completely isolated himself."[38] He also began to sense that the political tide was turning against him. In May, he told Bergmann that he had the feeling forces were at work that wanted him out of the way. If this were the case, he would return to Bolivia, and Bergmann could accompany him.

On May 29, Foreign Minister Neurath told the British ambassador that Hitler had given orders that all SA military exercises should cease. The Reichswehr and Hindenburg believed that the French and British governments would be more likely to accept a 300,000-man army and other defensive requirements if the SA were to disappear. Hitler was inclined to agree, hence his consideration of not recalling most of the SA after their July leave. Röhm's response, according to Neurath, was that Hitler was putting his head in a noose if he put his future in the hands of the Reichswehr before the army had really been Nazified.[39] Neurath's comments indicated that Hitler was not only holding firm on his decision that the Reichswehr leadership would have sole responsibility for the expanded German army, but also that he had decided that the role of the SA overall would diminish.

On June 4, Röhm and Hitler met in Berlin in a meeting that lasted four hours. After the war, Papen's adjutant, Fritz Günther von Tschirschky, claimed to have heard Röhm yelling at Hitler during the meeting, but neither Hitler himself nor Röhm described the meeting as heated. By Hitler's own testimony, Röhm agreed to stop any activity that might give rise to suspicion.[40] The purpose of the meeting was unclear. Did Hitler hope to provoke Röhm into action? Was he seeking to lull Röhm and the SA leadership into a false sense of security? Did Hitler persuade Röhm that he and the SA needed to take a temporary back seat to ease Hitler's internal and foreign policy difficulties? We only have Hitler's word for what happened at the meeting: we cannot know what he actually told Röhm.

We do know Röhm's response. On June 8, he issued an announcement to the SA that he was on leave to recover his health and that Ritter von Krausser would act in his place in June. Röhm's order was full of bluster, warning the SA's enemies that his leave and that of the entire SA in July did not mean that they would not return stronger than ever. The fact that Röhm's order was not signed "Heil Hitler" was neither unusual nor a sign of disloyalty. Internal SA orders, which Röhm modeled on military orders, never used "Heil Hitler,"[41]

Röhm left for the small Bavarian resort of Bad Wiessee to undertake an iodine cure. He did not seem to have any inkling of the danger he faced. Did Hitler's long unstinting support of him from 1931 to 1933 leave him too trusting of Hitler's friendship? Röhm stayed under medical care at the Pension Hanselbauer by the shores of the Tegernsee until June 30, accompanied by a small entourage of his friends. As in 1925 and 1932, Röhm's ill health was aggravated by the stress he was under. He had "many heart complaints and suffered from neuralgia."[42] Elisabetta Cerruti remembered his being treated for neuritis; Phipps believed Röhm was "suffering . . . from rheumatism accentuated by over-indulgence in food and drink and his irregular mode of life."[43]

Röhm spent his time in Bad Wiessee quietly walking and taking the baths. The local SA was instructed to take no notice of him. Reports that Hitler attempted unsuccessfully to visit Röhm in Bad Wiessee on June 25, calling in unannounced, must be regarded as not proven. On June 26, Schreyer visited, and on June 28, Bergmann arrived and was invited by Röhm to stay on. On June 28, while Epp and his SA adjutant Prinz von Ysenburg were visiting, Hitler called Röhm from Essen. Hitler was angry about a reported SA attack on a foreign diplomat in the Rhineland, and asked Röhm to call a conference of SA leaders in Bad Wiessee on Saturday, June 30. Röhm was pleased at the prospect of seeing Hitler, of being able to discuss his complaints face-to-face, and told Epp he would use the meeting to unmask Goebbels' intrigues. Röhm's heart complaint had intensified, and before Epp and Ysenburg left, the SA doctor Emil Ketterer gave Röhm an injection to make sure he slept.[44]

Friday June 29 passed quietly. Röhm and Bergmann went for a bath at the spa, and in the afternoon, took a long walk to Bad Kreuth. Bergmann remembered Röhm as preoccupied with his thoughts. That night they played Tarock, a game played with tarot cards. Martin Schätzl, now a SA-Obertruppführer, brought Röhm's uniform from his Munich residence, and some SA leaders, including Edmund Heines, arrived for the next day's meeting. Heines was concerned that the SA and Reichswehr were being encouraged into mutual suspicion by an unknown third party, and he may have raised his concerns with Röhm. The party had an early night in preparation for the meeting the next day. Röhm was "completely calm."[45]

CHAPTER 15

The Revolution Devours Its Children
June 30–July 2, 1934

Between 6:00 a.m. and 6:30 a.m. on the morning of Saturday, June 30, 1934, Hitler and his entourage arrived unexpectedly in Bad Wiessee while the guests of the Pension Hanselbauer slept and the staff began their preparations for the SA leaders' conference later that morning. Five cars carried Hitler, Propaganda Minister Josef Goebbels, SS-Gruppenführer Sepp Dietrich, Hitler's adjutants Schaub and Brückner, and about twenty-five SS men. Lutze and two SA men had arrived earlier. Hitler, accompanied by his driver, Julius Schreck, and a Munich detective, Kriminalkommissar Schmidbauer, was the first to enter the hotel and Röhm's room on the first floor of the hotel. Hitler had the hotel's headwaiter knock on the door of Room 31, Röhm's bedroom. Hitler greeted Röhm with "Röhm! You are arrested!"[1] As Hitler accused Röhm of treason, Röhm, who had opened the door himself, protested his innocence. Soon after, a witness observed that "Röhm sat completely consternated in his pyjamas at the edge of the bed."[2] Hitler left Röhm to dress himself and be led down into the foyer by two detectives.

Hitler tore Bergmann's insignia from his SS tunic, as he and the SA leaders in the hotel were arrested. Nazi accounts claimed that Heines was found in bed with a male companion. Some twelve men, including Heines, Bergmann, Schätzl, and Uhl, were temporarily imprisoned in the hotel's linen room. Röhm was left sitting in the hall between two guards, and eventually accepted a cup of coffee from Mrs. Hanselbauer, the wife of the proprietor. According to Mabire, when greeted by the SA doctor Ketterer with "*Heil Hitler*," Röhm responded with the traditional Bavarian greeting of "*Grüss Gott*." By 7:00 a.m., the prisoners other than Röhm were led to a coach that had been ordered to transport them to Stadelheim prison in Munich. Both Röhm and Hitler had served short terms of imprisonment there during the

Weimar Republic. Röhm's bodyguard had been commanded to Bad Wiessee to provide security for the meeting of senior SA leaders with Hitler. When they arrived, Hitler told them he had personally taken over SA leadership for the day and added that he knew he could rely on them. They responded with enthusiastic shouts of "Heil" and returned to Munich on Hitler's orders. Röhm was driven to Stadelheim with Hitler's entourage.[3]

The first SA prisoners to arrive at Stadelheim on June 30 were those arrested in Munich—Munich SA leaders August Schneidhuber and Wilhelm Schmid. Other senior SA leaders heading for the conference were seized as they arrived at Munich railway station (Manfred von Killinger and Georg Detten) at 7:30 a.m. At 10:45 a.m., seven further prisoners arrived (Ritter von Krausser, Schragmüller, Hayn, Falkenhausen, Spreti, Egger, and Vollner). The thirteen prisoners conveyed from Bad Wiessee, including Röhm, Heines, Bergmann, Uhl, Schätzl and Röhm's driver, König, were admitted at 11:00 a.m. Röhm was entered as prisoner 4034 and held in cell 474. Some sources claimed that this was the same cell he occupied in 1923.[4]

Meanwhile, Hitler and his entourage went to the party headquarters in Munich, the Braunes Haus. There, toward midday in the so-called Senatorial room, Hitler gave a twenty-minute speech to assembled SA and SS leaders, some of whom would later be imprisoned. Hitler told them that Röhm had planned a putsch against him and the Reichswehr, and therefore, Hitler had had him arrested. All participating SA leaders would be shot. According to Schreyer, Hitler described Röhm's act as "the greatest disloyalty in world history . . . Röhm, to whom he had always been loyal in all difficulties, had committed high and national treason toward him in that he wanted to arrest him and have him killed in order to deliver Germany to its enemies."[5] That evening, a party press statement announced that Hitler had removed Röhm from his position as Chief of Staff, expelled him from the NSDAP and SA, and appointed Obergruppenführer Viktor Lutze in his place.

The regime's difficulties in the spring and summer of 1934 and the question of the future role of the SA in the Third Reich had come together in a crisis that was resolved by the purge of the SA leadership. While Röhm had been spending June quietly in Bad Wiessee, the "crisis of the regime" had reached its peak. Hitler, characteristically, had delayed taking decisions until this point, and then resolved the situation by striking out under pressure from Hindenburg, the army leadership, and possibly Göring and Himmler.[6]

As spring 1934 drew to a close, the political position of the regime was under strain. Unemployment was still high, there was little sign of economic recovery, and the population was restive under the restrictions of dictatorship. The regime's response was to launch a large-scale propaganda campaign against its critics, whom it labeled as "alarmists and carpers" and "faultfinders."[7]

Both Hermann Göring and the army leadership had been collecting evidence of SA lack of cooperation and indiscipline for months. In his moves against the SA, Göring had been willing to concede more power to Reichsführer-SS Heinrich Himmler and Reinhard Heydrich. In April 1934, he had transferred to Himmler the Secret Police Office (*Geheimes Staatspolizeiamt*— Gestapa) that he had created in 1933. By early June, the SS in Munich was preparing lists of those to be arrested.[8]

The army leadership was simultaneously putting pressure on Hitler to remove any threat to them from the SA and moving to reassure him that the army could be relied on politically. The introduction of the "Aryan paragraph" and Nazi insignia on uniforms were followed by the introduction of ideological education in National Socialist values into the military. Bennecke believed that Krüger also intensified the Reichswehr's suspicions of the SA to strengthen his own position rather than seeking to reduce them.[9]

Army support was critical as other developments threatened the stability of the regime. Hindenburg's health was failing. In early June, he left Berlin for his East Prussian estate at Neudeck. Hitler was advised that Hindenburg's health was such that he would not return. A new president could be a check on the power of the regime. Some in Papen's office were seeking to revive the failed tactic of "taming" Hitler. They hoped to gain army support for a restoration of the monarchy, either directly, or by appointing one of the Royal princes as a regent. They sounded out senior army commanders and von Hindenburg's son Oskar.[10]

On June 18, Papen made the crisis more acute when he gave a speech at Marburg University in which he criticized various excesses of the regime. The speech had been written by Edgar Jung, a conservative intellectual in Papen's office. The regime banned publication of the speech by the press, but the text had already been published in the *Frankfurter Zeitung*. On June 19, Papen met Hitler and protested the banning of his speech by Goebbels. He threatened to go to Hindenburg with his resignation. Hitler pacified von Papen and hastened to Neudeck on June 21 to see Hindenburg on his own. There, Hitler was met by Blomberg. At this meeting, Hindenburg and Blomberg were believed to have put more pressure on Hitler to act against the SA.[11]

Both the army leadership and the conservatives around Papen were opponents rather than supporters of Röhm. Was Hitler led to believe that Röhm might have been willing to support the restoration of the monarchy, possibly with the SA officer "Auwi," Prince August Wilhelm of Prussia, the Kaiser's fourth son, as Regent? At least one of his later justifications of his actions suggested this.[12]

Hitler was already contemplating Röhm's dismissal as Chief of Staff. Röhm's ill health, the reason for his leave, could have been used to justify this. Probably on June 19, Hitler told Lutze to follow his orders only and indicated to Lutze that he intended to replace Röhm. Other observers were also expecting Röhm's dismissal when his leave ended.[13]

The decision that this removal would be by force was not taken until the final week of June. On Saturday, June 23, Fritsch ordered all army commands to a state of heightened readiness. The next day, he warned the commander in Breslau, Generalleutnant von Kleist, of a possible SA attack. That same day, Himmler began his preparations for the purge.[14]

Various senior military leaders were shown a "death list" allegedly prepared by Röhm or those close to him. In reality, the only death lists being prepared were by the SS. An inbuilt time pressure was now operating. Those who wanted the SA removed forcefully had to act before July 1, when the SA went on leave. It would be hard, after that date, to characterize the organization as an imminent threat. Röhm's office expected him to remain on leave in July, since they declined a dinner invitation by the U.S. ambassador for July for this reason.[15]

While Röhm continued to recover his health in Bad Wiessee, Edgar Jung was arrested in Berlin on June 25. The same day, Rudolf Hess gave a speech in the anti-grumbler campaign in which he also warned Nazis not to think that they knew better than Hitler how to make a revolution. This was later interpreted as being a warning to Röhm. On June 26, army commanders were shown an alleged order from Röhm, ordering the illegal arming of SA groups. No copies of this order survived.[16]

On Thursday June 28, Hitler left Berlin with Göring for the Rhineland to attend the wedding of Gauleiter Terboven in Essen. That day, Fritsch ordered all barracks to hold emergency ammunition ready. The Defense Ministry agreed to give the SS access to army weapons. From Essen, Hitler called Röhm to ask for a meeting of senior SA commanders on June 30. Hindenburg's health was such that Fritsch found, when he visited him in Neudeck on June 28, he could discuss nothing of substance. Oskar von Hindenburg told Papen, Bose, and Tschirschky that his father was too ill to become involved in any planning for the succession.[17]

The SA in Silesia had been alerted to the claims that they were planning a putsch by the statements of Reichswehr officers, and Edmund Heines had been informed. Heines commented that "it was an old putschist trick"[18] to accuse the other side of what one was planning oneself. In Breslau, the local army commander Generalleutnant von Kleist called Heines in for talks. Observing army activities around his SA headquarters, Heines had ordered defensive measures. Kleist had seen these as suspicious and had, in turn, taken countermeasures. Heines assured Kleist that he and the SA had no plans to move against the army. Earlier, on June 26, Berlin SA commander Karl Ernst had called on Landespolizei head Kurt Daluege to assure him the SA was not planning a putsch. Heines had also warned Göring of an imminent Reichswehr putsch led by Fritsch and had received assurances from Göring that there was no need for concern.

In the course of their conversation, both Kleist and Heines realized that they had been the victims of mutual distrust of each other's motives. Both men suspected that these suspicions had been fomented by other parties. On the night of June 28–29, Heines telephoned Kleist to say that his enquiries had revealed that the same process was under way across Germany. Heines and Kleist not only relaxed their countermeasures, but decided to bring their realization to the attention of their superiors. Heines may have raised the process with Röhm when he arrived in Bad Wiessee on June 29, and Kleist reported to Fritsch in Berlin the same day.[19]

Another senior officer later suggested that Heines' word of honor that he and the SA were not planning a putsch was worthless, and Kleist would not have believed it. Yet, Heines clearly did convince Kleist that he was genuine. When Kleist reported to Fritsch and Beck, Fritsch had him repeat his comments to Reichenau. Reichenau answered, "'that may well be right, but it is too late now.'"[20] While many army officers may have sincerely believed they faced a genuine threat from the SA, Blomberg, Fritsch, and Reichenau were consciously moving to remove the SA as a power factor and were aware that any danger the organization presented was past. On June 29, the *Völkischer Beobachter* published an article by Blomberg on the role of the Reichswehr in the National Socialist state. This was Blomberg's first ever article for the *Völkischer Beobachter* and a conscious signal of the alliance between the army leadership and the regime. In the article, Blomberg proclaimed Hitler to be "one of us" as a former soldier in the Bavarian Army and Reichswehr.[21]

Various steps were taken to ensure tensions did not relax. New alleged SA murder lists appeared that reached down the ranks of officers. An unnamed "SA officer" appeared at the headquarters of Wehrkreiskommando VI and claimed the SA would be taking over the building. Finally, on the evening of June 29–30, the SA in Munich and Stuttgart were brought onto the streets by mysterious orders informing them Hitler was against them. The Munich SA was sent back to their quarters by a SA officer who told them to obey Hitler even if he disarmed them. The Munich SA commanders Schmid and Schneidhuber were able to prove to Interior Minister Wagner, in the course of the evening, not only that they had not issued these orders but also that they had countermanded them. The written proofs they provided to Wagner subsequently vanished.[22]

It has been suggested that this last minute "evidence" may also have been intended to force a wavering Hitler to act. Hitler had told Lutze he would replace Röhm; he had told Blomberg at Neudeck he would arrest Röhm. Yet, on June 27, he allegedly told Ritter von Krausser that he would be keeping Röhm in his position and would overcome all differences and misunderstandings with the SA leadership. This last statement may have been a maneuver to keep the SA leadership unwary. By the end of June, the SA was largely leaderless and defenseless.[23]

"Evidence" that Röhm was conspiring with a foreign power to overthrow him was brought to Hitler late on the evening of June 29. Hitler flew to Munich in the early hours of the next day, where he met with Bavarian Interior Minister Adolf Wagner, senior army officers, and the police before setting off for Bad Wiessee. Across the country, SS and police units moved to arrest SA leaders. The move against the SA was simultaneously a move against the conservative opposition—Herbert von Bose was killed in Papen's office, and Papen himself narrowly escaped death—a move against political rivals (Schleicher, Gregor Strasser), an opportunity to settle personal feuds (Bernhard Stempfle), and to seek revenge against old enemies (Gustav von Kahr). The killings centered on Berlin, Munich, and Breslau. Men who had personal and political links to Röhm were particularly vulnerable. Both Crown Prince Rupprecht, who left the country for a visit to Britain before SS attempts to stop him could succeed, and General von Lossow, who was advised to lie low, may have been warned by army officers.[24]

When Bavarian Minister Hermann Esser went to the Braunes Haus to find out what was going on on June 30, he found Epp and Bavarian Minister President Siebert sitting in the mess in a depressed mood. While they sat there, Christian Weber, Viktor Brack, Julius Schaub, and various SS officers appeared. "They reminded General von Epp and me in an insulting manner of our friendly relations with Röhm, whereupon they stated in an unmistakable way that they also knew to strike at Röhm's friends and backers."[25] Esser and Epp left the "extremely unpleasant atmosphere"[26] of the Braunes Haus as soon as possible.

Epp had already had a long and heated conversation with Hitler about the arrests earlier in the morning, from which Hitler emerged with his face mottled with anger. Epp was the only Nazi leader with the courage to intervene with Hitler in an attempt to save lives. Either at this meeting or later in the day, when he farewelled Hitler at the airport at 6:00 p.m., Epp gained Hitler's promise that he would spare Röhm and Krausser's lives. Hitler stated that he would spare Röhm because of his services to the movement, and Krausser on account of his order (the MMJO). Other accounts reported Hitler as saying he would spare Röhm's life for the sake of Röhm's aged mother.[27]

Toward 5:00 p.m. on June 30, a SS-Gruppenführer appeared in the office of the Stadelheim prison director, Dr. Koch, and enquired about a place in the prison suitable to execute some of the SA prisoners. Over an hour later, Sepp Dietrich appeared with an SS execution squad and gave Koch a typed list signed by Wagner on which, at the airport, Hitler had marked with a pencil stroke the names of the six men to be put to death immediately. Koch held up the executions until Bavarian Justice Minister Hans Frank arrived with two officials. Frank intended to give the condemned men the semblance of a hearing, and had his friend Schneidhuber brought to him. Schneidhuber protested his innocence energetically, demanded to speak to Hitler, and could not believe that Hitler had ordered the execution. Frank abandoned his efforts, probably recognizing that each condemned man would react similarly. He ordered Koch to hand the men over to Dietrich.[28]

Frank claimed, in his memoirs, to have visited Röhm in his cell at this time. He reported that he found Röhm resigned and philosophical, quoting the saying that "every revolution devours its children."[29] Frank may have invented his account of this meeting, as he was probably not in the prison long enough to have met Röhm.

Whether he saw Frank or not, like other prisoners, Röhm heard the shots of the SS execution squads in the evening of June 30. Six men were killed that night at Stadelheim—Heydebreck, Schneidhuber, Hayn, Heines, Spreti, and Schmid. Schneidhuber, Heines, Spreti, and Schmid, in particular, had to be killed immediately: Schneidhuber and Schmid could have proved the Munich SA were not called onto the streets by their leaders; Heines could prove that he had attempted to remove the atmosphere of mutual suspicion and allay the army's concerns; Spreti could prove that he had assured the conservatives around von Papen that the SA leadership had no putsch plans.[30]

At 7:30 p.m., the six men were brought into the prison yard, escorted by two Landespolizei men each. They were lined up opposite the church. Koch read out their names, they answered to them, and Koch then told them they were being handed over to Dietrich on Hitler's order. Dietrich then stepped forward to the prisoners and told them "'The Führer has sentenced you to death! Heil Hitler!'"[31] The execution squad of one SS officer and fourteen men assembled in the so-called exercise yard of the old building, separated by a wall from the church yard. The men wrote hasty messages to their families on pieces of paper torn out of notebooks.

Then, one by one, each SA leader was brought to the execution yard, placed against the wall next to the dissection room, and shot. Heydebreck was shot first, then Schneidhuber, who pushed himself out of the row of prisoners. Schneidhuber was still protesting his innocence as the orders to shoot were given. Heines, too, tried to speak as he was shot. One or two of those shot were given a coup de grâce by the officer in command. Each execution took about twenty minutes and then the corpse was brought to the dissection room. Toward midnight, the dead men were buried in the nearby cemetery at Perlacher Forst.[32]

In the morning of June 30, Emilie Röhm may have rung Röhm's friend, Karl Zehnter, the landlord of the "Nurnberger Bratwurstglöckl," in an effort to find out what was happening. Zehnter visited Mrs. Röhm that day before he himself was arrested and killed. Epp's sister, Marie Epp, visited Röhm's mother and sister on July 1.[33]

Shootings of prisoners continued on June 30 and July 1, particularly in Berlin and Breslau. In Berlin, Göring and Himmler had persuaded Hitler, by late on July 1, to break his promise to Epp, and had overcome Hitler's reluctance to order Röhm's execution. On Sunday, July 1, Röhm had breakfast and a midday meal in his cell. He had asked to speak to Hitler and to see his sister, as Lore Lippert learned at the prison later when she visited Röhm's cell. Between 2:00 and 3:00 p.m. on July 1, the prisoners were let out of their cells to take exercise in the prison yard. Röhm tried to cheer up his twenty-five fellow SA prisoners by making jokes as they walked along. His efforts were unsuccessful, as the other men knew what they faced. Bergmann recalled that he had mimed to Röhm a question whether Röhm knew what was going on, and Röhm had mimed back that he did not.[34]

At about 5:00 p.m. on Sunday, the prisoners were served supper in their cells. Röhm had paid for bread, sausage, and beer with his own money. In addition, he asked for writing paper to write to his mother. He was under constant surveillance, with extra Landespolizei stationed near his cell, with orders to shoot him immediately if the SA attacked the prison to free him. At this time, SS-Obergruppenführer Schmauser, the leader of the SS-Oberabschnitt-Süd, SS-Brigadeführer Theodor Eicke, then commandant of the concentration camp at Dachau, and SS-Sturmbannführer Michael Lippert appeared at the prison gate and demanded entry to Röhm's cell. Taken to Koch's office, Eicke told Koch he had a direct order from Hitler for access to the cell, though he could produce no written evidence; Koch responded that he had strict orders from Frank not to allow any access to the cell. Eicke gave his word of honor that Hitler had deputized him personally to give Röhm a loaded revolver with the order to shoot himself in ten minutes. If Röhm did not comply then Eicke had to shoot him.[35]

After a shouting match on the phone between Frank and Eicke, and assurances from the Bavarian Political Police that he could rely on Eicke's word of honor, during which an hour had passed, Koch finally allowed prison administrator Karl Lechler to give the three men access to Röhm's cell. Toward 6:00 p.m., Lechler led the men to Röhm's cell. Because of the extra guards, and the curiosity of the prison warders, Röhm's was a public death. Eicke had Lechler place Eicke's loaded pistol and a copy of the *Völkischer Beobachter* on the table in the cell. The special edition of the *Völkischer Beobachter* announced Röhm's removal as chief of staff and the executions of June 30 at Stadelheim. No words were exchanged and Lechler withdrew. The cell door was closed and Eicke counted off ten minutes on his wristwatch. Röhm may have spent part of this period writing. At least one witness claimed to have seen a slip of paper in Röhm's handwriting after his body was taken out of the cell. This subsequently disappeared.[36]

A certain loyalty complex on Hitler's part, or a reluctance to have Röhm's death directly on his hands, led Hitler to give Röhm the opportunity to commit suicide. Indirectly, this allowed Röhm to convey a message by the decision he took. He did not commit suicide, nor did he attempt to use Eicke's pistol in a futile attempt to break out of the cell. His family believed that he refused to do so because such courses of action implied a guilt that he did not accept. Röhm bared his upper body in anticipation of being shot.[37]

After ten minutes, on Eicke's instructions, Lechler entered the cell in trepidation and removed the pistol from the table. Eicke and Lippert stood with drawn pistols in the open cell door. Röhm stood in the middle of the cell and called something out to the two men. They made hand gestures that they were not prepared to listen. The two men aimed at Röhm's heart. Eicke instructed Lippert "'Aim slowly and coolly!'"[38] Their shots were almost simultaneous. Röhm sank to the floor, gasping. One witness claimed Röhm said "'My Führer, my Führer!'"[39] but others recalled no such statement. One SS officer then entered the cell and shot Röhm again. Röhm's corpse had three shots in the chest, neck, and heart. Eicke told the prison officials that medical help for Röhm was forbidden. Eicke and Lippert left, taking four SA prisoners with them to Dachau. Prison records showed 6:00 p.m. on July 1 as the time of Röhm's death. His body was put in a coffin after twilight and buried toward 10:00 p.m. in section 1, plot number 24 at the Perlacher Forst cemetery.

Killings ceased on July 2, apparently after Hitler had promised Hindenburg they had stopped. In Berlin, Karl Schreyer's life was saved when the order to stop killing arrived just as he was being led to his execution at the barracks at Lichterfelde. Perhaps the last killings took place at Dachau concentration camp. Dachau records backdated the deaths to 4:00 a.m. on July 1 to suggest that the killings took place before Hitler's order to stop was received. Stadelheim prison records, however, indicate that SA-Standartenführer Julius Uhl from Ingolstadt, Röhm's chauffeur, Johann Heinrich König, and SA-Obertruppführer Martin Schätzl were not transferred from Stadelheim to Dachau until July 2. They were then killed there.[40]

The money and goods the executed men had brought with them to prison appeared to have been returned to their relatives. Röhm had with him a key, watch, pencil, two handkerchiefs, a cigarette lighter, a pair of cufflinks, and an open-ended tie. Between them, the men killed at Stadelheim had left behind 3,249.93 Reichsmarks in cash.[41]

On July 10, Wagner instructed the Munich police to exhume and cremate the corpses of the SA leaders buried at Perlacher Forst. The ashes were then released to their families with strict instructions as to how and when they could be buried. Röhm's ashes were buried in the same grave as his father on July 21, 1934. Röhm's grave was watched, and those who visited it came under surveillance.[42]

On July 16, 1934, the Amtsgericht München issued a death certificate for Ernst Röhm, giving his place of death as Stadelheimerstrasse 12 in Munich, and describing him as a "single, retired captain,"[43] since he had been stripped of his office as Chief of Staff by Hitler on June 30. Röhm died without leaving a will, with an estate of some 41,600 marks. Initially, his entire estate was confiscated by the political police, and then the Oberste SA-Führung. His personal papers and those of his Ministerial Office vanished. Since no material from these was kept or publicized, one can assume that no incriminating material was found. The *Geschichte eines Hochverräters* and other books by executed SA leaders were removed from public circulation.

On February 1, 1935, in its capacity as an inheritance court, the Amtsgericht ruled that Röhm's mother would inherit half the estate, and his siblings one-quarter each. Before this ruling was handed down, however, Emilie Röhm had died from heart trouble, aged seventy-seven, on January 6, 1935. Only one doctor had been willing to treat her. She had rejected the pension Hitler had offered direct dependents of those killed, saying "I will not take money from the murderer of my son."[44] Robert Röhm and his family fell under suspicion, and were subject to surveillance and harassment until 1945.

Hitler gave several explanations for the purge of Röhm and the SA leadership. Historians have given the most attention to the explanation he gave in his speech to the Reichstag on July 13, when Hitler spoke of a plot by Röhm and others to overthrow the regime in connection with an unnamed foreign power, by which he meant France. Hitler's earliest explanation was given to a ministerial meeting of July 3 under the immediate impact of events. At this meeting, Hitler stated he had been watching Röhm's activities for a year and had delayed his intervention out of consideration for Germany's foreign policy position. Röhm had gathered a clique of SA leaders around him who were held together by personal ambition and a particular inclination, that is, homosexuality. This exaggerated the extent to which senior SA leaders were homosexual. Hitler stressed that he had repeatedly protected Röhm, a reference to the period from 1931 to 1933. The clique around Röhm saw his tolerance as weakness, Hitler claimed.[45]

Hitler stated that in his four hour meeting with Röhm in early June, Röhm had promised to desist from his activities. Yet, he had not done so, nor had he kept to the agreement between the Reichswehr and the SA. Hitler's comments indicated that he either believed, or made himself believe, in the faked documents and orders that the SA was about to overthrow the regime. As von Salomon observed, "the fiction that there had been such a putsch was rigidly maintained."[46]

Hitler's presentation of Röhm's involvement with Schleicher was particularly incoherent. He claimed that Röhm had been involved with Schleicher and Gregor Strasser in plans for a change of government in Germany, and that contact had been made with France to ensure it made no difficulties. Yet, Hitler continued that Schleicher had rejected either forming a new government or being part of it.[47]

Hitler also revealed to the ministers that Röhm had been seeking the same way out of the impasse that he had taken in 1925. Röhm had asked him either to give him an independent position as Chief of Staff or to let him resign. Röhm was seeking a way out of an impossible situation, but Hitler considered "this threat of his resignation was nothing more than shameless blackmail."[48] Did Hitler see Röhm's offer to resign as too independent a step, as removing his prerogative as leader to dismiss and appoint? Why did he not accept Röhm's resignation and allow him to leave the country, perhaps to return to Bolivia? He could even have allowed Röhm to retire on health grounds. Did he want Röhm to oversee the SA's diminution in power? Did Hitler experience the pressure from Röhm for a continuing position for the SA as a form of blackmail? There is no evidence to support Machtan's claim that Röhm and those around him may have been blackmailing Hitler privately. Nothing in Röhm's past history, personality or attitude toward his own, and others', sexuality supports this interpretation.

Hitler concluded that there could be no question of a retrospective trial. Blomberg thanked Hitler in the name of the cabinet for his decisive and courageous action that had saved the German people from civil war. The cabinet agreed to the proposed Law for Measures of State Defense, the only article of which read, "The measures taken on 30 June and on 1 and 2 July 1934 to suppress high and national treasonous attacks are justified as defense of the State."[49]

Hitler's comments suggested why men who were—either correctly or incorrectly—linked to Röhm's homosexuality were targets on June 30, 1934, and why some men, like Zehnter and Schätzl, died solely because they were

Röhm's personal friends. Others, such as Du Moulin-Eckart, survived only by accident. After Röhm was killed, the laws against male homosexuality were tightened, and SS and police persecution of male homosexuals increased.[50]

The extent to which the moves were designed by the SA's rivals to move against the power of the SA, rather than to stamp out an actual conspiracy, could be seen in one significant detail. Except for in East Prussia, where one SS commander was killed in a power struggle within the SS, no SS officer, however close he was to Röhm, was executed. Robert Bergmann and Rolf Reiner survived when Edmund Heines and Martin Schätzl did not. Röhm's friends in the SS were stripped of their positions and disgraced, but Himmler protected them from execution.[51]

In 1931, Hitler had persuaded himself that Stennes was in league with his political enemies. He observed, "'I could only come to the conclusion that if anyone opposed me or my movement, he must have been a paid agent.'"[52] Once Hitler and others had convinced themselves that Röhm was plotting against them, the paranoid Nazi worldview made innocent actions seem suspicious. The bluster and wild talk of SA leaders and men, a product of the SA's sense that it was being outmaneuvered, was interpreted as evidence of their plans to stage a putsch. Röhm's efforts to obtain information about developments in Austria through von Alvensleben, if in fact he made them, may have come about because Habicht blocked the Austrian SA's attempts to inform Röhm accurately about developments in Austria. Later, this was interpreted as evidence that Röhm was intriguing with Dollfuss. Röhm had entertained lavishly in his new headquarters in the Standartenstrasse, but he was not the only Nazi leader to do so. After June 30, 1934, Röhm was attacked for his dinners with diplomats; in January, Bülow, of the Foreign Ministry, urged Röhm to attend a diplomatic dinner precisely so he could meet François-Poncet. This paranoid worldview was illustrated by von Neurath's comment to François-Poncet that he should not be surprised at being suspected of being part of Röhm's conspiracy because he had met with Röhm and Schleicher. As François-Poncet responded, it was not normally suspicious for a diplomat to meet a minister of his host government.

German public reaction to the purge was generally positive. Many hoped that it marked the beginning of the end to the regime's excesses. The SA had served as a lightning rod for resentment of the regime's abuses of power and excesses, though these were not confined to the SA. The purge also carried a message to every German. It signaled the regime's willingness to stay in power no matter what the cost. Foreign public and governmental opinion was more reserved. The foreign press highlighted the discrepancies and contradictions in the official story of the alleged plot.[53]

The SA was reduced to unimportance in the months that followed. Its weapons were handed in, and large numbers of SA men were disciplined for various offences. Its numbers were cut from about 4 million men in May-June 1934, to some 2.6 million by September 1934, 1.6 million by October 1935, and 1.2 million by April 1938. The SA's ministerial and political offices were dissolved, and its special representatives and plenipotentiaries abolished. Its lack of influence on the course of Nazi decision-making was such that its counsel at the Nuremberg war crimes trials could argue successfully that it was not a criminal organization. Viktor Lutze, whom Hitler appointed as Chief of Staff on June 30, 1934, came to recognize and resent that the purge had allowed the SS to rise at the expense of the SA. The more professional, methodical, and ideologically disciplined SS took the place of the spontane-ous, erratic, and amateurish SA. The SS increasingly came to fulfill both the function previously exercised by the SA—the use of force at home—and the function aimed for by the SA leadership—creating its own armed forces in the Waffen-SS.[54]

The immediate effects of the purge in 1934 were two-fold. On July 25, 1934, the Austrian SS and Nazis attempted to seize power in Vienna in a botched putsch. They possibly hoped to induce the Austrian army to come over to their side. Historians are still undecided whether Hitler and the Ger-man government knew of, or initiated, the rising. Austrian government offices were seized, Chancellor Dollfuss was captured, shot, and let bleed to death. Elements of the Austrian SS and party crossed the German-Austrian border to participate. There were Nazi uprisings with SA participation in regional cities. The Austrian SA in Vienna was only involved at the periphery of the planning of the attempted putsch, which was quickly suppressed by the Austrian army. Were they not involved because they were not trusted by the plotters and thus excluded? Was the Austrian SA leadership unwilling to par-ticipate in a putsch they judged likely to fail? Did the events of June 30–July 2, 1934, in the Reich play a role in this reluctance? Historians' opinions are divided.[55]

The second immediate effect was of more importance for the future of the regime. Hindenburg died at Neudeck at 9:00 a.m. on August 2. Hitler announced he would be assuming the office of President under the title of Führer as well as Chancellor, and seeking retrospective ratification by the elec-torate in a referendum. Not only did the army leadership accept this develop-ment, but on their own initiative, Blomberg and Reichenau introduced an (unconstitutional) personal oath of loyalty to Hitler as Führer, sworn by all the armed forces on August 2 and 3. The oath was intended to bind Hitler closer to the armed forces but, instead, it bound the armed forces to Hitler.[56] The army leadership's successful defeat of the SA as a potential rival had led it to Nazify voluntarily the armed forces more and more. The oath of loyalty to Hitler was the final step in this process.

Hitler's own role in the development of the crisis that led to the killing of Röhm and the purge of the SA is still debated. Did he really believe that Röhm posed a threat or was he manipulated by others? Two former SA leaders who had themselves fallen out with Hitler, Pfeffer and Stennes, believed that Hitler himself had been the driving force behind the moves against Röhm. Looking back in 1953, Röhm's predecessor, Franz von Pfeffer, judged:

> Röhm was a strong, indeed very strong, personality of excellent organizational and leadership qualities . . . AHi [Adolf Hitler] made a first-rate choice in him, in that he led the entire SA well through the seizure of power . . . right up to the moment when it became superfluous and up to its liquidation . . . Röhm was not at all equal to the game of AHi [Adolf Hitler] and could not be.[57]

When Hitler refused to accept Röhm's offer of his resignation, was this because he sensed that Röhm's continuation in his position served his purposes? The "Bolivian option" might have saved Röhm's life, but it did not suit Hitler. Was the Army's belief that the threat the SA posed was real the final service of the SA to Nazi control of Germany? Were Röhm and the SA, in representing such a threat, also "working towards the Führer"?[58] The SA leadership's continued pressure for a role for the SA, and Hitler's hesitation before the competing power groups had led the military leadership to make more and more concessions to the regime, concessions they might otherwise not have given. Ultimately, in his death and the SA's defeat, Röhm and the SA made their last decisive contribution to the Nazi consolidation of power.

CHAPTER 16

Conclusion:
Röhm and the Myth of Röhm

Ernst Röhm's reputation survived as much as myth and symbol as reality. Röhm's sister, Lore Lippert, believed Röhm appeared in the visions of the German medium Gerda Walther. Walther claimed to have felt a spiritual radiation emanating from a photo of Röhm on public display in Munich before his death. On July 3, 1934, during a Christian Community religious ceremony, she felt the same radiation and heard inside her, Röhm's voice saying "'I am not a scoundrel, I am not a scoundrel! I wanted the best, perhaps I made mistakes. To make mistakes is human, but I am not a scoundrel!'"[1] Over the next few days, Walther felt impelled by Röhm's spirit to go to the party headquarters and to find out all she could about what had happened on June 30. As 1934 continued, she had visions of Röhm's last moments and experienced the feeling, which she resisted, that Röhm wanted her to let Hitler know he had forgiven him. Röhm and other SA leaders also appeared in a vision to one of her other friends, and Röhm's spirit possessed a third friend on Christmas Eve 1934. On January 8, 1935, Walther had a vision of Emilie Röhm, then of Röhm kneeling before his mother, stroking her hands and speaking to her. This drove Walther to contact first Robert Röhm, and then Lore Lippert, who was more open to her reported spiritual experiences than Robert Röhm. Lore Lippert confirmed from her knowledge of her brother many of the impressions Walther believed that she received from Röhm's spirit.

On June 30, 1935, the two women visited Röhm's grave to find it covered with flowers, as it would be repeatedly close to the anniversary of his death. Undeterred by police observation, flowers heaped his grave as a silent demonstration.[2] This was a symbolic protest at Röhm's fate and a commemoration by his supporters. Later, SA leaders and Röhm's friends put his side of the story both at the postwar Nuremberg trial of the major Nazi war criminals and organizations, and in the 1957 trial of Sepp Dietrich and Michael Lippert for the 1934 killings.

These were signs of the way in which Ernst Röhm attained a symbolic significance in death. After his death, for loyal Nazis, he was a traitor; for others, he came to stand for the thwarted second revolution in Nazism and for the Nazi as homosexual. Some surviving SA leaders at Nuremberg claimed that the SA constituted the first resistance to Nazism. Leftist homophobia led to the development of a powerful exiled anti-Nazi critique of Nazism as both a homosexual movement and one that hypocritically killed some of its members on those grounds.[3]

After 1945, Röhm, who was killed before the Holocaust began, could stand for a National Socialism untainted by the regime's later crimes. Because Röhm died only a year and a half into the life of the National Socialist regime, he shared responsibility only for the very earliest of its violence and crimes, those committed in the seizure and consolidation of power. This allowed his friends and supporters to believe that, had Röhm lived and stayed at the top of the regime, he could have influenced its development in either a more or less radical manner, depending on their own personal preferences. The strength of their belief in Röhm also came from their sense of Röhm's humanity. He was a good friend and companion, socially adept, and capable of winning the respect and liking of many. Sefton Delmer recalled, "I had liked this gay and expansive old gangster despite his thuggery and his outrageous private life."[4]

Röhm's friends' and supporters' tendency to believe Röhm favored the policies they wanted him to support makes ascertaining Röhm's own political views more difficult.[5] Many Germans who had supported or voted for National Socialism, envisaging a National Socialist Germany as different from the reality, could imagine that under Röhm as leader, or with Röhm advising Hitler, National Socialism might be closer to their wishes.

However much Röhm may have agreed privately with criticisms of the regime's policies, he took no action to stop them. He may not have had strong views on racial issues by Nazi standards, but he never took action to lessen the impact of Nazi anti-Semitic policies when asked to intervene. Indeed, his willingness to listen to criticism and receive people of opposing views was a personal characteristic that did not necessarily mean he shared these views. In 1933–34, Röhm was prepared to receive the secretary of the Jewish Front Fighters' League for talks, but he did not soften SA policies as a result.[6] Even in the case of the policy toward male homosexuals in 1933–34, it is not clear whether Röhm took any active steps to prevent their persecution, or whether it was more that male homosexuals were protected because other leaders were wary of his reaction.

Ernst Röhm became, in a sense, the "lost leader," the man who stood for unrealized potential alternative directions in Nazism. This view is psychologically and humanly understandable, but unsubstantiated. Nothing in Röhm's role in the Nazi movement up to 1934 suggests that he was capable of playing the central role that this concept of him would require.

There is, however, a psychological basis for this view of Röhm. It is clear that he was in some respects more relaxed and flexible about National Socialist ideology than some of his fellow leaders. It could be argued that many Germans who supported National Socialism wanted a regime that was closer to Italian fascism in its impact on society than National Socialism, that is a regime that embodied nationalism, discipline, and authority but without the radicalizing momentum and extremism of National Socialism. Röhm, too, would have been at home in such a regime. His concept of National Socialist ideology and many of the policies he supported, even the concept of a Swiss-style militia army, were more national-conservative or fascist than National Socialist. This, of course, was also a key reason for his political failure.

Even before the purge of the SA and Röhm's death, his major contributions to the success of National Socialism were clearly past. It was not clear what future role he or the SA could fill in the Nazi state. Kemal Atatürk observed that the SA did not stand for a second revolution. Instead, what occurred in Germany from June 30—July 2, 1934 "were, rather, events of a kind which had followed other revolutions and which made the elimination of old fellow-combatants necessary as soon as they endeavored to obtain a special position for themselves on the strength of their past services."[7]

Röhm's protection, his financial and logistical support, had allowed the party to survive in its early years. His organizational skills found their fullest expression in his work as SA Chief of Staff from 1931 to 1933. In that capacity, he "rode the tiger" of the expanding SA. He was able to keep the SA under sufficient control to keep it responsive to the demands of the political leadership. It was the unceasing work and sacrifice of the ordinary SA man that enabled the NSDAP to fight four national elections in 1932 and keep up its relentless appearance of activity and momentum. Equally, Röhm's style of leadership of the SA allowed the organization to make its key contribution—violence and the threat of violence—to the success of the Nazi seizure of power.

The irony for Röhm and the SA was that their very success in achieving and consolidating the seizure of power made them superfluous. Had the Nazi takeover been far more strongly resisted, there would have been a continuing role for the SA. Had economic recovery arrived earlier than it did, SA men would have found employment and much of the pressure on the SA leadership from below would have dissipated. Instead, between 1933 and 1934, the balance that Röhm had maintained between SA adventurism and discipline broke down.

Röhm's own self-definition and orientation as a soldier meant that, in 1933–34, he missed a possible opportunity to have the SA fill the role of a political police, leaving the SS to seize this role. Instead, Röhm cast around looking for military and quasi-military roles for the SA—as a reserve army, as a Swiss-style militia, as a means of continuing the National Socialist revolution in the "hearts and minds" of German men.

In this last capacity, the SA probably had more of a contribution in the "Nazification" of German society than is usually recognized. Between January 1933 and June 1934, some four million men passed through the SA. Under Röhm, *Der SA-Mann* preached nationalism and military values. Biological racism was not highlighted in its feature articles, though racist stereotypes and anti-Semitism were present in the paper's stories and jokes. The paper concentrated on drawing the political lessons of the front experience. These ideas formed a subtle preparation for the more radical message elsewhere in Nazism for men coming to National Socialism for the first time.

Röhm's contribution to the SA had also always benefited from the duality and ambivalence of his emphasis on discipline and the signal his own life sent that discipline was not always absolute. So it was too, in 1933–34, when the SA's indiscipline unwittingly served the purposes of the Nazi movement for one last time despite itself. In sacrificing the SA, the rest of the Nazi movement could remove the final checks to Nazi power, the role of the President and the independence of the armed forces.

Röhm was loyal to Hitler, but—as was the case in all his relations with his superiors—he was loyal "in his fashion." His National Socialism was a further expression of Protestantism or non-conformism—he interpreted it through his individual personal conscience. Equally, he was "nonconformist" as a soldier in his attitude to discipline, to obeying orders, and to the officer's honor code where this ran counter to his sexuality.

Röhm's lawyer, Luetgebrune, reportedly observed that Röhm "was the only one with the courage to contradict Hitler. When Hitler shouted, Röhm shouted back even louder. But he was loyal to Hitler. That was certain. Röhm might completely forget that Hitler had once been his protégé—Hitler never forgot."[8] Was Röhm, ultimately, too independent? It has been argued that "Röhm was not amenable to Hitler's hypnotic influence. He was loyal to Hitler, but not dependent on him."[9]

In the 1933–34 crisis of the regime, Röhm's position suffered because of the long-term effect of the sustained political campaign against him from 1931 to 1933. This campaign weakened his position inside Nazism and made him more dependent on Hitler for support. The publicity given to his sexuality also isolated him from other members of the leadership,[10] and therefore made the moves against him more of a surprise. Hitler had been willing to allow Röhm the long leash he needed as a subordinate from 1931 to 1933, but in the 1934 crisis, the stakes were too high for this to continue. Hitler, too, may have felt that because he had given Röhm so much protection earlier, he could expect less trouble from Röhm in 1934. Paradoxically, Hitler's steadfast support in the earlier period led Röhm to maintain his trust in Hitler's good faith long after such trust was justified.

In his study of the SS, Koehl concludes that Röhm failed as a military commander in 1934 because he and the organization he headed were so comprehensively taken by surprise on June 30, 1934. "Röhm remained an amateur to the last, the amateur leader of an amateur army."[11] Röhm did not seem to recognize the danger he was in. Because of their long friendship, and Hitler's support of him from 1931 to 1933, he may have trusted Hitler's assurances too readily. Because, in actuality, he did not pose a real threat to the regime, Röhm underestimated the hostility of his opponents. Despite Dornheim's description of him as ruthless, Röhm ultimately was not ruthless enough to survive in National Socialist infighting.

In the dispute between the SA and the Reichswehr that led to Röhm's killing, Röhm's proposals seemed radical and threatening to the Reichswehr leadership. They were, in fact, conservative, and therefore doomed to fail. A Swiss-style militia, whether Röhm envisioned it as a substitute for the Reichswehr or an addition to it, would have only been capable of national defense. For this reason, the concept could be expected to be welcome to France, a receptiveness that the paranoid National Socialist world view could see as treason on Röhm's part.

It is particularly surprising that Hitler's claim in his Reichstag speech after June 30, 1934—that Röhm and those around him believed in constant revolution—was accepted. Röhm was a committed monarchist, a supporter of rapprochement with Britain and France, and a religiously observant Protestant.[12] Röhm often spoke of revolution, but after the takeover of power, he used the term to signify the conquest of hearts and minds in Germany and establishing the people's community. That is, he used the term in the conventional Nazi sense and not in any sense as a social revolutionary. On close examination, there is something chimerical and mythical about the Nazi left.

Why, then, did Röhm gain the lasting reputation of being a Nazi revolutionary and a member of the Nazi left? Have Hitler's self-justifications in his Reichstag speech had a lasting effect? Have historians been too influenced by Göring's "downright grotesque and cynical"[13] distortion of Röhm's political views at Nuremberg, where Göring depicted Röhm as a man who wanted to follow a strongly revolutionary path "consciously more placed to the left,"[14] strongly against the church and Jews?

The threat that Röhm's claims posed to the Reichswehr leadership, and the unwitting threat they posed to Hitler's continuing hold on power, contributed to Hitler depicting Röhm and the men around him as revolutionaries. Hitler's self-serving explanation served the interests of Nazis and non-Nazis alike in 1934. For Nazis, particularly those involved in the plot against Röhm and in the murders of the purge, it justified and excused that involvement and those murders. Opponents of Nazism wanted to believe that there were genuine social revolutionaries in the ranks of the NSDAP and that conflict had broken out within the regime. They hoped to use this and popular dissatisfaction at continuing economic problems to undermine the regime.

Röhm was psychologically believable as a revolutionary as well. It was his sexuality and the consequences that he drew from it that placed him in opposition to conventional contemporary social and moral values, that made him a self-conscious outsider in what he saw as a hypocritical society, and that prompted his most "revolutionary" statements. If Ernst Röhm was at all revolutionary, he was revolutionary in his demand that National Socialism and German society accept him as he was—a man who desired other men.

Ernst Röhm saw himself first and foremost as a soldier. It was the soldier's values of honor and courage that marked his behavior in the last day of his life—seeking to keep up his fellow prisoners' spirits by joking with them, refusing to commit suicide because it would imply an admission of guilt, his real and self-conscious physical courage. He lived up to his own self-image.

He died like a soldier.

Note on Sources

After June 30, 1934, all Röhm's private papers, as well as the records of his ministerial office, were seized. They have since vanished, and may have been destroyed in 1945, if not earlier. This is a considerable loss to his biographer, since, as late as 1923, Röhm kept a diary at least in note form.[1] Only fragmentary personal papers survive, some held by the Röhm family and others scattered in more official archival holdings.

Friends, political allies, and official acquaintances, as well may have destroyed valuable sources for self-preservation. I have been unable to trace the papers of Röhm's best friend, Robert Bergmann, for example. Of his other close friends, Graf Carl Léon Du Moulin-Eckart never recorded his memories of Röhm, and Josef Seydel died at the end of the Second World War.[2]

On the other hand, many of those who knew Röhm less well left their impressions in memoirs and interviews. Sometimes these memories were less reliable, or were influenced by conscious or unconscious homophobia or by Röhm's notoriety. Some witnesses, particularly those who were involved in purging the SA in 1934, were motivated by the need to justify their actions. Where possible, the views of Röhm's contemporaries, even if influenced by hindsight, have been reproduced to give a sense of how he appeared to others.

Unfortunately, I was not given permission to consult the diary of Viktor Lutze, held in the Friedrich-Ebert-Stiftung in Bonn, nor was I able to interview Hildegard Huber. In both cases, I have drawn on the work of earlier historians who had such access.

In his autobiography, *Saying Life: The memoirs of Sir Francis Rose*, the English painter Sir Francis Rose claimed to have been a close friend of Röhm, yet his statements about him were inaccurate in almost every detail. For example, he alleged that Hindenburg and Papen had great faith in Röhm, Röhm had no liking for Wagner, and that Röhm had a house at Bad Wiessee. Accordingly, I have not made use of the memoirs, though it is possible that the two men did know each other.[3]

Röhm's historical prominence, his notoriety, and death have resulted in some accounts of his stay in Bolivia by some Bolivian historians. These are not always accurate, particularly where they deal with Röhm's career outside Bolivia. I have used them where they draw directly or indirectly on testimony from Röhm's Bolivian contemporaries.

Some recent studies of Röhm's role in Bolivia have relied on the assertion of one of his German colleagues in Bolivia, Adolf Röpnack, that Röhm planned the June 1930 military uprising there. There is no evidence to support this. Röhm's private and public comments at the time and later also give no backing for this interpretation. Had Röhm played such a role, he would have revealed it at some time: he never did. The well-informed reports of the German ambassador Marckwald also do not substantiate the claim. Röpnack's assertion seems to have arisen from a combination of his hostility to Röhm, a reading of Röhm's alleged "revolutionary" stance of 1934 back into his actions in 1930, and his admiration of Kundt. Both Röpnack and the historians of Bolivia who have accepted his claim give too much credence to Röhm's reputation as a revolutionary.[4]

In addition, I have not drawn on evidence that is in my opinion extremely problematic. For example, both Richardi and Schumann, and Dornheim, have used an unsigned and undated typed memorandum, allegedly written by Martin Schätzl, which suggested Du Moulin-Eckart and Uhl plotted to kill Hitler in 1931 and make Röhm leader without Röhm knowing of the alleged plot.[5] This memorandum did not surface until after 1945; it has no known provenance but was posted anonymously to a Bavarian court. The most telling evidence against its authenticity is that this memorandum— allegedly written by Martin Schätzl before his own killing on July 2, 1934— contains anachronistic claims to the events of June 30–July 1, 1934, that he could not have known. It is significant that Du Moulin-Eckart did not claim to have planned to assassinate Hitler in his own postwar de-Nazification proceedings when such a claim would have been to his advantage.

In many cases, particularly with the reorganization of the Bundesarchiv, the Bayerisches Hauptstaatsarchiv, and the Landesarchiv Berlin, files have been moved from one archive to another, file groups have been reorganized or renumbered, and some file groupings have been renamed since I consulted them. The file and archive references are those as at the time when I used the files. The papers from the archive assembled by Dr. Otto Gritschneder that I consulted using his organization can now be seen in the Staatsanwaltschaft holdings of the Staatsarchiv München.

Appendix

Equivalent Ranks

SA	German Army	SS	U.S. Army	British Army
Stabschef der SA	Generalfeldmarschall	Reichsführer-SS	General of the Army	Field Marshal
	Generaloberst	SS-Oberstgruppenführer		
Obergruppenführer	General	SS-Obergruppenführer	General	General
Gruppenführer	Generalleutnant	SS-Gruppenführer	Lieutenant General	Lieutenant General
Brigadeführer	Generalmajor	SS-Brigadeführer	Brigadier general	Brigadier
Oberführer		SS-Oberführer		
Standartenführer	Oberst	SS-Standartenführer	Colonel	Colonel
Obersturmbannführer	Oberstleutnant	SS-Obersturmbannführer	Lieutenant Colonel	Lieutenant Colonel
Sturmbannführer	Major	SS-Sturmbannführer	Major	Major
Sturmhauptführer	Hauptmann	SS-Hauptsturmführer	Captain	Captain
Obersturmführer	Oberleutnant	SS-Obersturmführer	First lieutenant	Lieutenant
Sturmführer	Leutnant	SS-Untersturmführer	Lieutenant	2nd lieutenant
Haupttruppführer	Stabsfeldwebel	SS-Sturmscharführer	Sergeant major	Regimental Sergeant Major
Obertruppführer	Oberfeldwebel	SS-Hauptscharführer	Master sergeant	Sergeant Major

Equivalent Ranks (continued)

SA	German Army	SS	U.S. Army	British Army
Truppführer	Feldwebel	SS-Oberscharführer	Technical Sergeant	Quartermaster-Sergeant
Oberscharführer	Unterfeldwebel	SS-Scharführer	Staff sergeant	Staff Sergeant
Scharführer	Unteroffizier	SS-Unterscharführer	Sergeant	Sergeant
Rottenführer	Gefreiter	SS-Rottenführer	Corporal	Corporal
		SS-Sturmmann		Lance-Corporal
Sturmmann	Obersoldat	SS-Oberschütze	Private first class	Senior Private
SA-Mann (Anwärter)	Soldat	SS-Schütze	Private	Private

Adapted from: Campbell, *The SA Generals and the Rise of Nazism*, 163; Heinz Höhne, *The Order of the Death's Head: The Story of Hitler's SS* (New York: Ballantine Books, 1971), 744.

Abbreviations

AA: Auswärtige Angelegenheiten
AdR: Archiv der Republik
ALP: Archivo de La Paz
AMEMG: Archivo Militar del Estado Mayor General
AMRREE: Archivo del Ministerio de Relaciones Exteriores
ARF: Altreichsflagge
BAK: Bundesarchiv Koblenz
BA MA: Bundesarchiv Abteilung Militärarchiv, Freiburg i. B.
BAR: Bundesarchiv Abteilung Deutsches Reich, Berlin-Lichterfelde
BHSA/II: Bayerisches Hauptstaatsarchiv Abteilung II
BHSA/III: Bayerisches Hauptstaatsarchiv Abteilung III Geheimes Hausarchiv
BHSA/V: Bayerisches Hauptstaatsarchiv Abteilung V Nachlässe und Sammlungen
BHSA/KA: Bayerisches Hauptstaatsarchiv Abteilung IV Kriegsarchiv
DBF: Documents on British Foreign Policy
DGFP: Documents on German Foreign Policy
FO: Foreign Office
FZM: Feldzeugmeisterei
GP RA: Gritschneder Papiere Röhm-Akten
HKN: Hauptkammer Nürnberg
IfZ: Institut für Zeitgeschichte Munich
ISA: Ingolstadt Stadt Archiv
KPD: Kommunistische Partei Deutschlands (Communist Party of Germany)
LAB: Landesarchiv Berlin
LoC RSS: Library of Congress Recorded Sound Section
NA: National Archives Washington
NPA: Neues Politisches Archiv
NSDAP: Nationalsozialistische Deutsche Arbeiterpartei (National Socialist German Workers" Party)
ÖSA: Österreichisches Staatsarchiv
PA AA: Politisches Archiv des Auswärtigen Amtes
p.c.: press clipping
RFP: Röhm family papers
SA: Sturmabteilungen (assault detachments)

SAM: Staatsarchiv München
SAN: Staatsarchiv Nürnberg
SM: Stadtarchiv München
SMB: Schwules Museum Berlin
SPD: Sozialdemokratische Partei Deutschlands (Social Democratic Party of Germany)
SS: Schutzstaffel (protective squadron)
TNA: The National Archives of the United Kingdom (formerly Public Record Office)
VB: Völkische Beobachter

Notes

Chapter 1

1. Heinrich Bennecke, *Hitler und die SA* (Munich: Günter Olzog Verlag, 1962), 23. Joachim C. Fest, *Hitler* (London: Weidenfeld & Nicolson, 1974), 468.
2. Meyer Oberst u. Regimentskommandeur and others, December 15, 1906, "Dienst-Zeugnis für den Fahnenjunker/i Unteroffizier Ernst Julius Günther Röhm der 2. Kompagnie K.10.Infanterie Regiment Prinz Ludwig," and "Personalbogen," 1: BHSA/KA OP32380; Ernst Röhm to Emilie Röhm, July 27, 1929, RFP, 2; *The Daily Telegraph*, April 20, 1934, p.c., BAK Zsg. 117/435.
3. Alfonso Crespo Rodas, *Hernando Siles, el poder y su angustia* (La Paz: Empreso Editor Sigla, 1985), 240; *Illustrierter Beobachter*, November 25, 1933, p.c., BHSA/V Slg P 3653; Ernst Röhm, *Die Geschichte eines Hochverräters* (Munich: Eher Verlag, 1928), 86.
4. Konrad Heiden, *Der Fuehrer: Hitler's Rise to Power* (London: Victor Gollancz Ltd., 1944), 575, 577; Fest, *Hitler*, 450–51; George C. Browder, *Foundations of the Nazi Police State: The Formation of Sipo and SD* (University Press of Kentucky, Lexington, 1990), 81, 138.
5. Heiden, *Fuehrer*, 28–31; Fest, *Hitler*, 127–28, 473; Joachim C. Fest, "Ernst Röhm and the Lost Generation," *The Face of the Third Reich* (Harmondsworth: Penguin, 1972), 209, 211–12; Peter Longerich, *Die braunen Bataillone: Geschichte der SA* (Munich: Verlag C. H. Beck, 1989), 15–22; Conan Fischer, "Ernst Julius Röhm—Stabschef der SA und unentbehrlicher Außenseiter," in Ronald Smelser and Rainer Zitelmann, ed., *Die braune Elite: 22 biographische Skizzen* (Darmstadt: Wissenschaftliche Buchgesellschaft, 1989), 212–22; Jean Mabire, *Röhm l'homme qui inventa Hitler* (Paris: Fayard, 1983), 162.
6. Mabire, *Röhm, passim*.
7. Burkhard Jellonnek, *Homosexuelle unter dem Hakenkreuz: Die Verfolgung von Homosexuellen im Dritten Reich* (Paderborn: Ferdinand Schöningh, 1990), chap. 5; Lothar Machtan, *Hitlers Geheimnis: Das Doppelleben eines Diktators* (Berlin: Alexander Fest Verlag, 2001), chap. 3 and 5; Suzanne zur Nieden, "Aufstieg und Fall des virilen Männerhelden: Der Skandal um Ernst Röhm und seine Ermordung," in Suzanne zur Nieden, ed., *Homosexualität und Staatsräson, Männlichkeit,*

Homophobie und Politik in Deutschland 1900–1945 (Frankfurt am Main: Campus Verlag, 2005), 147–92.

8. Ian Kershaw, *Hitler 1889–1936: Hubris* (London: Allen Lane, 1998), xi–xii, xxvi–xxvii.

9. Trutter to the Amtsgericht München Nachlassgericht, July 16, 1934, SAM AM Nr. 1934/1767, 1; discussions with Dr. Reinhard Weber, SAM.

10. Röhm, *Geschichte*, 326. Heinrich Bennecke, "Die Memoiren des Ernst Röhm: Ein Vergleich der verschiedenen Ausgaben und Auflagen," *Politische Studien*, 14/I, 1963, 179–88.

11. Ian Kershaw, *The Nazi Dictatorship: Problems and Perspectives of Interpretation*, 4th ed. (London: Arnold, 2000), 5.

Chapter 2

1. Röhm, *Geschichte*, 11.

2. Advice from Frau Richter-Nachtigal, Evangelische Kirche Registeramt, Munich, September 10, 1997; Röhm to Dr Heimsoth, February 25, 1929, in Dr. Helmuth Klotz, ed., *Drei Briefe Ernst Röhms an Dr. Heimsoth, Berlin* (Berlin: Dr. H. Klotz, 1932), BAK Sammlung Schumacher 402, 7; SM PME R 139/140; Ernst Röhm, *Stammtafel der Familie Röhm abgeschlossen Juni 1927.* (Leipzig: Verlag Degener & Co., 1927).

3. September 13, 1997, "Wortwörtlicher Auszug aus dem Taufregister der protestantischen Stadtpfarrei München aus dem Jahre 1887 Seite 289 Nr. 1112," "Nr. 231/97/RN"; Hans Fehn, "I. Das Land Bayern und seine Bevölkerung seit 1800," in Max Spindler et al., ed., *Handbuch der bayerischen Geschichte Vierter Band Das neue Bayern 1800–1970*, vol. 4, pt. 2 (Munich: C. H. Beck, 1975), 685; Friedrich Prinz, "Annäherung an München: Postmoderne Rückblicke auf die Geburt einer Großstadt," and Hugo Maser, "Die protestantische Gemeinde," in Friedrich Prinz and Marita Krauss ed., *München, Musenstadt mit Hinterhöfen: die Prinzregentenzeit 1886–1912* (Munich: C. H. Beck, 1988), 16 and 206–12, respectively; Hermann Rumschöttel, *Das bayerische Offizierkorps 1866–1914* (Berlin: Duncker & Humblot, 1973), 237–38; Röhm, *Geschichte*, 52.

4. Sigrid Amedick, *Männer am Schienenstrang: Sozialgeschichte der unteren bayerischen Eisenbahnbeamten 1844–1914* (Stuttgart: Klett-Cotta, 1997), 235–37; Ernst Röhm, "Aus meinem Leben.," BHSA/V/ Slg P 3653; SM PME R139/140.

5. Röhm, *Geschichte*, 11. Röhm to Heimsoth, February 25, 1929; Klotz, *Drei Briefe*, 8; information from the Röhm family.

6. Röhm, *Geschichte*, 11; Christian Lankes, *München als Garnison im 19. Jahrhundert: die Haupt- und Residenzstadt als Standort der bayerischen Armee von Kurfürst Max IV. Joseph bis zur Jahrhundertwende* (Berlin: E. S. Mittler, 1993), 470–71, 481–82, 492–94, 497, 500.

7. Ekkehard Wiest, *Gesellschaft und Wirtschaft in München, 1830–1920: die sozioökonomische Entwicklung der Stadt dargestellt anhand historischer Adressbücher*

(Pfaffenweiler: Centaurus-Verlagsgesellschaft, 1991), 42–43; Röhm, *Stammtafel der Familie Röhm;* Dr. Wecklein, *Jahresbericht über das K. Maximiliansgymnasium in München für das Schuljahr 1898/99* (Munich: Akademische Buchdruckerei, 1898), SAM, 53; Winfried Bauer, "Chronik des Maximiliansgymnasiums nach den Jahresberichten und Festschriften sowie nach den Archivunterlagen der Schule," in Winfried Bauer, ed., *Chronik 150 Jahre Maximiliansgymnasium 1849–1999* (Munich: Maximiliansgymnasium, 1999), 15, 18–19, 20; Dr. Wecklein, "III. Verzeichnis der Schüler," *Jahresbericht über das K. Maximiliansgymnasium in München für das Schuljahr 1897/98* (Munich: Akademische Buchdruckerei, 1898), 46–50; Dr. Wecklein, "III. Verzeichnis der Schüler," *Jahresbericht über das K. Maximiliansgymnasium in München für das Schuljahr 1905/06* (Munich: Akademische Buchdruckerei, 1906), 27–28, 57.

8. Karl A. Schleunes, *Schooling and Society: The Politics of Education in Prussia and Bavaria 1750–1900* (Oxford: Berg, 1991), chap. 7; Dr. Wecklein, *Jahresbericht über das K. Maximiliansgymnasium in München für das Schuljahr 1904/05* (Munich: Akademische Buchdruckerei, 1905), 3–4; Bauer, "Chronik des Maximiliansgymnasiums," 19; Wecklein, *Jahresbericht . . . 1905/06*, 6–22; Dr. Wecklein, *Jahresbericht . . . 1897/98*, 5–21; IfZ ZS 539.

9. Röhm, *Geschichte*, 12.

10. K. Maximilians-Gymnasium in München, "Noten- und Zensurbogen für den Schuler der 9. Klasse Ernst Röhm. Oster=Zeugnis," transcript copy attached to September 9, 1998, Hamm, Direktorat, Maximiliansgymnasium to author, 3.

11. Wecklein, *Jahresbericht . . . 1905/06*, 57; Röhm, *Geschichte*, 12; Dr. Wecklein and Dr. Wohyek(?), July 13, 1906, "Königliches Maximilians-Gymnasium in München. Gymnasial-Absolutorium," 1–2; Dr. Wecklein, K. Rektorat des k. Maximilians-Gymnasiums, March 15, 1906, "LEUMUNDS-ZEUGNIS": BHSA/KA OP 32380.

12. Wolfgang Zorn, "Die Sozialentwicklung der nichtagrarischen Welt (1806–1970)," in Spindler et al., *Handbuch der bayerischen Geschichte*, vol. 4, pt. 2, 852.

13. Röhm, *Geschichte*, 13. Meyer Oberst u. Regimentskommandeur and others, December 15, 1906, "Dienst-Zeugnis für den Fahnenjunker/i Unteroffizier Ernst Julius Günther Röhm der 2. Kompanie K.10.Infanterie Regiment Prinz Ludwig," BHSA/KA OP 32380.

14. Röhm, *Geschichte*, 16. Lankes, *München als Garnison*, 157, 218; BHSA/KA Nachlaß Frauenholz/1, 44, 46, 48.

15. Vogel, Hauptmann, und Kompagniechef, 2. Kompagnie, 10. Infanterie Regiment, February 10, 1907, "Vertrauliche Mitteilungen über den Fahnenjunker Ernst, Julius, Günther Röhm.," BHSA/KA OP 32380, 1.

16. Fr. v. Horn, Kriegsministerium, Nr. 2561, "An die K. Generalkommandos und obersten Waffenbehörden. Verteilt nach Klasse I für die Kommandobehörden und Truppenteile. Betreff: Offiziersprüfung 1908," December 14, 1908, 4; signature [Kiehl?], Major & Kommandeur, January 25, 1908, "Abgangs-Zeugnis von der königlichen Kriegsschule für den Fähnrich Ernst Röhm vom K.10.

Infanterie-Regiment."; K. B. Kriegsschule, December 4, 1908, "Ergebnis der Offiziersprüfung für den Fähnrich Röhm, Ernst, K.10.Infanterie Regiment"; signature (Fasbender), Generalmajor und Chef des Generalstab der Armee, February 15, 1908, "Zeugnis der Reife zum Offizier für den Fähnrich Ernst Röhm": BHSA/KA OP 32380.

17. January 25, 1908, signature, Major & Kommandeur, "Abgangs-Zeugnis von der königlichen Kriegsschule für den Fähnrich Ernst Röhm vom K.10. Infanterie-Regiment.," BHSA/KA OP 32380.

18. "Verhandlung aufgenommen bei der Abstimmung des Offiziers-Korps des 10. Infanterie-Regiments über den zur Beförderung zum Leutnant vorzuschlagenden Fähnrich Ernst Röhm.," February 17, 1908; K.B.10 Infanterie-Regiment. Prinz Ludwig, "Verhandlung aufgenommen über die Verpflichtung des zum Leutnant beförderten Fähnrichs Ernst Röhm.," March 14, 1908, 1–3: BHSA/KA OP 32380.

19. Mehrere Mitkämpfer, *Das K.B. 10. Infanterie Regiment König* (Munich: Verlag Bayerisches Kriegsarchiv, 1925), 9–10; Röhm, *Geschichte*, 13, 17.

20. The following paragraphs are based on Gerhard Heyl, "Einführung Bayern und seine Armee," in Generaldirektion der Staatlichen Archive Bayerns, *Bayern und seine Armee: Eine Ausstellung des Bayerischen Hauptstaatsarchivs aus den Beständen des Kriegsarchivs* (Munich: Selbstverlag der Generaldirektion der Staatlichen Archive Bayerns, 1987), 8–10; Lankes, *München als Garnison*, 18, 54–55; Rumschöttel, *Das bayerische Offizierkorps*, 39–74, 94–103; Bernd Steger, *Berufssoldaten oder Prätorianer: die Einflußnahme des bayerischen Offizierskorps auf die Innenpolitik in Bayern und im Reich 1918–1924* (Frankfurt am Main: Rita G. Fischer Verlag, 1980), 19–29; Kai Uwe Tapken, *Die Reichswehr in Bayern von 1919 bis 1924* (Hamburg: Verlag Dr. Kovač, 2002), 45–47; Wolfgang Zorn, *Bayerns Geschichte im 20. Jahrhundert: Von der Monarchie zum Bundesland* (Munich: Verlag C. H. Beck, 1986), 40; BHSA/KA Nachlaß Frauenholz/1, 75–76, 85, 111.

21. Heyl, "Einführung Bayern und seine Armee," 10; Röhm, *Geschichte*, 23; Ingolstädter Tagblatt, November 7, 1913, 1–2; Reinhard Bauer and Ernst Piper, with Elisabeth Lukas-Götz, *München: die Geschichte einer Stadt* (Munich: Deutscher Taschenbuch Verlag, 1996), 246.

22. Hans Fegert, *Ingolstadt in alten Ansichten* (Zaltbommel: Europäische Bibliothek, 1986), 23; Christian Dittmar, *Ingolstadt in alten Ansichtskarten* (Frankfurt am Main: Flechsig Verlag, 1979), 68–69; Siegfried Hofmann, *Alt Ingolstadt: Bilder einer Donaustadt* (Tübingen: Verlag Gebr. Metz, 1988), 8–9; B., "Die Landesfestung Ingolstadt," *Bayern und seine Armee*, 226; Markus Ingenlath, "'meinem König Otto I. treu zu dienen' Militärdienst in München," Prinz and Krauss, *München, Musenstadt mit Hinterhöfen*, 146.

23. Röhm's duty and leave patterns are set out in BHSA/KA OP 32380, and in the regimental and battalion reports also held in BHSA/KA; Röhm, *Geschichte*, 24.

24. Quoted in Rumschöttel, *Das bayerische Offizierkorps*, 111. K. 10. Infanterie-Regiment Prinz Ludwig, III Bataillon, "Nachweisung der Gehaltsverhältnisse des

Ernst Röhm Leutnant im 10. Infanterie-Regiment, Patent vom 9. März 1909.";
Kriegsministerium No. 18194, Abteilung für Persönliche Angelegenheiten, September 25, 1909, "Gehaltseinweisung und Festsetzung des Besoldungs-Dienstalters.," : BHSA/KA OP 32380, 2; Rumschöttel, *Das bayerische Offizierkorps*, 116–20.

25. Röhm, *Geschichte*, 22–23; Rumschöttel, *Das bayerische Offizierkorps*, 120–21; BHSA/KA Nachlaß Frauenholz/1, 27, 30, 94.

26. Röhm, *Geschichte*, 17, 19–24; *Ingolstädter Tagblatt*, 1910–14, *passim*, and *Ingolstädter Zeitung*, 1910–14, *passim*; *Ingolstädter Zeitung*, May 7, 1934, 2; Röhm to Emilie Röhm, April 23, 1929, RFP, 2; information from the Röhm family.

27. Röhm, *Geschichte*, 17, 18, 20–22.

28. Ibid., 19. "K. B. Gericht der 6. Division empf. 9.3.11 Nr. 284," March 9, 1911; "Vormerkungen zur Personal-Akte: Ernst Röhm," 1; Weiß, Oberstltn. U. Regts. Kdr., 10. Infanterie-Regiment Prinz Ludwig to the K.11. Inf. Brigade, March 14, 1911, "Betreff: Mißhandlung Untergebener Untersuchungssache Röhm": BHSA/KA OP 32380.

29. BHSA/KA Nachlaß Frauenholz/1, 36; Ingenlath, "'meinem König Otto I. treu zu dienen,'" 149–50; Lankes, *München als Garnison*, 636–43; signature, Gen. Kdo.III.Bay.A.Corps No. 143 II g, "Zum K. Kriegs-Ministerium," March 23, 1911, BHSA/KA MKr. 1102; von Kirschbaum, 10. Infanterie-Regiment Prinz Ludwig, to the K. 11. Inf. Brigade, March 14, 1911, "Betreff: Mißhandlung Untergebener Untersuchungssache Röhm," BHSA/KA OP 32380, 2–3.

30. Information on the case is taken from BHSA/KA OP 32380 and BHSA/KA MKr 11029; Mrs. Bauernschäfer, Stadtarchiv Nürnberg, September 25, 1997, "Landgericht Eichstätt und Staatanwaltschaft bei dem Landgericht Eichstätt hier: Verbleib der einschlägigen Akten."

31. "Qualifikations-Bericht zum 1. Januar 1913 über den Leutnant Ernst Röhm im K.10.Infanterie Regiment.," BHSA/KA OP 32380, 1.

32. Schleicher, Kompagniechef, undated, "Qualifikations-Bericht zum 1. Januar 1913 über den Leutnant Ernst Röhm im K.10.Infanterie Regiment.," BHSA/KA OP 32380, 3.

33. Ibid.

34. Weißmüller, Reg. Kdr., November 3, 1912, "Qualifikations-Bericht zum 1. Januar 1913 über den Leutnant Ernst Röhm im K.10.Infanterie Regiment.," BHSA/KA OP 32380, 2.

35. Rumschöttel, *Das bayerische Offizierkorps*, 174, 187, 214.

36. IfZ ZS 357/I, 1.

37. IfZ ZS 70, 2.

38. Ibid.; Röhm, *Geschichte*, 22, 41; Herr Edmund Hausfelder, stellv. Leiter, Stadtarchiv Ingolstadt, to the author, March 15, 1999; Dr. Fridolin Hug, Eichstätt, fax to the author, September 17, 2000.

39. Röhm to Dr. Heimsoth, February 25, 1929, Klotz, *Drei Briefe*, 7–8. István Déak, *Beyond Nationalism: A Social and Political History of the Habsburg Officer Corps, 1848–1918* (New York: Oxford University Press, 1990), 143; John C.

Fout, "Sexual Politics in Wilhelmine Germany: The Male Gender Crisis, Moral Purity, and Homophobia," *Journal of the History of Sexuality* 2, no. 3 (1992): 388–421.

40. Rumschöttel, *Das bayerische Offizierkorps*, 222–34; Vogel, Hauptmann, und Kompagniechef, 2. Kompagnie, 10. Infanterie Regiment, February 10, 1907, "Vertrauliche Mitteilungen über den Fahnenjunker <u>Ernst</u>, Julius, Günther Röhm," BHSA/KA OP 32380, 1; Röhm, *Geschichte*, 23–4.

41. B., "Juden in der Armee," *Bayern und seine Armee*, 47–49.

42. Rumschöttel, *Das bayerische Offizierkorps*, 222, 223, 227, 233, 239–43, 253–54; BHSA/KA Nachlaß Frauenholz/1, 103.

43. Zorn, *Bayerns Geschichte*, 40–41, 44, 48, 61; David Blackbourn, *The Fontana History of Germany 1780–1918: The Long Nineteenth Century* (London: Fontana, 1997), chap. 7–9.

44. Lankes, *München als Garnison*, 457–67; *Ingolstädter Zeitung*, January 14, 1912, 1.

45. Röhm, *Geschichte*, 24.

Chapter 3

1. Undated, Röhm, "<u>Denkschrift über den Frontbann.</u>," SAM STAW 14360, 3.

2. IfZ ZS 357/I, 1–2.

3. *Ingolstädter Zeitung*, August 2, 1914.

4. Bayerisches Kriegsarchiv, *Die Bayern im Großen Kriege 1914–1918. Auf Grund der Kriegsakten dargestellt* (Munich: Verlag des bayerischen Kriegsarchivs, 1923), 6–8; "6th Bavarian Division," *Histories of Two Hundred and Fifty-One Divisions of the German Army which participated in the War (1914–1918), Compiled from Records of Intelligence Section of the General Staff, at General Headquarters: Chaumont, France: 1919* (Washington, DC: Government Printing Office, 1920), 134.

5. Holger H. Herwig, *The First World War: Germany and Austria-Hungary 1914–1918*, 2nd impression (London: Arnold, 1997), 46–50, 60–62, 96–106; Robin Prior and Trevor Wilson, *The First World War* (London: Cassell, 2001), 39, 47–48.

6. Bayerisches Kriegsarchiv, *Bayern im Großen Kriege*, 55.

7. Mehrere Mitkämpfer, *K.B.10 Infanterie-Regiment König*, 150–53; Röhm, *Geschichte*, 28–30.

8. Herwig, *First World War*, 105.

9. Mehrere Mitkämpfer, *K.B.10 Infanterie-Regiment König*, 164–68, 173–74.

10. Röhm, *Geschichte*, 34–36; signature, February 15, 1915, "Militärärztliches Zeugnis.," BHSA/KA OP 32380.

11. Bergmann to Weiss, May 14, 1949, SAM STAW 28793, 2.

12. IfZ ZS 70, 1–2; IfZ ZS 8, 1.

13. *Ingolstädter Zeitung*, October 20, 1914; "Vormerkungen.," BHSA/KA OP 32380, 2; *Histories of Two Hundred and Fifty-One Divisions of the German Army*, 135.

14. Röhm, *Geschichte*, 36; *Der S.A.-Mann*, June 30, 1933, 4; Mehrere Mitkämpfer, *K.B.10 Infanterie-Regiment König*, 177, 196.
15. *Der S.A.-Mann*, December 16, 1933, 5.
16. Röhm, *Geschichte*, 37–40, 42–43; BHSA/KA 10 I.R./Bd. 12; Mehrere Mitkämpfer, *K.B.10 Infanterie-Regiment König*, 177, 198–99.
17. *Der S.A.-Mann*, June 24, 1933, 3.
18. Ibid., 4.
19. Röhm, *Geschichte*, 41.
20. Prior and Wilson, *First World War*, 113–14, 118–23.
21. Undated, "Beschreibung der Tat des Oberleutnants Ernst Röhm im 10. Infanterie-Regiment.," BHSA/KA MMJO VII K 24/9, 1.
22. Röhm, *Geschichte*, 47.
23. Ibid.
24. Ibid.
25. BHSA/KA 12. b.I.D./Bd. 41 Akt 4, 3; undated, "Beschreibung der Tat . . .," BHSA/KA MMJO VII K24/9, 2.
26. BHSA/KA MMJO VII K 24/9.
27. Röhm, *Geschichte*, 48–49.
28. Quoted in "Beschreibung der Tat . . .," BHSA/KA MMJO VII K24/9, 2.
29. "Vorgeschichte," "Krankenblatt.," "Hauptkrankenbuch Nr. 1443," July 16, 1916, 4–5, and Reserve-Lazarett VI Frankfurt a.m., June 30, 1916, "Krankenblatt Hauptkrankenbuch Nr. 6029," 1; "Vorgeschichte," August 14, 1916, 2; Reservelazarett München B, Ohren-Kehlkopfstation (C.), October 17, 1916 and November 16, 1916, "Krankenblatt.," 2; "Krankengeschichte," August 12, [1916], 7; signature, Ambulatorium d.Sr.B II für organisch Nervenkranke, letter to a colleague, October 16, 1916; signature, Ridlerschule, to the Chefarzt d. Res. Laz. München R, December 2, 1916: BHSA/KA OP 32380.
30. Röhm, *Geschichte*, 50–52, 55; I.V., Kriegsministerium to the K. stellv. Generalkommando III A.K., November 8, 1916, "No. 123563," BHSA/KA OP 32380.
31. Von Kreß, "Qualifikations-Bericht zum 29. Mai 1917 über den Hauptmann Ernst Röhm des 10. Infanterie-Regiments," BHSA/KA OP 32380.
32. V. Hellingrath to Generalkommando III. A.K., May 25, 1917, BHSA OP 32380; *Histories of Two Hundred and Fifty-One Divisions of the German Army*, 222–23.
33. Robert Ruchte, *Das K.B. 27. Infanterie-Regiment* (Munich: Verlag Max Schick, 1932), 98–110.
34. V. Nagel, 12. bayer. Inf.-Division, February 15, 1918, "Beurteilung über den Hauptmann Ernst Röhm, Kompagnieführer im 10. Inf.Rgt.," BHSA/KA OP 32380.
35. Ernst Kern, *Das K.B. 26 Infanterie-Regiment* (Munich: Verlag Bayerisches Kriegsarchiv, 1926), 72–78.
36. Röhm, *Geschichte*, 58, 62; "12. Bayer. Infanterie Division.," BHSA/KA 3 Inf. Div. aktiv 10–16, 2; Alois Früchtl, *Das K.B. 28 Infanterie-Regiment* (Munich: Verlag Bayerisches Kriegsarchiv, 1924), 44–46.

37. Röhm, *Geschichte*, 59; April 24, 1949, Schreyer, "Eidesstattliche Erklärung," AM HKN/574, 1.
38. Ruchte, *K.B. 27. Infanterie-Regiment*, 136, 141, 163–64; *Histories of Two Hundred and Fifty-One Divisions of the German Army*, 224; v. Boehm, July 2, 1918, "IIc Nr. 97 pers.," 1 plus added at the bottom of this order and counter-signed by Röhm, July 8, 1918, Frhr. von Nagel, "Abtlg. Ib Nr. 9264," "Zusatz der Division," 2: BHSA/KA 12 b.I.D./Bd. 44 Akt 8.
39. Röhm, *Geschichte*, 62.
40. Prior and Wilson, *First World War*, 184–85.
41. Röhm, *Geschichte*, 63–64.
42. Röhm, *Geschichte*, 64; Ruchte, *K.B. 27. Infanterie-Regiment*, 174, 176, 177, 180–82.
43. Röhm, *Geschichte*, 65–66.
44. Quoted in IfZ ZS 357/I, 1–2.
45. Röhm, *Geschichte*, 68–69.

Chapter 4

1. Röhm, *Geschichte*, 164.
2. Georg Fischer, "Revolution und Rathausbrand 1918 in Ingolstadt im Spiegel der Erinnerung," *Ingolstädter Heimatblätter* 41, no. 4 (1978): 13–14; Willy Albrecht, "Das Ende des monarchisch-konstitutionellen Regierungssystems in Bayern: König, Regierung und Landtag im Ersten Weltkrieg," in Karl Bosl ed., *Bayern im Umbruch: Die Revolution von 1918, ihre Voraussetzungen, ihr Verlauf und ihre Folgen* (Munich: R. Oldenbourg Verlag, 1969), 290–93.
3. Karl-Ludwig Ay, "Volksstimmung und Volksmeinung als Voraussetzung der Münchner Revolution von 1918," *Bayern im Umbruch*, 345–86.
4. Martin Hobohm, "Soziale Heeresmißstände im Ersten Weltkrieg," in Wolfram Wette ed., *Der Krieg des kleinen Mannes: Eine Militärgeschichte von unten*, 2nd ed. (Munich: Piper, 1995), 136–45; Richard Bessel, *Germany after the First World War* (Oxford: Clarendon Press, 2002), chap. 1.
5. Andreas Kraus, *Grundzüge der Geschichte Bayerns*, 2nd ed. (Darmstadt: Wissenschaftliche Buchgesellschaft, 1992), 202; Karl-Ludwig Ay, *Die Entstehung einer Revolution: Die Volksstimmung in Bayern während des Ersten Weltkrieges* (Berlin: Duncker & Humblot, 1968), 134–48.
6. BHSA/KA M.Kr. 2330; BHSA/KA M.Kr. 2331; Röhm, *Geschichte*, 52–55, 58; Karl Demeter, "Otto von Kress als bayerischer Kriegsminister," *Zeitschrift für bayerische Landesgeschichte* 6 (1933): 85–110.
7. Longerich, *Die braunen Bataillone*, 20; Röhm, *Geschichte*, 69, 72.
8. Röhm, *Geschichte*, 73.
9. Zorn, *Bayerns Geschichte*, 131–32; Steger, *Berufssoldaten oder Prätorianer*, 52.
10. Wilhelm Deist, "Verdeckter Militärstreik im Kriegsjahr 1918?" Wette, *Der Krieg des kleinen Mannes*, 146–67; Bessel, *Germany after the First World War*, chap. 1 and 3.

11. Bessel, *Germany after the First World War*, 7, 88–89, 265; Fischer, "Revolution und Rathausbrand 1918 in Ingolstadt," 14; Zorn, *Bayerns Geschichte*, 148.

12. Eleanor Hancock, "Ernst Röhm and the Experience of World War I," *The Journal of Military History* 60, no. 1 (1996): 54, 57.

13. Röhm, *Geschichte*, 71–72; Steger, *Berufssoldaten oder Prätorianer*, 55.

14. Röhm, *Geschichte*, 71–85; "No. 311858 Note. Betreff: Stellenbesetzungen," December 12, 1918, BHSA/KA OP 32380.

15. Zorn, *Bayerns Geschichte*, 139, 141, 147.

16. Ibid., 166–67.

17. Röhm, *Geschichte*, 80.

18. Ibid., 79–81.

19. Ibid., 79–80.

20. Stefan Hofbauer, "Die Revolution von 1918/19 in Ingolstadt," Schriftliche Hausarbeit zur Wissenschaftlichen Prüfung für das Lehramt an Gymnasien im Fruhjahr 1978 in München, *passim*; *Ingolstädter Tagblatt*, January-March 1919, *passim*; *Ingolstädter Zeitung*, January–June 1919, *passim*. Hofbauer notes the problematic nature of Röhm's claims about the revolution in Ingolstadt, but observes that they provide indirect evidence of the lack of opposition to the revolution, including on the part of the bourgeoisie: Hofbauer, "Revolution von 1918/19 in Ingolstadt," 63. Edmund Hausfelder, "Kommunalpolitik und Verwaltung in Ingolstadt während der Weimarer Republik," in Stadtarchiv, Wissenschaftliche Stadtbibliothek and Stadtmuseum, *Ingolstadt im Nationalsozialismus: Eine Studie* (Ingolstadt: Dokumentation zur Zeitgeschichte Band 1, Stadtarchiv, 1995), 25.

21. Hofbauer, "Revolution von 1918/19 in Ingolstadt," 140; Röhm, *Geschichte*, 82–83; Zorn, *Bayerns Geschichte*, 169.

22. Zorn, *Bayerns Geschichte*, 170–72; Röhm, *Geschichte*, 84.

23. *Ingolstädter Tagblatt*, February 23, 1919; Hofbauer, "Revolution von 1918/19 in Ingolstadt," 152–56; Röhm, *Geschichte*, 85.

24. "Verpflichtung der Freiwilligen des Bayrischen Freikorps für den Grenzschutz Ost.," April 8, 1919, BHSA/KA Sch. Brig. 21/Nr. 236/I; Röhm, *Geschichte*, 85–87; Tapken, *Reichswehr in Bayern*, 117–21.

25. Hagen Schulze, *Freikorps und Republik 1918–1920* (Boppard: Harald Boldt Verlag, 1969), 25, 30; Hannsjoachim W. Koch, *Der deutsche Bürgerkrieg: Eine Geschichte der deutschen und österreichischen Freikorps 1918–1933* (Berlin: Ullstein, 1978), chap. 2; BHSA/KA HS 2176.

26. Röhm, *Geschichte*, 86; BHSA/KA HS 925, 13–17.

27. Kraus, *Grundzüge*, 215; BHSA/KA HS2283; Bauer and Piper, with Lukas-Götz, *München*, 264; BHSA/KA HS 2176; Röhm, *Geschichte*, 88–89.

28. IfZ ZS 70; "Anlage 1. Kriegsgliederungen.," Im Auftrage des Oberkommandos der Wehrmacht bearbeitet und herausgegeben von der Kriegsgeschichtlichen Forschungsanstalt des Heeres, *Die Niederwerfung der Räteherrschaft in Bayern, 1919* Vierter Band (Berlin: E. S. Mittler & Sohn, 1939), 200; Bauer and Piper, with Lukas-Götz, *München*, 264; BHSA/KA RWGrKdo4 Bd. 2; BHSA/KA RWGrKdo 4/No. 48.

29. Von Epp, Bayr. Schützenkorps, May 1, 1919, "Befehl.," BHSA/KA Sch. Brig. 21/Nr. 6; Röhm, *Geschichte*, 90; Bauer and Piper, with Lukas-Götz, *München*, 266; Heinrich Hillmayr, *Roter und Weißer Terror in Bayern nach 1918: Ursachen, Erscheinungsformen und Folgen der Gewalttätigkeiten im Verlauf der revolutionären Ereignisse nach dem Ende des Ersten Weltkrieges* (Munich: Nusser, 1974), 120–57.

30. Röhm, *Geschichte*, 91–2.

31. Ibid., 93.

32. Ibid., 96, 99.

33. Ibid., 98.

34. Ibid.

35. Frederic Raphael and Kenneth McLeish, *The List of Books* (London: Mitchell Beazley, 1981), 22.

Chapter 5

1. Adolf Hitler, quoted in "P.N.D. Nr. 727," SAM Pol. Dir. München Nr. 6809, 2.

2. Quoted in Röhm, *Geschichte*, 140.

3. BHSA/KA RWGrKdo 4/No. 316; Tapken, *Reichswehr in Bayern*, 37–56.

4. BHSA/KA Sch. Brig. 21/Nr. 18; Tapken, *Reichswehr in Bayern*, 165–268, 321–31; Steger, *Berufssoldaten oder Prätorianer*, 117–18.

5. BHSA/KA Sch.Brig. 21/ Nr. 21/1 u. 2, 38, 51, 69, 88, 92, 102, 111, 126; BAK NL101/3, 38; SM PME R 139/140.

6. Röhm, handwritten draft, to Gruppenkommando 4, December 24, 1919, "Betreff: Neuorganisation der Heeresverwaltung.," and the final version signed by von Epp on the same date: BHSA/KA Sch. Brig. 21/Nr. 38.

7. Karl Schreyer, April 24, 1949, "Eidesstattliche Erklärung.," Amtsgericht München HKN/574, 1.

8. BHSA/KA HS 925, 17. See also ibid., 15–16; Röhm, *Geschichte*, 100.

9. David Clay Large, *The Politics of Law and Order: A History of the Bavarian Einwohnerwehr, 1918–1921* (Philadelphia: transactions of the American Philosophical Society 70, pt. 2, 1980), 9–17, 19–21, 24–25, 31, 34, 39; BHSA/KA HS 920, 61–66a; BHSA II Minn 66135.

10. BHSA/KA Sch. Brig. 21/Nr. 97; BHSA/KA Sch. Brig. 21/Nr. 126; Röhm, *Geschichte*, 100; Clay Large, *Politics of Law and Order*, 29–30, 47–48; BHSA/KA Sch. Brig. 21/Nr. 99; BHSA/KA RWGrKdo 4/No. 20; BHSA/KA Infanterieführer 21 Bd. 1; BHSA/II M Inn 66135.

11. Clay Large, *Politics of Law and Order*, 31, 66–67; BHSA/KA EW Bd. 3/Ic; Steger, *Berufssoldaten oder Prätorianer*, 137–50.

12. BHSA/KA Infanterie Führer 21/Bund 1 Akt 7; Tapken, *Reichswehr in Bayern*, 333–35; BHSA/KA Sch. Brig. 21/Nr.13.

13. Harold J. Gordon, Jr., *The Reichswehr and the German Republic, 1919–1926* (Princeton: Princeton University Press, 1957), 165; Röhm, *Geschichte*, 107.

14. Röhm, *Geschichte*, 107, 108; BAR NS 26/230; A. Joachimsthaler, *Korrektur einer Biographie: Adolf Hitler 1908–1920* (Munich: Herbig, 1989), 252; Tapken, *Reichswehr in Bayern*, 316–17; Bennecke, *Hitler und die SA*, 23.

15. Röhm, *Geschichte*, 108. BAR NS 26/76; Joachimsthaler, *Korrektur einer Biographie*, 251; Reginald H. Phelps, "Hitler and the *Deutsche Arbeiterpartei*," *American Historical Review* 68, no. 4 (1963): 978–82.

16. Georg Franz, "Munich: Birthplace and Center of the National Socialist German Workers' Party," *The Journal of Modern History* 29, no. 4 (1957): 331. BHSA/ II MA 103476, 41; Bennecke, *Hitler und die SA*, 23, 25–34; Röhm, *Geschichte*, 108; Andreas Werner, "SA und NSDAP: SA: 'Wehrverband,' 'Parteitruppe' oder 'Revolutionsarmee' Studien zur Geschichte der SA und der NSDAP 1920–1933," Inaugural Dissertation der Philosophischen Fakultät der Friedrich-Alexander-Universität zu Erlangen-Nürnberg, 1964, 22–23; BAK N1101/42.

17. Röhm, *Geschichte*, 100–101; Benjamin Ziemann, "Wanderer zwischen den Welten—Der Militärkritiker und Gegner des entschiedenen Pazifismus Major a.D. Karl Mayr (1883–1945)," in Wolfram Wette, with Helmut Donat, ed., *Pazifistische Offiziere in Deutschland 1871–1933, ed.* (Bremen: Donat Verlag, 1999), 273–85; "Mayr, Karl," in Werner Roder and Herbert A. Strauss ed., *Biographisches Handbuch der deutschsprachigen Emigration nach 1933 Band I Politik, Wirtschaft, Öffentliches Leben, ed.* (Munich: K. G. Saur, 1980), 486; Tapken, *Reichswehr in Bayern*, 313–16.

18. IfZ ZS 263, 1.

19. Röhm, *Geschichte*, 101; Eberhard Kolb, *The Weimar Republic* (London: Unwin Hyman, 1988), 36–37; Koch, *Der deutsche Bürgerkrieg*, chap. VI; Schulze, *Freikorps und Republik*, 244–304.

20. Kolb, *Weimar Republic*, 37–38; Schulze, *Freikorps und Republik*, 297–301, 304–18; BAR R 43 I/2715, 2716, 2717, and 2718; BHSA/KA RWGrKdo 4/ No. 11, Sch. Brig. 21/Nr. 143, 317.

21. Clay Large, *Politics of Law and Order*, 36; Röhm, *Geschichte*, 102–4; BHSA/KA HS 920, 224–338; BHSA II M Inn 66286.

22. Kolb, *Weimar Republic*, 38; "Tagebuch," March 19, 1920 entry, BHSA/KA Sch. Brig. 21/1, 2, 8; Epp, "Kriegstagebuch.," BAK N1101/33, 1–2.

23. Epp, "Kriegstagebuch.," March 31–April 2, 1920 entries, BAK N1101/33, 4–6; BHSA/KA Sch. Brig. 21/Nr. 56; BHSA/KA Sch. Brig. 21/Nr. 42.

24. Haas, Gruppe Haas, "Abt. Ib Nr. 467 mob.," April 8, 1920, BHSA/KA Sch. Brig. 21/Nr. 59; Oberst Bayer, Schützen-Brig. Epp Abt. Ic to Gruppe Haas, April 14, 1920, BHSA/KA Sch. Brig. 21/Nr. 56.

25. Röhm, *Geschichte*, 105–7.

26. Kolb, *Weimar Republic*, 38; BHSA/KA RWGrKdo 4/No. 28; BHSA/KA RWGrKdo 4/No 25; BHSA/KA RWGrKdo 4/No. 282; Röhm, *Geschichte*, 104.

27. BHSA/KA RWGrKdo 4/No. 837; BHSA/KA OP 32380.

28. IfZ ZS 263, 1. Röhm, *Geschichte*, 110, 118.

29. Clay Large, *Politics of Law and Order*, 49–66; Werner, "SA und NSDAP," 15, 16; BHSA/KA RWGrKdo 4/Bd. 499.

30. Clay Large, *Politics of Law and Order*, 52–53, 63, 67; BHSA/KA RWGrKdo 4/ No. 499; BHSA/II MInn 66139; PRO FO 371/4740, 4757, 4758, 4759, 5855, 5856, and 5865; BHSA/KA RWGrKdo 4/No. 60, 61, 68, 76, 78; BHSA/II M Inn 66139; BHSA/II MA 104087; BHSA/II M Ju 10973; Steger, *Berufssoldaten oder Prätorianer*, 137–47; Werner, "SA und NSDAP," 18.

31. Röhm, *Geschichte*, 117–18; Harold R. Gordon, Jr., *Hitler and the Beer Hall Putsch* (Princeton: Princeton University Press, 1972), 161–62; Steger, *Berufssoldaten oder Prätorianer*, 150; BHSA/KA B. u. R. Bd. 36.

32. Howard Stern, "The *Organisation Consul*," *Journal of Modern History* 35, no.1 (1963): 21; BAR R 43 I/2263.

33. Röhm, *Geschichte*, 109–10; IfZ ZS 1738.

34. Kraus, *Grundzüge*, 223; Röhm, *Geschichte*, 120; Steger, *Berufssoldaten oder Prätorianer*, 146, 149; Werner, "SA und NSDAP," 19; Kurt Sendtner, *Rupprecht von Wittelsbach, Kronprinz von Bayern* (Munich: Richard Pflaum Verlag, 1959), 507; Gordon, *Putsch*, 19, 90.

35. Röhm, *Geschichte*, 122–23; Unsigned, "Abschrift. Königsputsch," September 11, 1922, BHSA/KA B.u.R. Bd. 35, I-III (a) 4; Sendtner, *Rupprecht von Wittelsbach*, 461–64, 499–502.

36. Röhm, *Geschichte*, 110–11.

37. Ibid., 135–37; ZStAP R 15.07/67119 Nr. 231; Steger, *Berufssoldaten oder Prätorianer*, 157–61.

38. Röhm, *Geschichte*, 138; Steger, *Berufssoldaten oder Prätorianer*, 153; Sendtner, *Rupprecht von Wittelsbach*, 514.

39. Quoted in "Abschrift!" Freih. v. Berchem, Der Chef des Stabes, Wehrkreiskommando VII to Infanterieführer VII, July 27, 1922, "Ib No. 4847 Pers.," BAK N1101/92: Röhm, *Geschichte*, 139–43; BAK NL1101/42; Kolb, *Weimar Republic*, 45; Steger, *Berufssoldaten oder Prätorianer*, 154; papers on BAK N1101/92; BAK N1101/21; BA MA RH 53–7/v. 393. Röhm did not discuss the *Heimatlandbriefe* incident in the *Geschichte*.

40. Generalmajor Ritter von Epp, "Denkschrift zum "Tausch" Röhm-Hanneken.," December 1922, BAK NL1101/21, 1–11; Röhm, *Geschichte*, 143.

41. Generalmajor Ritter von Epp, "Denkschrift zum "Tausch" Röhm-Hanneken.," December 1922, BAK NL1101/21, 7; Röhm, *Geschichte*, 144.

Chapter 6

1. Röhm, *Geschichte*, 164.

2. Ibid., 144, 147; Gordon, *Putsch*, 147–48.

3. BHSA/KA HS 925, 3.

4. Kolb, *Weimar Republic*, 46–50.

5. BAR R431/2231; BAR R 43 I/2681; Kershaw, *Hitler*, 192; Röhm, *Geschichte*, 148–50.

6. Röhm, *Geschichte*, 150. BHSA/II MA 99518; Kershaw, *Hitler*, 192; Gordon, *Putsch*, 190; Steger, *Berufssoldaten oder Prätorianer*, 176–77.

7. Röhm, *Geschichte*, 148.
8. V. Lossow, Befehlshaber, Bayer. Wehrkreiskommando VII to Hauptmann im Generalstab Röhm, March 6, 1923, "Hpt. Nr. 7912 IIa Nr. 1340," 1; Oberstleutnant Stollberger to Herr Befehlshaber, enclosing "Gutachten und Schlussurteil.," February 21, 1923, 1–6: BA MA RH 53–7/v. 394a.
9. Röhm to Freiherr von Berchem, January 16, 1923, "Betreff: Meldung," BA MA RH 53–7/v. 394a, 2.
10. V. Lossow, der Befehlshaber, Bayer. Wehrkreiskommando VII, July 17, 1923, "Hpt. Nr. 21625/IIa Nr. 4315. Pers.," enclosing July 12. 1923, Oberstlt. Stollberger, Hptm Rüdel, Major Dollmann, report of the commission, BA MA RH 53–7/v. 394a, 6.
11. Ibid., 3.
12. Ibid., 1, 4, 7, 8, 9–11.
13. Von Epp to von Lossow, April 23, 1923, '"Betreff: Dienstliches Verhalten des Hauptmanns Röhm.," BA MA RH 53–7/v. 394a, 1–6; "Unterredung mit Hauptmann Röhm 6.IV.23 nachmittag.," BAK N 1101/25, 1–2.
14. Kommission in Ehrenhandel zwischen Gen.Majr. Ritter von Epp u. Minis.R. Dr. Roth an den Herrn Befehlshaber, June 21, 1923, "Betreff: Verhalten des Hauptmanns Röhm.," BA MA RH 53–7/v. 394a, 2.
15. Röhm to von Lossow, June 12, 1923, "Betreff: Persönliche Angelegenheit.," 1–3 with 4 attachments; v. Lossow, June 28, 1923, "Hpt. Nr. 203040/IIa Nr. 4047" to Epp: BA MA RH 53–7/v. 394a.
16. Von Lossow to Röhm, June 29, 1923, BA MA RH 53–7/v. 394a, 3.
17. Ibid.
18. Röhm, *Geschichte*, 164.
19. Ibid., 166.
20. Steger, *Berufssoldaten oder Prätorianer*, 177–79; BHSA/II MA 103476, 22–29; Gordon, *Putsch*, 151–54, 157–59.
21. Röhm, *Geschichte*, 153–57.
22. Ibid., 158; Kershaw, *Hitler*, 194; IfZ ZS 1900; Steger, *Berufssoldaten oder Prätorianer*, 179.
23. Röhm, *Geschichte*, 153, 161; Gordon, *Putsch*, 191–92.
24. Röhm, *Geschichte*, 159–62; Steger, *Berufssoldaten oder Prätorianer*, 182, 184–85, 193.
25. BHSA/II MA 103476, 95–96.
26. Röhm, *Geschichte*, 171.
27. Ibid., 175.
28. Ibid., 177.
29. Quoted in ibid., 177.
30. Ibid., 177, 179; BHSA/II MA 103476, 51, 107, 130; Gordon, *Putsch*, 196, note 37.
31. BHSA/II MA 103476, 29–31, 51, 54.
32. Ibid., 110, 135, 136.
33. Ibid., 189, 190.

34. Röhm, *Geschichte*, 180–81: BHSA/II MA 103476, 195–96.
35. Röhm, *Geschichte*, 181; Gordon, *Putsch*, 198, 200.
36. Steger, *Berufssoldaten oder Prätorianer*, 191; BHSA/II MA 103476, 197, 199, 200; Gordon, *Putsch*, 201–2, 204.
37. Gordon, *Putsch*, 202.
38. Ibid., 202–4; BA MA RH 53–7/v. 394a; BHSA/KA RWGrKdo4/No. 784; Röhm, *Geschichte*, 182–83.
39. BHSA/KA RWGrKdo4/No. 784; Röhm, *Geschichte*, 184, 190–91.
40. Röhm, *Geschichte*, 184–85.
41. Steger, *Berufssoldaten oder Prätorianer*, 200–201; Röhm, *Geschichte*, 191.
42. Röhm, *Geschichte*, 191–94.
43. Ibid., 185, 196; BHSA/KA RWGrKdo4/No. 784.
44. Kraus, *Grundzüge*, 226; Gordon, *Putsch*, 94; Steger, *Berufssoldaten oder Prätorianer*, 199.
45. SAM STAW I/3103; Röhm, *Geschichte*, 199.
46. Gordon, *Reichswehr and the German Republic*, 196–97; Gordon, *Putsch*, 514–15.

Chapter 7

1. "5. Verhandlungstag: Samstag, den 1. März 1924, Vormittag," Lothar Gruchmann and Reinhard Weber, eds., with Otto Gritschneder, *Der Hitler-Prozess 1924: Wortlaut der Hauptverhandlung vor dem Volksgericht München Teil 2: 5.-11. Verhandlungstag* (Munich: K. G. Saur, 1998), 380.
2. Röhm, *Geschichte*, 208; Kershaw, *Hitler*, 202; Kolb, *Weimar Republic*, 47, 48, 199.
3. Kershaw, *Hitler*, 202; Kraus, *Grundzüge*, 226; Gordon, *Putsch*, 224; Röhm, *Geschichte*, 204.
4. Gordon, *Putsch*, 150, 228–29; Kraus, *Grundzüge*, 226; Röhm, *Geschichte*, 204; Lothar Gruchmann, "Der Weg zum Hitler-Putsch: Das Reich und Bayern im Krisenjahr 1923," in Lothar Gruchmann and Reinhard Weber, eds., with Otto Gritschneder, *Der Hitler-Prozess 1924: Wortlaut der Hauptverhandlung vor dem Volksgericht München Teil 1: 1.-4. Verhandlungstag* (Munich: K. G. Saur, 1997), LVIII.
5. Röhm, *Geschichte*, 199–200, 202–3; Sendtner, *Rupprecht von Wittelsbach*, 522.
6. Röhm, *Geschichte*, 200.
7. Ibid., 202–3; SAM AG München 19209; *Völkische Zeitung*, October 11, 1923, p.c., ZStAP/R 15.07/67185 file Nr. 374.
8. Gruchmann, "Weg zum Hitler-Putsch," *Hitler-Prozess*, 1, LIX-LX; Gordon, *Putsch*, 247, 249.
9. Gruchmann, "Weg zum Hitler-Putsch," *Hitler-Prozess*, 1, LXI, LXII-LXIII; Gordon, *Putsch*, 252–53; Steger, *Berufssoldaten oder Prätorianer*, 202–13; BAR NS 26/125.
10. Kershaw, *Hitler*, 202–3; Hans Mommsen, *Die verspielte Freiheit: Der Weg der Republik von Weimar in den Untergang 1918 bis 1933* (Frankfurt am Main: Propyläen, 1990), 177.

11. Gordon, *Putsch*, 249, 251, 257; Steger, *Berufssoldaten oder Prätorianer*, 213–17.

12. Röhm, *Geschichte*, 201–2, 207; Gordon, *Putsch*, 102, 103, 442; SAM STAW 3101.

13. VIa, December 6, 1923, unheaded memorandum, containing a letter written by Osswald to Röhm on November 18, 1923, SAM Pol. Dir. München 10162, 1.

14. Röhm, *Geschichte*, 201–2; Gordon, *Putsch*, 102; SAM Pol. Dir. München 6712.

15. Gordon, *Putsch*, 255–56, 259.

16. Gordon, *Putsch*, 259; Kershaw, *Hitler*, 205; BHSA/KA HS 925, 25.

17. "2. Verhandlungstag: Mittwoch, den 27. Februar 1924 vorm.," *Hitler-Prozess*, 1, 81. Gordon, *Putsch*, 259–60; Kershaw, *Hitler*, 205; unsigned, January 3, 1924, "Röhm.—Die Zusammenstellung fasst auf den Sonderakten Röhm und die mir sonst gekommenen Schriftstücken. Ergänzungen werden die Zusammenstellungen der Collegen Dresse und Ehard bringen.," SAM STAW 3108, 1; December 1937, Johann Aigner, "Ein Beitrag zur Geschichte der nationalen Erhebung im November 1923. Als Ordonnanz bei Hochverrätern.," BAR NS 26/116, 3–4.

18. Gordon, *Putsch*, 274–75, and 274, footnote 16; BHSA/KA HS 925, 37.

19. Kraus, *Grundzüge*, 227; Kershaw, *Hitler*, 205; unsigned, January 3, 1924, "Röhm.—Die Zusammenstellung fasst auf den Sonderakten Röhm . . .," SAM STAW 3108, 2, 3; Gordon, *Putsch*, 260–62.

20. Gordon, *Putsch*, 267.

21. Ibid., 270–72.

22. BAR NS 26/125; SAM Pol. Dir. München 6712.

23. "Der Putsch am 8. November 1923 Vorgeschichte und Verlauf.," "Anlage 4.," "Vorgänge beim Stab der 7. Division am 8.11. abends u. 9.11. vom Verlassen des Bürgerbräukellers bis zur Wiedereinbesitznahme des Kriegs-Ministeriums.," BHSA/KA HS 2401, 13; Röhm, *Geschichte*, 209; Gordon, *Putsch*, 283–91.

24. Signatures (Rudolf Schmäling and Lorenz Reithmeier), November 27, 1923, "VId/131," "Betreff: Versammlung der 'Reichskriegsflagge' im Löwenbräukeller am Donnerstag, den 8. November 1923 abends 8 Uhr.," SAM Pol. Dir. München Nr. 6.709, 1–3; Röhm, *Geschichte*, 210, 211; John Dornberg, *Munich 1923: The Story of Hitler's First Grab for Power* (New York: Harper & Row, 1982), 25–26, 72, 83, 84, 105; "Der Putsch am 8. November 1923. Vorgeschichte und Verlauf.," "C. Die Ereignisse am 8.1.1 abends in den Kasernen usw. bis zur Ueber-nahme der Leitung der Gegenmassnahmen durch den Befehlshaber.," BHSA/KA HS 2401, 9.

25. Röhm, *Geschichte*, 211; Dornberg, *Munich 1923*, 118–19; SAM Pol. Dir. München 6712; Gordon, *Putsch*, 291–92; SAM Pol. Dir. München 6712; SAM STAW 3099; SAM Pol. Dir. München 10066.

26. Röhm, *Geschichte*, 211–12.

27. November 13, 1923, "Abschrift von Abschrift. Hauptmann Daser, Offz.v.Dienst 8./9.XI.", "Bericht über die Vorgänge 8./9.11.23 im Wehrkreiskommando.," SAM Pol. Dir. München 10066, 2. Röhm, *Geschichte*, 212; SAM Pol. Dir. 6713.

28. Gordon, *Putsch*, 289, 317–18, 320, 322–24, 332–35.

29. Röhm, *Geschichte*, 212–13.

30. Ibid., 212; BA MA Sg 1/91 963; SAM Pol. Dir. München 67121; unsigned, January 3, 1924, "Röhm.—Die Zusammenstellung fasst auf den Sonderakten Röhm . . .," SAM STAW 3108, 5.

31. Georg [Raithel] to Richard [Reinhardt], November 16, 1923 "Brief-Abschrift," SAM Pol. Dir. München 6712, 1. SAM STAW 3101; Röhm, *Geschichte*, 214; BHSA/KA HS 925, 48; SAM STAW 3101; Gordon, *Putsch*, 344; unsigned, January 3, 1924, "Röhm.—Die Zusammenstellung fasst auf den Sonderakten . . .," SAM STAW 3108, 6–7.

32. Gordon, *Putsch*, 343–44, 346. Röhm, *Geschichte*, 215–16. Röhm exaggerated the strength of the attacking force in his autobiography.

33. Gordon, *Putsch*, 346–47, and 346, note 109; BHSA/KA HS 925, 51–52.

34. Gordon, *Putsch*, 347, 350–65.

35. Ibid., 347–48.

36. Ibid., 348; Dornberg, *Munich 1923*, 304; SAM Pol. Dir. München 6712; Röhm, *Geschichte*, 221.

37. Röhm, *Geschichte*, 228–29.

38. *Bay. Staatsanzeiger*, November 14, 1923, SAM Pol. Dir. München 6721; "Beilage zum Briefe an Röhm Ernst, datiert vom 18.11.23.," Karl Osswald, Kommandeur, Reichskriegsflagge to various örtliche Kommandos, November 11, 1923, 1; and VIa, unheaded memorandum, December 6, 1923, 1–3: SAM Pol. Dir. München 10162; Gordon, *Putsch*, 427–36; Röhm, *Geschichte*, 255–56.

39. Quoted in signature (Munz?), February 16, 1924, "Herrn Ersten Staatsanwalt wiedervorgelegt.," SAM STAW 3108, 2. Röhm, *Geschichte*, 234, 241, 243–44, 248; SAM STAW 3101; SAM Pol. Dir. München 6713.

40. SAM STAW 3099; Röhm, *Geschichte*, 272.

41. Otto Gritschneder, "Das mißbrauchte bayerische Volksgericht," *Hitler-Prozess*, 1, XIX-XLI; Otto Gritschneder, *Bewährungsfrist für den Terroristen Adolf H. Der Hitler-Putsch und die bayerische Justiz* (Munich: Verlag C. H. Beck, 1990), Part II, chap. 4 and 5; Otto Gritschneder, *Der Hitler-Prozeß und sein Richter Georg Neithardt: Skandalurteil von 1924 ebnet Hitler den Weg* (Munich: Verlag C. H. Beck, 2001), *passim*; Gordon, *Putsch*, 479–85.

42. "4. Verhandlungstag: Freitag, den 29. Februar 1924 nachm. 3 Uhr.," *Hitler-Prozess*, 1, 281. Gritschneder, *Hitler-Prozeß und sein Richter*, 164; *Hitler-Prozess*, 1, 80–81, 215.

43. "5. Verhandlungstag: Samstag, den 1. März 1924, Vormittag.," *Hitler-Prozess*, 2, 378.

44. "24. Verhandlungstag: 27. März 1924, vorm. 9. Uhr.," Lothar Gruchmann and Reinhard Weber, eds., with Otto Gritschneder, *Der Hitler-Prozess 1924: Wortlaut der Hauptverhandlung vor dem Volksgericht München Teil 4: 19.-25. Verhandlungstag* (Munich: K. G. Saur, 1999), 1592.

45. "10. Verhandlungstag, Samstag, den 8. März 1924, vorm. 1/2 9 Uhr.," ibid., 2, 692. BA MA RH 37/602; SAM STAW 3099.

46. Röhm, *Geschichte*, 219–28, 269.

47. Gordon, *Putsch*, 520–21.

48. Röhm, *Geschichte*, 225.
49. Gritschneder, *Bewährungsfrist*, 67–94; Gritschneder, *Hitler-Prozeß und sein Richter*, 55–57; SAM Pol. Dir. München Nr. 15540.
50. Quoted in September 10, 1924, signature (Kundt), Krim.-Kommissar, "VIa 2500/23," SAM STAW 14344, 1.
51. "Anhang Dokument 10 Urteil des Volksgerichts München I vom 1. April 1924 im Hitler-Prozeß," *Hitler-Prozess*, 1, 342–43; Röhm, *Geschichte*, 275–76.

Chapter 8

1. Röhm, *Geschichte*, 289.
2. Ibid., 289; Adolf Hitler, handwritten card, April 1, 1925, BAK NS 26/1258.
3. David Jablonsky, *The Nazi Party in Dissolution: Hitler and the Verbotzeit 1923–1925* (London: Frank Cass, 1989), 85; Kershaw, *Hitler*, 228–29; Röhm, *Geschichte*, 277, 283; Roger Manvell and Heinrich Fraenkel, *Doctor Goebbels* (London: New English Library, 1968), 83.
4. "Urlaubsliste 1924—Mai 1924–Sept. 1924," BAR R01.01/3708, 25; Röhm, *Geschichte*, 283–84; "Enclosure in No. 26. *Record of Leading Personalities in Germany*.," in Sir E. Phipps to Sir John Simon, January 16, 1934, PRO FO 408/64, 67.
5. Kershaw, *Hitler*, 225, 226, 227; Jablonsky, *Nazi Party*, 55.
6. Kurt G.W. Ludecke, *I Knew Hitler: The Story of a Nazi Who escaped the Blood Purge* (New York: Charles Scribner's Sons, 1937; New York: AMS Press, 1982), 245. Röhm, *Geschichte*, 289, 290; SAM STAW 14358.
7. Röhm, *Geschichte*, 291–92; Rossbach to Röhm, July 26, 1924, SAM Pol. Dir. München 10138; Jablonsky, *Nazi Party*, 201–2, footnote 180.
8. Röhm, May 24, 1924, "Richtlinien für die Neuorganisation der S.A. der N.S.D.A.P.," SAM Pol. Dir. München Nr. 10138, 1–2. Longerich, *Die braunen Bataillone*, 46; SAM STAW 14358; SAM STAW 14353; Jablonsky, *Nazi Party*, 90; SAM STAW 14359; IfZ ZS 128; SAM Pol. Dir. München Nr. 10138; SAM Pol. Dir. München Nr. 15540; SAM STAW 14361.
9. SAM STAW 14360; SAM STAW 14359; SAM STAW 14353; SAM STAW 14358.
10. SAM Pol. Dir. München 6692; Röhm, *Geschichte*, 292; SAM STAW 14360; *Amberger Tageblatt*, August 12, 1924, p.c., BHSA/V Slg P 3653.
11. Bruce Campbell, *The SA Generals and the Rise of Nazism* (Lexington: University Press of Kentucky, 1998), 27; Longerich, *Die braunen Bataillone*, 46.
12. Witness statements in SAM STAW/14360; Röhm, *Geschichte*, 293.
13. SAM STAW 14360; SAM STAW 14358.
14. Kellerer, "Zeugen-Vernehmung mit Adolf Hitler in der Voruntersuchung gegen gegen Oßwald Karl, Student in München und 9 Genossen, wegen Geheimbündelei. Aufgenommen in der Gefangenen= und Festungshaftanstalt Landsberg am Lech am 1. Dezember 1924," SAM STAW 14360, 3.

15. Kellerer, "Zeugen-Vernehmung mit Dr Weber Friedrich in der Voruntersuchung gegen Oßwald Karl, Student in München, und 9 Gen. wegen Geheimbündelei. Aufgenommen zu Landsberg a.lech Gefangenen= und Festungshaftanstalt am 2ten Dezember 1924," ibid., 6.

16. Kellerer, "Zeugen-Vernehmung mit Adolf Hitler . . . am 1. Dezember 1924," ibid., 4.

17. Robert Holtzmann, summer 1949, "Tragik zweier überragender Persönlichkeiten.," BAK NL 79/21/1, 6.

18. Witness statements in SAM STAW 14358, SAM STAW 14359, SAM STAW 14360, and SAM STAW 14344; Röhm, Geschichte, 293.

19. "Aufruf des Frontringes und Frontbannes," SAM STAW 14344, 3. SAM STAW 14354; SAM STAW 14344; BAK NS 26/1258; Röhm, Geschichte, 294; SAM STAW 14361.

20. "Nr. 33/1924. Niederschrift aufgenommen in der Ministerratssitzung vom 2. August 1924 im Staatsministerium des Aeußern zu München.," BHSA MA 99519, 5–6.

21. Röhm to Stützel, August 5, 1924, BAK NS 26/1258, 1–2.

22. Witness statements in SAM STAW 14360.

23. Kellerer, "Zeugen-Vernehmung mit nachbenannten Personen in der Voruntersuchung gegen Oßwald Karl, Student in München, und 9 Gen. wegen Geheimbündelei. Aufgenommen zu Nürnberg, Justizpalast, Fürtherstrasse am 28ten November 1924," ibid., 5.

24. Campbell, SA Generals, 27–28; Bennecke, Hitler und die SA, 111; Röhm, Geschichte, 297–98; Jablonsky, Nazi Party, 115; BHSA/II MA 101235/1.

25. Osswald to Schramm, August 19, 1924, SAM STAW 14364, 1–3; Osswald to Seydel, July 1, 1924, SAM STAW 14344, 2.

26. Röhm to Stützel, August 27, 1924, BAK NS 26/1258; SAM STAW 14353; Stützel to Röhm, September 5, 1924, BAK NS 26/1258.

27. SAM STAW 14357; SAM STAW 14359; Jablonsky, Nazi Party, 131; SAM Pol. Dir. München Nr. 15540.

28. Röhm, Geschichte, 297; witness statements in SAM STAW 14360 and SAM STAW 14359; SAM STAW 14353.

29. SAM STAW 14353; Röhm, Geschichte, 299.

30. "von Hptm Röhm," undated (October 1924), "Denkschrift über den Frontbann.," SAM STAW 14360, 7, 13; Röhm, Geschichte, 300–301; Völkischer Kurier, September 21–22, 1924, p.c., BHSA MA 100423; signature, Mitarbeiter im Hauptarchiv der N.S.D.A.P., August 23, 1935, "Bericht," BAR NS 26/116, 1–2; SAM STAW 14359.

31. Signature, der Staatsanwalt bei dem Landgericht München I. an den Herrn Oberreichsanwalt beim Staatsgerichtshof in Leipzig, September 19, 1924, "Haftbeschwerden!" SAM STAW 14353, 1; Röhm, Geschichte, 302; SAM STAW 14344; Jablonsky, Nazi Party, 147.

32. "von Hptm Röhm," undated (October 1924), "Denkschrift über den Frontbann.," SAM STAW 14360, 1–2, 3.

33. Röhm, October 15, 1924, "Erklärung.," SAM STAW 3099; Ludendorff, October 15, 1924, "Erklärung.," SAM STAW 14344; *Völkischer Kurier*, October 16, 1924, p.c., BHSA/II MA 100423; Röhm, *Geschichte*, 304; Lorenz, Conze, Maenner, undated, "Beschluß.," "St.R.Tgb.1128/25.," SAM STAW 14361.

34. Röhm, *Geschichte*, 296, 307; Longerich, *Die braunen Bataillone*, 50; Jablonsky, *Nazi Party*, 151; BAR R 43 I/2236; IfZ ZS 539.

35. Röhm to Kellerer, November 7, 1924, SAM STAW 14359, 1; IfZ ZS 263; SM PME R 139/40; *Münchener Post*, June 2, 1931, p.c., BHSA/V Slg P 3653.

36. Röhm to Kellerer, November 7, 1924, SAM STAW 14359, 1; Ketterer, October 14, 1924, "Ärztl. Zeugnis," SAM STAW 14359.

37. Röhm, *Geschichte*, 307–8; Jablonsky, *Nazi Party*, 152.

38. Röhm, *Geschichte*, 308–9; Jablonsky, *Nazi Party*, 170; Adolf Hitler, March 29, 1925, "Anordnung," *Völkischer Beobachter* (henceforth *VB*), April 8, 1925, p.c., SAM Pol. Dir. München 6805; BAR R 15.01/462; "P.N.D. Nr. 546. Komp.-Appell der S.A. Schwabing der N.S.D.A.P. am 21. Juli im Fäustlergarten.," [1926], SAM Pol. Dir. München 6810, 1.

39. Röhm, *Geschichte*, 309–11; *Völkischer Kurier*, March 28, 1925, p.c., BAR R 15.07/462; *Kurier für Niederbayern*, March 24, 1925, p.c., BHSA/V Slg P 3653; SAM Pol. Dir. München 1020.

40. Röhm, *Geschichte*, 313.

41. Ibid., 314.

42. Ibid.

43. Ibid., 316. *Völkischer Kurier*, May 5, 1925, p.c., SM ZA Pers. Röhm; Röhm to Kommandeure der Gruppen Nord, Mitte, Süd and Ost, May 1, 1925, BAK NL 79/28; *Völkischer Kurier*, May 2, 1925, p.c., BHSA/II MA 103475.

44. David Jablonsky, "Röhm and Hitler: The Continuity of Political-Military Discord," *Journal of Contemporary History* 23, no. 3 (1988), 367–86; Longerich, *Die braunen Bataillone*, 48; James M. Diehl, *Paramilitary Politics in Weimar Germany* (Bloomington: Indiana University Press, 1977), 160.

45. Kershaw, *Hitler*, 224–25, 261, 267; Jablonsky, *Nazi Party*, 171.

Chapter 9

1. Röhm, *Geschichte*, 320.

2. Ibid.; Gerda Walther, *Zum anderen Ufer: Vom Marxismus und Atheismus zum Christentum* (Remagen: Der Leuchter, Otto Reichl Verlag, 1960), 517–18; IfZ Sp. 2/1; Röhm to Emilie Röhm, June 11, 1929, RFP, 2.

3. Röhm, *Geschichte*, 320–21; IfZ Sp 2/1; *VB*, November 24, 1928, p.c., SM ZA Pers. Röhm.

4. *Münchener Post*, June 2, 1931, p.c., BHSA/V Slg P 3653; Ernst Röhm, *Geschichte eines Hochverräters*, 5. Auflage, Volksaufgabe (Munich Eher Verlag, 1934), 358; SAM Bayer. Amtsgericht München Nr. 1926/396.

5. Reichskommissar [für] Ueberwachung der öffentlichen Ordnung Nr. 1272/26 I to Reichsminister des Innern, February 20, 1926, BAR R 15.01/13508, 3–6.

6. Reports on BAR R43I/2242 and BAR R 15.01/13508; *Berliner Tageblatt*, December 10, 1926, #583, p.c., BAR R 72/1874.
7. Haniel to the Reichskanzlei, October 11, 1926, BAR R43I/2243, 1; Röhm, *Geschichte*, 322.
8. Röhm, *Geschichte*, 322; *VB*, February 27, 1927, p.c.; *VB*, February 11, 1927, p.c.: BHSA/V Slg P 3653; Haniel to the Reichskanzlei, February 10, 1927, BAR R43I/2245.
9. BHSA/II MA 101235/2; SAM Pol. Dir. München Nr. 6809; signature, Krim. Kom., Polizeidirektion Abt. Via, January 25, 1928, "Auszug aus dem Personalakt des Kaufmanns Edmund Heines, geb. 21.7.97 in München.," BHSA/II M Inn 71525, 6–7.
10. BAP 61 Sta 1/66; BAR R 72/1874; SAM Pol. Dir. München 6739; BHSA/V Slg P 3653.
11. "N/No. 67.," June 13, 1928, BHSA/II MA 101235/2, 12.
12. Dr. Max Werner. quoted in IfZ ZS 268, 20.
13. Giuseppe Renzetti, "Dall' Albania, all'Alta Silesia e a Berlina," BAK N 1235/16, 6.
14. Ibid., 1. Röhm to Emilie Röhm, February 28, 1929, 1; Röhm to Emilie Röhm, October 5, 1929, 1: RFP; *VB*, December 15, 1933, p.c., BHSA/V Slg P 3653; *Münchner Illustrierte Presse*, undated p.c. [December 1933], BHSA/KA OP 32380; Eleonore Lippert to Weiss, May 7, 1949, SAM STAW 28793; Walther, *Zum anderen Ufer*, 528.
15. Information from the Röhm family; Reichel to Crown Prince Rupprecht, April 13, 1929, BHSA/III Geh. Hausarchiv Nachlaß Kronprinz Rupprecht 820, 1; Röhm, *Geschichte*, 324; IfZ ZS 539.
16. Reichel to Crown Prince Rupprecht, July 28, 1928, 1, and Reichel to Crown Prince Rupprecht, August 27, 1928, 1–2: BHSA/III Geh. Hausarchiv Nachlaß Kronprinz Rupprecht 820; Georg Wacha, "Zu Carl Anton Reichel Der Briefwechsel mit Kronprinz Rupprecht von Bayern." *Kunstjahrbuch der Stadt Linz*, 15 (1976), BHSA/III NL Kronprinz Rupprecht 84, 56; Röhm, *Geschichte*, 324–25; Mr. Günter Fischer, Bibliothek und Archiv, Richard-Wagner-Museum, Bayreuth, to the author, August 25, 2000; information from the Röhm family.
17. Bergmann to Weiss, May 14, 1949, SAM STAW 28793, 5.
18. Bennecke, "Die Memoiren des Ernst Röhm," 180–81. Walther Darré, "Drehbühne mit Nürnberger Aufzeichnungen," "Dr. Merkel," BAK NL 94 I/28, reverse of 65; April 24, 1949, Karl Schreyer, "Eidesstattliche Erklärung," Amtsgericht München HKN/574, 1.
19. IfZ ZS 539, 12.
20. Röhm, *Geschichte*, 323–24; SAM Pol. Dir. München Nr. 10138; SAM Pol. Dir. München 6781; BHSA/V Slg P 3653; LAB Rep. 58/517.
21. Ernst von Salomon, *The Answers of Ernst von Salomon to the 131 Questions in the Allied Military Government "Fragebogen"* (London: Putnam, 1954), 271. Röhm, *Geschichte*, 226, 239, 285, 326; *Münchener Post*, October 6, 1932, p.c., SAM Pol. Dir. München 6783.

22. Sefton Delmer, *Trail Sinister. An Autobiography*, vol. 1 (London: Secker & Warburg, 1961), 120. BHSA/II MA 103476, 56.

23. Röhm, *Geschichte*, 241. Ibid., 9, 10, 12, 96, 229, 239, 240, 248, 249, 282, 313, 318, 326, 327.

24. Röhm, *Geschichte*, 76–77; BHSA/KA HS 925, 16; Mabire, *Röhm*, 207.

25. Sendtner, *Rupprecht von Wittelsbach*, 515.

26. Ibid., 643. Robert S. Garnett, Jr., *Lion, Eagle, and Swastika: Bavarian Monarchism in Weimar Germany, 1918–1933* (New York: Garland Publishing, 1991), 256.

27. Röhm, *Geschichte*, 231–33, 319; BHSA/KA HS 2401; Röhm, December 28, 1931, "Pr. Nr. 7579/31," BHSA/II MA 101235/3, 1–2.

28. Delmer, *Trail Sinister*, 105; Darré, "Drehbühne mit Nürnberger Aufzeichnungen," "Dr. Merkel," BAK NL 94 I/28, 64, 65; LoC RSS RYH 8616 John Toland Collection Interview with Robert and Annalies Röhm at Socking, October 14, 1971.

29. Heinrich Hoffmann, *Hitler wie ich ihn sah: Aufzeichnungen seines Leibfotografen* (Munich: Herbig, 1974), 69. Sir John Wheeler-Bennett, *Knaves, Fools and Heroes in Europe between the Wars* (London: Macmillan, 1974), 80; BAK N1120/14, 132.

30. Eleanor Hancock, "'Only the Real, The True, The Masculine Held its Value': Ernst Röhm, Masculinity, and Male Homosexuality," *Journal of the History of Sexuality* 8, no. 4 (1998): 632–33; August 2, 1931, "'Rechtsbewegung.," "l. Nr. 103.," BHSA/II MA 10235/3, 1.

31. Röhm to Dr. Heimsoth, Klotz, February 25, 1929, *Drei Briefe*, 7.

32. Wolfgang Theis and Andreas Sternweiler, "Alltag im Kaiserreich und in der Weimarer Republik," Berlin Museum, *Eldorado: Homosexuelle Frauen und Männer in Berlin 1850–1950* (Berlin: Frölich und Kaufmann, 1984), 63; LAB Rep. 58/517; Helmuth Klotz, "Wir gestalten durch unser Führerkorps die Zukunft!" (Berlin: Selbstverlag des Herausgebers Dr. Helmut Klotz, Berlin-Tempelhof, Hohenzollern Korso 38a, May 1932), 26–27; Helmuth Klotz, *Ehrenrangliste* (Berlin: APK, 1932), 34–5; Herbert Heinersdorf, "Akten zum Falle Röhm (1. Teil)," SMB *Mitteilungen des wissenschaftlich-humanitären Komitees E.V.*, Nr. 32, (January/March 1932), 367.

33. Röhm to Dr. Heimsoth, August 11, 1929, Klotz, *Drei Briefe*, 16. Hancock, "'Only the Real, the True, the Masculine Held Its Value,'" 616–41; Manfred Herzer, "Communists, Social Democrats and the Homosexual Movement in the Weimar Republic," Gert Hekma, Harry Oosterhuis, and James Steakley, ed., *Gay Men and the Sexual History of the Political Left*, ed. (New York: Harrington Park Press, 1995), 209; Andreas Sternweiler, "III.6 Schwules Selbstbewusstsein," Andreas Sternweiler and Hans Gerhard Hannesen, ed., *Goodbye to Berlin? 100 Jahre Schwulenbewegung: eine Ausstellung des Schwulen Museums und der Akademie der Künste, 17. Mai bis 17. August 1997*, ed. (Berlin: Verlag Rosa Winkel, 1997), 123–28.

34. Delmer, *Trail Sinister*, 122. Interview with Frau Annalies Röhm in the BBC documentary, *Night of the Humming Bird, Hitler's 1934 Massacre* (BBC TV, first broadcast, June 30, 1981); telephone conversation with Dr. Gräfin Eva du Moulin-Eckart, September 1997; Röhm to Heimsoth, February 25, 1929, Klotz, *Drei Briefe*, 7–10; IfZ ZS 357/I; IfZ ZS 70; Herzer, "Communists, Social Democrats, and the Homosexual Movement in the Weimar Republic," 224–25, note 45; BAR NS 26/324; SAM Pol. Dir. München Nr. 15540.

35. See Chapter 10.

36. See, for example, Ernst Röhm, *Warum SA? Rede des Reichsministers Stabschef Röhm in Berlin am 7. XII. 1933 vor dem Diplomatischen Korps* (Berlin: Liebheit u. Thiesen, 1933), 10.

37. Röhm, *Geschichte*, 237–38. BAK Slg Schumacher/414; Röhm to Dr. Heimsoth, December 3, 1928, Klotz, *Drei Briefe*, 6; Andreas Sternweiler, "III.3 Die Freundschaftsbünde—eine Massenbewegung," Sternweiler and Hannesen, ed., *Goodbye to Berlin?* 100; "III. Die Schwulenbewegung in der Weimarer Republik," Sternweiler and Hannesen, ed., ibid., *passim*.

38. LAB Rep. 58/517; Manfred Herzer, "34. Asexuality as an element in the selfpresentation of the right wing of the German gay movement before 1933. (Elisar von Kupfer, Benedict Friedlaender, Hans Blüher, Karl Günther Heimsoth).," in Matthias Duyves et al., ed., *Among men, among women: sociological and historical recognition of homosocial arrangements: Gay-studies and Women's studies, University of Amsterdam Conference, 22th-26th June 1983, Oudemanhuispoort, Amsterdam* (Amsterdam: Sociologisch Instituut, undated), 319–21, 581; Manfred Herzer, "III. 2 Die Gemeinschaft der Eigenen," Sternweiler and Hannesen, ed., *Goodbye to Berlin?* caption on 91; Röhm to Dr. Heimsoth, December 3, 1928, Klotz, *Drei Briefe*, 6.

39. Röhm, *Geschichte*, 258; Harry Oosterhuis, "V. Political Issues and the Rise of Nazism Introduction" and "VI. Epilogue Male Bonding and Homosexuality in German Nationalism," Harry Oosterhuis and Hubert Kennedy, ed., *Homosexuality and Male Bonding in Pre-Nazi Germany: The Youth Movement, the Gay Movement, and Male Bonding Before Hitler's Rise: Original Transcripts from Der Eigene, The First Gay Journal in the World*, ed. (New York: Harrington Park Press, 1991), 185–87 and 243–44, respectively.

40. Du Moulin-Eckart, undated [1946], "Zeugen-Vernehmung in der Untersuchung gegen Kuchler Ludwig aus Rosenheim wegen Mordes," IfZ Gt 01.02/1, 2; Röhm, *Geschichte*, 256–59.

41. Hans-Joachim Schoeps, *Ja—Nein—und Trotzdem: Erinnerungen—Begegnungen—Erfahrungen* (Mainz: v. Hase & Koehler Verlag, 1974), 129–30.

42. Röhm, *Geschichte*, 259, 320–21.

43. Ibid., 55, 59–60.

44. *VB*, November 29, 1928, p.c., and *VB*, June 3–4, 1928, p.c., BHSA/V Slg P 3653; Röhm to Emile Röhm, April 5, 1929, 1–2; Röhm to Emilie Röhm, February 26, 1930, 1: RFP.

45. June 13, 1928, "N/No. 67.," BHSA/II MA 101235/2, 12; Röhm to Emilie Röhm, February 12, 1930, RFP, 2; Garnett, *Lion, Eagle, and Swastika*, 247.

46. Sendtner, *Rupprecht von Wittelsbach*, 515. Signatures, May 19, 1949, unheaded statement of Graf Josef Maria von Soden-Fraunhofen, SAM STAW 28793, 2; Alfons Beckenbauer, "Wie Adolf Hitler durch einen niederbayerischen Grafen zu einem Wutausbruch gebracht wurde: Aus den unveröffentlichen Memoiren des Joseph Maria Graf von Soden-Fraunhofen –zugleich ein Beitrag zur Geschichte des monarchischen Gedankens in Bayern während der Weimarer Zeit," Sonderdruck aus *Verhandlungen des Historischen Vereins für Niederbayern*, Band 103, Landshut, 1977, 27; Reichel to Crown Prince Rupprecht, August 27, 1928, in Georg Wacha, "Zu Carl Anton Reichel: Der Briefwechsel mit Kronprinz Rupprecht von Bayern," *Kunstjahrbuch der Stadt Linz*, 1976, BHSA/III Geheimes Hausarchiv NL Kronprinz Rupprecht 820, 58; Sendtner, *Rupprecht von Wittelsbach*, 439.

47. Signatures, May 19, 1949, unheaded statement of Graf Josef Maria von Soden-Fraunhofen, SAM STAW 28793, 2.

48. "N/Nr. 71.," November 28, 1928, BHSA/II MA 101235/2, 19. "Auszug aus dem P.N.D. Bericht vom 28.7.28 Nr. 623.,"and "Auszug aus dem P.N.D. Bericht vom 23.10.28 Nr. 632.," SAM Pol. Dir. München 10162.

49. "N/Nr. 71," November 28, 1928, BHSA/II MA 101235/2, 17.

50. "Abschrift!" Ernst Röhm, "Wehrpolitische Vereinigung.," November 28, 1928, SAM Pol. Dir. München Nr. 6874, 2.

51. Ibid., 1.

52. "Auszug aus dem P.N.D. Bericht v. 21.12.1928 Nr. 640.," SAM Pol. Dir. München 10080, 1.

Chapter 10

1. Röhm to Crown Prince Rupprecht, February 7, 1929, BHSA/III Geh. Hausarchiv Nachlaß Kronprinz Rupprecht 822 (†1955), 1.

2. Signature, Ministro de Guerra to the Ministerio de Estado en el Despacho de Relaciones Exteriores y Culto, enclosing letter from the Chief of the General Staff, January 11, 1928, AMRREE MIN-1-70. Röhm to Crown Prince Rupprecht, February 7, 1929, BHSA/III Geh. Hausarchiv Nachlaß Kronprinz Rupprecht 822, 1; Röhm to Emilie Röhm, December 31, 1928, RFP, 3; IfZ Sp. 2/1.

3. Schätzl to Käte Schätzl, October 14, 1930, SAM STAW 28792, 1, 2. Röhm to Dr. Heimsoth, February 25, 1929, Klotz, *Drei Briefe*, 8; *El Diario*, September 27, 1930, 7.

4. *Hamburger Echo*, December 14, 1928; Röhm to Emilie Röhm and Eleonore Lippert, December 14, 1928, 4; Röhm to Emilie Röhm, December 15, 1928, 1; Röhm to Emilie Röhm, December 17, 1928, 1; Röhm to Emilie Röhm, December 27, 1928,1; Röhm to Emilie Röhm, December 31, 1928, 1; Röhm to Emilie Röhm, January 5, 1929, 1: all RFP; *Hamburger Echo*, January 2, 1929, Nr. 2; January 5, 1929, *El Diario*, 5.

5. Ernst Röhm, *Geschichte*, 5th ed., 357; John R. Thomas, Jr., Colonel, General Staff, Military Attaché, December 21, 1928, "Report No. 23745," "BOLIVIA

(MILITARY), Subject: Military Strength," "6020.,," NA 2005–35/2; Reinhard Wolff and Harmut Fröschle, "Die Deutschen in Bolivien," in Harmut Fröschle, ed., *Die Deutschen in Lateinamerika: Schicksal und Leistung* (Tübingen: Horst Erdmann Verlag, 1979), 146; R. C. Michell to Rt. Hon. Sir Austen Chamberlain, "CONFIDENTIAL (13410) BOLIVIA Annual Report, 1927," February 14, 1928, TNA FO 371/12741, 21; Herbert S. Klein, *Parties and Political Change in Bolivia 1880–1952* (Cambridge: Cambridge University Press, 1969), 167.

6. Klein, *Parties and Political Change in Bolivia*, 160–61; James Dunkerley, "The Politics of the Bolivian Army: Institutional Development to 1935," (PhD diss., University of Oxford, 1979), 104; Mariano Baptista Gumucio, *Historia contemporánea de Bolivia 1930–1976*, vol. 2 (La Paz: Gisbert & Cía, 1976), 396.

7. Dunkerley, "Politics of the Bolivian Army," 163–64; Klein, *Parties and Political Change in Bolivia*, 108.

8. Klein, *Parties and Political Change in Bolivia*, 19, 24, 167–68; Marten Willem Brienen, "The Liberal Crisis and Military Socialism in Bolivia: Bolivian History from 1930 to 1939," Vakgroep Talen en Culturen van Latijns Amerika, Faculteit der Letteren, Rijksuniversiteit Leiden, August 26, 1996, 18; Dunkerley, "'Politics of the Bolivian Army," 157.

9. C. J. Allen, G. S. Major, M. A. Peru, June 28, 1929, "Report No. 3590," "BOLIVIA (Combat) Subject: Distribution of Troops.," NA 2005–35 $_3$, 1–2. NA 644/14 Roll 14; PA AA R 78893; NA 2005–35 $_4$; Dunkerley, "Politics of the Bolivian Army," 157.

10. Brienen, "Liberal Crisis and Military Socialism in Bolivia," 24; James Dunkerley, *Orígenes del poder militar: Historia política e institucional del ejército boliviano hasta 1935* (La Paz: Quipus, 1987), 127; Waltraud Q. Morales, *A Brief History of Bolivia* (New York: Facts on File, Inc., 2003), 99–103.

11. Léon E. Bieber, "La política militar alemana en Bolivia, 1900–1935," *Latin American Research Review* 29, no. 1 (1994): 88; Dunkerley, "Politics of the Bolivian Army," 131, 132–33; Dunkerley, *Orígenes del poder militar*, 94–96.

12. Stefan Rinke, *"Der letzte freie Kontinent": Deutsche Lateinamerikapolitik im Zeichen transnationaler Beziehungen 1918–1933*, Teilbände 1 and 2 (Stuttgart: Akademischer Verlag, 1996) 170, 177 and 577, 620, respectively; Röhm to Emilie Röhm, May 7, 1929, RFP, 2; Dunkerley, *Orígenes del poder militar*, 115; R. R. Craigie, note on April 4, 1929, "Activities of General Hans Kundt, Commander-in-Chief of Bolivian Army.," August 1 [1929], TNA FO 371/13465, 3; signature (W. Burberry?), FO "Memorandum," TNA FO 371/13465, 1–2.

13. Rinke, *"Der letzte freie Kontinent,"* 2, 621–62, 628, 630, note 170; Marckwald, Deutsche Gesandtschaft in Bolivien, to the Auswärtiges Amt, Berlin, July 3, 1928, "B. 130. Betrifft: Deutsche Instrukteure für Bolivien.," PA AA R 78893, 1–8; R.C. Michell to Sir Austen Chamberlain, "CONFIDENTIAL (13410) BOLIVIA. Annual Report, 1927.," February 14, 1928, TNA FO 371/12741, 5; R. C. Michell to Rt. Hon. Sir Austen Chamberlain, July 12, 1928, TNA FO 126/37, 1–4.

14. Rinke, *"Der letzte freie Kontinent,"* 2, 620, 622; Jesse S. Cottrell, La Paz, Bolivia to Secretary of State, Washington, August 12, 1922, "No. 68.," NA 644/14

Roll 14, 4; Bieber, "La politica militar alemana en Bolivia, 1900–1935," 88–89; Dunkerley, "Politics of the Bolivian Army," 172; Dunkerley, *Orígenes del poder militar*, 116, 125, 127; November 12, 1926, Marckwald, Deutsche Gesandtschaft, La Paz, to the Auswärtiges Amt, Berlin, "B. 184.," "Betrifft: Deutsche Militärinstrukteure im bolivianischen Heere.," PA AA R 78893, 2; "BOLIVIA. Annual Report, 1927.," TNA FO 371/12941, 21; R. C. Michell to Sir Austen Chamberlain, "CONFIDENTIAL. (13543) Bolivia Annual Report, 1928.," "Enclosure. *Annual Report on Bolivia for* 1928," February 1, 1929, TNA FO 371/13466, 26; Kundt and Martinez Vargas, January 1929, one page renewal of contract, AMEMG Legajo No. 1 52 Organización del Estado Mayor General; "EXTRACTO de presupuestos de haberes pagados por el Tesoro Nacional, al señor General H. Kundt en su carácter de jefe del E.M.G., es como sigue," June 3, 1931, AMEMG Legajo No. 1 52 Organización del Estado Mayor General, 3–4.

15. F. Osorio, Ayudante General, Teniente Coronel Ernst Roehm, "COPIA LEGAL-IZADA" attachment, 1–3, to April 12, 1929, signature, Ayudante General, Ministro de Guerra to Ministro de Estado en el Despacho de Relaciones Exteriores y Culto, AMRREE MIN-1–72; Dunkerley, *Orígenes del poder militar*, 235, note 21.

16. Röhm, *Geschichte* (5th ed.), 363. Bennecke, "Die Memoiren des Ernst Röhm," 181; Röhm to Crown Prince Rupprecht, February 7, 1929, BHSA/III Geh. Hausarchiv Nachlaß Kronprinz Rupprecht 822, 1; Röhm to Adolf Hitler, February 1, 1929, BAR 62 KA 1/51/1, 1; Röhm to Emilie Röhm, March 19, 1929, 2; Röhm to Emilie Röhm, April 29, 1929, 2: RFP; Röhm to Himmler, September 19[29], BAR NS 19/2668, 1.

17. Marckwald, Deutsche Gesandtschaft, La Paz, to the Auswärtiges Amt, Berlin, July 3, 1928, "B. 130," PA AA R 78893, 7.

18. Röhm to Emilie Röhm, November 2, 1929, 1, and Röhm to Emilie Röhm, April 23, 1929, 1, RFP; Marckwald to Auswärtiges Amt, April 11, 1929, "Inhalt: Französischer Protest wegen Anstellung des Hauptmann Röhms im bolivianischen Heere.," PA AA R 78893; Le Mallier's protests on AMRREE LE-3-R-132 and Bolivian Government responses on AMRREE LE-3-E-37, especially May 2, 1929, note from Bolivian Ministry of External Relations to Mr. André le Mallier, Ambassador of France, ibid.; R. C. Michell to Rt. Hon. A. Henderson M.P., March 12, 1930, TNA FO 126/54, 1.

19. Röhm, *Geschichte* (5th ed.), 360; Röhm to Emilie Röhm, 1; and Röhm to Emilie Röhm, May 7, 1929, 1: RFP; Röhm to Schätzl, June 1, 1929, SAM STAW 28792, 1.

20. Röhm to Dr. Heimsoth, August 14, 1929, Klotz, *Drei Briefe*, 15. Crespo Rodas, *Hernando Siles, el poder y su angustia*, 241; Oficina Nacional de Estadística Financiera, *Sinopsis estadística de la República de Bolivia* (La Paz: July 10, 1930), 1; Röhm to Dr. Heimsoth, February 25, 1929, Klotz, *Drei Briefe*, 8–9.

21. Röhm to Hitler, February 1, 1929, BAR 62 KA1/51/1, 1; Ernst Röhm, La Paz, Bolivia, to Crown Prince Rupprecht, February 7, 1929, BHSA/III Geh. Hausarchiv Nachlaß Kronprinz Rupprecht 822, 2; Carl Anton Reichel to

Crown Prince Rupprecht, April 13, 1929, BHSA/III Geh. Hausarchiv Nachlaß Kronprinz Rupprecht 820, 1; Röhm to Emilie Röhm, April 9, 1929, RFP, 2.

22. Röhm to Emilie Röhm, April 5, 1929, 2; Röhm to Emilie Röhm, June 18, 1929; Röhm to Emilie Röhm, July 24, 1929, 1; Röhm to Emilie Röhm, July 24,1929, 1; Röhm to Emilie Röhm, September 20, 1929, 1: RFP; Röhm to Schätzl, June 1, 1929, SAM STAW 28792, 1.

23. H. Kundt, el general, Jefe del Estado Mayor General, September 7, 1929, "ORDEN GENERAL NO. 238," AMEMG Ordenes Generales del Ejército 1928–1929; Röhm to Emilie Röhm, September 14, 1929, 1–2; Röhm to Emilie Röhm, September 20, 1929, 1: RFP; AMEMG A-148 C-027 Elevación de Recortes de Prensa-Impresos 1929–1930, 1932; AMEMG A-154 C-028 1929; October 20, 1929, 5; October 25, 1929, 7; October 26, 1929, 6; October 29, 1929, 6; November 5, 1929, 7; November 6, 1929, 7; November 7, 1929, 9; November 8, 1929, 4: all El Diario.

24. Röhm to Emilie Röhm, December 5, 1929, RFP, 1–2; December 20, 1929, El Diario, 7.

25. Quoted in Crespo Rodas, Hernando Siles, el poder y su angustia, 241.

26. Ibid., 241.

27. Röhm to Hitler, February 1, 1929, BAR 62 KA 1/51/1, 2; Röhm to Crown Prince Rupprecht, April 9, 1930, BHSA/III Geh. Hausarchiv Nachlaß Kronprinz Rupprecht 822, 4.

28. Röhm to Emilie Röhm, January 15, 1930; Röhm to Emilie Röhm, May 7, 1930, 1; Röhm to Emilie Röhm, June 3, 1930; Röhm to Emilie Röhm, January 25, 1930, 1–2: RFP; "Geschäftsjahr 1930.," Libro de actas del Club Alemán en Oruro desde 1928–1974.

29. Röhm to Crown Prince Rupprecht, April 9, 1930, BHSA/III Geh. Hausarchiv Nachlaß Kronprinz Rupprecht 822, 2.

30. Ibid., 3–4; Röhm to Emilie Röhm, August 2, 1930, RFP, 1–2.

31. Röhm to Crown Prince Rupprecht, April 9, 1930, BHSA/III Geh. Hausarchiv Nachlaß Kronprinz Rupprecht 822, 3.

32. Ibid., 3–4.

33. Reports by R. C. Michell on TNA FO 371/14197; reports by Marckwald on PA AA R 78889 and PA AA R 78883; Dunkerley, Orígenes del poder militar, 129; Klein, Parties and Political Change in Bolivia, 111; Hibbard, telegram to Secretary of State, June 28, 1930, NA II Department of State 824.00/507, 2–3.

34. Reports by R. C. Michell on TNA FO 371/14197 and TNA FO 371/14198; reports by Marckwald on PA AA R 78883; Rinke, "Der letzte freie Kontinent," 2, 631; Marckwald, Deutsche Gesandtschaft in Bolivien, note to Señor General Carlos Blanco Galindo, Presidente del Consejo de Ministros, July 3, 1930, AMRREE LE-3-R-134, 1–5.

35. Dunkerley, "Politics of the Bolivian Army," 213; Klein, Parties and Political Change in Bolivia, 114, 127; Dunkerley, Orígenes del poder militar, 132–37.

36. Marckwald, Deutsche Gesandschaft in Bolivien, an das Auswärtige Amt Berlin, "Betr.: Bolivianische Revolution und Deutschtum.," July 23, 1930, PA AA R 78883, 4–5. El Diario, July 25, 1930, 4; Röhm to Crown Prince Rupprecht,

August 22, 1930, BHSA/III Geh. Hausarchiv Nachlaß Kronprinz Rupprecht 822, 2.

37. *El Diario*, August 15, 1930, 7. Röhm, *Geschichte* (5th ed.), 361; Röhm to Emilie Röhm, July 5, 1930, RFP, 1–2; signature, el General de Brigada, Jefe del Estado Mayor General, July 3, 1930, "ORDEN GENERAL No 257," AMEMG Órdenes Generales del Ejército 1930–1931, 1–2; "Vorstandssitzung vom 12. Juli 1930," *"Geschäftsjahr 1930.,"* Libro de actas del Club Alemán en Oruro desde 1928–1974, 1–2.

38. Miguel Arteaga Aranibar, "Ernst Roehm" (unpublished manuscript, La Paz, June 30, 1984), 6. Röhm to Emilie Röhm, July 9, 1930, RFP.

39. Röhm to Himmler, August 27, 1930, BAK NS 19/2668, 2. Röhm to Crown Prince Rupprecht, August 22, 1930, BHSA/III Geh. Hausarchiv Nachlaß Kronprinz Rupprecht 822, 1–2.

40. Röhm to Hühnlein, undated telegram, received in Munich, September 27, 1930, BAR NS 26/1258.

41. Marckwald to Auswärtiges Amt, October 16, 1930, "B. 230," PA AA R 78893, 3–4.

42. Röhm, *Geschichte*, 5th ed., 359–60; Louis P. Lochner, *What about Germany?* (London: Hodder and Stoughton, 1943), 79.

43. Correspondence and reports on AMRREE MIN-2–53; AMRREE ALEM-1-R-11; and AMRREE MIN-1–78; Crespo Rodas, *Hernando Siles, el poder y su angustia*, 245; Röhm, *Geschichte*, 5th ed., 362; Jill Halcomb, *The SA: A Historical Perspective* (Overland Park: Crown Agincourt, 1985), 105, 107; *N.S. Kurier*, February 10, 1932, p.c., BHSA/V Slg P 3653; *Fränkischer Kurier*, November 23, 1930, and *Der Stürmer*, undated, p.c., BHSA/V Slg P 3653; signature, Deutsche Gesandtschaft, La Paz, January 14, 1931, "B. 9.," PA AA R 78894, 1; *Der Angriff*, August 19, 1932, p.c., PA AA R 78862; Röhm to the Auswärtiges Amt, May 24, 1934, PA AA R 79816, 1–2; *El Diario*, April 8, 1934, final page.

44. Marckwald, Deutsche Gesandtschaft in Bolivien to Auswärtiges Amt, October 16, 1930, "B. 230," PA AA R 78893, 4.

45. *VB*, November 8, 1932, p.c., BHSA/V Slg P 3653; Röhm, *Geschichte*, 5th ed., 362; *El Diario*, September 27, 1930, 7; *El Diario*, October 3, 1930, 6; Schätzl to Käte Schätzl, October 14, 1930, SAM STAW 28792, 1; *Hamburger Echo*, November 5, 1930; *Hamburger Echo*, November 11, 1930.

Chapter 11

1. Röhm, quoted, *Der SA-Mann*, June 30, 1933, 4.

2. "Auszug aus dem P.N.D.—Bericht vom 17.11.30 Nr. 715.," SAM Pol. Dir. München Nr. 10020; undated, *Der Stürmer*, p.c., BHSA/V Slg P 3653; "P.N.D.," "Führerbesprechung der S.A. am 29. und 30.11.30 in München.," SAM Pol. Dir. München Nr. 6809, 1; *VB*, January 1, 1931, p.c., SAM Pol. Dir. München 6805.

3. Richard Evans, *The Coming of the Third Reich* (London: Allen Lane, 2003), 233–37, 247–52.

4. Dietrich Orlow, *The History of the Nazi Party: 1919–1933* (Pittsburgh: University of Pittsburgh Press, 1969), 132–86.

5. Bennecke, *Hitler und die SA*, 119–42, 145–49, 151; Osaf Stellv. Süd, September 19, 1930, "Stellungnahme zur vorgesehenen Um-Organisation der SA-Führung.," BAK Slg Schumacher/403, 1–10; Longerich, *Die braunen Bataillone*, 56, 107–8; K. D. Bracher et al, *Die nationalsozialistische Machtergreifung: Studien zur Errichtung des totalitären Herrschaftssystems in Deutschland 1933/34*, 2nd, enlarged ed. (Cologne: Westdeutscher Verlag, 1962), 851; "Abschrift. Tagebuch Reichsführerschule der N.S.D.A.P., München, Schwanthalerstr. 68.," SAM Pol. Dir. München Nr. 6812, 26.

6. Longerich, *Die braunen Bataillone*, 62–64, 74–77, 97–100.

7. Ibid., 81–86, 93, 111; Conan Fischer, *Stormtroopers: A Social, Economic and Ideological Analysis, 1929–35* (London: George Allen and Unwin, 1983), chap. 3; Eric G. Reiche, *The Development of the SA in Nürnberg, 1922–1934* (Cambridge: Cambridge University Press, 1986), 103–16, 139; IfZ ZS 1685; BAK Slg. Schumacher 415; Richard Bessel, *Political Violence and the Rise of Nazism: the Stormtroopers in Eastern Germany 1925–1934* (London: Yale University Press, 1984), 46–47.

8. This section is derived from the following studies of the SA: Thomas Balistier, *Gewalt und Ordnung: Kalkül und Faszination der SA* (Münster: Verlag Westfälisches Dampfboot, 1989); Bessel, *Political Violence and the Rise of Nazism;* Campbell, *SA Generals;* Fischer, *Stormtroopers;* Longerich, *Die braunen Bataillone;* Sven Reichardt, *Faschistische Kampfbünde: Gewalt und Gemeinschaft im italienischen Squadrismus und in der deutschen SA* (Cologne: Böhlau Verlag, 2002); Dirk Walter, *Antisemitische Kriminalität und Gewalt: Judenfeindschaft in der Weimarer Republik* (Bonn: Verlag J. H. W. Dietz Nachfolger, 1999), chap. VIII.

9. BAR R 15.01/25791; Longerich, *Die braunen Bataillone*, 102–5.

10. Adolf Hitler, February 3, 1931, "Erlaß Nr. 1.," BAK Slg Schumacher/403. The section on Hitler's motives for supporting Röhm is based on Campbell, *SA Generals*, 84–86. *Vorwärts*, February 21, 1931, p.c., BAR R 8034 II/9243; *Der Jungdeutsche*, March 28, 1931; *Der Jungdeutsche*, January 8, 1931: p.c., BHSA/V Slg P 3653; *Vorwärts*, January 1, 1931, p.c., BAR R 15.01/25791.

11. IfZ ZS 177 Bd. 1, 4.

12. Ludecke, *I Knew Hitler*, 478.

13. IFZ ZS 177 Bd. 1; Orlow, *History of the Nazi Party: 1919–1933*, 213–14; IfZ ZS 2084; Campbell, *SA Generals*, 88.

14. Longerich, *Die braunen Bataillone*, 112–13; Fest, *Hitler*, 293–94; Röhm, March 31, 1931, "Verfügung," "Nr. 1190/31," BAR NS 23 neu/1; BAR Sammlung Schumacher/403, 404, 405, and 406; signature, Polizeidirektion München to the Staatsministerium des Innern, June 15, 1931, BHSA/II M Inn 81606, 1–2, with 70-page attachment; Hitler, February 10, 1931, "Verordnung," SAM Pol. Dir. München 6826, 1–2; Röhm, September 27, 1931, "Ch. Nr. 2684/32," BAR NS 23 neu/2, 1–2.

15. Andreas Dornheim, *Röhms Mann fürs Ausland: Politik und Ermordung des SA-Agenten Georg Bell* (Münster: LIT Verlag, 1998), 77. Campbell, *SA Generals*, 105, 110; Bennecke, *Hitler und die SA*, 160.

16. Lehmann to Stellrecht, September 15, 1932, BAK NS 51/14, 6; Fest, *Hitler*, 294; Hans-Georg Stümke and Rudi Finkler, *Rosa Wimpel, Rosa Listen: Homosexuelle und "Gesundes Volksempfinden" von Auschwitz bis heute* (Reinbek bei Hamburg: Rowohlt, 1981), 125; IfZ ZS 539; Mathilde Jamin, *Zwischen der Klassen: Zur Sozialstruktur der SA-Führerschaft* (Wuppertal: Peter Hammer Verlag, 1984), *passim*; Longerich, *Die braunen Bataillone*, 115, 144–47; Fischer, *Stormtroopers*, 58–63; Reiche, *Development of the SA in Nürnberg*, 114, 116, 142.

17. "Die Stennes-Revolte.," ZStAP R. 15.01/26073, 3–8; entries for March 25, 1931, March 28, 1931, March 29, 1931, March 31, 1931, April 2, 1931, April 4, 1931, April 6, 1931, and April 17, 1931, Elke Fröhlich, ed., *Die Tagebücher von Joseph Goebbels: Sämtliche Fragmente Teil I Aufzeichnungen 1924–1941 Band 2 1.1.1931–31.12.1936* (Munich: K. G. Saur, 1987), 38, 40, 40–41, 42, 42–43, 43–44, 44, 50–51, respectively; Orlow, *History of the Nazi Party: 1919–1933*, 217–19; Bernhard Sauer, *Schwarze Reichswehr und Fememord: Eine Milieustudie zum Rechtsradikalismus in der Weimarer Republik* (Berlin: Metropol, 2004), 296.

18. Dornheim, *Röhms Mann fürs Ausland, passim.* Dornheim's careful research supersedes the more sensational claims of Hans-Günter Richardi and Klaus Schumann, *Geheim Akte Gerlich/Bell: Röhms Pläne für ein Reich ohne Hitler* (Munich: W. Ludwig Verlag, 1993); Drs. Steppacher and Prechtl to Landgericht München I 7. Zivilkammer, December 23, 1932, "VII A 487/32.," "Schriftsatz der Rechtsanwälte Dres. Steppacher und Prechtl München in Sachen Bell./. Röhm wegen Forderung.," SAM STAW 29791, 1–4; Dornheim, *Röhms Mann für Ausland*, 50–1; IfZ Gt 01.02/1.

19. Dornheim, *Röhms Mann fürs Ausland, passim.*

20. Röhm to Bell, April 15, 1931, IfZ Gt 01.02/1; Drs. Steppacher and Prechtl to Landgericht München I 7. Zivilkammer, December 23, 1932, SAM STAW 29791, 3–4; Delmer, *Trail Sinister*, 105–8, 111–17, 118–21; Franz von Hörauf, June 24, 1946, "Abschrift. Affidavit. Eidesstattliche Versicherung.," GP RA/27, 1–2; SA-Affidavit No. 77 May 15, 1946, SAN KV-Prozesse IMT C-185; July 1, 1946, "I. Kommission," SAN KV-Prozesse IMT A 403–19 3621–25.

21. Ernst Röhm, "Abschrift," IfZ Gt 01.02/1, 1–7; Dornheim, *Röhms Mann fürs Ausland*, 87–88; Winfried Süss, "Beiträge und Berichte: Über Röhms angebliche Pläne 'für ein Reich ohne Hitler,'" *Historisches Jahrbuch* Sonderdruck 115. Jahrgang Zweiter Halbband 1995 (Freiburg: Verlag Karl Alber, 1995), 489; information from the Röhm family; Delmer, *Trail Sinister*, 122–24.

22. Dornheim, *Röhms Mann fürs Ausland*, 91; Süss, "Beiträge und Berichte: Über Röhms angebliche Pläne 'für ein Reich ohne Hitler,'" 489; Delmer, *Trail Sinister*, 120; Bennecke, *Hitler und die SA*, 204–6.

23. Dornheim, *Röhms Mann fürs Ausland*, 52–53; Richardi and Schumann, *Geheim Akte Gerlich/Bell*, 217; SAM Pol. Dir. München 68253.

24. *Münchener Post*, June 2, 1931, p.c., BHSA/V Slg P 3653; *Münchener Post*, 45/140, June 22, 1931, p.c., BAR NS 26/87, 1; SAM AG 37005; SAM Pol. Dir. München 11998; *VB*, June 24, 1931, p.c.; Röhm, "Erklärung," *VB*, June 24, 1931, p.c.: SAM Pol. Dir. München 6782; *Münchener Post*, June 24, 1931, p.c.; *8 Uhr Abend Blatt*, June 25, 1931, p.c.: BHSA/V Slg P 3653; *Münchener Post*, June 26, 1931, p.c., SAM Pol. Dir. München 6782; *Münchener Post*, June 29, 1931, p.c., SAM Pol. Dir. München 6783; "Kundgebung des Vorstandes des WHK an die deutschen Presse betr. den Fall Röhm," SMB *Mitteilung des wissenschaftlich-humanitären Komitees e.V.*, Nr. 31 (September/December 1931): 315–16; Herbert Heinersdorf, "Akten zum Falle Röhm (I. Teil)," ibid., January/March 1932, Nr. 32, 349–68; Herbert Heinersdorf," Akten zum Falle Röhm (II. Teil)," ibid., April/August 1932, Nr. 33, 387–96; Herbert Heinersdorf, "Akten zum Falle Röhm (III. Teil)," ibid., September 1932/February 1933, Nr. 34, 419–28; Hancock, "Only the Real, the True, the Masculine Held Its Value," 616–41; Harry Oosterhuis, "The 'Jews' of the Antifascist Left: Homosexuality and Socialist Resistance to Nazism," Hekma, Oosterhuis, and Steakley, ed., *Gay Men and the Sexual History of the Political Left*, 227–57.
25. "Ausschnitt aus Lagebericht Nr. 103 v. 2. August 1931 Nationalsozialistische Deutsche Arbeiterpartei (NSDAP.)," SAM Pol. Dir. München 6780. Herbert Linder, *Von der NSDAP zur SPD: Der politische Lebensweg des Dr. Helmuth Klotz (1894–1943)* (Konstanz: Universitätsverlag Konstanz, 1998), 168–70; Richardi and Schumann, *Geheim Akte Gerlich/Bell*, 219.
26. Hoffmann, *Hitler wie ich ihn sah*, 69; entry for January 6, 1931, *Die Tagebücher von Joseph Goebbels*, 2, 4; Anton Joachimsthaler, *Hitlers Liste: Ein Dokument persönlicher Beziehungen* (Munich: Herbig, 2003), 335–36.
27. Kolb, *Weimar Republic*, 116–17; Volker R. Berghahn, *Der Stahlhelm Bund der Frontsoldaten 1918–1935* (Dusseldorf: Droste, 1966), 179–86.
28. Bessel, *Political Violence and the Rise of Nazism*, chap. V; Bennecke, *Hitler und die SA*, 157–59; BAK Kl. Erw. 242/6, 1–2.
29. Alan Bullock, *Hitler: A Study in Tyranny*, rev. ed. (Harmondsworth: Penguin, 1968) 183, 187, 192; Dornheim, *Röhms Mann fürs Ausland*, 80; BA MA N 97/2.
30. Dornheim, *Röhms Mann fürs Ausland*, 74.
31. Joachim von Stülpnagel, *75 Jahre Meines Lebens*, BA MA N 5/27, 307.
32. Brüning quoted in Dornheim, *Röhms Mann fürs Ausland*, 81–82.
33. The *Münchener Post* story is summarized in SAM Pol. Dir. München 6787. *Münchener Post*, November 28–29, 1931, p.c., BAR NS 26/87, 1; "Polizeipres-sebericht.," November 28, 1931, SAM Pol. Dir. München 6787; *Münchener Neueste Nachrichten*, April 6, 1932, p.c., SAM Pol. Dir. München 6787; Douglas C. Morris, *Justice Imperilled: The Anti-Nazi Lawyer Max Hirschberg in Weimar Germany* (Ann Arbor: University of Michigan Press, 2005), 289–91; Röhm, January 25, 1932, "Stabsbefehl.," "Qu. Nr. 114/32 a,"BAR NS 23 alt/505, 1–24; Du Moulin-Eckart, "Mein Lebenslauf 1921 bis 1946.," IfZ Sp. 2/1, 3; Bell to Röhm, March 24, 1933, BAR R 15.01/2576/1; Karl Buchheim and Karl Otmar

von Aretin, eds., Erwein von Aretin, *Krone und Ketten: Erinnerungen eines bay-erischen Edelmannes* (Munich: Süddeutscher Verlag, 1955), 63.

34. Entry for February 22, 1932, *Tagebücher von Joseph Goebbels*, 2, 130–31; Kolb, *Weimar Republic*, 117; Röhm, "Tagesbefehl," *Der SA-Mann*, March 14, 1932, p.c., SAM Pol. Dir. München Nr. 6812.

35. Linder, *Von der NSDAP zur SPD*, 171, and more generally chap. III.3; press clip-pings in SM ZA Pers. Röhm, BAR R 15.01/26064, and BHSA/V Slg P 3653; Hancock, "'Only the Real, the True, the Masculine Held Its Value,'" 629–30.

36. Dr. Schoch im Auftrage, "Beglaubigte Abschrift aus den Akten XIII, b. 913–15/31 der St.A. München," undated, LAB Rep. 58/517, 4, and other papers on the same file; signatures, LP.-Posten Kaufering, Kaufering Landpolizei Oberbay-ern, Bez. Insp. Landsberg/L., October 7, 1949, "Vernehmungsniederschrift.," interrogation of Leonhard Sedlmayer, GP RA/2, 1–2; *Münchener Neueste Nach-richten*, November 8, 1932, p.c., BHSA/V Slg P 3653; Dr. Helmuth Klotz, "Tatsachen!" September 12, 1932, *Der Fall Röhm*, 2nd ed. (Berlin: Selbstverlag des Herausgebers Dr. Helmut Klotz, Berlin-Tempelhof, Hohenzollern Korso 38a, 1932), 1–4; Linder, *Von der NSDAP zur SPD*, 173–74, 180–84; Dr. med. K. G. Heimsoth and Dr. Walter Luetgebrune, September 3, 1932, BAK Slg Schumacher/407; IfZ ZS 70; IfZ ZS 319.

37. BAR NS 26/324; SAM Pol. Dir. München 11998 and SAM Pol. Dir. München 15540; *Frankfurter Volksstimme*, June 24, 1932, p.c., BHSA/V Slg P 3653; undated, Dr. Schoch im Auftrage, "Beglaubigte Abschrift aus den Akten XIII, b. 913–15/31 der St.A. München," LAB Rep. 58/517, 1–8; signature, der Ober-staatsanwalt bei dem Landgerichte München I to the Generalstaatsanwalt bei dem Oberlandesgerichte München, December 10, 1931, "Betreff: Das Strafver-fahren gegen den Hauptmann a.D. Ernst Röhm und Genossen wegen wider-natürlicher Unzucht.," BAK R 22/5006, 1–2; Dr. Luetgebrune, *Ein Kampf um Röhm* (Diessen: Verlag Jos. C. Huber, 1933), 10.

38. Hancock, "'Only the Real, the True, the Masculine Held Its Value,'" 631–32; *Münchener Neueste Nachrichten*, April 8, 1932, p.c., SAM Pol. Dir. München 6783; Peter D. Stachura, *Nazi Youth in the Weimar Republic* (Santa Barbara: Clio Books, 1975), 161–62.

39. Hierl to Hitler, March 24, 1932, SAM Pol. Dir. München 10080, 1–2; Polizei-direktion VIa 155, April 13, 1932, "Zeugenvernehmung.," SAM Pol. Dir. München 11998, 1–4; signature, i.A., RefVI, Polizeidirektion München to Staats-anwaltschaft, Karlsruhe, July 1932, "VIa 1101/32.," SAM Pol. Dir. München Nr. 15513, 1; unsigned, undated, "Denkschrift! (2. Bearbeitung!)," BAR NS 26/1935, 8, 11, 12–14; BHSA/II MInn 71712; BHSA/II MInn 71525; *Das andere Deutschland*, October 3, 1932, p.c., BHSA/V Slg P 3653.

40. Unsigned, undated, "Denkschrift! (2. Bearbeitung!)," BAR NS 26/1935, 10–11, 14–15; signature, Polizeidirektion, April 11, 1932, "I. Vormerkung.," BHSA/II M Inn 71525, 1; der Oberstaaatsanwalt bei dem Landgerichte München I to the Generalstaatsanwalt bei dem Oberlandesgerichte München, April 20, 1933, ibid., 3; "Zeugen-Vernehmung in der Untersuchung gegen

Kuchler Ludwig aus Rosenheim wegen Mordes," 1946, IfZ Gt 01.02/1, 2; Oberführer, I. A. Der Chef des Stabes to the Reichsorganisationsleiter I, April 8, 1932, "Abschrift," SAM Pol. Dir. München 6831a; Röhm, Der Chef des Stabes, Der Oberste SA-Führer, September 17, 1932, "II. Nr. 2514/32.," "Verfügung.," BAR NS 23 neu/2; signature, i.a., Ref VI, Polizeidirektion München to Staatsanwaltschaft Karlsruhe, July 1932, "VIa 1101/32," SAM Pol. Dir. München Nr. 15513, 2.

41. *Klassenkampf*, October 12, 1932, p.c., BHSA/V Slg P 3653.

42. *VB*, October 6, 1932, p.c., BAR R 8034 II/9249; *VB*, October 8, 1932, p.c., SAM Pol. Dir. München 6787; Delmer, *Trail Sinister*, 124–25.

43. *Münchener Post*, October 6, 1932, p.c., BAR R 8034 II/9249. *Münchener Neueste Nachrichten*, October 7, 1932, p.c., BHSA/V Slg P 3653; *Münchener Post*, October 6, 1932, p.c., SAM Pol. Dir. München 6783.

44. *NSK-Folge*, 9[?].10 [1932], p.c., BHSA/V Slg P 3653; *VB*, October 8, 1932, p.c., SAM Pol. Dir. München 6787; *NSK-Folge*, October 5, 1932, p.c., BHSA/V Slg P 3653.

45. Bell to Du Moulin-Eckart, April 20, 1932, SAM Pol. Dir. München 11998; Dornheim, *Röhms Mann furs Ausland*, 136, 137; "Sitzung im Reichsministerium des Innern am 5. April 1932 unter Vorsitz von Reichsminister Exz. Groener.," BHSA/II M Inn 81607, 1–9; Bennecke, *Hitler und die SA*, 171, 176–85; Richardi and Schumann, *Geheim Akte Gerlich/Bell*, 220–21.

46. *NSK [Nationalsozialistische Korrespondenz]*, May 17, 1932, p.c., BAR R 8034 II/9248; LAB Rep. 58/Nr. 2526; Linder, *Von der NSDAP zur SPD*, 174–79, 187–89; *Berliner Volks-Zeitung*, May 17, 1932, p.c.; Erich Ludendorff, *Heraus aus dem braunen Sumpf* (Munich: Ludendorffs Volkswarte-Verlag, 1932): BAR R 8034III/291; "Röhm-Skandal wächst!" Der Tannenberger, 8, no. 1, Nebelung 1932, BAK N 1079/3, 120.

47. Quoted in *Westfälische Allgemeine Volkszeitung*, June 9, 1932, p.c., BHSA/V Slg P 3653. Kolb, *Weimar Republic*, 118–19, 120; entry for May 8, 1932, *Tagebücher von Joseph Goebbels*, 2, 165.

48. Evans, *Coming of the Third Reich*, 285; *Deutsche Zeitung*, June 17, 1932, p.c., BAR R 1501/25794; Kolb, *Weimar Republic*, 120–21, 195.

49. Hitler to von Schleicher, Meissner and Planck, enclosing Röhm, Frick, Hitler, "Besprechung in der Reichskanzlei am 13.8.32 Dauer insgesamt von 16,15 Uhr bis 16,25 Uhr," August 18, 1932, BAK NS 51/14, 1–4; Kolb, *Weimar Republic*, 121; "No. 14 Sir H. Rumbold (Berlin) to Sir J. Simon," August 15, 1932, E. L. Woodward and R. Butler, eds., *Documents on British Foreign Policy 1919–1939 Second Series Volume IV 1932–3* (London: HMSO, 1950), 30–33; entries for August 12 and 13, 1932, *Tagebücher von Joseph Goebbels*, 2, 223–25; Delmer, *Trail Sinister*, 167–68; BAK Kl. Erw. 569, 80; Bessel, *Political Violence and the Rise of Nazism*, 87–92.

50. Bessel, *Political Violence and the Rise of Nazism*, 91; BAR R 1501/25794; "L. Nr. 112a," October 20, 1932, BHSA/II MA 101235/3, 9; Reiche, *Development of the SA in Nürnberg*, chap. 5.

51. Ludecke, *I Knew Hitler*, 492. *VB*, October 9–10, 1932, p.c., SAM Pol. Dir. München Nr. 6812.

52. "Auszug aus dem Morgenrapport des Ref. VI/N vom 8.10.32," SAM Pol. Dir. München Nr. 6812.

53. Röhm, October 28, 1932, "Ch. Nr. 3151/32. Befehl.," SAM Pol. Dir. München Nr. 6823; Evans, *Coming of the Third Reich*, 297–98; Dornheim, *Röhms Mann für Ausland*, 149–50; December 23, 1932, Drs. Steppacher and Prechtl to Landgericht München I 7. Zivilkammer, SAM STAW 29791, 1–4; *Münchener Post*, October 18, 1932, p.c., SAM Pol. Dir München 6781; Eduard Oskar Püttmann, "Aussprüche über die mann männliche Liebe," SMB *Blätter für Menschenrechte*, 10/6–7 (June/July 1932): 11–12; "Kleine Unterschlagungen," ibid., Nr. 10/11 (October/November 1932): 11–13; Herbert Heinersdorf, "Akten zum Falle Röhm (III. Teil)," SMB *Mitteilungen des wissenschaftlich-humanitären Komitees e.V.*, Nr. 34 (September 1932/February 1933): 419–28.

54. Evans, *Coming of the Third Reich*, 299, 302–3; Kolb, *Weimar Republic*, 122–23; entry for December 8, 1932, *Tagebücher von Joseph Goebbels*, 2, 295.

55. BAR NS 26/328; Morris, *Justice Imperilled*, 291–92; *Neue freie Volkszeitung*, November 20–21, 1932, p.c., SM ZA Pers Röhm; entry for December 1, 1932, *Tagebücher von Joseph Goebbels*, 2, 287.

56. Kolb, *Weimar Republic*, 123–24; entry for January 30, 1933, *Tagebücher von Joseph Goebbels*, 2, 358.

57. IfZ ZS 1147/II, 39, 41.

Chapter 12

1. January 2, 1934, *VB*, 2.

2. Wienstein, "Niederschrift über die Ministerbesprechung am 31. Januar 1933 5 Uhr nachm. in der Reichskanzlei.," BAR R43I/1459, 4.

3. General Liebmann, "Hitler am 3.II.1933 bei Hammerstein (Ansprache an die versammelten Befehlshaber von Heer und Marine.)," IfZ ED 1 Liebmann Aufzeichnungen, 1. Klaus-Jürgen Müller, "Die Reichswehr und die 'Machtergreifung,'" in Wolfgang Michalka ed., *Die nationalsozialistische Machtergreifung* (Paderborn: Ferdinand Schöningh, 1984), 143; Bracher, *Die nationalsozialistische Machtergreifung*, 51.

4. Hitler, December 9, 1931, "Nr. 7525/31," SAM Pol. Dir. München Nr. 6822.

5. Signature, July 26, 1932, "Akten-Notiz.," BA MA N 97/1, 3.

6. Wienstein, "Niederschrift über die Ministerbesprechung am 31. Januar 1933 5 Uhr nachm. in der Reichskanzlei.," BAR R43I/1459, 1–6; Wienstein, "Niederschrift über die Ministerbesprechung am 3. Februar 1933 6,30 Uhr nachm. in der Reichskanzlei.," BAR R43I/1459, 3–6; Martin Faatz, *Vom Staatsschutz zum Gestapo-Terror: Politische Polizei in Bayern in der Endphase der Weimarer Republik und der Anfangsphase der nationalsozialistischen Diktatur* (Würzburg: Echter Verlag, 1995), 356, 358; Klaus Mlynek, "Der Aufbau der Geheimen Staatspolizei in Hannover und die Errichtung des Konzentrationslagers Moringen," in Anke

Dietzler et al., *Hannover 1933: Eine Großstadt wird nationalsozialistisch: Beiträge zur Ausstellung* (Hannover: Historisches Museum am Hohen Ufer, 1981), 70.

7. Longerich, *Die braunen Bataillone*, 166; BAR NS 23 neu/3; Bracher, *Die nationalsozialistische Machtergreifung*, 136.

8. Oliver Gliech, "Die Spandauer SA 1926 bis 1933 Eine Studie zur nationalsozialistischen Gewalt in einer Berliner Bezirk," in Wolfgang Ribbe, ed., *Berlin-Forschungen III* (Berlin: Colloquium Verlag, 1988), 147–49; Kurt Schilde, Rolf Scholz, and Sylvia Wallecsek, *SA-Gefängnis Papestraße: Spuren und Zeugnisse* (Berlin: Overall Verlag, 1996), *passim*.

9. Evans, *Coming of the Third Reich*, 328–31; Wienstein, "Niederschrift über die Ministerbesprechung am 28. Februar 1933, nachm. 4^{15} Uhr.," BAR R43I/1459, 2; Bracher, *nationalsozialistische Machtergreifung*, 84–88; Wienstein, "Niederschrift über die Ministerbesprechung am 28. Februar 1933 vorm. 11 Uhr.," BAR R43I/1459, 2–4.

10. Evans, *Coming of the Third Reich*, 518–19, note 58; Uwe Backes et al, *Reichstagsbrand—Aufklärung einer historischen Legende*, 2nd ed. (Munich: Piper, 1987), *passim*; Kershaw, *Hitler*, 456–59.

11. Herbert Obenaus, "Die Märzwahlen 1933 in Hannover: Terror und Gegenwehr, Jubel und Resignation," in Dietzler, *Hannover 1933*, 39, 56; Faatz, *Vom Staatsschutz zum Gestapo Terror*, 363–65; Wolfram Selig, *Aspekte der nationalsozialistische Machtergreifung in München Aus der Stadtchronik und anderen Quellen zusammengestellt* (Munich: Stadtarchiv München, 1983), 13.

12. Evans, *Coming of the Third Reich*, 340.

13. Evans, *Coming of the Third Reich*, 339–40; Wienstein, "Niederschrift über die Ministerbesprechung am 7. März 1933, nachm. 415 Uhr.," BAR R43I/1459, 4.

14. Evans, *Coming of the Third Reich*, 350–53; Bracher, *Die nationalsozialistische Machtergreifung*, 152–68.

15. Bracher, *Die nationalsozialistische Machtergreifung*, 141–44, 722–24.

16. Evans, *Coming of the Third Reich*, 348.

17. Winfried Becker, "Die nationalsozialistische Machtergreifung in Bayern. Ein Dokumentarbericht Heinrich Helds aus dem Jahr 1933," *Historisches Jahrbuch* 112, no. 1 (1992): 413–14; Erwein von Aretin, "Die Frühjahrstage 1933," BHSA/KA HS 3263, 2–9; Sendtner, *Rupprecht von Wittelsbach*, 547–54; Karl Otmar Freiherr von Aretin, "Der bayerische Adel von der Monarchie zum Dritten Reich," in Andreas Kunz and Martin Vogt, ed., *Nation, Staat und Demokratie in Deutschland: Ausgewählte Beiträge zur Zeitgeschichte von Karl Otmar Freiherr von Aretin zum 70. Geburtstag des Verfassers* (Mainz: Verlag Philipp von Zabern, 1993), 25–35; IfZ F 52.

18. Becker, "Die nationalsozialistische Machtergreifung in Bayern," 415, 423, 426–28; BHSA/II MA 105247; BHSA/II MA 105255; BHSA/KA HS 3263.

19. BAR R 43II/1315; Selig, *Aspekte der nationalsozialistischen Machtergreifung in München, passim*; Falk Wiesemann, *Die Vorgeschichte der nationalsozialistischen Machtübernahme in Bayern 1932/1933* (Berlin: Duncker & Humblot,

1975), *passim;* Becker, "Die nationalsozialistische Machtergreifung in Bayern," 428–31.

20. Becker, "Die nationalsozialistische Machtergreifung in Bayern," 432.

21. Epp, diary entry for March 9, 1933, BHSA/II RS 63, 2, 3; Becker, "Die nationalsozialistische Machtergreifung in Bayern," 432–44.

22. Epp, diary entry, March 9, 1933, BHSA/II RS 63, 3–4; Browder, *Foundations of the Nazi Police State,* 63–64. The University Press of Kentucky, 1990), 63–64.

23. Epp, diary entry, March 10, 1933, BHSA/II RS 63, 4–5.

24. Becker, "'Die nationalsozialistische Machtergreifung in Bayern," 434–35.

25. BHSA/II MA 105255; Faatz, *Vom Staatsschutz zum Gestapo Terror,* 389–92.

26. Dornheim, *Röhms Mann fürs Ausland,* 167–75, 175–80; IfZ Gt 01.02/1; BAR R15.01/125769/1; Richardi and Schumann, *Geheim Akte Gerlich/Bell,* 139–46; Oberlandesgericht München I. Strafsenat, December 7, 1948, "Urteil.," GP RA/27, 1–5; Weiß, Erster Staatsanwalt, Im Auftrag des Generalstaatsanwalts, to the 5. Strafkammer des Landgerichts München I, July 4, 1956, "VIII 3324/55," "Betreff Strafverfahren gegen Josef Dietrich und Michael Lippert wegen Beihilfe zum Mord (Mordaktion vom 30. Juni 1934.)," GP RA/46, 46, note 3; Linder, *Von der NSDAP zur SPD,* 224–25.

27. Max Hirschberg, *Jude und Demokrat: Erinnerungen eines Münchener Rechtsanwalts 1883 bis 1939,* bearbeitet von Reinhard Weber (Munich: Oldenbourg Verlag, 1998), 282.

28. BAR ehem BDC Parteikartei Heimsoth, Karl Günther; Mrs B. (?) Heimsoth, Dortmund, to von Fritsch, September 13, 1934, 1–2, and von Fritsch to Mrs Heimsoth, September 19, 1934: IfZ MA 260.

29. Faatz, *Vom Staatsschutz zum Gestapo-Terror,* 440–42; BHSA/KA Landespolizei-Inspektion Bund 80.

30. Browder, *Foundations of the Nazi Police State,* 52, 67–68, 99; Bracher, *Die nationalsozialistische Machtergreifung,* 437–42, 883–84; IfZ ZS 357/II.

31. Faatz, *Vom Staatsschutz zum Gestapo-Terror,* 483, 505–6; Gliech, "Die Spandauer SA 1926 bis 1933," *Berlin-Forschungen III,* 170–71, 173.

32. Ulrich Klein, "SA-Terror und Bevölkerung in Wuppertal 1933/34," in Detlev Peukert and Jürgen Reulecke, ed., with Adelheid Gräfin zu Castell Rüdenhausen, *Die Reihen fast geschlossen: Beiträge zur Geschichte des Alltags unterm Nationalsozialismus, ed.* (Wuppertal: Peter Hammer Verlag, 1981), 45; Evans, *Coming of the Third Reich,* chap. 4 and 5, *passim;* Richard J. Evans, *The Third Reich in Power 1933–1939* (London: Allen Lane, 2005), 40–41, 114–18; Bessel, *Political Violence and the Rise of Nazism,* 108, 111–12; BAR R 15.01/25794/2.

33. BAR R43I/1460; BAR R 43 II/603 and R 43 II/1195; Orlow, *History of the Nazi Party: 1919–1933,* 218, note 160; BAR NS 23 neu/3.

34. Evans, *Coming of the Third Reich,* 358–67, 431–37; BHSA/II MA 105476; Gliech, "Die Spandauer SA 1926 bis 1933," *Berlin-Forschungen III,* 170–71; Henryk Skryzypczak, "Das Ende der Gewerkschaften," in Michalka, ed., *Die*

nationalsozialistische Machtergreifung, 97–110; Bracher, *Die nationalsozialistische Machtergreifung*, 212.

35. Berghahn, *Stahlhelm*, 242–67; Evans, *Coming of the Third Reich*, 373; Bessel, *Political Violence and the Rise of Nazism*, 121.
36. Bracher, *Die nationalsozialistische Machtergreifung*, 214.
37. Campbell, *SA Generals*, 119.

Chapter 13

1. Röhm, quoted, Sir E. Phipps to Sir John Simon, December 12, 1933, "No. 122.," TNA FO 408/63, 262.
2. Walther Darré, "Drehbühne II," BAK NL 94 I/28, 227.
3. Röhm, March 20, 1933, "Ch.-Nr. 800/33," "Verfügung.," BAK Slg Schumacher/407, 1.
4. Berghahn, *Stahlhelm*, 266–70; Bessel, *Political Violence and the Rise of Nazism*, 121; Campbell, *SA Generals*, 124–26; Reiche, *Development of the SA in Nürnberg*, 191–93; Bracher, *Die nationalsozialistische Machtergreifung*, 891–93; Röhm, September 12, 1933, "Ch. Nr. 3517/33," BAR NS 23 neu/5; Renzetti, Berlin, unheaded report, September 25, 1933, BAK N1235/12, 1–3; B. C. Newton to Sir Simon, September 27, 1933, "No. 930.," TNA FO 371/16709, 1–5; Phipps to Simon, May 30, 1934, No. 92, TNA FO 408/64, 124–25; Röhm, August 10, 1933, "Ch. Nr. 1456/33," BAR NS 31/303.
5. Campbell, *SA Generals*, 126. *Der Führer*, May 15, 1934, p.c., BAR 61 Sta 1/487; Bessel, *Political Violence and the Rise of Nazism*, 122.
6. Campbell, *SA Generals*, 122.
7. Bessel, *Political Violence and the Rise of Nazism*, 125–29.
8. IfZ ZS 145 Bd. 1; BAR R 2/18740a.
9. Röhm, der Chef des Stabes, der Oberste SA-Führer, May 30, 1933, "Ch. Nr. 1233/33," "Verfügung," BAK Slg Schumacher/414, 1.
10. *Deutsche Zeitung*, July 3, 1933, p.c., BAR 61 Sta 1/480; Bracher, *Die nationalsozialistische Machtergreifung*, 870, 898; Evans, *Third Reich in Power*, 20–21.
11. *The Times*, July 8, 1933, 12; Bracher, *Die nationalsozialistische Machtergreifung*, 473–76, 880; Evans, *Third Reich in Power*, 21.
12. *The Times*, July 8, 1933, 11; Norbert Frei, *National Socialist Rule in Germany: The Führer State 1933–1945* (Oxford: Blackwell, 1993), 60.
13. *Berliner Börsen-Zeitung*, July 2, 1933, p.c., BAR 61 Sta 1/480; Röhm, June 2, 1933, "Ch. Nr. 1236/33," BAR NS 23 neu/4, 1–2.
14. Röhm, September 8, 1933, "Ch. Nr. 149/33," BAK Slg Schumacher/414; Röhm, January 10, 1934, "Ch. Nr. 80/34," BAK NS 23 neu/7.
15. Kraußer, Obergruppenführer I.V. Der Chef des Stabes, July 20, 1933, "I. Nr. 1379./33.," BAR NS 23 neu/5; Richard Stegmann-Gall, *The Holy Reich: Nazi Conceptions of Christianity, 1919–1945* (Cambridge: Cambridge University Press, 2004), 159–60; Eberhard Röhm and Jörg Thierfelder, "Die evangelische Kirche und die Machtergreifung," in Michalka, *Die nationalsozialistische Machtergreifung*, 175–78.

16. Röhm, September 6, 1933, "Tagesbefehl," BAK NS 23 alt/vorl. 189; entries for September 1 and 2, 1933, respectively, *Tagebücher von Joseph Goebbels*, 2, 462–63; *The Times*, October 9, 1933, 13; notes by Sir Maurice Hankey to Wigram, October 24, 1933, "Hitler's External Policy in Theory and Practice," TNA FO 371/16744, 69.

17. I. A., signature, Gruppenführer, Chef der Abteilung IV, September 23, 1933, "IV Nr. 3316/33," BAK Slg Schumacher/414, 1–4; Röhm, October 7, 1933, "Ch. Nr. 1547/33," BHSA/II MA 106288, 2; Browder, *Foundations of the Nazi Police State*, 82–84; signature, i.V. Reichsstatthalter in Bayern an den Herrn Bayer. Ministerpräsidenten, November 24, 1933, "Betreff: Feldjägerkorps," BHSA/II MA 106288, and other papers on this file; "Vormerkung über die Besprechungen des Staatsministers Adolf Wagner in Berlin am Donnerstag, 12.4.1934 im Reichsministerium des Innern," BHSA/II Bayer. Gesandtschaft Berlin 1789, 3; "Auszug.," undated [1934], BHSA/II MA 106288.

18. Quoted in *Der SA-Mann*, June 30, 1933, 4; *Cumhuriyet*, June 9, 1933, 3; *Milliyet*, June 9, 1933; *Der S.A.-Mann*, July 8, 1933, 5; October 28, 1933, "Enclosure in No. 1," Consul-General Gainer to Phipps, November 2, 1933, Phipps to Simon, "Germany. Confidential.," "No. 1," TNA FO 371/16709, 1.

19. Epp, Reichsstatthalter in Bayern, to Reichsminister des Innern, July 12, 1933, "betr. Haushalte der Reichsstatthalter im Rechnungsjahr 1933.," BHSA/II RS 787; Pfundtner i.V., Reichsminister des Innern to Staatssekretär, Reichskanzlei, July 19, 1933, BAR R43II/1378; BHSA/II RS 165; Epp, "an die Herren Präsidenten der Regierungen a) von Ober- und Mittelfranken b) von Niederbayern und der Oberpfalz. Betreff: Ostmarkreise.," July 16, 1933, BHSA/II RS 64, 2; Epp diary, entry for August 27, 1933, BHSA/II RS 63, 67.

20. Bracher, *Die nationalsozialistische Machtergreifung*, 893–96; IfZ ZS 44; Robert J. O'Neill, *The German Army and the Nazi Party, 1933–1939*, 2nd ed. (London: Cassell, 1968), 33–34; Heinrich Bennecke, *Die Reichswehr und der "Röhm-Putsch"* (Munich: Günter Olzog Verlag, undated [1964]), 26–30; I. A. & I. V. v. Reichenau, der Reichswehrminister, July 27, 1933, "TA Nr. 533/33 g. Kdos. T 4 III Richtlinien für die vormilitärische Ausbildung. Jugend=, Gelände= und S.A.=Sport.," BA MA RH 12–5/7, 1–10; Immo von Fallois, *Kalkül und Illusion: Der Machtkampf zwischen Reichswehr und SA während der Röhm-Krise 1934* (Berlin: Duncker & Humblot, 1994), 90.

21. Gerhard L. Weinberg, *The Foreign Policy of Hitler's Germany: Diplomatic Revolution in Europe 1933–36* (Chicago: University of Chicago Press, 1970), 36–52, 159–66. Military Attaché to M.I.3, "Military training of Nazi stormtroops in Germany," June 16, 1933, TNA FO 371/16706, 2–6; "Besprechung mit den Reichsstatthaltern am 28. September 1933 in Berlin, Reichskanzler-Palais, 5 Uhr Nachmittag. Darlegungen des Reichskanzlers Adolf Hitler.," BHSA/II RS Epp 148, 4–5; Seydel, I. A. Der Chef des Stabes, July 25, 1933, "Z. Nr. 1393/33," BAR NS 23 neu/5.

22. *Deutsche Allgemeine Zeitung*, August 20, 1933, p.c., BAR 61Sta1/1998; *Neue Zürcher Zeitung*, August 23 [1933], p.c., BAR R 8034 II/9252; signature, Berlin to Simon, September 27, 1933, TNA FO 371/16709, 1–5.

23. Von Neurath, September 15, 1933, "R.M. 1302," PA/AA R 70511, 2; v. Neurath, May 9, 1933, "R.M. 642.," PA/AA R 33636; Mr. B.C. Newton to Simon, enclosing a report of the Military Attaché Colonel Thorne, "Germany. confidential," September 6, 1933, TNA FO 371/16708, 1–12.

24. "Niederschrift über die Reichsstatthalterkonferenz am 28. September 1933 415 Uhr nachmittags in der Reichskanzlei.," BA R43II/1392, 2–5.

25. V. Reichenau I.A. Der Reichswehrminister, September 22, 1933, "Nr. 460 WIII. geh," BA MA RH 46/107, 3; Fallois, *Kalkül und Illusion*, 93.

26. Weinberg, *Foreign Policy of Hitler's Germany*, 69; Dietrich Orlow, *The History of the Nazi Party: Volume II 1933–1945* (Newton Abbot: David & Charles, 1973), 91; Reichstag IX. Wahlperiode 1933, *Verzeichnis der Mitglieder des Reichstags und der Reichsregierung sowie der Bevollmächtigten zum Reichsrat*. Abgeschlossen am 12. December 1933, BHSA/II RS 54, 48.

27. Phipps to Simon, October 10, 1933, TNA FO 371/16709, 3. *Deutsche Staatsbürger-Zeitung*, October 5, 1933, p.c., BHSA/V Slg P 3653; *Deutsche Allgemeine Zeitung*, October 4, 1933, p.c., BAR 8034 II/9252; "Stabschef Röhm über Aufgaben und Wesen der SA," October 4, 1933, Wolff's Telegraphisches Büro, 84/ Nr. 2431, BAR R 15.01/25794/2; Phipps to Simon, October 10, 1933, TNA FO 371/16709, 1–4; notes by Sir Maurice Hankey to Wigram, October 24, 1933, "Hitler's External Policy in Theory and Practice," TNA FO 371/16744, 69.

28. Dieter Ross, *Hitler und Dollfuß: Die deutsche Österreich-Politik 1933–1934* (Hamburg: Leibniz-Verlag, 1966), chap. 1.

29. Bülow to Neurath, August 25, 1933, PA AA R 30406k, 2; Gerhard Jagschitz, *Der Putsch: Die Nationalsozialisten 1934 in Österreich* (Graz: Verlag Styria, 1976), 36.

30. Comments of Professor Gerhard Schulz, "Zweite Arbeitssitzung Errichtung und Stabilisierung einer totalitären Diktatur Erste Diskussionsrunde," in M. Broszat et al. eds., *Deutschlands Weg in die Diktatur: Internationale Konferenz zur nationalsozialistischen Machtübernahme im Reichstagsgebäude zu Berlin Referate und Diskussionen* (Berlin: Siedler Verlag, 1983), 207; Ross, *Hitler und Dollfuß*, 114–18; Jagschitz, *Putsch*, 61; Dieter Anton Binder, *Dollfuss und Hitler: Über die Außenpolitik des autoritären Ständestaates in den Jahren 1933/34* (Graz: Verlag für die Technische Universität Graz, 1979), 173–74; "No. 49 Memorandum by an Official of Department II," November 8, 1933, Hüffer, Berlin, "SECRET," *Documents on German Foreign Policy 1918–1945. Series C (1933–1937) The Third Reich: First Phase Volume II October 14, 1933—June 13,1934* (London: HMSO, 1959), 87; Document 7, "Gesandtschaftsbericht Berlin 9. Oktober 1933," Binder, *Dollfuss und Hitler*, fol. 76–77; Neurath to Reichsminister des Innern, May 24, 1934, PA/AA R 30406k, 1–4. The documents that Dr. Gregory Weeks of Webster University in Vienna uncovered for me in the Austrian State Archives do not substantiate Binder's interpretation.

31. D. St. Clair Gainer, Munich, to Phipps, November 11, 1933, "Enclosure in No. 62," No. 62, Phipps to Simon, November 14, 1933, TNA FO/108/63, 134.

Germania, November 8, 1933, p.c., BAR R 15.01/25794/2; Renzetti, "CONFI-DENZIALE," unheaded report, November 10, 1933, BAK N 1235/12, 2; Epp diary, entry for November 8, 1923, BHSA/II RS 63, 81; Röhm, November 2, 1933, "II. Nr. 1638/33," BAR NS 23 neu/6, 1; Röhm, November 2, 1933, "II. Nr. 1635/33," ibid., 1.

32. *VB*, November 28, 1933, 1–2; *VB*, November 29, 1933, p.cs, BHSA/V Slg P 3653; *VB*, November 30, 1933, 2; December 2, 1933, *Der S.A.-Mann*, 4.

33. November 21, 1933, No. 60, Phipps to Simon, E. L. Woodward and Rohan Butler, eds., *Documents on British Foreign Policy 1919–1939, Second Series Volume VI 1933–34* (London: HMSO, 1957), 86. November 9, 1933, No. 26, Phipps to Simon, ibid., 24.

34. Der Reichspräsident, December 4, 1933, "Abschrift zu Rk. 13802.," BAR R43II/141; Lammers to Röhm, December 7, 1933, BAR NS 26/328, 1; "Niederschrift über die Reichsstatthalterkonferenz am 28. September 1933 415 Uhr nachmittags in der Reichskanzlei.," BA R43II/1392, 6–8; Bracher, *Die nationalsozialistische Machtergreifung*, 217–18; Wienstein, Willuhn, and Killy, "Niederschrift über die Ministerbesprechung und Kabinettssitzung am 27. Juni 1933, nachm 530 Uhr," BAR R 43 I/1463, 4; "Niederschrift, aufgenommen in der Ministerratssitzungen vom 5. und 6. Dezember 1933 in der Staatskanzlei des Freistaates Bayern zu München," BHSA/II RS 165, 1, 2; "Ministerratssitzungen vom 5. und 6. Dezember 1933," BAK Slg. Schumacher/272, 2; "No. 105 memorandum by the State Secretary," Bülow, December 2, 1933, *DGFP, Series C Volume II*, 184–85; December 6, 1933, No. 101, Phipps to Simon, No. 276 Telegraphic, *DBFP*, 157; December 7, 1933, No. 105, Simon to Phipps, ibid., 167.

35. *Warum SA?*, 17.

36. Phipps to Simon, December 12, 1933, "No. 122," TNA FO 408/63, 262.

37. Ibid.

38. Phipps to Simon, December 9, 1933, No. 120, *DBFP*, 179.

39. *Ingolstädter Zeitung*, December 11, 1933, 2; *Ingolstädter Zeitung*, December 14,1933, 1; Röhm, December 13, 1933, "Ch-II Nr. 1724/33 Betrifft: Urlaub," "Verfügung," BAK Slg Schumacher/415; *Ingolstädter Zeitung*, December 16, 1933, 1; *Der Donaubote*, December 18, 1933, 5; Renzetti, December 10, 1933, unheaded report, BAK N 1235/12, 1–2. It is not clear when Röhm returned to Germany. According to a colorful account of Röhm's visit to Capri by Ernst's adjutant, the party stayed on and went to Ragusa (Dubrovnik) in Yugoslavia in the New Year: IfZ ZS 268.

40. Renzetti, December 10, 1933, unheaded report, BAK N 1235/12, 2; *VB*, December 15, 1933, p.c., BHSA/V Slg P 3653; undated press clipping [December 1933], *Münchner Illustrierte Presse*, BHSA/KA OP 32380; *Neue freie Volkszeitung*, November 24, 1933, p.c., SM ZA Pers. Röhm.

41. Röhm, "Neujahrsbefehl 1934," BAR NS 23 neu/6.

42. Bennecke, *Reichswehr und der "Röhm-Putsch*," 36–37; Bracher, *Die nationalsozialistische Machtergreifung*, 805–6; "Besprechung in Berlin am 21. und 22.12.33.," BA MA RH 53-7/v. 1086, 1–2.

Chapter 14

1. Hermann Esser, October 10, 1949, "Eidesstattliche Erklärung.," SAM STAW 28793, 2.

2. Longerich, *Die braunen Bataillone*, 198, 202; BHSA/II M Ju 16998; Bessel, *Political Violence and the Rise of Nazism*, 122–29; Mathilde Jamin, "Das Ende der 'Machtergreifung': Der 30. Juni 1934 und seine Wahrnehmung in der Bevölkerung," in Michalka, *Die nationalsozialistische Machtergreifung*, 208; Bracher, *Die nationalsozialistische Machtergreifung*, 931.

3. Bessel, *Political Violence and the Rise of Nazism*, 125; IfZ ZS 44; BAK NS 23 neu/7; BAK R 19/390; BAR R 2/18518; BAR R 15.01/25794/3.

4. Thomsen, February 20, 1934, "No. 271 Memorandum kept by an official of the Reich Chancellery," *DGFP, Series C Volume II*, 516; Kershaw, *Hitler*, 506.

5. "No. 129 The Ambassador in France to the Foreign Ministry," July 27, 1934, Köster, Paris, *DGFP, Series C Volume II*, 259–65; June 28, 1949, Stölzle to Weiss, GP RA/4a, 5–8; Wheeler-Bennett, *Knaves, Fools and Heroes*, 80–81; SAM STAW 28793; IfZ ZS 251 Bd. I; Library of Congress Martha E. Dodd Family Papers, Box 1 Folder 6; IfZ ZS 357/I; BAR R 54/138.

6. BAR R 15.01/25749/2.

7. BA MA RH 26–7/744; BA MA RH 53–7/v. 1086; IfZ ZS 44; IfZ Fa 74; Fallois, *Kalkül und Illusion*, 103.

8. Stölzle to Weiss, June 28, 1949, GP RA/4a, 9; Bracher, *Die nationalsozialistische Machtergreifung*, 738–39; IfZ ZS 208 Bd 1.

9. IfZ ZS105, 9–10.

10. May 29, 1933, "Guide to lesser known personalities in the Nazi party," Berlin Chancery to Central Department, TNA FO 371/16750, 316.

11. February 12, 1934, No. 72, Phipps to Simon, enclosing a memorandum by D. St Clair Gainer, January 22, 1934, TNA FO 408/64, 161.

12. The Rt. Hon. The Earl of Avon, *The Eden Memoirs: Facing the Dictators* (London: Cassell, 1962), 71.

13. BA MA N 265/149; Fallois, *Kalkül und Illusion*, 105–7.

14. Field Marshal Maximilian von und zu Weichs an der Glon, "Erinnerungen Band 1—Potsdam und Weimar 1933–1937" Band 1, BA MA N 19/5, 11.

15. BAK Rep. 501 XXXVII C; Bergmann to Weiss, May 14, 1949, SAM STAW 28793, 5; Fredrich Haselmayr, June 22, 1946, "Eidesstattliche Versicherung," Staatsarchiv Nürnberg KV-Prozesse IMT C 186 SA-Affidavits, 1–2; IfZ ZS 70; Salomon, "*Fragebogen*," 272; Bracher, *Die nationalsozialistische Machtergreifung*, 938; Fest, *Hitler*, 791, note 37.

16. Berlin, K[rüger], February 23, 1934, "Aktenvermerk. Betrifft: Denkschrift Reichsverteidigung.," BAR (ehem.BDC) O.421 SA Chef AW; unsigned and undated report, "Vorschlag für Zusammenarbeit mit SA.," BA MA RH 26–7/377, 1–6.

17. BA MA N 19/5, 11–13.

18. Ibid., 14; Fallois, *Kalkül und Illusion*, 107–8.

19. Nachlaß von Weichs, BA MA N 19/5, 14.

20. No. 335 Berlin, Phipps to Simon, March 7, 1934, *DBFP*, 532.

21. Charles K. Harris, "'After the Ball'" lyrics," "History Wired," http://historywired .si.edu/detail.cfm?ID=286, accessed November 10, 2006.

22. Italics in the original: Röhm, March 12, 1934, "Dienstanweisung für die Inspekteure Ost, Südost, Mitte und West der SA.," BA MA RH 26–7/377, 1.

23. BAR NS 23 neu/8; BAR NS 23 neu/9; Bessel, *Political Violence and the Rise of Nazism*, 127–28.

24. "Vormerkung über die Besprechungen des Staatsministers Adolf Wagner in Berlin am Donnerstag, 12.4.1934 im Reichministerium des Innern," BHSA/II Bayer. Gesandtschaft Berlin 1789, 3.

25. "GERMANY: 'Self-Help' of Mob Stops Film Starring Jewess," *Newsweek*, March 17, 1934, 15.

26. Papers on PA AA 73123.

27. "Wachsendes Verständnis für Deutschland in Jugoslawien," *Der Deutsche*, April 8, 1934, p.c., PA AA R 73123; *VB*, April 12, 1934, p.c., SM Zeitungsauschnitte Personen Röhm.

28. Marxer to Kanzlei des Führers, April 12, 1934, BAK NS 23 neu/8; BAR NS 1/8; BAK NS 23 neu/8.

29. Elisabetta Cerruti, *Ambassador's Wife* (London: George Allen and Unwin, 1953), 146.

30. Ibid.

31. *VB*, April 16, 1934, p.c., BHSA/V Slg P 3653; *VB*, April 19, 1934, p.c., BAR R 8034III/113; BA MA N 265/149.

32. April 19, 1934, No. 38, Phipps to Simon, TNA FO 408/64, 56–58.

33. BAR NS 23 neu/8; *Ingolstädter Tagblatt*, May 8, 1934, 2; *Der S.A.-Mann*, May 26, 1934, 1–2, 4; Bracher, *Die nationalsozialistische Machtergreifung*, 937; Bessel, *Political Violence and the Rise of Nazism*, 130; BAR NS 23 neu/5.

34. *Ingolstädter Zeitung*, May 7, 1934, 2. ISA A III/6d; *Münchner Neueste Nachrichten*, May 7, 1934, p.c., BHSA/V Slg P 3653; ISA AIII/6g; ISA A III/6i; Bracher, *Die nationalsozialistische Machtergreifung*, 882–84.

35. June 28, 1949, Stölzle to Weiss, GP RA/4a, 26.

36. "No. 129 The Ambassador in France to the Foreign Ministry," July 27, 1934, Köster, Paris, *Documents on German Foreign Policy 1918–1945. Series C (1933–1937) The Third Reich: First Phase Volume III June 14, 1934–March 31, 1935* (London: HMSO, 1959), 263. Regendanz to Brendler, Geheime Staatspolizei, Berlin, July 2, 1934, William E. Dodd Papers, Box 45 General Correspondence. 1934 – R, 10; Fest, *Hitler*, 456, 458.

37. BA MA RH 53–7/v.1324; Fallois, *Kalkül und Illusion*, 124, 125, 129; O'Neill, *German Army and the Nazi Party*, 44–45; IfZ ZS 251 Bd. I.

38. IfZ ZS 177 Bd. 1, 7. Bessel, *Political Violence and the Rise of Nazism*, 126, 129, 131–32; Jamin, "Ende der 'Machtergreifung,'" Michalka, *Die nationalsozialistische Machtergreifung*, 208; Browder, *Foundations of the Nazi Police State*, 30–31; BAK Slg Schumacher/403; BAR NS 23 neu/9; BAR NS 26/328; Bergmann to Weiss, May 14, 1949, SAM STAW 28793, 3.

39. May 30, 1934, No. 433, Telegram Phipps to Sir R. Vansittart, *DBFP*, 715.

40. IfZ ZS 568/I; IfZ ZS 568/II; Bracher, *Die nationalsozialistische Machtergreifung*, 952; Stölzle to Weiss, June 28, 1949, GP RA/4a, 26; Max Domarus, *Hitler Speeches and Proclamations 1932–1945 The Chronicle of a Dictatorship Volume One The years 1932 to 1934* (London: I. B. Tauris, 1990), 495.

41. June 9, 1934, *Ingolstädter Tagblatt*, 1; Anlage 1, Bennecke, *Reichswehr und der "Röhm-Putsch*,*"* 81. The Munich Schwurgericht trying Dietrich and Lippert after the war for murders on June 30 and July 1, 1934, saw the failure to append "Heil Hitler" to the order as suspicious and gave more weight to this than it should have: Drs Graf, Bartsch, Schlicker, das Schwurgericht beim Landgericht München I, "Urteil:," May 1957, GP RA/13, 73.

42. *8 Uhr-Blatt*, May 9, 1957, p.c., BHSA/KA HS 2656; July 4, 1956, Weiß "VIII 3324/55" to the 5. Strafkammer des Landgerichts München I, GP RA/10, 56; July 10, 1934, signature, Aerztliche Verrechnungsstelle e.V., Gauting-München to Nachlassgericht beim Amtsgericht München, SAM Amtsgericht München Nr. 1934/1767; Bergmann to Weiss, May 14, 1949, SAM STAW 28793, 2; Cerruti, *Ambassador's Wife*, 146.

43. Phipps to Simon, June 8, 1934, No. 447, *DBFP*, 742.

44. M. H., "30. Juni 1934—'Röhm-Putsch' in Bad Wiessee. Tod eines Badegastes," handout from Bad Wiessee Bücherei, 17; IfZ MS 200/170; Altdorf, signatures, February 1, 1949, Landpolizei Ober- u. Mittelfranken Kriminalaussenstelle, "Vernehmungsniederschrift," GP RA/29, 3. Both sources from contemporary eyewitnesses in Bad Wiessee reproduce hearsay as well as evidence, but make it clear that Röhm spent his time there peacefully taking the cure: M. H., "30. Juni 1934—'Röhm-Putsch' in Bad Wiessee. Tod eines Badegastes," handout from Bad Wiessee Bücherei, 17; IfZ MS 200/170. Schreyer to Polizeipräsidium München, May 27, 1949, GP RA/57, 3–4; Epp diary, June 28, 1934, BHSA/II RS 65, 33; Ferdinand Paul, Prinz v. Ysenburg, January 3, 1950, "Betreff: Mordaktion vom 30.VI.34," GP RA/2 [IfZ Fa 442/5 II], 2–3.

45. Altdorf, signatures, February 1, 1949, Landpolizei Ober- u. Mittelfranken Kriminalaussenstelle, "Vernehmungsniederschrift.," GP RA/29, 4. Bergmann to Weiss, May 14, 1949, SAM STAW 28793, 4; April 27, 1949, K. 7B, "Vernehmungsniederschrift.," ibid., 2; Gritschneder, *"Der Führer hat Sie zum Tode verurteilt . . . ,"* 143; Munich, K. 7B, signatures, May 17, 1949, "Vernehmungsniederschrift.," SAM STAW 28793, 6–7.

Chapter 15

1. Schaub, quoted in *Münchner Merkur*, May 8, 1957, p.c., BHSA/KA HS 2656. IfZ MS 200/170; Drs. Graf, Bartsch, Schlicker, Schwurgericht beim Landgericht München I, May 1957, "Urteil:," GP RA/13, 77.

2. *Münchner Merkur*, May 9, 1957, p.c., BHSA/KA HS 2656, 3.

3. Bergmann to Weiss, May 14, 1949, SAM STAW 28793, 4; entry for July 7, 1934, Hans-Günther Seraphim, ed., *Das politische Tagebuch Alfred Rosenbergs*

aus den Jahren 1934/35 und 1939/40 (Göttingen: Musterschmidt Verlag, 1956), 33–34; *Münchner Merkur*, May 9, 1957, p.c., BHSA/KA HS 2656, 3; Mabire, *Röhm*, 392; "100 Jahre Justizvollzugsanstalt München," undated handout, from Stadelheim Prison Director Kronzücker, September 8, 1997, 1.

4. Dr. Koch, Direktion des Strafsvollstreckungsgefängnisses, July 2, 1934, "Eingeliefert und aufgenommen wurden hier am 30. Juni 1934," SAM St. Anw. 28792, 1–2; unheaded page copied from 1934 register of inmates, *Grundbuch* v. 2.6.1934 b. 25.4.1935, Verzeichnis der in Verwahrung genommenen Sache der Gefangenen, from Stadelheim Prison Director Kronzücker in September 1997; Siegel, September 4, 1934, "Das letzte Kapitel zu dem Buch Röhm's 'Aus dem Leben eines Hochverräters,'" SAM STAW 28793, 3; discussion with prison director, Mr. Kronzücker, Stadelheim prison, September 8, 1997.

5. Schreyer to Polizeipräsidium München, May 27, 1949, GP RA/57, 5; Graf, Bartsch, Schlicker, May 1957, "Urteil:," GP RA/13, 79; Adolf Hitler, "Abschrift! (Sondernummer des Völkischen Beob. V. 1.7.34)," BAK Slg Schumacher/407, 1–3; Phipps to Simon, by telephone, June 30, 1934, TNA FO 408/64, 2–3.

6. Heinz Höhne, *Mordsache Röhm: Hitlers Durchbruch zur Alleinherrschaft 1933–1935* (Reinbek: Spiegel-Buch, 1984), chap. 4–6; Fallois, *Kalkül und Illusion*, chap. C and D; IfZ ZS 317/I, 3–4.

7. Frei, *Führer State*, chap. 1; Höhne, *Mordsache Röhm*, 215.

8. Fallois, *Kalkül und Illusion*, 125–26; BAR R 43v II/1202; Browder, *Foundations of the Nazi Police State*, 128–31; IfZ ZS 317/I, 4; July 4, 1956, Weiß to the 5. Strafkammer des Landgerichts München I, "VIII 3324/55," GP RA/46, 49–50.

9. Fallois, *Kalkül und Illusion*, 106–12, 125–27; Bracher, *Die nationalsozialistische Machtergreifung*, 917–20; Bennecke, *Reichswehr und der "Röhm-Putsch,"* 46–47.

10. BAK R 53/45; IfZ ZS 321; Frei, *Führer State*, 15–16.

11. BHSA/II RS 51; IfZ ZS 568/I; Frei, *Führer State*, 17–18.

12. *Deutsche Tagespost*, May 14, 1957, p.c., SM ZA Pers Röhm; Bracher, *Die nationalsozialistische Machtergreifung*, 910–13; Lothar Machtan, *Der Kaisersohn bei Hitler. Prinz August Wilhelm im Hexenkessel der deutschen Geschichte* (Hamburg: Hoffmann und Campe, 2006).

13. Höhne, *Mordsache Röhm*, 242, 246; Heinrici to "Liebe Eltern, liebe Mutter Alice," June 23, 1934, BA MA N 265/149, 2; signature, der Führer der S.A.-Standarte 76, Hamburg to SA Brigade 12 (Hamburg), June 29, 1934, BAK Slg Schumacher 402, 1–2.

14. Fallois, *Kalkül und Illusion*, 134–35; Browder, *Foundations of the Nazi Police State*, 14; July 4, 1956, Weiß to the 5. Strafkammer des Landgerichts München I, GP RA/46, 49; Bracher, *Die nationalsozialistische Machtergreifung*, 955.

15. Foertsch to the Generalstaatsanwalt beim Oberlandesgericht München, April 16, 1957, GP RA/57; von Holtzendorff to the Generalstaatsanwalt beim Oberlandesgericht München, April 16, 1957, BA MA N 264/14, 2; formal note on behalf of the Stabschef der SA, Berlin to U.S. Ambassador Dodd, June 29,1934, LoC William E. Dodd Papers, Box 45, General Correspondence 1934-R.

16. Höhne, *Mordsache Röhm*, 247; Hess, "Kölner Rede (Gau Essen) am 25.6.1934.," BAR NS 6/70, 1–17; Weiß to the 5. Strafkammer des Landgerichts München I, July 4, 1956, GP RA/46, 54; Drs Graf, Bartsch, Schlicker, "Urteil:," May 1957, GP RA/13, 69.

17. Höhne, *Mordsache Röhm*, 246; Fallois, *Kalkül und Illusion*, 135, 136; Ysenburg, January 3, 1950, "Betreff: Mordaktion vom 30.VI.34," GP RA/ 2, 2–3; Altdorf, signatures, Landpolizei Ober- u. Mittelfranken Kriminalaussenstelle, February 1, 1949, "Vernehmungsniederschrift," GP RA/29, 3; IfZ ZS105; IfZ ZS 568/ II.

18. Quoted in K. 7B, signatures, "Vernehmungsnieder-schrift.," May 17, 1949, Munich, SAM STAW 28793, 5. Anlage 4, Bennecke, *Reichswehr und der "Röhm-Putsch*," 85; O'Neill, *German Army and the Nazi Party*, 47–48; Weiß, unheaded statement of Wilhlem Ott, October 12, 1949, GP RA/ 2, 2; Bracher, *Die nationalsozialistische Machtergreifung*, 957–58.

19. O'Neill, *German Army and the Nazi Party*, 47–48; Weiß, unheaded statement of Wilhlem Ott, October 12, 1949, GP RA/2, 3; May 17, 1949, Munich, K. 7B, signatures, "Vernehmungsniederschrift.," SAM STAW 28793, 7.

20. Anlage 4, Bennecke, *Reichswehr und der "Röhm-Putsch*," 85. Patzig, Admiral a.D., April 11, 1957, SAM STAW 28794, 2; O'Neill, *German Army and the Nazi Party*, 47; testimony of Jodl, June 3, 1946, Internationaler Militärgerichtshof Nürnberg, *Der Prozess gegen die Hauptkriegsverbrecher vor dem Internationalen Militärgerichtshof Nürnberg 14. November 1945–1. Oktober 1946* (1947, Nuremberg; repr. Delphin Verlag, Munich, 1984), vol. 15, 336; Heinrici to "Liebe Eltern, liebe Mutter Alice!" July 7, 1934, BA MA N 265/149, 1–7; Heinrici, "Der 30. Juni 1934.,"BA MA N 465/v. 4, 1–6; *8 Uhr-Blatt*, May 10, 1957, p.c., SM ZA Pers Röhm; Fallois, *Kalkül und Illusion*, 84, 134–35.

21. *VB*, June 29, 1934, p.c., BAR 62 Sta 1/1230. The claim that Röhm had been expelled from various retired officers' organizations at the end of June seems to have originated in a story in the Austrian newspaper, *Die Wiener Zeitung*, as reported by the Swiss paper, *Der Bund*, July 7, 1934, p.c., BAR R 8034 III/9255, 1.

22. Höhne, *Mordsache Röhm*, 245, 260–63; June 23,1956, KD2 Munich, "Vernehmungsniederschrift," SAM STAW 28794, 1–3; Weiß to the 5. Strafkammer des Landgerichts München I, July 4, 1956, GP RA/46, 58–59; May 6–10, 1957, May 13–14, 1957, "Protokoll geführt in öffentlicher Sitzung der 4. Tagung des Schwurgerichts beim Landgericht München I in dem Strafverfahren gegen Dietrich Josef und Lippert Michael wegen Beihilfe zum Totschlag," SAM STAW 29791, 18; Mrs. Martina Schmid to Staatsanwalt, August 12, 1949, GP RA/2, 1–4.

23. Höhne, *Mordsache Röhm*, 227, 239–409, 245–56; Schreyer to Polizeipräsidium München, May 27, 1949, GP RA/57, 7–8; "2. April 1935" (briefing note), BAR R 22/603, 5; Weiß to the 5. Strafkammer des Landgerichts München I, July 4, 1956, GP RA/46, 56; May 14, 1949, Bergmann to Weiss, SAM STAW 28793, 5.

24. Weiß to the 5. Strafkammer des Landgerichts München I, July 4, 1956, GP RA/46, 60–61; BHSA/KA Landespolizeiinspektion Südwest; BA MA RH 57/9; BHSA/KA Landespolizei München Bd. 1; BA MA RH 26–7/397a; Höhne, *Mordsache Röhm, passim;* Otto Gritschneder, *"Der Führer hat Sie zum Tode verurteilt . . .": Hitlers "Röhm-Putsch"-Morde vor Gericht* (Munich: C. H. Beck, 1993), *passim;* June 26, 1934, comment written on June 19, 1934, Lammers to von Epp, "St.S. Nr. 1531/34. Persönlich!" BHSA/II RS 788, 1–2; BHSA/KA HS 925, 71.

25. Hermann Esser, October 10, 1949, "Eidesstattliche Erklärung," SAM STAW 28793, 2.

26. Ibid.

27. Ysenburg, handwritten paper, undated, "Betreff: Mordaktion vom 30.VII.34," GP RA/2, 2, 4–7. Ysenburg described Hitler as emerging from the meeting literally "with riven color" (*"mit zerrissener Farbe"*). 1934 Tagebuch, June 30, 1934 entry, BHSA/II RS 65, 33–34; Hermann Esser, October 10, 1949, "Eidesstattliche Erklärung," GP RA/57, 3; signature (Siebert), Bayerische Ministerpräsident, unheaded note, July 5, 1934, BHSA/II MA 107579; Walter Kurreck, Dusseldorf, August 18, 1949, "Betr.: Röhm Putsch," SAM STAW 28793, 2; IfZ ZS 28; von Epp, handwritten, July 4, 1934, "R.In.Mi Dr. Frick vorgetragen E," BDC 402 Röhm Röhmputsch Reichstagsbrand, i–iv.

28. Koch, Direktion der Strafvollstreckungsgefängnisses, June 30, 1934, "Niederschrift," Stadelheim prison records; signature, Oberregierung-srat, der Vorstand der Vorstand der Strafanstalten München to Staatsanwalt Dr. Wörle, January 18, 1949, Beilage 1, June 30,1934, Koch, Wagner, "Abschrift," GP RA/1; Weiß to the 5. Strafkammer des Landgerichts München I, July 4, 1956, GP/RA 10, 68–69.

29. Quoted in Fest, *Face of the Third Reich,* 224. Weiß to the 5. Strafkammer des Landgerichts München I, July 4, 1956, GP RA/10, 68 note 1; Friedrich Döbig, Oberlandesgerichtsrat Nürnberg to Herrn Generalstaatsanwalt bei dem Oberlandesgericht München, June 1, 1949, SAM STAW 28793, 2.

30. Weiß to the 5. Strafkammer des Landgerichts München I, July 4, 1956, GP RA/10, 68–69; Wolfram Selig, "Ermordet im Namen des Führers. Die Opfer des Röhm-Putsches in München," Sonderdruck aus *Staat, Kultur, Politik—Beiträge zur Geschichte Bayerns und des Katholizismus Festschrift zum 65. Geburtstag von Dieter Albrecht* (Kallmünz/Opf.: Verlag Michael Laßleben, 1992), 344; Joachim Petzold, *Franz von Papen: Ein deutsches Verhängnis* (Munich: Buchverlag Union, 1995), 289.

31. Weiß to the 5. Strafkammer des Landgerichts München I, July 4, 1956, GP RA/10, 69. Wolfram Selig, "Ermordet im Namen des Führers," 344.

32. Weiß to the 5. Strafkammer des Landgerichts München I, July 4, 1956, GP RA/10, 69–70; Direktion des Vollstreckungsgefängnis München, unheaded page, Stadelheim prison records.

33. Signatures, unheaded report of statement of Maria Weinmayer, geb. Witt, June 14, 1949, SAM Pol.Dir. München 10007, 1; Weiß, Erster Staatsanwalt, Im

Auftrag Der Generalstaatsanwalt, an die 5. Strafkammer des Landgerichts München I, July 4, 1956, "VIII 3324/55 (GenStA) Betreff: Strafverfahren gegen Josef <u>Dietrich</u>, Michael <u>Lippert</u>, Dr. Werner <u>Best</u> und Karl Albrecht <u>Oberg</u> wegen Beihilfe zum Totschlag (Mordaktion vom 30. Juni 1934)," GP RA/10, 3; Eleonore Lippert to Weiss, May 7, 1949, SAM STAW 28793, 1.

34. May 1957, Graf, Bartsch, Schlicker, "<u>Urteil</u>:," GP RA/13, 61; Kershaw, *Hitler*, 516; Höhne, *Mordsache Röhm*, 292–94; May 6–10, 1957, May 13–14, 1957, "<small>PROTOKOLL</small> . . .," GP RA/12, 10–11; Dr. Robert Koch, January 25, 1949, "1 a Js 68/49," "<u>Vernehmungsniederschrift</u>.," GP RA/1, 7; Walther, *Zum anderen Ufer*, 526; Siegel, "Das letzte Kapitel," September 4, 1934, SAM STAW 28793, 4–5; Bergmann to Weiss, May 14, 1949, SAM STAW 28793, 8.

35. Landerer, K. K., Kriminalpolizei KD2, Polizeipräsidium München and Jakob Schlicher, "Vernehmungsniederschrift," April 12, 1957, SAM STAW 28794 1; Weiß to the 5. Strafkammer des Landgerichts München I, July 4, 1956, GP RA/10, 77; signature (Koch), Direktion des Strafvollstreckungs-gefängnisses, "Niederschrift.," July 1, 1934, Stadelheim prison records, 1–2.

36. Weiß to the 5. Strafkammer des Landgerichts München I, July 4, 1956, GP RA/10, 79; Walter Kopp, Sonthofen to the Staatsanwaltschaft München I, March 7, 1949, BHSA/KA HS 2656.

37. Weiß to the 5. Strafkammer des Landgerichts München I, July 4, 1956, GP RA/10, 81, note 3; "Niederschrift aufgenommen vor dem Untersuchungsrichter beim Landgericht München I in dem Untersuchungsverfahren gegen Dietrich Josef und 3 A. wegen Verbrechens des Totschlags u.a.," June 22,1953, GP RA/57, 1–4; LoC RSS RYH 8616 John Toland Collection Interview with Robert and Annalies Röhm.

38. *Bild-Zeitung*, May 8, 1957, p.c., BHSA/KA HS 2656; "<u>Niederschrift</u> aufgenommen vor dem Untersuchungsrichter beim Landgericht München I in dem Untersuchungsverfahren gegen Sepp Dietrich u.A. wegen Totschlags bzw. Mordes," May 27, 1953, GP RA/6, 1–4; Weiß to the 5. Strafkammer des Landgerichts München I, July 4, 1956, GP RA/10, 81, note 3.

39. Testimony of Johann Mühlbauer, quoted in *Süddeutsche Zeitung*, May 14, 1957, p.c., SM ZA Pers. Röhm. Weiß to the 5. Strafkammer des Landgerichts München I, July 4, 1956, GP RA/10, 81, 82; undated, Strafvollstreckungsgefängnis München, "Betreff: Säuberungsaktion," SAM St Anw 28792, 2; 1997, Direktion des Vollstreckungsgefängnis München, unheaded page, Stadelheim prison records.

40. Schreyer to Polizeipräsidium München, May 27, 1949, GP RA/57, 10. IfZ ZS 317/I, 10; Schreyer to Polizeipräsidium München, May 27, 1949, GP RA/57, 1; Schwarzmann, Bürgermeister, Prittlbach, to the Stadtrat München Polizeipräsidium Kriminaluntersuchungsabteilung, June 7, 1949, SAM Pol.Dir. München 10007, 1–3; signature, Oberregierungsrat, der Vorstand der Vorstand der Strafanstalten München to Staatsanwalt Dr. Wörle, January 18, 1949, Beilage 7, GP RA/1, 2; Weiß, Erster Staatsanwalt, i.A. Auftrag, Der Generalstaatsanwalt, an die 5 Strafkammer des Landgerichts München I, July 4, 1956, "VIII

3324/55(GenStA) Betreff: Strafverfahren gegen Josef Dietrich und Michael Lippert, Dr. Werner Best und Karl Albrecht Oberg wegen Totschlags (Mordaktion vom 30. Juni 1934)," GP RA/46, 82 note 1; Siegel, "Das letzte Kapitel," September 4, 1934, SAM STAW 28793, 11.

41. Signature (A? Schneidhuber), July 18, 1934, "Empfangsbestätigung"; July 5, 1934, signature, "Empfangsbescheinigung über 5 große Couvertpackungen,": SAM Pol.Dir. München 8547.

42. Signature i.V., Polizeidirektion, July 19, 1934, "I. Vormerkung," SAM Pol. Dir. München 8547, 1–2; information from the Röhm family; Richter, I. V. Evang. Luth. Kirchengemeindeamt München, letter to the author, September 13, 1997.

43. "Todes-Anzeige," July 16, 1934, SAM Amtsgericht München Nr. 1934/1767. BHSA/II MA 107579; BAR R 58/935.

44. Quoted in LoC RSS RYH 8616 John Toland Collection Interview with Robert and Annalies Röhm. SAM Amtsgericht München Nr. 1934/1767. SAM AG-Nr. München Nr. 1935/115; "Wortwörtlicher Auszug aus dem Beerdigungsbuch der Evang.-Luth. Pfarrei St Matthäus, München aus dem Jahre 1935 Seite 226 Nr. 4 Nr. 230/97/RN," September 13, 1997; *Prester Lloyd*, April 2, 1935, p.c., BHSA/V Slg P 3653; information from the Röhm family.

45. Hitler's speech to the Reichstag, July 13, 1934, Domarus, *Hitler Speeches and Proclamations*, Vol. 1, 495–96; LoC RSS RYH 8616, John Toland, interview with André François-Poncet; Dr. Thomsen, "Niederschrift über die Ministerbesprechung am 3. Juli 1934 vorm. 10 Uhr.," BAR R 43I/1469, 2–3. See also Hitler's later comments on Röhm in a speech to Kreisleiter in Vogelsang, April 29, 1937, Domarus, *Hitler Speeches and Proclamations 1932–1945 Vol. 1*, 501 and 606, note 177.

46. Salomon, *"Fragebogen,"* 271.

47. Dr. Thomsen, "Niederschrift über die Ministerbesprechung am 3. Juli 1934 vorm. 10 Uhr.," BAR R 43I/1469, 4–6.

48. Ibid., 5. Bracher, *Die nationalsozialistische Machtergreifung*, 947; Machtan, *Hitlers Geheimnis*, 248; Geoffrey J. Giles, "Fuehrer Fantasy" (review of Lothar Machtan, *The Hidden Hitler*), *The Washington Post*, November 25, 2001, 4–5; Hans Mommsen, "Viel Lärm um nichts," *Die Zeit*, 42, 2001, 1–4, accessed at http://zeus.zeit.de/text/archiv/2001/42/200142_p-mommsen.xml on October 2, 2005.

49. Dr. Thomsen, "Niederschrift über die Ministerbesprechung am 3. Juli 1934 vorm. 10 Uhr.," BAR R 43I/1469, 8; Hindenburg to Hitler, July 2, 1934, BAR R 43 II/1202.

50. Jamin, "Das Ende der 'Machtergreifung,'" 210–12; IfZ Sp. 2/1; Gritschneder, *"Der Führer hat Sie zum Tode verurteilt . . .,"* 108; BAR R 22/973, BAR R 22/854 and BAR R 22/865; Evans, *Third Reich in Power*, 531–35; Jellonnek, *Homosexuelle unter dem Hakenkreuz*, section 6.1.3, *passim*.

51. Höhne, *Mordsache Röhm*, 284–87; IfZ ZS 317/I; Bergmann to Weiss, May 14, 1949, SAM STAW 28793, 8.

52. Quoted in Orlow, *History of the Nazi Party: 1919–1933*, 218, note 160. Browder, *Foundations of the Nazi Police State*, 140, 142–43; Bessel, *Political Violence and the Rise of Nazism*, 131–32, 145–46; Stölzle to Weiss, June 28, 1949, GP RA/4a, 5–8; "No. 17 The Inspector of the National Socialist Party in Austria, Habicht, to Counsellor of Legation Hüffer," June 18, 1934, *DGFP, Series C Volume III*, 4; "No. 220 Memorandum by the State Secretary," January 26, 1934, ibid., 422; von Neurath, "No. 64 Memorandum by the Foreign Minister," July 5, 1934, ibid., 134–35.

53. BAR R 58/660; "[Nr. 3] Juni/Juli 1934," *Deutschland-Berichte der Sozial-demokratischen Partei Deutschlands (Sopade) 1934–1940 Erster Jahrgang 1934* (Salzhausen: Verlag Petra Nettelbeck, 1980), 191–204, 248–67; Jamin, "Ende der 'Machtergreifung,'" 207–19; BAK NS 19/4002; BAR R0901/60952; BAR R43II/1448; BAR R43II/1426; BAR R43II/1448.

54. BHSA/KA Landespolizei Nürnberg-Fürth Bund 2; BA MA RH 26–7/377; BA MA RH 57/9; BHSA/II MA 107579; BHSA/II M Inn 72426; Longerich, *Die braunen Bataillone*, 222–23; BAK Slg Schumacher/403; BAR ehem. BDC O 421 SA—Chef A.W. A-H; BHSA/II MA 105256; IMT Nürnberg, *Prozess gegen die Hauptkriegsverbrecher*, Vol. 22, 160; Judgement of the International Military Tribunal on the SA, October 1, 1946, ibid., 1, 307–9; BAK Slg Schumacher/402; Bracher, *Die nationalsozialistische Machtergreifung*, 686.

55. Jagschitz, *Putsch*, 84–85; Gerhard L. Weinberg, "Die deutsche Außenpolitik und Österreich 1937/38," and "Diskussion zu den Beiträgen Weinberg, Kindermann," Gerald Stourzh and Birgitta Zaar, eds., *Österreich, Deutschland und die Mächte: Internationale und Österreichische Aspekte des "Anschlusses" vom März 1938* (Vienna: Verlag der Österreichischen Akademie der Wissenschaften, 1990), 62–63 and 97–110, respectively; Norbert Schausberger, *Der Griff nach Österreich: Der Anschluss* (Vienna: Jugend und Volk, 1978), 287–88; Ross, *Hitler und Dollfuß*, 216; Evans, *Third Reich in Power*, 621; Gottfried-Karl Kindermann, *Hitlers Niederlage in Österreich: Bewaffneter NS-Putsch, Kanzlermord und Österreichs Abwehrsieg von 1934* (Hamburg: Hoffmann und Campe, 1984), 159–66, 254–56.

56. Evans, *Third Reich in Power*, 42–43, 110–17; Karl Otmar Freiherr von Aretin, "Der Eid auf Hitler: eine Studie zum moralischen Verfall des Offizierkorps der Reichswehr," Kunz and Vogt, ed., *Nation, Staat und Demokratie in Deutschland*, 175–94.

57. Von Pfeffer to Institut für Zeitgeschichte, March 10, 1953, IfZ ZS 177 Bd I, 1.

58. Kershaw, *Hitler*, 530.

Chapter 16

1. Walther, *Zum anderen Ufer*, 511.

2. Ibid., 529.

3. August 2, 1946, Freund to Dr. Böhm, GP RA/4a, 4; Drexel A. Sprecher, *Inside the Nuremberg Trial: A Prosecutors' Comprehensive Account* (Lanham: University

Press of America, c. 1999), vol. 1, 482–83, 488; Alexander Zinn, *Die soziale Konstruktion des homosexuellen Nationalsozialisten: zu Genese und Etablierung eines Stereotyps* (Frankfurt a.M.: Lang, 1997), *passim*.

4. Delmer, *Trail Sinister*, 236.

5. Betz's claim that Röhm was opposed to close links with Italy, and refused to visit there, was incorrect. It was probably retrospectively influenced by the course of the German-Italian relationship in World War II: *Deutsche Tagespost*, May 14, 1957, p.c., SM ZA Pers. Röhm. Even Bergmann claimed Röhm was close to Gregor Strasser, which was not the case: Bergmann to Weiss, May 14, 1949, SAM STAW 28793, 5–6. Schreyer's claims about Röhm's political opinions also seemed designed to make him more palatable to postwar sensibilities: Schreyer to Polizeipräsidium München, May 27, 1949, GP RA/57, 2–3; April 24, 1949, Schreyer, "Eidesstattliche Erklärung.," AM HKN/574, 1. Equally, Röhm's brother Robert claimed that Röhm was seeking to put an end to Hitler's criminal goals: "Robert Röhm (1949) 4.4. (I45)," SAM STAW 28792.

6. Röhm to Epp, May 27, 1933, BHSA/II RS 38/2; Seydel, February 26, 1934, "Z. Nr. 3724/34," BAK NS 23 neu/7; Stölzle to Weiss, June 28, 1949, GP RA/4a, 16; Lorant, *I Was Hitler's Prisoner*, 67; Schoeps, *Ja– Nein –und Trotzdem*, 129–30.

7. "No. 59 Fabricius, Chargé d'Affaires, Tarabiya Turkey to Foreign Ministry," *DGFP, Series C Vol. III*, 128.

8. Salomon, "*Fragebogen*," 272.

9. Bracher, *Die nationalsozialistische Machtergreifung*, 936.

10. R. L. Koehl, *The Black Corps: the structure and power struggles of the Nazi SS* (Madison: University of Wisconsin Press, 1983), 97.

11. Ibid.

12. IMT Nürnberg, August 15, 1946, *Prozess gegen die Hauptkriegsverbrecher*, vol. 21, 224; Jüttner to "Kamerad Freund," May 14, 1948, IfZ ZS 251 Bd II, 2.

13. Weiß, Erster Staatsanwalt, "1 Js Gen. 1 ff/49'," January 28, 1952, GP RA/46, 5.

14. Hermann Göring, IMT Nürnberg, March 14, 1946, *Prozess gegen die Hauptkriegsverbrecher*, vol. 9, 301.

Notes on Sources

1. V. Danner I.V. to the Heerespersonalamt, August 22, 1923, "Hpt. N. 24918/ IIa Nr. 4848," BA MA RH 53-7/v. 394a, 2; Dr. Trutter to the Amtsgericht München Nachlassgericht, July 16, 1934, SAM Amtsgericht München Nr. 1934/1767, 1; discussions with Dr. Reinhard Weber, SAM.

2. Telephone conversation by author with Dr. Gräfin Eva Du Moulin-Eckart, September 1997.

3. Sir Francis Rose, *Saying Life: The Memoirs of Sir Francis Rose* (London: Cassell, 1961), 196, 213, and 229.

4. Adolph Röpnack, "B. Im Wirrwarr von Politik und Wirtschaft. Blanco Galindo.," extract from his unpublished memoirs in BHSA/KA OP 32380, 1–3; Charles W. Arnade, "German Military Missions and Advisers to Bolivia," *Escenas y episodios de la historia: Estudios Bolivianos, 1953–1999* (La Paz: Los Amigos del Libro, 2004), 204; Robert Brockmann, "Libro I. Soldado, rebelde, marica: Ernst Röhm en Bolivia" (unpublished manuscript: La Paz, 2006), 43–45; Luis F. Sánchez Guzmán, *Hans Kundt Luces y sombras* (no publisher listed: La Paz, 2006), 139. I am grateful to Professor Arnade and Mr. Brockmann for sending me copies of their works.

5. Richardi and Schumann, *Geheim Akte Gerlich/Bell*, 72–74; Dornheim, *Röhms Mann für Ausland*, 179–80, 285, note 673. Dornheim does admit that this source has problems.

Select Bibliography

Only sources actually mentioned in the reduced endnotes have been included in the select bibliography. A full bibliography containing all works consulted has been placed online at: http://www.unsw.adfa.edu.au/hass/staff/hancock .html.

Primary Sources

Archives

Austria
Österreichisches Staatsarchiv, Vienna
Archiv der Republik

Bolivia
Archivo de El Diario, La Paz
El Diario, 1929–34
Archivo de La Patria, Oruro
La Patria, 1929–30
Archivo Militar del Estado Mayor General, La Paz
Archivo de La Paz
Archivo del Ministerio de Relaciones Exteriores y Culto, La Paz

Germany
Amtsgericht München
Auswärtiges Amt Archiv
Bayerisches Hauptstaatsarchiv Abteilung II
    M Ju Staatsministerium der Justiz
    M Inn Staatsministerium des Innern
    MA Akten des Staatsministerium des Äussern and Akten der Bayerischen
        Staatskanzlei
    RS Reichsstatthalter

Bayerisches Hauptstaatsarchiv Abteilung III Geheimes Hausarchiv
Bayerisches Hauptstaatsarchiv Abteilung IV Kriegsarchiv
    B. u. R. Bund Bayern und Reich
    EWW Einwohnerwehr
    HS Handschriften
    MKr. Kriegs Ministerium
    MMJO Militär-Max-Joseph-Orden
    OP Personal files
    RWGrkdo4 Reichswehrgruppenkommando 4
    Sch. Brig. 21. Schützenbrigade 21
    Stadt. Kdtr. Stadt Kommandantur München
    10 IR 10. bayerisches Infanterie-Regiment
    12.b.I.D. 12. bayerische Infanterie-Division
Bayerisches Hauptstaatsarchiv Abteilung V
Berlin Document Center
Bundesarchiv Abteilung Deutsches Reich, Berlin-Lichterfelde
    61 Sta 1 Stahlhelm, Bund der Frontsoldaten
    62 Di 1 Dienststelle Rosenberg
    62 Ka 1 Kanzlei des Führers.
    NS 1 Reichsschatzmeister der NSDAP
    NS 8 Kanzlei Rosenberg.
    NS 23 alt Sturmabteilungen der NSDAP
    NS 23 neu Sturmabteilungen der NSDAP
    NS 26 Hauptarchiv der NSDAP.
    NS 43 Außenpolitisches Amt der NSDAP
    NS 51 Kanzlei des Führers der NSDAP (Dienststelle Bouhler)
    R 0901 Auswärtiges Amt
    R 2 Anh. Reichsfinanzministerium
    R 15.07 Reichskommissar für die Überwachung der Öffentlichen
        Ordnung
    R 43 Alte Reichskanzlei
    R 58 Reichssicherheitshauptamt
    R 8034 II Reichslandbund – Pressearchiv
    R 8034 III Reichslandbund/Pressearchiv – Personalia
    Slg Schumacher Sammlung Schumacher
Bundesarchiv Abteilung Potsdam (BAP). Ehemalige Deutsches Zentralarchiv
der DDR
    07.01 Neue Reichskanzlei
    15.01 Reichministerium des Innern
Bundesarchiv Filmarchiv, Berlin
Bundesarchiv Koblenz

KE Kleine Erwerbungen
N, NL Nachlässe
NS 8 Kanzlei Rosenberg
NS 10 Adjutantur des Führers
NS 19 Persönlicher Stab Reichsführer-SS
NS 20 NS Kleine Erwerbungen
NS 22 Reichsorganisationsleiter
NS 23 alt Sturmabteilungen der NSDAP
NS 23 neu Sturmabteilungen der NSDAP
NS 26 Hauptarchiv der NSDAP
NS 33 SS-Führungshauptamt
NS 36 Oberstes Parteigericht der NSDAP
NS 46 Nationalsozialistische Reichstagsfraktion
NS 51 Kanzlei des Führers der NSDAP (Dienststelle Bouhler)
R 19 Hauptamt Ordnungspolizei
R 53 Stellvertreter des Reichskanzlers
R 54 Büro des Reichspräsidenten
Slg Schumacher Sammlung Schumacher
Zsg. 2 Allgemeine Drucksachen-Sammlung
Bundesarchiv Militärarchiv
M Sg Militärgeschichtliche Sammlungen
N Nachlässe
RH 1 Adjutantur des Chefs der Heeresleitung/Oberbefehlshabers des
Heeres
RH 2 Chef des Truppenamts/Generalstab des Heeres
RH 15 OKH/Allgemeines Heeresamt
RH 26–7 Infanterie-Division
RH 53–7 Wehrkreiskommando VII
RH 57 Landespolizei-inspektion Südwest
RW 1 Reichswehrministerium
RW 5 Amt Ausland/Abwehr
RW 6 Wehrmachtsabteilung Reichswehrministerium
RWD 6 Reichswehrministerium/Reichskriegsministerium
RWD 12 OKW/Allgemeines Wehrmachtsamt
Ingolstadt Stadtarchiv
Der Donaubote 1933–34
Ingolstädter Zeitung 1933–34
Institut für Zeitgeschichte Munich
ED Sammlungen und Nachlässe
Gt. Landgerichtsakten
MS Manuskripte

Sp. Spruchkammerakten
ZS Zeugenschriftum
Landesarchiv Berlin
Staatsarchiv München
   Pol. Dir. München Polizeidirektion München
   STAW Staatsanwaltschaften München
Staatsarchiv Nürnberg
   KV Prozesse IMT Kriegsverbrecherprozesse Internationaler
   Militärgerichtshof
Stadelheim Prison Records
Stadtarchiv München

United Kingdom
Churchill Archives, Churchill College, University of Cambridge
Institute of Historical Research, University of London
Liddell-Hart Archives, King's College, University of London
The National Archives of the United Kingdom, Kew
   FO Foreign Office

United States of America
National Archives II, College Park Maryland
National Archives, Washington, DC

Libraries

Australia
Baillieu Library, University of Melbourne
   Der SA-Mann, 1933–34
   Völkischer Beobachter, 1927–34

Bolivia
Biblioteca Municipal, La Paz
   La Rázon, 1929–31

Germany
Bayerische Staatsbibliothek, Munich
   Ingolstädter Tagblatt, 1910–14, 1919
   Ingolstädter Zeitung, 1910–14, 1919
Schwules Museum, Berlin
   Blätter für Menschenrecht, 1932
   Mitteilungen des Wissenschaftlich-humanitären Komitees e.V., 1927–33

United States of America
Library of Congress
Africa & Middle East Reading Room
  Cumhuriyet, 1933
Manuscript Reading Room
  Martha E. Dodd Family Papers
  William E. Dodd Papers
Music Reading Room
  "The Hitler Tapes": Interviews by John Toland

Private Papers

Bolivia
Papers of the Club Alemán de Oruro, Mrs Irma de Bollweg

Germany
Gritschneder Papiere Röhm – Akten
Röhm Family Papers

Articles

Beckenbauer, Alfons, "Wie Adolf Hitler durch einen niederbayerischen Grafen zu einem Wutausbruch gebracht wurde: Aus den unveröffentlichen Memoiren des Joseph Maria Graf von Soden-Fraunhofen—zugleich ein Beitrag zur Geschichte des monarchischen Gedankens in Bayern während der Weimarer Zeit," Sonderdruck aus *Verhandlungen des Historischen Vereins für Niederbayern*, Band 103, Landshut (1977): 5–29

Becker, Winfried, "Die nationalsozialistische Machtergreifung in Bayern Ein Dokumentarbericht von Heinrich Helds aus dem Jahr 1933." *Historisches Jahrbuch*, 112, no.1 (1992): 412–35.

"Der amtliche Bericht über den Rathaussturm 1918 verfaßt vom damaligen Ingolstädter Oberbürgermeister Königlichen Hofrat und Geheimen Rat Jakob Kroher." *Ingolstädter Heimatblätter* 41, no. 4 (1978): 15.

"Der amtliche Bericht über den Rathaussturm 1918 verfaßt vom damaligen Ingolstädter Oberbürgermeister Königlichen Hofrat und Geheimen Rat Jakob Kroher (1. Fortsetzung und Schluß)." *Ingolstädter Heimatblätter* 41, no. 5 (1978): 17–18.

Röpnack, Generalmajor a.D. Adolph, "Aus den Memoiren eines deutschen Offiziers in bolivianischen Diensten." *Deutscher Soldatenkalender* 10 (1962): 231–241.

Books

Avon, The Rt. Hon. The Earl of. *The Eden Memoirs: Facing the Dictators.* London: Cassell, 1962.

Bayerisches Kriegsarchiv. *Die Bayern im Großen Kriege 1914–1918. Auf Grund der Kriegsakten dargestellt.* Munich: Verlag des Bayerischen Kriegsarchivs, 1923.

Buchheim, Karl and Aretin, Karl Otmar von, ed., Aretein, Erwein von. *Krone und Ketten: Erinnerungen eines bayerischen Edelmannes.* Munich: Süddeutscher Verlag, 1955.

Cerruti, Elisabetta. *Ambassador's Wife.* London: George Allen and Unwin, 1953.

Delmer, Sefton. *Trail Sinister. An Autobiography*, Vol. 1. London: Secker & Warburg, 1961.

Deutschland-Berichte der Sozialdemokratischen Partei Deutschlands (Sopade) 1934–1940. Erster Jahrgang 1934, Salzhausen: Verlag Petra Nettelbeck & Zweitausendeins, 1980.

Documents on German Foreign Policy 1918–1945. Series C (1933–1937) The Third Reich: First Phase Volume October 14, 1933–June 13, 1934, London: Her Majesty's Stationery Office, 1959.

Documents on German Foreign Policy 1918–1945. Series C (1933–1937) The Third Reich: First Phase Volume III June 14, 1934–March 31, 1935, London: Her Majesty's Stationery Office, 1959.

Domarus, Max. ed. *Hitler Speeches and Proclamations 1932–1945 The Chronicle of a Dictatorship. Vol. One, The years 1932 to 1934.* London: I. B. Tauris, 1990.

Fröhlich, Elke, ed. im Auftrag des Instituts für Zeitgeschichte und in Verbindung mit dem Bundesarchiv. *Die Tagebücher von Joseph Goebbels: Sämtliche Fragmente Teil I Aufzeichnungen 1924–1941, Band 2, 1.1.1931–31.12.1936.* Munich: KG Saur, 1987.

Gruchmann, Lothar, and Weber, Reinhard, eds. with the collaboration of Gritschneder, Otto, *Der Hitler-Prozess 1924: Wortlaut der Hauptverhandlung vor dem Volksgericht München I*, Vols. 1–4. Munich: K G Saur, 1997–99.

Hirschberg, Max., Weber, Reinhard ed., *Jude und Demokrat: Erinnerungen eines Münchener Rechtsanwalts 1883 bis 1939.* Munich: Oldenbourg Verlag, 1998.

Histories of Two Hundred and Fifty-One Divisions of the German Army which Participated in the War (1914–1918), Compiled from Records of Intelligence Section of the General Staff, at General Headquarters: Chaumont, France, 1919. Washington, DC: Government Printing Office, 1920.

Hoffmann, Heinrich. *Hitler wie ich ihn sah: Aufzeichnungen seines Leibfotografen.* Munich: Herbig, 1974.

Internationaler Militärgerichtshof Nürnberg. *Der Prozess gegen die Hauptkriegsverbrecher vor dem Internationalen Militärgerichtshof Nürnberg 14. November 1945–1. October 1946*, Bände I–XXII. Original edition Nuremberg 1946, Munich: Delphin Verlag, 1984 reprint.

Klotz, Dr. Helmuth, ed. *Drei Briefe des Ernst Röhms an Dr. Heimsoth, Berlin.* Selbstverlag des Herausgebers Dr. Helmut Klotz, Berlin-Tempelhof, Hohenzollern Korso 38a, 1932.

————. *Der Fall Röhm*, 2nd ed., Selbstverlag des Herausgebers Dr. Helmut Klotz, Berlin-Tempelhof, Hohenzollern Korso 38a, 1932.

Lochner, Louis P. *What about Germany?* London: Hodder and Stoughton, 1943.

Lorant, Stefan. *I Was Hitler's Prisoner: Leaves from a Prison Diary*, first published April 1935. Harmondsworth: Penguin, 1939.

Ludecke, Kurt G. W. *I Knew Hitler: The Story of a Nazi Who Escaped the Blood Purge.* New York: Charles Scribner's Sons, 1937. Facsimile reprint. New York: AMS Press, 1982.

Ludendorff, Erich. *Heraus aus dem braunen Sumpf.* Munich: Ludendorffs Volkswarte-Verlag, 1932.

Oficina Nacional de Estadística Financiera, *Sinopsis estadística de le Républica de Bolivia.* Mimeograph, La Paz, July 10, 1930.

Oosterhuis, Harry, and Kennedy, Hubert, eds. *Homosexuality and Male Bonding in Pre-Nazi Germany: the Youth Movement, the Gay Movement, and Male Bonding Before Hitler's Rise: Original Transcripts from Der Eigene, The First Gay Journal in the World.* New York: Harrington Park Press, 1991.

Röhm, Ernst. *Die Geschichte eines Hochverräters.* Munich: Franz Eher Verlag, 1928.

————. *Die Geschichte eines Hochverräters.* 5. Auflage, Volksausgabe, Munich: Eher Verlag, 1934.

————. *Stammtafel der Familie Röhm abgeschlossen Juni 1927.* Leipzig: Verlag Degener & Co., 1927.

————. *Warum SA? Rede des Reichsministers Stabschef Röhm in Berlin am 7. XII. 1933 vor dem Diplomatischen Korps.* Berlin: Liebheit u. Thiesen, 1933.

Rose, Sir Francis. *Saying Life: The Memoirs of Sir Francis Rose.* London: Cassell, 1961.

Salomon, Ernst von. *The Answers of Ernst von Salomon to the 131 Questions in the Allied Military Government "Fragebogen."* London: Putnam, 1954.

Schoeps, Hans-Joachim. *Ja–Nein–und Trotzdem: Erinnerungen–Begegnungen–Erfahrungen.* Mainz: v. Hase & Koehler Verlag, 1974.

Seraphim, Dr. Hans-Günther, ed. *Das politische Tagebuch Alfred Rosenbergs aus den Jahren 1934/35 und 1939/40.* Göttingen: Musterschmidt Verlag, 1956.

Sprecher, Drexel A. *Inside the Nuremberg Trial: A Prosecutor's Comprehensive Account*, Vols. 1 and 2. Lanham: University Press of America, c. 1999.

Walther, Gerda. *Zum anderen Ufer: vom Marxismus und Atheismus zum Christentum.* Remagen: Der Leuchter, Otto Reichl Verlag, 1960.

Wecklein, Dr. *Jahresbericht über das K. Maximiliansgymnasium in München für das Schuljahr 1897/98.* Munich: Akademische Buchdruckerei, 1898.

————. *Jahresbericht über das K. Maximiliansgymnasium in München für das Schuljahr 1898/99.* Munich: Akademische Buchdruckerei, 1898.

————. *Jahresbericht über das K. Maximiliansgymnasium in München für das Schuljahr 1904/05.* Munich: Akademische Buchdruckerei, 1905.

————. *Jahresbericht über das K. Maximiliansgymnasium in München für das Schuljahr 1898/99.* Munich: Akademische Buchdruckerei, 1899.

————. *Jahresbericht über das K. Maximiliansgymnasium in München für das Schuljahr 1905/06.* Munich: Akademische Buchdruckerei, 1906.

Wheeler-Bennett, Sir John. *Knaves, Fools and Heroes in Europe between the Wars.* London: MacMillan, 1974.

Woodward, E. L., and Butler, Rohan, eds. *Documents on British Foreign Policy 1919–1939, Second Series Volume VI 1933–34.* London: Her Majesty's Stationery Office, 1957.

Secondary Sources

Articles and Papers

Arnade, Charles W. "German Military Missions and Advisers to Bolivia." In *Escenas y episodios de la historia: Estudios Bolivianos, 1953–1999.* La Paz: Los Amigos del Libro, 2004.

Bennecke, Heinrich. "Die Memoiren des Ernst Röhm: Ein Vergleich der verschiedenen Ausgaben und Auflagen." *Politische Studien* 14, no. 1 (1963): 179–88.

Bieber, Léon E. "La política militar alemana en Bolivia, 1900–1935." *Latin American Research Review* 29, no.1 (1994): 85–106.

Demeter, Karl. "Otto von Kress als bayerischer Kriegsminister." *Zeitschrift für bayerische Landesgeschichte* 6 (1933): 85–110.

Fischer, Conan. "Ernst Julius Röhm—Stabschef der SA und unentbehrlicher Außenseiter." In Ronald Smelser and Rainer Zitelmann, ed., *Die braune Elite: 22 biographische Skizzen*, 212–22. Darmstadt: Wissenschaftliche Buchgesellschaft, 1989.

Fischer, Georg. "Revolution und Rathausbrand 1918 in Ingolstadt im Spiegel der Erinnerung." *Ingolstädter Heimatblätter* 41, no. 4 (1978): 13–14, 18.

Fout, John C. "Sexual Politics in Wilhelmine Germany: The Male Gender Crisis, Moral Purity, and Homophobia." *Journal of the History of Sexuality* 2, no. 3 (1992): 388–421.

Franz, Georg. "Munich: Birthplace and Center of the National Socialist German Workers' Party." *The Journal of Modern History* 29, no. 4 (1957): 319–34.

Giles, Geoffrey J. "Fuehrer Fantasy." Review of *The Hidden Hitler* by Lothar Machtan. *The Washington Post*, November 25, 2001, 4–5.

Hancock, Eleanor. "A Question of Honour? Ernst Röhm and the Officer's Honour Code, 1922–24." In John Perkins and Jürgen Tampke, ed., *Europe: Retrospect and Prospects. Proceedings of the 1995 Biennial Conference of the Australasian Association of European Historians (University of New South Wales, July 1995*, 30–40. Manly East: Southern Highlands Publishers, undated, c. 1996.

———. "Ernst Röhm and the Experience of World War I." *The Journal of Military History* 60 (1996): 39–60.

———. "'Only the Real, The True, The Masculine Held its Value': Ernst Röhm, Masculinity, and Male Homosexuality." *Journal of the History of Sexuality* 8, no. 4 (1998): 616–41.

Herzer, Manfred. "34. Asexuality as an element in the selfpresentation of the right wing of the German gay movement before 1933. (Elisar von Kupfer, Benedict Friedlaender, Hans Blüher, Karl Günther Heimsoth)." In Matthias Duyves et al., eds., *Among Men, Among Women: Sociological and Historical Recognition of Homosocial Arrangements: Gay-studies and Women's studies, University of Amsterdam Conference, 22th-26th June 1983, Oudemanhuispoort, Amsterdam.* Amsterdam: Sociologisch Instituut, undated.

Jablonsky, David. "Röhm and Hitler: The Continuity of Political-Military Discord." *Journal of Contemporary History* 23, no. 3 (1988): 367–86.

"Mayr, Karl." In Roder, Werner and Strauss, Herbert A., eds., *Biographisches Handbuch der deutschsprachigen Emigration nach 1933*, Band I Politik, Wirtschaft, Öffentliches Leben, KG Saur, Munich, 1980.

Mommsen, Hans. "Viel Lärm um nichts." *Die Zeit* 42 (2001):1–4, accessed at http://zeus.zeit.de/text/archiv/2001/42/200142_p-mommsen.xml 2/10/2005.

Phelps, Reginald H. "Hitler and the Deutsche Arbeiterpartei." *The American Historical Review* 68, no. 4 (1963): 974–86.

Selig, Wolfram. "Ermordet im Namen des Führers. Die Opfer des Röhm-Putsches in München." Sonderdruck aus *Staat, Kultur, Politik – Beiträge zur Geschichte Bayerns und des Katholizismus Festschrift zum 65. Geburtstag von Dieter Albrecht*, Verlag Michael Laßleben, Kallmünz/Opf., 1992, 341–356.

Stern, Howard. "The *Organisation Consul.*" *Journal of Modern History* 35, no. 1 (1963): 20–32.

Süss, Winfried. "Beiträge und Berichte: über Röhms angebliche Pläne 'für ein Reich ohne Hitler,'" *Historisches Jahrbuch* Im Auftrag der Görres-Gesellschaft Sonderdruck 115. Jahrgang Zweiter Halbband 1995, Verlag Karl Alber, Freiburg/München: 486–490.

Wacha, Georg. "Zu Carl Anton Reichel: Der Briefwechsel mit Kronprinz Rupprecht von Bayern." *Kunstjahrbuch der Stadt Linz* 15 (1976): 53–65.

Wolff, Reinhard, and Hartmut Fröschle. "Die Deutschen in Bolivien." In Harmut Fröschle, ed., *Die Deutschen in Lateinamerika: Schicksal und Leistung.* Tübingen: Horst Erdmann Verlag, 1979: 146–168.

Ziemann, Benjamin. "Wanderer zwischen den Welten—Der Militärkritiker und Gegner des entschiedenen Pazifismus Major a.D. Karl Mayr (1883–1945)," In Wolfram Wette, ed., with the collaboration of Helmut Donat, *Pazifistische Offiziere in Deutschland 1871–1933.* Bremen: Donat Verlag, 1999: 273–85.

Books

Amedick, Sigrid. *Männer am Schienenstrang: Sozialgeschichte der unteren bayerischen Eisenbahnbeamten 1844–1914.* Industrielle Welt Schriftenreihe des Arbeitskreises für moderne Sozialgeschichte Band 57, Klett-Cotta, Stuttgart, 1997.

Ay, Karl-Ludwig. *Die Entstehung einer Revolution: Die Volksstimmung in Bayern während des Ersten Weltkrieges*, Beiträge zu einer historischen Strukturanalyse Bayerns im Industriezeitalter Band 1, Duncker & Humblot, Berlin, 1968.

Backes, Uwe, Karl-Heinz Janßen, Eckhard Jesse, Henning Köhler, Hans Mommsen, and Fritz Tobias. *Reichstagsbrand – Aufklärung einer historischen Legende*, 2nd ed. Munich: Piper, 1987.

Balistier, Thomas. *Gewalt und Ordnung: Kalkül und Faszination der SA*. Münster: Verlag Westfälisches Dampfboot, 1989.

Baptista Gumucio, Mariano. *Historia contemporánea de Bolivia 1930–1976*, Vol. II. La Paz: Gisbert & Cía, 1976.

Bauer, Reinhard, and Ernst Piper, with the collaboration of Elisabeth Lukas-Götz. *München: Geschichte einer Stadt*. Munich: Deutscher Taschenbuch Verlag, 1996.

Bauer, Winifried, ed. *Chronik 150 Jahre Maximiliansgymnasium 1849–1999*. Munich: Maximiliansgymnasium, 1999.

Bennecke, Heinrich. *Die Reichswehr und der "Röhm-Putsch."* Beiheft der Zeitmonatschrift Politische Studien, Munich Günter Olzog Verlag, undated (1964).

———. *Hitler und die SA*. Munich: Günter Olzog Verlag, 1962.

Berghahn, Volker R. *Der Stahlhelm Bund der Frontsoldaten 1918–1935*. Beiträge zur Geschichte des Parlamentarismus und der politischen Parteien Band 33, Düsseldorf: Droste, 1966.

Berlin Museum. *Eldorado: Homosexuelle Frauen und Männer in Berlin 1850–1950: Geschichte, Alltag und Kultur*. Berlin: Frölich und Kaufmann, 1984.

Bessel, Richard. *Germany after the First World War*. Oxford: Clarendon Press, 2002.

———. *Political Violence and the Rise of Nazism: The Stormtroopers in Eastern Germany 1925–1934*. London: Yale University Press, 1984.

Binder, Dieter Anton. *Dollfuss und Hitler: Über die Außenpolitik des autoritären Ständestaates in den Jahren 1933/34*. Graz: Verlag für die Technische Universität Graz, 43, 1979.

Blackbourn, David. *The Fontana History of Germany 1780–1918: The Long Nineteenth Century*. London: Fontana, 1997.

Bosl, Karl, ed. *Bayern im Umbruch: Die Revolution von 1918, ihre Voraussetzungen, ihr Verlauf und ihre Folgen*. Munich: R. Oldenbourg Verlag, 1969.

Bracher, K. D. *Die Auflösung der Weimarer Republik: Eine Studie zum Problem des Machtverfalls in der Demokratie*. Schriften des Instituts für politische Wissenschaft, Band 4, Stuttgart: Ring Verlag, 1955.

Bracher, Karl Dietrich, Wolfgang Sauer, and Gerhard Schulz. *Die nationalsozialistische Machtergreifung: Studien zur Errichtung des totalitären Herrschaftssystems in Deutschland 1933/34*, 2nd rev. ed. Cologne: Westdeutscher Verlag, 1962.

Broszat, Martin, Ulrich Dübber, Walther Hofer, Horst Möller, Heinrich Oberreuter, Jürgen Schmädeke, Wolfgang Treue, eds. Im Auftrage der Historischen Kommission zu Berlin, des Instituts für Zeitgeschichte, München, der Deutscher Vereinigung für Parlamentsfragen, Bonn. *Deutschlands Weg in die Diktatur: Internationale Konferenz zur nationalsozialistischen Machtübernahme im Reichstagsgebäude zu Berlin Referate und Diskussionen Ein Protokoll*. Berlin: Siedler Verlag, 1983.

Browder, George C. *Foundations of the Nazi Police State: The Formation of Sipo and SD*. Lexington: University Press of Kentucky, 1990.

Bullock, Alan. *Hitler: A Study in Tyranny*, rev. ed. Harmondsworth: Penguin, 1968.

Campbell, Bruce. *The SA Generals and the Rise of Nazism*. Lexington: University Press of Kentucky, 1998.

Crespo Rodas, Alfonso. *Hernando Siles, el poder y su angustia*. La Paz: Empresa Editora Siglo Ltda., 1985.

Déak, István. *Beyond Nationalism: A Social and Political History of the Habsburg Officer Corps, 1848–1918.* New York: Oxford University Press, 1990.

Diehl, James M. *Paramilitary Politics in Weimar Germany.* Bloomington: Indiana University Press, 1977.

Dietzler, Anke et al. *Hannover, 1933. Eine Großstadt wird nationalsozialistisch Beiträge zur Ausstellung.* Hannover: Historisches Museum am Hohen Ufer, 1981.

Ditmar, Christian. *Ingolstadt in alten Ansichtskarten.* Frankfurt am Main: Flechsig Verlag, 1979.

Dornberg, John. *Munich 1923: The Story of Hitler's First Grab for Power.* New York: Harper & Row, 1982.

Dornheim, Andreas. *Röhms Mann für Ausland: Politik und Ermordung des SA-Agenten Georg Bell.* Münster: LIT Verlag, 1998.

Dunkerley, James. *Orígenes del poder militar: historia política e institucional del ejército boliviano hasta 1935.* La Paz: Quipus, 1987.

Evans, Richard J. *The Coming of the Third Reich.* London: Allen Lane, 2003.

———. *The Third Reich in Power 1933–1939.* London: Allen Lane, 2005.

Faatz, Martin. *Vom Staatsschutz zum Gestapo-Terror: Politische Polizei in Bayern in der Endphase der Weimarer Republik und der Anfangsphase der nationalsozialistischen Diktatur.* Würzburg: Echter Verlag, 1995.

Fallois, Immo von. *Kalkül und Illusion: Der Machtkampf zwischen Reichswehr und SA während der Röhm-Krise 1934*, Beiträge zur Politischen Wissenschaft Band 75. Berlin: Duncker & Humblot, 1994.

Fegert, Hans. *Ingolstadt in alten Ansichten.* Zaltbommel: Europäische Bibliothek, 1986.

Fest, Joachim C. *Hitler.* London: Weidenfeld and Nicolson, 1974.

———. *The Face of the Third Reich.* Harmondsworth: Penguin, 1972.

Fischer, Conan. *Stormtroopers: A Social, Economic and Ideological Analysis, 1929–1935,* London: George Allen and Unwin, 1983.

Frei, Norbert. *National Socialist Rule in Germany: The Führer State 1933–1945.* Oxford: Blackwell, 1993.

Früchtl, Alois, *Das K.B. 28 Infanterie-Regiment,* Nach den amtlichen Kriegstagebüchern bearbeitet im Auftrage des bayerischen Kriegsarchivs, Erinnerungsblätter deutscher Regimenter Bayerische Armee Heft 25. Munich: Verlag Bayerisches Kriegsarchiv, 1924.

Garnett, Robert S., Jr. *Lion, Eagle, and Swastika: Bavarian Monarchism in Weimar Germany, 1918–1933.* New York: Garland Publishing, 1991.

Generaldirektion der Staatlichen Archive Bayerns. *Bayern und seine Armee: Eine Ausstellung des Bayerischen Hauptstaatsarchivs aus den Beständen des Kriegsarchivs,* Ausstellungskataloge der Staatlichen Archive Bayerns Nr. 21. Munich: Selbstverlag der Generaldirektion der Staatlichen Archive Bayerns, 1987.

Gordon, Harold R., Jr. *Hitler and the Beer Hall Putsch.* Princeton: Princeton University Press, 1972.

———. *The Reichswehr and the German Republic 1919–1926.* Princeton: Princeton University Press, 1957.

Gritschneder, Otto. *Bewährungsfrist für den Terroristen Adolf H. Der Hitler-Putsch und die bayerische Justiz.* Munich: Verlag C. H. Beck, 1990.

———. *"Der Führer hat Sie zum Tode verurteilt . . .": Hitlers "Röhm-Putsch"-Morde vor Gericht.* Munich: Verlag C. H. Beck, 1993.

———. *Der Hitler-Prozeß und sein Richter Georg Neithardt: Skandalurteil von 1924 ebnet Hitler den Weg.* Munich: Verlag C. H. Beck, 2001.

Halcomb, Jill. *The SA: A Historical Perspective.* Overland Park: Crown Agincourt, 1985.

Heiden, Konrad. *Der Fuehrer: Hitler's Rise to Power.* London: Victor Gollancz, 1944.

Hekma, Gert, Harry Oosterhuis, and James Steakley, eds. *Gay Men and the Sexual History of the Political Left.* New York: Harrington Park Press, 1995.

Herwig, Holger H. *The First World War: Germany and Austria-Hungary 1914–1918,* 2nd impr. London: Arnold, 1997.

Hillmayr, Heinrich. *Roter und Weißer Terror in Bayern nach 1918: Ursachen, Erscheinungsformen und Folgen der Gewalttätigkeiten im Verlauf der revolutionären Ereignisse nach dem Ende des Ersten Weltkrieges,* Reihe Moderne Geschichte Band II. Munich: Nusser Verlag, 1974.

Höhne, Heinz. *Mordsache Röhm: Hitlers Durchbruch zur Alleinherrschaft 1933–1934.* Reinbek bei Hamburg: Spiegel-Buch, 1984.

———. *The Order of the Death's Head: The Story of Hitler's S. S.* New York: Ballantine Books, 1971.

Hofmann, Siegfried. *Alt Ingolstadt: Bilder einer Donaustadt.* Tübingen: Verlag Gebr. Metz, 1988.

Im Auftrage des Oberkommandos der Wehrmacht bearbeitet und herausgegeben von der Kriegsgeschichtlichen Forschungsanstalt des Heeres. *Die Niederwerfung der 240 Räteherrschaft in Bayern, 1919,* Vierter Band, Darstellungen aus den Nachkriegskämpfen deutscher Truppen und Freikorps. Berlin: Verlag von E. S. Mittler & Sohn, 1939.

Jablonsky, David. *The Nazi Party in Dissolution: Hitler and the Verbotzeit 1923–1925.* London: Frank Cass, 1989.

Jagschitz, Gerhard. *Der Putsch: Die Nationalsozialisten 1934 in Österreich.* Graz: Verlag Styria, 1976.

Jamin, Mathilde. *Zwischen den Klassen: Zur Sozialstruktur der SA-Führerschaft.* Wuppertal: Peter Hammer Verlag, 1984.

Jellonnek, Burkhard. *Homosexuelle unter dem Hakenkreuz: Die Verfolgung von Homosexuellen im Dritten Reich.* Paderborn: Ferdinand Schöningh, 1990.

Joachimsthaler, Anton. *Hitlers Liste: Ein Dokument persönlicher Beziehungen.* Munich: Herbig, 2003.

———. *Hitlers Weg begann in München 1913–1923,* Überarbeitete und um die Jahre 1920–1924 erweiterte Neuauflage des 1989 erschienenen Titels, *Korrektur einer Biographie: Adolf Hitler 1908–1920.* Munich: Herbig, 2000.

———. *Korrektur einer Biographie: Adolf Hitler 1908–1920.* Munich: Herbig, 1989.

Kern, Ernst. *Das K.B. 26 Infanterie-Regiment,* Nach den amtlichen Kriegstagebüchern bearbeitet, Erinnerungsblätter deutscher Regimenter Bayerische Armee Band 46. Munich: Verlag Bayerisches Kriegsarchiv, 1926.

Kershaw, Ian. *Hitler 1889–1936: Hubris*. London: Allen Lane The Penguin Press, 1998.

———. *The Nazi Dictatorship: Problems and Perspectives of Interpretation*, 4th ed. London: Arnold, 2000.

Kindermann, Gottfried-Karl. *Hitlers Niederlage in Österreich: Bewaffneter NS-Putsch, Kanzlermord und Österreichs Abwehrsieg von 1934*. Hamburg: Hoffmann und Campe, 1984.

Klein, Herbert S. *Parties and Political Change in Bolivia 1880–1952*. Cambridge: Cambridge University Press, 1969.

Koch, Hanns Joachim W. *Der deutsche Bürgerkrieg: Eine Geschichte der deutschen und österreichischen Freikorps 1918–1923*. Berlin: Ullstein, 1978.

Koch, Stephen. *Double Lives: Spies and Writers in the Secret Soviet War of Ideas Against the West*. New York: The Free Press, 1994.

Koehl, Robert L. *The Black Corps: The Structure and Power Struggles of the Nazi SS*. Madison, WI: University of Wisconsin Press, 1983.

Kolb, Eberhard. *The Weimar Republic*. London: Unwin Hyman, 1988.

Kraus, Andreas, *Grundzüge der Geschichte Bayerns*, 2nd ed. Darmstadt: Wissenschaftliche Buchgesellschaft, 1992.

Kunz, Andreas, and Martin Vogt, eds. *Nation, Staat und Demokratie in Deutschland: Ausgewählte Beiträge zur Zeitgeschichte von Karl Otmar Freiherr von Aretin zum 70. Geburtstag des Verfassers*. Mainz: Verlag Philipp von Zabern, 1993.

Lankes, Christian. *München als Garnison im 19. Jahrhundert: Die Haupt- und Residenzstadt als Standort der bayerischen Armee von Kurfürst Max IV. Joseph bis zur Jahrhundertwende*, Militärgeschichte und Wehrwissenschaften Band 2. Berlin: Verlag E. S. Mittler & Sohn, 1993.

Large, David Clay. *The Politics of Law and Order: A History of the Bavarian Einwohnerwehr, 1918–1921*. Philadelphia: American Philosophical Society, 1980.

Linder, Herbert. *Von der NSDAP zur SPD: Der politische Lebensweg des Dr. Helmuth Klotz (1894–1943)*, Karlsruher Beiträge zur Geschichte des Nationalsozialismus 3. Konstanz: Universtätsverlag Konstanz, 1998.

Longerich, Peter. *Die braunen Bataillone: Geschichte der SA*. Munich: Verlag C. H. Beck, 1989.

Mabire, Jean. *Röhm l'homme qui inventa Hitler*. Paris: Fayard, 1983.

Machtan, Lothar. *Der Kaisersohn bei Hitler. Prinz August Wilhelm im Hexenkessel der deutschen Geschichte*. Hamburg: Hoffmann und Campe, 2006.

———. *Hitlers Geheimnis: Das Doppelleben eines Diktators*. Berlin: Alexander Fest Verlag, 2001.

Manvell, Roger and Heinrich Fraenkel. *Doctor Goebbels*. London: New English Library, 1968.

McMeekin, Sean. *The Red Millionaire: A Political Biography of Willi Münzenberg, Moscow's Secret Propaganda Tsar in the West*. New Haven: Yale University Press, 2003.

Mehrere Mitkämpfer. *Das K.B.10 Infanterie-Regiment König*, Nach der amtlichen Kriegstagebüchern und privaten Aufzeichnungen bearbeitet Errinnerungsblätter deutscher Regimenter, Band 36. Munich: Verlag Bayerisches Kriegsarchiv, 1925.

Michalka, Wolfgang, ed. *Die Nationalsozialistische Machtergreifung.* Paderborn: Ferdinand Schöningh, 1984.

Mommsen, Hans. *Die verspielte Freiheit: Der Weg der Republik von Weimar in den Untergang 1918 bis 1933.* Frankfurt am Main: Propyläen, 1990.

Morales, Waldtraud Q. *A Brief History of Bolivia.* New York: Facts on File, Inc., 2003.

Morris, Douglas G. *Justice Imperiled: The Anti-Nazi Lawyer Max Hirschberg in Weimar Germany.* Ann Arbor: University of Michigan Press, 2005.

Nieden, Suzanne zur, ed. *Homosexualität und Staatsräson, Männlichkeit, Homophobie und Politik in Deutschland 1900–1945.* Frankfurt am Main: Campus Verlag, 2005.

O'Neill, Robert J. *The German Army and the Nazi Party, 1933–1939,* 2nd ed. London: Cassell, 1968.

Orlow, Dietrich. *The History of the Nazi Party: 1919–1933.* Pittsburgh: University of Pittsburgh Press, 1969.

———. *The History of the Nazi Party: Volume II 1933–1945.* Newton Abbot: David & Charles, 1973.

Petzold, Joachim. *Franz von Papen: Ein deutsches Verhängnis.* Munich: Buchverlag Union, 1995.

Peukert, Detlev and Jürgen Reulecke, eds., with the collaboration of Adelheid Gräfin zu Castell Rüdenhausen. *Die Reihen fast geschlossen: Beiträge zur Geschichte des Alltags unterm Nationalsozialismus.* Wuppertal: Peter Hammer Verlag, 1981.

Prinz, Friedrich and Marita Krauss, eds. *München, Musenstadt mit Hinterhöfen: die Prinzregentenzeit 1886–1912.* Munich: Verlag C. H. Beck, 1988.

Prior, Robin and Trevor Wilson. *The First World War.* London: Cassell History of Warfare, 2001.

Raphael, Frederic, and Kenneth McLeish. *The List of Books.* London: Mitchell Beazley, 1981.

Reichardt, Sven. *Faschistische Kampfbünde: Gewalt und Gemeinschaft im italienischen Squadrismus und in der deutschen SA.* Cologne: Böhlau Verlag, 2002.

Reiche, Eric G. *The Development of the SA in Nürnberg, 1922–1934.* Cambridge: Cambridge University Press, 1986.

Ribbe, Wolfgang, ed. *Berlin-Forschungen III.* Einzelveröffentlichungen der Historischen Kommission zu Berlin Band 66, Publicationen der Sektion für die Geschichte Berlins, Band 5, Colloquium Verlag, Berlin, 1988.

Richardi, Hans-Günter, and Klaus Schumann. *Geheim Akte Gerlich/Bell: Röhms Pläne für ein Reich ohne Hitler.* Munich: W. Ludwig Verlag, 1993.

Rinke, Stefan. *"Der letzte freie Kontinent": Deutsche Lateinamerikapolitik im Zeichen transnationaler Beziehungen, 1918–1933* Teilbände 1 and 2, Hans-Joachim König and Stefan Rinke (eds), *Historamericana* Band 1. Stuttgart: Verlag Hans-Dieter Heinz, 1996.

Ross, Dieter. *Hitler und Dollfuß: Die deutsche Österreich-Politik 1933–1934,* Hamburger Beiträge zur Zeitgeschichte, Band III. Hamburg: Leibniz-Verlag, 1966.

Ruchte, Robert. *Das K.B. 27. Infanterie-Regiment*, Erinnerungsblätter deutscher Regimenter Band 77, Auszüge aus den amtlichen Kriegstagebüchern Herausgegeben für den Anteil der bayerischen Armee vom bayerischen Kriegsarchiv. Munich: Verlag Max Schick, 1932.

Rumschöttel, Hermann. *Das bayerische Offizierkorps 1866–1914*. Beiträge zu einer historischen Strukturanalyse Bayerns im Industriezeitalter Nr. 9. Berlin: Duncker & Humblot, 1973.

Sánchez Guzmán, Luis F. *Hans Kundt Luces y sombras*. La Paz: no publisher listed, 2006.

Sauer, Bernhard. *Schwarze Reichswehr und Fememorde: Eine Milieustudie zum Rechtsradikalismus in der Weimarer Republik*, Reihe Dokumente-Texte-Materialien Veröffentlicht vom Zentrum für Antisemitismusforschung der Technischen Universität Berlin, Band 50. Berlin: Metropol, 2004.

Schausberger, Norbert. *Der Griff nach Österreich: Der Anschluss*. Vienna: Jugend und Volk, 1978.

Schilde, Kurt, Rolf Scholz, and Sylvia Walleczek. *SA-Gefängnis Papestraße: Spüren und Zeignisse*. Berlin: Overall Verlag, 1996.

Schleunes, Karl A. *Schooling and Society: The Politics of Education in Prussia and Bavaria 1750–1900*. Oxford: Berg, 1995.

Schulze, Hagen. *Freikorps und Republik 1918–1920*. Militärgeschichtliche Studien herausgegeben vom Militärgeschichtlichen Forschungsamt 8. Boppard am Rhein: Harald Boldt Verlag, 1969.

Selig, Wolfram. *Aspekte der nationalsozialistischen Machtergreifung in München; aus der Stadtchronik und anderen Quellen zusammengestellt von Wolfram Selig*. Munich: Stadtarchiv München, 1983.

Sendtner, Kurt. *Rupprecht von Wittelsbach, Kronprinz von Bayern*. Munich: Richard Pflaum Verlag, 1954.

Smelser, Ronald and Rainer Zitelmann, eds. *Die braune Elite: 22 biographische Skizzen*. Darmstadt: Wissenschaftliche Buchgesellschaft, 1989.

Spindler, Max, ed. *Handbuch der Bayerischen Geschichte Vierter Band Das neue Bayern: 1800–1970*. Zweiter Teilband. Munich: CH Beck'sche Verlagsbuchhandlung, 1975.

Stachura, Peter D. *Nazi Youth in the Weimar Republic*. Santa Barbara, CA: Clio Books, 1975.

Stadtarchiv, Wissenschaftliche Stadtbibliothek and Stadtmuseum. *Ingolstadt im Nationalsozialismus: Eine Studie*, Dokumentation zur Zeitgeschichte Band 1. Ingolstadt: Stadtarchiv, 1995.

Steger, Bernd. *Berufssoldaten oder Prätorianer: die Einflußnahme des bayerischen Offizierskorps auf die Innenpolitik in Bayern und im Reich 1918–1924*. Frankfurt am Main: Rita G. Fischer Verlag, 1980.

Stegmann-Gall, Richard. *The Holy Reich: Nazi Conceptions of Christianity, 1919–1945*. Cambridge: Cambridge University Press, 2004.

Sternweiler, Andreas, and Hans Gerhard Hannesen, eds. *Goodbye to Berlin? 100 Jahre Schwulenbewegung: eine Ausstellung des Schwulen Museums und der Akademie der Künste, 17. Mai bis 17. August 1997*. Berlin: Verlag Rosa Winkel, 1997.

Stourzh, Gerald, and Birgitta Zaar, eds. *Österreich, Deutschland und die Mächte: Internationale und Österreichische Aspekte des "Anschlusses" vom März 1938*. Band 16 Veröffentlichungen der Kommission für die Geschichte Österreichs. Vienna: Verlag der Österreichischen Akademie der Wissenschaften, 1990.

Stümke, Hans-Georg, and Rudi Finkler. *Rosa Wimpel, Rosa Listen: Homosexuelle und "Gesundes Volksempfinden" von Auschwitz bis heute*. Reinbek bei Hamburg: Rowohlt, 1981.

Tapken, Kai Uwe. *Die Reichswehr in Bayern von 1919 bis 1924*, Schriftenreihe Studien zur Zeitgeschichte Bd. 26. Hamburg: Verlag Dr. Kovač, 2002.

Walter, Dirk. *Antisemitische Kriminalität und Gewalt: Judenfeindschaft in der Weimarer Republik*. Bonn: Verlag J. H. W. Dietz Nachfolger, 1999.

Weinberg, Gerhard L. *The Foreign Policy of Hitler's Germany: Diplomatic Revolution in Europe 1933–36*. Chicago: University of Chicago Press, 1970.

Wette, Wolfram, ed. *Der Krieg des kleinen Mannes: Eine Militärgeschichte von unten*, 2nd ed. Munich: Piper, 1995.

Wiesemann, Falk. *Die Vorgeschichte der nationalsozialistischen Machtübernahme in Bayern 1932/1933*. Beiträge zu einer historischen Strukturanalyse Bayerns im Industriezeitalter Band 12. Berlin: Duncker & Humblot, 1975.

Wiest, Ekkehard. *Gesellschaft und Wirtschaft in München, 1830–1920: Die sozioökonomische Entwicklung der Stadt dargestellt anhand historischer Adreßbücher*. Aktuelle Beiträge zur Sozialwissenschaftlichen Forschung, Bd. 3. Pfaffenweiler: Centaurus-Verlagsgesellschaft, 1991.

Zorn, Wolfgang. *Bayerns Geschichte im 20. Jahrhundert: Von der Monarchie zum Bundesland*. Munich: Verlag C. H. Beck, 1986.

Zinn, Alexander. *Die soziale Konstruktion des homosexuellen Nationalsozialisten: zur Genese und Etablierung eines Stereotyps*. Frankfurt am Main: Lang, 1997.

Other Media

BBC Television, Night of the Humming Bird, Hitler's 1934 Massacre, first broadcast, June 30, 1981.

"History Wired," "After the Ball" lyrics, http://historywired.si.edu/detail.cfm?IC=286, accessed November 11, 2006.

Papers and Theses

Brienen, Marten Willem. "The Liberal Crisis and Military Socialism in Bolivia: Bolivian History from 1930 to 1939." Vakgroep Talen en Culturen van Latijns Amerika, Faculteit der Letteren, Rijksuniversiteit Leiden, August 26, 1996.

Dunkerley, James. "The Politics of the Bolivian Army: Institutional Development to 1935." PhD diss., University of Oxford, 1979.

Hofbauer, Stefan. "Die Revolution von 1918/19 in Ingolstadt." Schriftliche Hausarbeit zur Wissenschaftlichen Prüfung für das Lehramt an Gymnasien im Frühjahr 1978 in München.

Schmitz, Andreas Walter. "Die SA und ihr Selbstverständnis. Das Beispiel Viktor Lutze." Hausarbeit zur Erlangung des Magistergrades der Philosophischen Fakultät der Westfälischen Wilhelms-Universität zu Münster, 1992.

Werner, Andreas. "SA und NSDAP: SA: 'Wehrverband,' 'Parteitruppe,' oder 'Revolutionsarmee' Studien zur Geschichte der SA und der NSDAP 1920–1933." Inaugural Dissertation der Philosophischen Fakultät der Friedrich-Alexander-Universität zu Erlangen-Nürnberg, 1964.

Unpublished Manuscripts

Arteaga Araníbar, Miguel. "Ernst Roehm." [La Paz], June 30, 1984.

Brockmann, Robert. "Libro I. Soldado, rebelde, marica: Ernst Röhm en Bolivia." [La Paz], 2006.

Index